I'm Feeling Lucky

I'm Feeling Lucky

The Confessions of Google
Employee Number 59

Douglas Edwards

ALLEN LANE
an imprint of
PENGUIN BOOKS

ALLEN LANE

Published by the Penguin Group

Penguin Books Ltd, 80 Strand, London WC2R ORL, England

Penguin Group (USA) Inc., 375 Hudson Street, New York, New York 10014, USA

Penguin Group (Canada), 90 Eglinton Avenue East, Suite 700, Toronto, Ontario,
Canada M4P 2Y3 (a division of Pearson Penguin Canada Inc.)

Penguin Ireland, 25 St Stephen's Green, Dublin 2, Ireland (a division of Penguin Books Ltd)

Penguin Group (Australia), 250 Camberwell Road, Camberwell, Victoria 3124, Australia
(a division of Pearson Australia Group Pty Ltd)

Penguin Books India Pvt Ltd, 11 Community Centre, Panchsheel Park,
New Delhi – 110 017, India

Penguin Group (NZ), 67 Apollo Drive, Rosedale, Auckland 0632, New Zealand
(a division of Pearson New Zealand Ltd)

Penguin Books (South Africa) (Pty) Ltd, 24 Sturdee Avenue, Rosebank, Johannesburg 2196,
South Africa

Penguin Books Ltd, Registered Offices: 80 Strand, London WC2R ORL, England

www.penguin.com

First published in the United States of America by Houghton Mifflin Harcourt Publishing
Company 2011
First published in Great Britain by Allen Lane 2011

2

Set in 11.99/14.58 pt Minion Pro
Printed in Great Britain by Clays Ltd, St Ives plc

A CIP catalogue record for this book is available from the British Library

HARDBACK ISBN: 978-1-846-14512-4
TRADE PAPERBACK ISBN: 978-1-846-14513-1

www.greenpenguin.co.uk

To Kristen, without whom the journey would have been impossible and the destination meaningless.

Nothing to tell now. Let the words be yours, I'm done with mine.

—"CASSIDY" BY JOHN BARLOW

Contents

Introduction

L ARRY PAGE IS an intense guy. At least he was in 1999 when I
first began working for the company he co-founded with Sergey
Brin.

Whenever I found myself in a room with Larry, I felt an urgent need
to do more, as though every second in which I wasn't communicating
vital information was a waste of his bandwidth.

One day in 2002, I ended up alone with Larry in his office after a long
and protracted battle over some policy or other. I had fought and I had
lost, and I had come to opine on what I had learned and to extend an
olive branch across what had been a turbulent time. Larry, dressed in
casual shades of gray, peered intently at his screen. Or rather, at his two
oversized adjacent monitors, filled with code and open web browser
windows. Sergey, with whom he shared the office, was not on hand.
Disassembled in-line skates, a crumpled hockey jersey, and a Japanese
geisha doll kept watch over his empty chair.

"Larry," I began, "I know I haven't always agreed with the direction you and Sergey have set for us. But I've been thinking about it
and I just wanted to tell you that, in looking back, I realize that
more often than not you've been right about things. I feel like I'm
learning a lot and I appreciate your patience as I go through that process."

I smiled inwardly. It was a well-framed corporate kiss-up. I'd hum-
bled myself and given Larry an opportunity to analyze my strengths
as a member of Google's management team and to reward me with
comforting words and reassurances about the value I added. Now he

would recount those occasions when my counsel had been sage and congratulate me on my perspicacity. I envisioned us engaging in the non-physical equivalent of a man hug before I trundled off to savor the moment with a freshly made cappuccino in the micro-kitchen. That's how you "manage up" in a large corporation.

Larry looked at me with the same stare he had directed at the code on his screen, as if he were trying to decipher some undigested bit of an equation that refused to resolve itself.

"More often than not?" he asked me. "When were we *ever* wrong?"

He didn't smile as he asked his question or arch an eyebrow to signify annoyance. He simply wanted to know when he had been wrong so he could feed that information into the algorithm that ran his model of the universe. If he had made a mistake, he needed to know the specifics so he could factor that into the next iteration of the problem if it reappeared.

"Oh. That's right," I thought, awakening from my reverie. "I don't work at a large corporation anymore. I work at Google."

Operating Principles

You know Google.

At least, you know what Google does. It finds stuff on the Internet. That's as much as I knew when I joined the company in 1999. I didn't know what a web indexer, a pageranker, or a spidering robot was. I didn't know how dogmatic engineers could be. I didn't know how many Internet executives could squeeze into a hot tub or how it felt to "earn" more in one day than I had in thirty years of hard work. I didn't know then, but I do now.

True, my story is one of rare opportunity and fortuitous timing, but not entirely so.

This book tells how it felt to be subjected to the g-force of a corporate ascent without precedent, to find myself in an environment where old rules didn't apply and where relying on what I knew to be true almost got me fired. It's not a complete history of everything Google did between 1999 and 2005, nor a completely objective retelling of Google's greatest hits. I wrote the official history of Google during that period and inscribed it on the company's website.* Most accounts since have merely embellished it, and I don't intend to cover all that old ground again. Instead I'll give my insider's view of how things worked (and didn't work) and how we changed as individuals and as a corporate entity.

This book won't delve deeply into Google's current imbroglios over censorship, regulation, and monopoly. I include only what happened between my first day in 1999 and the day I left in 2005. We weren't yet worried about network neutrality, street-view data gathering, or off-shore wind farms. Our big issues barely grazed the electrified moral fence of our "Don't be evil" credo: develop the best search technology, sell lots of ads, avoid getting killed by Microsoft.

While this story is told from a marketer's perspective and my title came to encompass "consumer brand management," this book is not just about marketing. I don't claim to have "built" Google's brand. The brand was built on the product, and the product was built by engineers — computer scientists who constructed systems as complex as any that ever launched a rocket into space, but powering instead a small rectangular search box that now appears in every corner of the Internet.

I'll describe the work habits that enabled them to accomplish a great deal in a short time and the shortcomings that developed in a company where every problem was viewed as solvable and every situation as reducible to a set of data points; where knowing you were right meant nothing should, could, or would stand in your way.

And I'll show how a company with a vision of providing access to all the world's information sometimes mishandled its own relationship with openness, honesty, and disclosure in ways that arose organically and inevitably from the attitudes of those in charge.

To start, I'll give you the background I wish someone had given me on my first day at Google, so you can appreciate the chaos without getting lost in it yourself.

Let's begin with a quick sketch of the company's founding. Google

---

* In Larry's binary world, literary license was the moral equivalent of sloppy engineering. I wrote that he was on a campus tour when he met Sergey for the first time. "It was a visit weekend, not a campus tour," he corrected me. The great stories I'd heard about him sleeping under his desk while working on developing Google? Sergey setting up a business office in his dorm room? The strain on Stanford's power grid created by their Google prototype? "It didn't happen that way," Larry told me. "Take it out."

started as a joint research project by Larry and Sergey in 1996, when they were graduate students at Stanford. They based their project on a new approach to search technology that Larry named PageRank in honor of himself and because, well, it ranked web pages according to their importance.* Their algorithm took into account all the hyperlinks pointing to a given web page from other websites, as if by linking to a page those other sites were declaring it worthy of attention. Most search engines just looked at the content of the pages themselves and based their results on how often the searched-for word appeared on them. It was the difference between judging a stranger by his looks and gathering opinions from everyone who knew him. Because Larry and Sergey's technology analyzed what was going on behind the scenes, they called their search engine "BackRub." For a while, a photo of Larry's hand caressing a bare shoulder was their logo, but even after they airbrushed out the dark hairs, it looked like a shot from a low-budget porn flick.

In 1997, they changed the name to Google, which played to their love of math and scale (a googol is 10^{100}). They chose the variant spelling for two reasons: the googol.com web domain was taken, and Larry thought they wouldn't be able to trademark a number. Larry was a very shrewd businessman — but we'll get to that.

Within a year, Larry and Sergey had taken leave from Stanford and set up in the Menlo Park garage of Susan Wojcicki, the college roommate of Sergey's girlfriend. Google's traffic began climbing and the company began hiring. They incorporated in September 1998, and when they outgrew Susan's garage in early 1999, they moved to an office at 165 University Avenue in Palo Alto. Six months later, having talked two venture capital firms out of $25 million, they moved into an industrial park at 2400 Bayshore Parkway in Mountain View. That's where I joined the company, which at the time had about fifty employees and was doing almost seven million searches a day. Even though that was a seventy thousand percent increase over the year before, it barely registered as a blip on the radar of major players like Yahoo, AOL, and MSN, which were each delivering on the order of half a billion page views per day.

---

*The PageRank patent is actually assigned to Stanford, and the university received 1.8 million shares of Google stock for granting Google an exclusive license to use it. Larry and Sergey described the core of the technology in their 1998 paper "The Anatomy of a Large-Scale Hypertextual Web Search Engine," available at http://infolab.stanford.edu/~backrub/google.html.

Yahoo was the Jabba the Hutt of the "search space" at the turn of the millennium, and it wasn't even a search engine. Yahoo was a "portal," a provider of mail and news and all kinds of services built around a hand-compiled directory of web pages arranged by categories. It had almost thirty million users, but it rented technology to power its search box from Inktomi, the leading provider of search to websites and corporate intranets.

Industry experts speculated, Would Google focus on growing its own site to compete with Yahoo, or would it become a technology supplier and compete with Inktomi? If we tried to do both — build a popular online search engine while providing search technology to other sites that hoped to do the same thing — we would end up competing with our customers. The question, however, betrayed ignorance of Larry and Sergey's aspirations and self-confidence. Why choose just to have cake when you could eat it too? Google would be both a supplier and a search site, because Larry and Sergey knew they were smart enough to isolate the part of the equation containing failure and work around it.

Their vision didn't end at winning the search wars. They would build a company to fix large-scale problems affecting millions of people and terraform the entire landscape of human knowledge. They would speed medical breakthroughs, accelerate the exploration of space, break down language barriers. Instead of putting a Band-Aid on global ignorance and confusion, they would clear the clogged arteries of the world's data systems and move information effortlessly to the point at which it was needed at exactly the time it was required. They would be, Larry believed, an information conglomerate on the scale of General Electric — the GE of IT. To do that, they would need better tools — starting with a search engine that actually delivered what people wanted to find.

Engineers rebel at inefficiency. Larry Page, more than anyone I ever met, hated systems that ate hours and produced suboptimal results. His burning passion was to help the world stop wasting his time.

That love of efficiency begat a fondness for frugality, because paying more than the bare minimum for something was by definition wasteful. Larry liked trimming unnecessary expenses, but it was Sergey who fully applied his razor-sharp intellect to cutting costs.

"That seems kind of expensive," Sergey said, looking at the hundred-dollar price for a cab from Malpensa airport to downtown Milan in

January 2003. He, his girlfriend, and I had flown in for the opening of our new Italian office, and I was looking forward to traveling in style with the president of a booming Internet company. The dot-com era was over for everyone else, but Google's financials were deep in the black. Even though we'd flown coach, surely now we'd be kicking loose a little change to let the Old World know we had indeed arrived.

"Maybe we should take the bus," Sergey suggested, standing in the middle of the baggage claim area squinting at the signage. "It's less than five Euros a person." The bus? What? Were we college kids backpacking on spring break? Maybe we could just hitchhike into town. It was pouring out, and a cab would take us right to our door, not to some run-down depot a short walk from nowhere.

We compromised on the train, which ended up saving us fifty dollars, not counting the cost to my inflated sense of importance.

Efficiency. Frugality. And oh yes, integrity.

Larry and Sergey had an intuitive feel for presenting data in a way that improved the ratio of signal to noise. That means they didn't believe in adding unnecessary crap to the information you actually wanted to see. So, no blinking banner ads in Google search results. No links to every service Google offered pasted all over the Google.com homepage. And no intermingling of ads with actual search results as our competitor GoTo.com was doing. To corrupt a working system would be to profane perfection.

"We could try a loyalty program," I once suggested in a meeting about getting users to search more often, "like a frequent flyer program."

Larry raised his eyebrows the way he does when he considers an idea so blatantly ridiculous you should be ashamed of yourself for even thinking it.

"Frequent flyer programs are evil," he said.

"They are?" I didn't recall my Mileage Plus number ending in 666.

"They incentivize people to take flights that are not the most direct or the cheapest, just so they can earn points. Their employers end up paying more, and people lose time traveling."

Loyalty programs promoted loyalty above efficiency, and that was just wrong, wrong, wrong.

Efficiency, Frugality, Integrity. I suppose if you had stitched that onto a flag, most Googlers would have saluted. There were other operating principles I unearthed picking my way along through trial and error, but those three constitute the mother lode from which they were mined.

And while we're in the mines, let's explore exactly what my fifty-plus honest Google colleagues were toiling to accomplish so cheaply and efficiently.

You Don't Say

I was Google employee number fifty-nine, as near as I can tell, but I started the same week as other people, so my number might have been higher or lower. It doesn't matter. We each contributed according to our ability to improve information access for the betterment of all mankind. That the lowliest engineer's capacity exceeded mine by a bazillion percent made no difference in our status-blind environment.

Theoretically.

In reality, if you weren't an engineer, your first directive was to avoid impeding the progress of those who were. I'm not a technical guy. No one at Google ever said, "Hey, let's ask Doug!" when the flux capacitor hiccupped. But you couldn't work at Google without learning something new every day, even if you weren't trying to. Most engineers opened up about their work when I sat next to them at lunch, and generally they didn't mind using little baby-English words to explain things to me. Given the pressure, though, the engineers were biased toward being productive rather than talking about their productivity. It was a "Don't talk. Do." kind of culture, which made communication about our technical achievements erratic.

For example, I ran our weekly TGIF meeting for a while. TGIF was an all-company affair at which Larry and Sergey recounted the wins of the previous week as we sipped beer and chewed food on skewers. The engineers were so reluctant to report what they had done that Sergey got annoyed because he ran out of things to talk about.

"You must have at least three hundred people," he said to an engineering manager one Friday. "So over the course of a week, that makes six man-years. If this were the list of my accomplishments after six years of work, I would be pretty embarrassed."

Communication issues appear as a recurring motif in the pages to come: issues between engineering and marketing and issues between

Larry and Sergey and everyone else. You'll recognize them when you see them.

So there you have it: the overview I *didn't* have that would have helped me understand something, at least, about the challenges that lay ahead for Google and for me. I still wouldn't have known our business strategy or how we would pay for all the engineers and hardware we needed. I still wouldn't have been prepared for Google's idiosyncratic rules of management, the atmosphere of constant pressure, or the environment that incubated extremism. But at least I'd have recognized which laws of physics applied — most of the time.

You're now better prepared than I was to undertake the Google adventure, which began for me in late 1999, a year after I crossed into my forties. I was due for a mid-life crisis, but what I got was a rebirth.

PART I

YOU ARE ONE OF US

I did things my way.
It was not the Google way.
One of us would change.

CHAPTER 1

From Whence I Came

I WAS NOT A young Turk. I was not a hotshot bred-for-success type who blew through business school, swung a gig at a consulting firm, and then leapt into a great management slot at a groundbreaking new tech company just as it went platinum. I had no desire to be that guy. You can tell, because I majored in English. I drifted through college without set plans for life after graduation and ended up in a series of short-term marketing roles until 1992, when I landed at the *San Jose Mercury News* (a.k.a. "The *Merc*"). I was thirty-four years old and ready to settle into something with a tinge of permanence.

"There's another baby on the way," my wife, Kristen, reminded me, "and he's going to need new shoes."

Seven years went by. It was 1999 and I was now forty-one. I had a steady paycheck and a third child, and I was set for life in a big, rock-solid company with a 150-year history and a handle on the future — but instead of hunkering down, I quit my job to join a startup with no revenue and no discernible business plan. What was I thinking? Why would I volunteer to take a twenty-five-thousand-dollar salary cut and a less impressive title to be with a bunch of college kids playacting at creating a company?

It seemed logical at the time, but only because logic at the time was warped and twisted by the expanding dot-com bubble.

Managing marketing and then online product development at the *Merc* ("The Newspaper of Silicon Valley") had given me a great view of the Internet explosion taking place outside our walls. Jerry Ceppos, the paper's executive editor, called it "the equivalent of the Italian Renaissance, happening right in our backyard." The region was rife with emerging e-Medicis and dot-Botticellis crafting new businesses from nothing but bits and big ideas. The *Merc* wanted desperately to join them and so launched a raft of new-media initiatives, including a tech news hub called Siliconvalley.com for which I'd written the business plan. I envisioned SV.com as a vibrant community center for anyone whose life was touched by technology. Yet, despite our air of optimism, I couldn't help but notice a spreading stench of tar pit–scented doom.

Over its century and a half, the *Mercury News* had layered on coat after coat of process, until whatever entrepreneurial spirit remained was obscured beneath the corporate craquelure of org charts and policy manuals. We saw newspapers as the first draft of history, and no one wanted to make missteps transitioning the historical record to the next mass medium. Every loose end and every blurry projection needed to be carefully wrapped up before our new product could be thrown onto the public's porch.

We did manage to launch a Siliconvalley.com store stocked with logo items from well-known tech companies like Dell, HP, and NetObjects. Our supplier asked if, as a favor to him, we'd also include a smaller firm from his client list.

"This Google," I asked him, "what do they make?"

"Internet search," he said.

"Search? Ha. Good luck with that," I thought, and immediately lost interest in them.

A Fire in the Valley

I grew tired of the struggles that went with dragging an old business into a new age. I wanted a fresh start. I wanted to get closer to the real Internet; close enough to grab the cable and feel the hum of millions of people communicating within the global hive. Worst-case scenario? I'd get in, build my high-tech chops, and get out. Perhaps I'd return like the prodigal son. It was 1999. It wasn't as if mainstream media were going away anytime soon.[*]

I scoured the tech press for leads on the next Yahoo, a business I had shortsightedly predicted would be a flash in the pan. Yahoo had shown a willingness to hire talent from the *Mercury News,* but by the time I grudgingly decided they might be on to something, they no longer needed my validation or my résumé. Even with former colleagues interceding, it took me weeks to get the attention of a Yahoo recruiter.

"Are we more like Macy's or Wal-Mart as a brand?" the hiring manager asked me over the phone. "What Yahoo services do you use? How could they be improved?"

He liked my answers well enough to call me in for face-to-face questioning that very afternoon. A large Plexiglas cow stood patiently in Yahoo's lobby, surrounded by big overstuffed purple furniture that looked as if it had been appropriated from *Pee-wee's Playhouse.* A t-shirted drone showed me to a windowless white room, where for the next three hours a series of marketing staffers jabbed at me with pointed questions. I kept my energy high and my answers short as my interrogators flitted from topic to topic and then flew off to more important meetings.

When it was over, Yahoo offered me a low-level position, a salary I couldn't live on, and the prestige of a purple badge. I politely declined, shook hands, and left. I was way too late for Yahoo.

I didn't give up.

I had been swept away by tales of a new legion of dot-com heroes and had happily contributed fables to the frenzy. Our ads for the *Mercury News* online service asked, "Why wait 'til you're twenty-seven to make your first million?" and urged executives to "Find out when your mailroom guy is going public." I embraced the hype. At night I murmured into my pillow that we needed to "win mind share" and "go big fast."

The dot-com energy in the Valley vibrated at a frequency visible everywhere, overwhelming and electrifying and so intoxicating that whole cities became drunk on it. High-tech gold was all around us; you could feel the weight of it displacing rationality. Houses sold overnight

---

[*] In 2006, the *Merc*'s owner Knight Ridder was sold and its assets divided up. The *Mercury News* is now owned by MediaNews Group, which filed for Chapter 11 bankruptcy in 2010.

for a million dollars above the asking price, paid in cash. Lamborghinis and Ferraris zipped past the Beamers and Benzes cruising Highway 280. Elvis Costello jammed at company parties and private fireworks displays lit up backyard barbeques.

I invested my minimal savings in companies I read about in *Red Herring* and the *Industry Standard*: JDS Uniphase and NetGravity and DoubleClick. I watched their value soar and became convinced I was a keen analyst of the burgeoning Internet economy. Relatives turned to me for stock tips and I began pontificating on the future of XML and push media as if I actually knew what I was talking about.

The millennium was ending and maybe civilization too. Y2K was almost here. A software bug would cause computer clocks to fail, and planes would fall from the sky. The power grid would shut down and cities go dark. Better day trade while the lights were still on.

The next big thing was out there, lurking in a renovated warehouse in San Francisco's Multimedia Gulch or hanging around in a rented one-room office, sharing utilities and a blackened Mr. Coffee machine with other aspiring successes. Brilliant schemes were cooking up like idea popcorn. Most died quietly; half-baked, warmed over, unpalatable. But occasionally one would explode into a wild success and the Valley would come running, throwing business cards and venture capital at the new marvel of fluff and air.

I talked to anyone who had a business plan with "Internet" scrawled in crayon across the top and enough backing to cover my salary for a month, from iTix and Bits2Go to AllBusiness and NexTag. I talked with Sinanet though every word on their site was in Chinese. I begged for an interview at InsWeb, a company offering insurance over the Internet, because somehow it didn't sound lame to say "I sell auto coverage" if you could add the magic word "online."

I lowered my standards and flung out another dozen résumés in hopes of locating a landing place, even aiming one at the little startup that had been part of our Siliconvalley.com store — what was it called? Oh yeah, "Google." It was likely a waste of buff-colored stationery and a thirty-three-cent stamp, because I was looking for the next big thing and I was pretty sure they weren't it. Search was so 1997.

Still, since I'd sent Google a résumé, I figured I should give their product a try. I went to their site and entered the name of a girl I'd known in high school but hadn't heard from in twenty years. Even AltaVista, which I viewed as the best search engine available, had never found a trace of her, so my expectations were low when I hit the enter key.

And there she was.

Google listed her current contact information as the first result. I tried more searches. They all worked better than they had on AltaVista. I no longer begrudged Google the stationery and the stamp.

Other signs pointed to something out of the ordinary. Sequoia Capital and Kleiner Perkins were the Montagues and Capulets of Silicon Valley venture capital (VC) firms. They had enviable success records individually — Yahoo, Amazon, Apple, Cisco Systems, Sun Microsystems — and an intense rivalry that usually kept them from investing in the same startup. Yet together they had poured twenty-five million dollars into the fledgling company. What did Google possess that induced them to set aside their ancient grudge?

I looked for clues in the bios of Google's founders and management team. An abundance of Stanford grads and advanced degrees, which wasn't uncommon. But members of Stanford's faculty had even invested their own money in the new venture — that was different. I didn't know diddly about search technology, but people who presumably did seemed to think Google had potential. When you're burning with startup fever, it doesn't take much to feed the visions playing in your head. So when Google agreed to interview me, I printed out some fresh résumés, tossed my briefcase in our old Taurus, and headed north to Mountain View to check out the new frontier.

A First Encounter

How does one interview for a job at a startup in Silicon Valley? I was well practiced by the time I pulled into Google's parking lot. It was another warm Bay Area November, and I wasn't surprised to see one section of the asphalt roped off with police tape and a roller hockey net at each end. The beige building and a herd of others just like it grazed in verdant fields interspersed with tasteful fountains and ambiguous sculptures. When I entered the first floor of the building, there were arrows printed on copy paper pointing the way to the stairs, which I followed to the second floor.

The curly-haired young receptionist smiled at me. I looked at her and recalled tales of secretaries walking off with millions from early stock options. Would she be one of them? She guided me to a small room decorated with a nine-foot whiteboard, a standard-issue circular table, and several inflated rubber balls large enough to sit on. Nothing here suggested rivers of currency dammed and waiting to burst forth in a torrential IPO. It was just a conference room in a generic office building on a lazy late-autumn afternoon. As I sat idly patting a three-foot ball, a number of folks on the business side of the company straggled in and introduced themselves.

Susan Wojcicki, who owned the garage that had been Google's first headquarters, had left Intel to join her tenants' company as a marketing manager. Cindy McCaffrey had come over from Apple to be director of public relations. Together they walked me through a general introduction to Google with the sort of positive energy that bubbled over everywhere in those days. At least they had facts on which to build their optimism. *Time* had written up the site, traffic was growing by leaps and bounds, and Google had ample financial backing, though no immediate source of revenue. That would come in time, they assured me. They asked about my experience, especially with viral marketing, which Cindy indicated was important to the company's founders, Larry Page and Sergey Brin.

"Oh sure, I've done viral," I assured them, whipping through my bulging portfolio to show them the "Nerd for the New Millennium" contest I'd worked up with the Tech Museum and the oval SV.com stickers the *Merc* had sent local venture capitalists to stick on their Porsches. It wasn't exactly "viral," but it was what I had.

They were equally orthogonal in answering my questions about Google's business model and corporate structure.

"Right now we license search technology," Susan informed me, "but we've got some other things in the works."

"We have a very flat organization," Cindy said. "We don't have very clearly defined roles, and everyone does everything."

I smiled and nodded to indicate that this made perfect sense to me, thanked them, and said it sounded as if Google had a marvelous future.

As the Taurus crept home along Highway 101, I turned up the radio and sang along. I had the impression that Cindy and Susan were interested and would call me back. That was a relief after so many months of throwing in my line and netting nothing. I felt my luck was turning.

I had been hungry for a long time and now scented an opportunity I could really sink my teeth into.

A Hard Question Rewarded with Raw Fish

Two days later, Leesa, the Google recruiter, called me back. Could I meet with more members of the staff? I could and I did. Scott Epstein, the interim VP of sales, wished me good luck. He was phasing out after proposing Google spend millions on an ad campaign — an idea that didn't sit well with Larry and Sergey. Urs Hölzle, Google's head of engineering, greeted me warmly and advised me not to lie on the floor and act like a chew toy near Yoshka, the wooly mammoth noisily slurping water from a bowl behind him.* Omid Kordestani, the newly hired head of sales and business development, forgave me for trash-talking AOL even though he had worked there.

Afterward, Cindy took me back to the conference room to wait for Sergey. I wasn't nervous. Sergey was about the age of my favorite t-shirt and a Russian by birth. I had lived in Russia and spoke some Russian. I had Russian friends and embraced their dark humor, their cynical views, and their sarcastic ways. I felt unusually confident that the interview would go well. Perhaps Sergey was seeking a mentor? I pictured us toasting our success and each other's health with fine Siberian vodka.

Sergey showed up wearing roller hockey gear: gym shorts, a t-shirt, and inline skates. He had obviously been playing hard. I had known better than to wear a tie, but he took office casual to a new level.† I sat back and resumed toying with one of the rubber balls, feeling so relaxed that I accidentally removed its stopper, causing half the air inside to rush out with a hiss. Sergey found that amusing. He pored over my résumé and began peppering me with questions. "What promotion did you do that was most effective?" "What metrics did you use to measure it?" "What types of viral marketing did you do?" "What was your GPA?" I was doing fine until that last one. I just looked at him.

---

* Yoshka, a Leonberger, was described by engineer Ron Dolin as "a cross between a lion, a horse, and a puppy."

† Another Googler recalled answering interview questions on Halloween while Sergey, attired in a full-size cow suit, absentmindedly stroked his rubber udder.

"My GPA?" I hadn't thought about my grade point average since the day they handed me my diploma in 1981. And given that my alma mater had allowed me to take as many classes as I wanted with a pass/fail option, I'm not sure I ever knew what my GPA was. I laughed, thinking Sergey was joking, but even after the company offered me a job, the HR people kept pestering me for a college transcript and my SAT scores. It was a classic Google moment. Your SAT score was the measure of your intellectual capability; your GPA represented your ability to execute on that potential. The value of your future contribution to Google could be plotted using just those two data points.

Sergey's desire to reduce every decision to an equation would cause me a fair amount of frustration in the years to come. While it forced me to discipline my thinking, it also went against my deeply held conviction that some things are not expressible with an algorithm, no matter how carefully derived.

"How much do you think a company our size should spend on marketing?" Sergey asked me. From his earlier questions, it was easy to guess what he wanted to hear.

"I don't think at this stage you should spend much at all," I said. "You can get good exposure with viral marketing and small budgets. Shooting gerbils out of a cannon in a Superbowl spot* is not a very effective strategy for building a brand."

Sergey nodded his agreement, then asked about my six months in Siberia, casually switching to Russian to see how much I had picked up. Finally, he leaned forward and fired his best shot, what he came to call "the hard question." "I'm going to give you five minutes," he announced. "When I come back, I want you to explain to me something complicated that I don't already know." He then rolled out of the room toward the snack area.

I looked at Cindy. "He's very curious about everything," she said. "You can talk about a hobby, something technical, whatever you want. Just make sure it's something you understand really well."

I reached for a piece of scrap paper as my mind raced. What complicated thing did I know well enough to describe to Sergey? Diaper changing didn't seem appropriate. How newspapers are printed? Kind of dull. I decided to go with the general theory of marketing, which was fresh in my mind because I'd only learned it recently.

---

* That was the premise of an Outpost.com spot.

One of my dirty little secrets was a complete lack of academic preparation for the business world. Instead of statistics and economics, I'd taken planetary geology, Latin, and Spenserian verse. Fortunately, Annie Skeet, my boss at the *Mercury News,* had a Harvard MBA and a desire to drive some business theory into my thick skull. She had given me a stack of her old textbooks along with strong hints that I should read them. I had found a couple of titles interesting, including Michael Porter's *Competitive Strategy* and David Aaker's books on branding.

I began regurgitating everything I could remember onto the paper in front of me: the five P's (or was it six?), the four M's, barriers to entry, differentiation on quality or price. By the time Sergey came back, I had enough to talk for ten minutes and was confident I could fill any holes with the three B's (Buckets of Baffling Bullshit). I went to the whiteboard and furiously drew circles and squares and unleashed arrows like Legolas. I was nervous, but not very. Sergey bounced on a ball and asked questions that required me to make things up on the spot.

"What's the most effective barrier to entry?"

"What's more important: product differentiation or promotion?"

"How does the strategy change if the price is zero?"

He seemed to be paying attention, and I began enjoying myself. We were developing a special rapport! Clearly, he wanted to hear what I had to say and valued my opinions. Later I found out that Sergey did this with everyone he interviewed. An hour wasted with an unqualified candidate wasn't a total loss if he gained insight into something new.

The light was fading by the time I finished, and Sergey invited me to join the staff for dinner, which was being brought into a small kitchen across from the conference room. A crowd of hungry engineers bounced from platter to platter with chopsticks picking at a large selection of sushi.

"We just hired a chef, so this is a temporary setup," Sergey confided. "And we've got a couple of massage therapists coming in as well."

A warning light flashed in my head. This was the guy who didn't think there should be a marketing budget, and he had hired a chef and dual massage therapists? But then I saw the platters of fatty tuna and shrimp and salmon and yellowtail. I grabbed some chopsticks and began loading my plate. Concerns about a business plan and revenue streams and organizational structure faded away. Google met most of my requirements. It offered at least the appearance of superior Internet-related technology, some eccentric genius types, funding that should last at least a year, and a fun consumer brand that I could help develop. And sushi. I could always bail for the next startup or get my old job back when Google ran out of money. In the meantime, I thought, I'll eat well and maybe learn something useful.

Two weeks later, on November 29, 1999, I started work as Google's online brand manager.

Day the First

On my first day, I showed up before nine to make sure I gave a good initial impression to my new teammates. My khakis were clean, my polo shirt wrinkle free. I'm not sure the three or four Googlers who straggled in before ten in their shorts, sandals, and Google t-shirts really noticed. It turns out that engineers prefer to phase-shift their work schedules and start after the morning rush hour is well past. It's more efficient to get to work when traffic is light and to go home when everyone else is already asleep. And anything that needs to be ironed is automatically on the losing end of a cost-benefit analysis. Efficiency, I would learn very quickly, is valued highly among those who live to make things work better.

The office space was even more Spartan in the daytime than it had appeared during my evening interview. One large room held a dozen desks made of wooden doors mounted on metal sawhorses. There were small offices scattered around the perimeter, each occupied by at least two workstations sporting large-screen monitors. Many of the screensavers displayed the raining green English and Japanese characters popularized by *The Matrix*. A single bookshelf crammed with programming books was tucked into a corner. I felt as if a crew of small-parts assemblers might show up any minute, cover the tables with soldering guns and pieces of metal, and begin making toasters or robot dogs or locking mechanisms for seat belts. Generically utilitarian would be a generous description.

Google was leasing the top floor of a two-story building and had originally occupied only half of the available area. The technical staff were all tucked into that space because the engineers were literally the core of the company. Great things would come from packing them tightly together so that ideas bounced into one another, colliding and recombining in new, more potent ways.

My new space was in "the annex," the other half of the floor. It was completely raw: cables draped from the ceiling above an uncarpeted concrete floor in a wide-open space interrupted only by cement pillars and, oddly enough, a disco ball left behind by a previous tenant. A couple of offices off to the side had been completed by the time I joined, and I was assigned to one with Aydin Senkut, another newbie, who worked in business development. Aydin lived on his constantly ringing cell phone, which he considerately stepped outside to answer so he could yell at the callers in Turkish without disturbing me. My laptop was new and very fast.

I had been hired during one of the company's first big staffing ramp-ups, and there were many new faces besides mine and Aydin's: Charlie Ayers, the Google chef; massage therapists Babette Villasenor and Bonnie Dawson; webmaster Karen White; and Shari Fujii, the offline marketing manager. We joined the forty engineers and operations staff already in place and the dozen or so business-side staffers who made up the rest of the company.

There was no organizational chart to consult for a quick status check, and the obvious signs demarcating relative importance to the organization were absent. Even Larry and Sergey shared an office, albeit a slightly larger one, just like everyone else. Titles were generic. The position both Shari and I had applied for was "Marketing Director" according to Google's website, though that position didn't actually seem to exist. Google preferred to call us "managers." I shrugged my shoulders and swallowed my pride.

"Titles aren't important," Sergey reminded us on a regular basis. "We'll all do better if we have a flat organization with few levels to facilitate communication and avoid bureaucracy." I accepted the startup assumption that success would float all boats and decided not to get hung up on traditional progress mileposts like money and prestige. After twenty years of working toward my next pay raise and a chance to level up on the corporate org chart, what I did in the office would become an end unto itself. I hadn't felt the same mixture of liberation and anxiety since the day I stuck my diploma in a drawer and first opened a help-wanted section.

I spent the next eight hours settling in, collecting Google's standard-issue mechanical pencils and quadrille-ruled lab books from a metal file cabinet and arranging my stapler and tape dispenser and docking station and inbox until my desk was exactly balanced. I was ready, but not sure for what.

I took a personal inventory. Two decades in marketing had taught me many practical things, from how to build consensus across divisions to how to write a CYA memo when I wanted to color outside the lines. I viewed that experience as an important asset but was beginning to suspect that within the walls of the Googleplex,* it might be valued differently. I had wanted to live the Silicon Valley startup life, with its complete lack of longstanding rules. Now, poised on the precipice of realizing that dream, I asked myself, "My God. What have I done?"

---

*Google is a play on "googol," which is the number one followed by a hundred zeroes. The nickname for our office is from "googolplex," ten raised to the power of a googol (one followed by a googol zeros).

CHAPTER 2

In the Beginning

HEY, WANT TO see something cool?" Jay asked me, standing in the micro-kitchen eating from a cup of yogurt, barefoot and sporting pajama pants, a well-loved sweatshirt, and a graying ponytail.

"Sure," I said, though I couldn't imagine anything cooler than the kitchen itself. One entire wall was lined with bins of granola and cereal. Other bins were filled with Gummi Bears, peach gels, M&Ms,* nutrition bars, and instant oatmeal. Caffeinated and carbonated beverages chilled inside illuminated Google-branded coolers. Boxes of soy milk and Rice Dream stood stacked in the corners. A toaster and a new white breadmaker gleamed on the counter next to the sink.

I'd been at work almost a week and was getting the lay of the land. Jay and Radhika, both engineers and parents, were the only ones who arrived at the office as early as I did, perhaps because we all had kids to drop off on the way. Jay was around my age and a veteran of the Valley who had already been at Google more than a month, making him a valuable source of knowledge about the corporate culture.

I followed him toward a row of glass offices in the engineering zone.

---

* Like many new Googlers, HR director Stacy Sullivan found the unlimited munchies irresistible. "The first week I couldn't believe having that much free candy. There were huge bowls of M&Ms. I ate so many I threw up."

He pointed to a large K'nex roller coaster stretching the length of two desks set end to end. "I built this one day when I needed a break from coding," he said as he turned it on. We watched as a little gray-wheeled cart climbed to the summit and then raced downhill into a loop de loop.

"That *is* pretty cool," I gushed, but not about the roller coaster. I'd already noticed that Jay worked what, to me, were reasonable hours and left in the late afternoon to pick up his kids. Despite the prevailing conception of startups as Silicon Valley's sweatshops, Jay's kick-back attitude convinced me I'd be able to work at Google, help raise our children, and even find time for my own personal development. Pretty cool indeed.

It was a happy fantasy.

My life balance was about to get knocked on its inner ear. In less than a year I would be working sixteen-hour days and Jay would depart Google to pursue personal goals that were at odds with those of the company.

What were Google's goals in late 1999? Hell if I knew. We were a search engine. What did search engines do? They searched. I assumed that we wanted to be the best damn search engine on the planet. Even better than AltaVista. It seemed unlikely we'd ever be a giant like Yahoo, given their head start, but maybe someday we'd be big enough to make Inktomi share the market for supplying portals with technology. There were no mouse pads imprinted with our mission statement or motivational posters on the walls urging us to surpass our sales targets as there had been at the *Merc*. If Googlers, or anyone else, had a clear vision of the company's future, they kept it hidden. And not just from me.

"I had lunch with Sergey and another engineer and it was clear they had a search engine," said engineer Ed Karrels, who in 1999 was trying to decide if he should leave SGI for a job at Google, "but everybody and their brother had a search engine in those days. I asked, 'Where are you going with this? How will you make money?' And Sergey said, 'Well . . . , we'll figure something out.' I asked, 'Do you already have a plan figured out and you're collecting smart people to make it happen?' And he said, 'Yeah, that's pretty much it.'" Very reassuring.

I had worked for a startup in the eighties, joining a group of former auditors with an idea that would revolutionize health-care marketing. They set up shop in San Francisco next to a former garage that now housed a Chinese restaurant. The place was soaked in adrenaline and constantly shifting direction. Change, change, change. Charge ahead. No back. I left after three months, and a few weeks later the company disappeared. I learned that hyperactivity wasn't the same as productivity. Google, however, gave off a different vibe.

A big part of that was the people I met.

"Hi, I'm Jim," said the guy who came by to give me my laptop and set up my phone. "Jim Reese. I should have this done in a jiffy." Something about him reminded me of Dustin Hoffman in *Rain Man:* the open and friendly attitude, the hair parted way over on one side, the whiff of geekiness I detected as he crawled under my desk, whipped out a screwdriver, and began adeptly fiddling with one of the jacks.

I later learned that Google had hired Jim as a systems administrator (sysadmin) because the early engineers were all coders and not so good with hardware. It wasn't what Jim had been trained to do at Harvard, at Yale Medical School, or in his neurosurgery residency at Stanford, but somewhere along the line he had developed an interest in computer networking and had ended up on the phone with Urs Hölzle, Google's head of engineering. Recruiters from other companies had spent their interview time selling him on the jobs they were offering. Not Urs.

"Urs said nothing about coming to the company," Jim recalls. "Every single question was like, 'Tell me how many bits there are in a netmask for a slash 28 network.' Then he started drilling down from there." That focus on the technology had convinced Jim to sign on.

The day in June 1999 when Jim started as Google employee number eighteen, his orientation took less than a minute. "Here's your space over here," Larry directed him. "There are a bunch of parts over there. Make your own computer." It was the same for the next guy hired: Larry "Schwim" Schwimmer, who took responsibility for Google's mail and security systems.

I stopped by the office Schwim shared with Jim so he could sign me up for a company email account. A large stuffed penguin, the mascot for the Linux operating system our engineers used instead of Windows, sat in a folding chair next to a model of the human skull left over from Jim's med school days. The room felt cramped, as most Google offices did, and was crowded with wires and RAM and computers in various states of assembly. Schwim peered from behind his monitor with the distracted look of someone whose mind was elsewhere — like John Malkovich in that movie where a puppeteer took command of his brain.

"You're the first Doug," Schwim told me. "Do you want doug@google

.com?" I did. I felt a strange tingle as I thought about the implication of that. The first Doug. Among certain sets in Silicon Valley, your email address indicates more about you than the car you drive or the clothes you wear. I liked the status doug@google conferred on me as an early adopter.

I'd see a lot of "Jim and Schwim," as they came to be called. Their group, known as operations or ops, took charge of building and maintaining all the machines running Google. Larry had given Jim a list on his second day, in priority order, of the top one hundred things he wanted done. Number one was "to make sure we had enough capacity to run the site and if there are problems, solve them or find someone to solve them."

"The first year I got nine done," Jim confessed with a hint of pride. "And in the subsequent five years, I got through fifteen of them." Jim's job wasn't defined by the list, however, just as I was about to learn that mine wasn't defined by my somewhat generic "marketing manager" title. As Jim pointed out, "When there were problems to be solved, whoever could solve them did, regardless of what their official title was."

CableFest '99

"We've got some work to do at our data center on Saturday," Cindy informed all of us in the marketing group toward the end of my first week on the job. "Bring warm clothes, because I understand it can get a bit chilly in there." It was our formal invitation to "volunteer" at Google's CableFest '99.

I was no expert on computer hardware. I had read an article or two about servers, hubs, and routers, but I pronounced "router" as if it rhymed with "tooter" instead of "outer." Given my profound lack of technical expertise and my bad computer karma, why would any company allow me in the same room as its computational nerve center? That requires a bit of explanation.

In late 1999, Google began accelerating its climb to market domination. The media started whispering about the first search engine that actually worked, and users began telling their friends to give Google a try. More users meant more queries, and that meant more machines to respond to them. Jim and Schwim worked balls-to-the-wall to add capacity. Unfortunately, computers had suddenly become very hard to get. At the height of the dot-com madness, suppliers were so busy with big customers that they couldn't be bothered fending off the hell-hounds of demand snapping at Google's heels. A global shortage of RAM (memory) made it worse, and Google's system, which had never been all that robust, started wheezing asthmatically.

Part of the problem was that Google had built its system to fail.

"Build machines so cheap that we don't care if they fail. And if they fail, just ignore them until we get around to fixing them." That was Google's strategy, according to hardware designer Will Whitted, who joined the company in 2001. "That concept of using commodity parts and of being extremely fault tolerant, of writing the software in a way that the hardware didn't have to be very good, was just brilliant." But only if you could get the parts to fix the broken computers and keep adding new machines. Or if you could improve the machines' efficiency so you didn't need so many of them.

The first batch of Google servers had been so hastily assembled that the solder points on the motherboards touched the metal of the trays beneath them, so the engineers added corkboard liners as insulation. It looked cheap and flimsy, but it prevented the CPUs (central processing units) from shorting out. Next, Larry focused on using space more efficiently and cutting out as many expensive parts as possible. He, Urs, and a couple of other engineers dumped out all the components on a table and took turns arranging the pieces on the corkboard tray like a jigsaw puzzle.* Their goal was to squeeze in at least four motherboards per tray. Each tray would then slide into a slot on an eight-foot-tall metal rack. Since servers weren't normally connected to displays, they eliminated space-hogging monitor cards. Good riddance — except that when something died the ops staff had no way to figure out what had gone wrong, because they couldn't attach a monitor to the broken CPU. Well, they could, but they'd have to stick a monitor card in while the machine was live and running, because Larry had removed the switches that turned the machines off.

"Why would you ever want to turn a server off?" he wondered.

---

* According to Urs, Gerald Ainger and Larry Page did most of the work on the corkboard design. First they ran performance tests on four commercial motherboards to see which was fastest, then they worked on fitting them together. Gerald was hired in May 1999, and the first machines were in service just a month later, replacing boards that had one (much bigger) server per tray.

Perhaps because plugging a monitor card into an active computer could easily short out the motherboard, killing the whole machine.

After the engineers crammed four boards onto each tray, the one in the back couldn't be reached from the front. To fix it the technician would have to pull the tray out of the rack, but the trays were packed so tightly that yanking on one would cause the trays directly above it and below it to start sliding. With cables wrapped around every surface like lovelorn anacondas, that could unplug everything and shut down the entire rack.

That's how my chance to perform bypass surgery on Google's still-beating heart came about. My comrades and I would be disconnecting the cables one by one and reconnecting them in tightly tied bundles running in plastic troughs along the side of the server trays instead of in front of them, making it easier to move the trays in and out of the racks. Even marketeers could use a twist-tie, so we were encouraged to get our hands dirty mucking out the server farm.

"CableFest '99 lays the groundwork for the frictionless exchange of information on a global scale and will increase the knowledge available to every sentient being on the planet," I assured my wife.

Kristen looked at me and sadly shook her head. She had a PhD in Soviet history, a job as a professor, and a very sensitive bullshit detector. She tried to be supportive, but her maternal instincts were primarily focused on the three children she now worried would see little of their father. "You took a giant pay cut, and now you're working weekends. You know, the *Merc* might still want you back."

Saturday morning came and I pulled into the almost empty parking lot of a large, gray, windowless edifice in Santa Clara. There was no sign in front, but it was Exodus, the co-lo that housed our data center.* I joined the movement of people straggling single file through a well-fortified security checkpoint. Marketing, finance, and facilities were all represented. Even Charlie Ayers, our newly hired chef, was there. Photo IDs were checked and badges issued. Stern warnings were given. We were not, repeat, *not* to touch anyone else's stuff.

And then we were in.

Unless you're a sysadmin, electrician, or NSA stenographer, you may never have been inside a server farm. Imagine an enormous, extremely

---

* "Co-lo" for "co-location center," a building housing the computers of more than one company.

well-kept zoo, with chain-link walls draped from floor to ceiling creating rows of large fenced cages vanishing somewhere in the far, dark reaches of the Matrix. Inside each cage is a mammoth case (or several mammoth cases) constructed of stylish black metal and glass, crouched on a raised white-tile floor into which cables dive and resurface like dolphins. Glowing green and red lights flicker as disks whir, whistle, and stop, but no human voices are ever heard as frigid air pours out of exposed ceiling vents and splashes against shiny surfaces and around hard edges.

The overwhelming impression, as Jim led us past cage after cage of cooled processing power, was of fetishistic efficiency. Clean, pristine, and smoothly sculpted, these were more than machines, they were totems of the Internet economy. Here was eBay. Here Yahoo. Here Inktomi. Welcome to Stonehenge for the Information Age.

The common design element seemed to be a mechanized monolith centered in each cage, surrounded by ample space to set up a desk and a few chairs, with enough room left over for a small party of proto-humans to dance about beating their chests and throwing slide rules into the air.

At last we arrived at Google's cage. Less than six hundred square feet, it felt like a shotgun shack blighting a neighborhood of gated mansions. Every square inch was crammed with racks bristling with stripped-down CPUs. There were twenty-one racks and more than fifteen hundred machines, each sprouting cables like Play-Doh pushed through a spaghetti press. Where other cages were right-angled and inorganic, Google's swarmed with life, a giant termite mound dense with frenetic activity and intersecting curves. Narrow aisles ran between the rows of cabinets, providing barely enough space to pass if you didn't mind shredding clothes and skin on projecting screws and metal shards.

It was improbably hot after our stroll through a freezer to get there, and we were soon sweating and shedding outerwear. On the floor, sixteen-inch metal fans vibrated and vainly pushed back against the heat seeping out from the racks around us—their feeble force doing little more than raise the temperature of Inktomi's adjacent cage by a few degrees.

We went to work. First the ops team attached Panduit cable troughs to the sides of the cabinets with adhesive tape. Then we began gently placing the free-hanging cables in the troughs and twist-tying them together so they no longer draped over the face of the machines like the bangs of a Harajuku Girl.

I tackled the rack labeled "U." It has long since been retired, but I like to think that those user queries routed to U got their answers a nanosecond or two faster because of my careful combing of the cables.

Why, you might ask, did Google do things this way? In addition to the efficiency gained by running cheap, redundant servers, Google was exploiting a loophole in the laws of co-lo economics. Exodus, like most hosting centers, charged tenants by the square foot. So Inktomi paid the same amount for hosting fifty servers as Google paid for hosting fifteen hundred. And the kicker? Power, which becomes surprisingly expensive when you gulp enough to light a neighborhood, was included in the rent. When Urs renegotiated the lease with Exodus, Jim spelled out exactly how much power he needed. Not the eight twenty-amp circuits normally allocated to a cage the size of Google's; he wanted fifty-six.

"You just want that in case there's a spike, right?" asked the Exodus sales rep with a look of surprise. "There's no way you really need that much power for a cage that size."

"No," Jim told him. "I really need all fifty-six to run our machines."

It's rumored that at one point Google's power consumption exceeded Exodus's projections fifty times over.[*] It didn't help that Google sometimes started all of its machines at once, which blew circuit breakers left and right until Google instituted five-second delays to keep from burning down the house.

Air-conditioning came standard, too. Again, Exodus based their calculations on a reasonability curve. No reasonable company would cram fifteen hundred micro-blast furnaces into a single cage, because that would require installing a separate A/C unit. Google did. We were a high-maintenance client.

CableFest '99 was the one and only time I entered a Google data center. It gave me an appreciation of the magnitude of what we were building and how differently we were doing it. I can't say it inspired confidence to lay my untrained hands on our cheap little generic servers, lying open to the controlled elements on crumbly corkboards,

---

[*] A different data center complained to an ops technician in 2001 that Google's cage drew more power and generated more heat than the entire rest of their operation. In 2002, engineer Amit Patel calculated Google's power usage curve and predicted, "We're going to destroy the universe in 143 years."

while next door, Inktomi's high priests tended to sleek state-of-the-art machines that loomed like the Death Star. But the arrangement seemed to work pretty well for us, and I decided not to worry about things that were beyond my ken.

Very smart people were obsessing about the viability of Google's back end, and unbeknownst to me, I would soon be obsessing about the viability of my own.

Meet the Marketers

"Once she had accomplished that," Cindy was explaining to our small marketing team, "she had the world by its oyster."

I smiled. New fodder for the quote board I'd pinned up on my cubicle wall, which still featured Cindy's last pronouncement, "That's what happens when that happens."

Our department consisted of a small cadre with mixed levels of experience in marketing. Cindy was the boss and acting VP. She was close to my age, very funny (usually intentionally), and always in a hurry, which led to an alarming number of emails in which her fingers failed to keep up with her thoughts. She had started as a print journalist, then done PR duty under some of the most notorious tycoons in the Valley, where she had become personally acquainted with every reporter who talked or typed about technology. She focused on public relations, which Larry and Sergey supported as the most cost-effective way to promote the company.

Cindy exuded a wholesome Laura Petrie vibe that I found comforting, and I felt a connection with her because of our common history at newspapers. As she bounced around the department, a whirling dynamo of positive energy, she urged us to take risks, try new things, and let nothing stand in our way. We started referring to her as "Small. But mighty." Those qualities cut both ways.

"Larry and Sergey were always skeptical about traditional marketing," Cindy recalls. "They wanted Google to stand apart from others by not doing what everyone else was doing . . . Let the other guys with inferior products blow their budgets on noise-making, while we stayed focused on building a better mousetrap." That skepticism translated into constant questioning about everything marketing proposed. The department only existed because someone (a board member or a friend from Stanford) had insisted the founders needed people to do all the stuff that wasn't engineering.

Cindy pushed back against the constant pressure to prove her department was not a waste of payroll, but she also let us know that expectations were high. When we performed below her professional standards, she rebuked us for "Mickey Mouse behavior" with an intensity as devastating and unexpected as the tornados that swept her native Nebraska. I learned to keep an eye out for storm warnings.

My counterpart on the offline branding side of things was Shari Fujii, a thin, thoughtful, hyperkinetic marketing professional with an MBA and a tendency to exclaim that the impact of any given action would be *"huge."* We often commiserated about Larry and Sergey's abysmal lack of regard for our department and its work. Coming out of a company run by journalists, I found it more of the same, but Shari struggled to make it fit with her experience at brand-driven companies, where marketing summoned the sun to begin each new day.

The other key player in my world was Karen White, the webmaster. Karen had been a casino dealer in North Dakota when she decided to teach herself the ins and outs of creating web pages. Cindy had discovered her at a previous job and brought her to Google. I soon understood why. Karen had the organizational skills and disposition of a NASA launch coordinator. Industrious, objective, unflappable, and willing to stretch her day across multiple time zones, Karen took all the words I threw together and arranged them in pretty columns on our website. She had more influence on the overall look of Google than anyone who worked on it after Larry and Sergey's original "non-design" design.

Other than Susan Wojcicki, who had put her MBA to work at Intel, our group was new to marketing. Google hired Stanford grads in bulk and set them loose in the halls. If they didn't secure a role elsewhere, they rolled downhill to our department, where the assumption seemed to be that no special skills were required.

"The founders were okay with a loose shag bag of marketing folks who were at the ready to execute on their whims," Cindy told me, "but a real marketing department with a VP, proper organization, funding, and a strategy was not a priority." As a result, our world was without form and confusion was on the faces of those who dwelled within it.

"Who's working on our letterhead?" I asked Cindy. "Who handles sponsorship requests?" Were these areas that fell into my domain? I was seeking more than organizational clarity. I wanted to be sure that there was some substance to my job, something I could cling to when people asked, as they inevitably would, "What exactly do you do here?"

"No structure, foundation, or control," is how Heather Cairns, Google's HR lead at the time, remembers the company's early days. "Even if someone had a manager, that manager was inexperienced and provided no leadership. People weren't used to authority and wouldn't adhere to it—it was a completely unmanaged workforce that was bouncing off the walls like a tornado. I didn't pretend to have any control over it . . . I just went home at night to drink, thinking, 'We're gonna crash and burn.'"

Keeping It Clean

"Our site is kind of a mess," Cindy said to Karen and me my second week on the job. "Can you work up some guidelines to clean it up?"

We had no rules governing what went on Google.com. Something new launched, it got mentioned on the homepage. We won an award, that went up too. Our other pages were equally devoid of planning and design. There were job listings, some help content, contact information, and brief profiles of the executive team. As with everything else at the company, our user interface (UI: the look and feel of our website) operated on the principle that we should minimize the time it took for users to find what they wanted.

Unlike Yahoo.

Yahoo's homepage had links to apparel, computers, DVDs, travel, TV listings, weather, games, yellow pages, stock quotes, and chat. It got busier with every passing day. The most prominent feature on the page was Yahoo's hand-built directory with its fourteen major categories from Arts & Humanities to Society & Culture, beneath which were links to all known points in the Dewey decimal system. Buried in the middle of all the text links was a search box powered by our nemesis Inktomi.

Inktomi hadn't always owned that space. AltaVista had provided search to Yahoo until 1998, but they made the fatal mistake of building their own portal site and stealing users from their customer (competing with your own distributor is known as "channel conflict"). Inktomi had no "consumer-facing" search site,* so they weren't Yahoo's competitors, which also gave them a clear shot at Microsoft's MSN network and America Online (AOL). Inktomi locked those customers up as well, completing their trifecta of high-traffic Internet sites and ensuring that the state of search across the web was commoditized. You could get any flavor of search you wanted, as long as it was Inktomi. They owned the search market and sat on it as fat and happy as the enormous customers they served.

Other portals wanted a piece of Yahoo's traffic: Excite, Lycos, and Disney's Go.com. And other search companies, like AlltheWeb, Teoma, and HotBot, fought alongside Google for the crumbs falling from Inktomi's table. While Wall Street focused on the portal wars, the struggle for search domination wasn't of much interest to anyone but a handful of analysts. There was no money in it. Well, not much money.

In February 1998, a small Pasadena company named GoTo started auctioning placement in search results they bought from other providers. Six months later, they claimed to have more than a thousand paying customers. According to GoTo, you didn't need fancy algorithms to determine relevance, just the invisible hand of the free market. Any company bidding for placement at the top of the results must be a good match for the term being searched. At Google, we found that concept ridiculous. Bidding-based ranking was clearly inferior to results based on an algorithm. Bidding was driven by imprecise humans. Humans bad. Math good. We knew about GoTo, but we discounted their "non-technological" approach. That proved to be unwise. We gave them a head start, and for the next four years we would fight them for supremacy in the online advertising market.

Codifying some UI guidelines† would be a good beginning project, I thought. How tough could it be to come up with some design rules for a page containing nothing but a search box, a hundred or so text

---

* Industry-speak for a site that was targeted to individual users and branded with a company's own name. Also referred to as a "destination site," because the owner tries to send people there.

† Not "branding guidelines," as we might have called them at another company. Functionality, not marketing, drove everything we did at Google.

characters, and some corporate shovelware behind it?* Besides, working with Karen was like drawing the right lab partner at school. Even if I screwed up, Karen wouldn't let us fail. We knocked a proposal together in less than a week.

Google was fast, accurate, and easy to use — that's what our users told us. Sergey wanted our site to be "fun" as well. Yeah, great, it's fine to have fun occasionally, but Karen and I agreed that whimsical elements shouldn't get in the way of users getting things done. We explicitly stated the obvious: "The personality of the site should under no circumstances interfere with the speed of results delivery, the accuracy of the results, or the ease in using the search functionality." An axiom we would unintentionally prove soon enough.

The rest of the proposal involved other obvious points — tweaks to what existed rather than a major overhaul — like adding decorative graphics to our corporate section. That didn't fly.

"Yahoo doesn't use images beyond the homepage," Larry reminded us, "and they have millions of users. Images take time to transfer across the Internet and slow things down." Larry and Sergey rolled on the floor rapturously speaking in tongues when we shaved a nanosecond off the time it took a page to load. Or to read. "I want all the content of the About Google section on one page," Larry said. "It would be faster to scroll up and down one page than to click from page to page and wait for it to load."

"But no one's going to scroll down a hundred pages," I said, not sure if he was joking. He wasn't, but we managed to argue him out of it. Other suggestions fell by the wayside, like a help link, a tagline, and an embarrassingly naive idea Sergey had to change the homepage logo every day to build user interest. Professional branding people were in the house now, and we would never abide such amateur antics. Overall, Larry and Sergey gave a thumbs-up, proclaiming our guidelines "sensible." High praise indeed.

I let out a sigh of relief. Now I got it. *This* was what I'd been hired to do. If I hadn't knocked my first project out of the park, at least I'd hit a solid double. Everyone seemed reasonable and receptive to new ideas,

---

* Sergey did Google's original design and explained its simplicity by saying, "We didn't have a webmaster, and I don't do HTML."

and the feedback made sense. I hadn't done anything terribly unconventional, yet my ideas had been accepted.

"Yep," I thought, "it's all going to work out just fine."

Birth of a Data Agnostic

"As of last night, Google's result font has become sans-serif," engineer Marissa Mayer announced to the company at large. "We tested the change and Larry and I reviewed it with some other engineers who were here and offered opinions about it."

I had seen Marissa's name on a note Sergey forwarded to the new marketing group a couple of days earlier. She had suggested we replace our temporary slogan — "Best Search Engine in the World. Promise" — with one Urs had come up with: "The Little Engine That Could." I didn't particularly like either line, though Marissa had constructed a detailed rationale for associating Google with the "scrappy," "determined," and ultimately "triumphant" children's book character. Besides, she pointed out, look at the importance of Ask Jeeves's tagline to their valuation.

Shari thanked Marissa and explained that we didn't have a slogan, just a phrase that was printed on some cards until we could properly research our brand character. Marketing had it under control.

Marissa, like Susan, was an old-timer who had come over from the Palo Alto office. Before that she had been a Stanford student. When I finally met her, I was struck by the intensity and scope of her interests. If everyone else at Google was a hundred-watt bulb illuminating a single corner of the company, Marissa was a flashing neon sign, casting light and shadow in all colors across the entire Googleplex. Trying to keep up with her could induce seizures. Her primary role was as a software engineer, but she was temporarily working on UI design. She had uncovered research indicating that sans-serif fonts were easier to read, so she and engineer Craig Silverstein had decided to change the results font to Verdana. It didn't happen because Karen and I had suggested a move to sans serif in our guidelines. In fact, Marissa may not have even seen our proposal.

"It would have been nice to know that engineering was already working on UI," I griped to Karen. It undermined what we had done and made me question our internal communication. No one else seemed terribly upset, so I dismissed the faint alarm bells and chalked it up to the newness of the marketing organization. It was great that our engineers made improvements. I just wanted to be sure we wouldn't be caught by surprise when they launched them.

I was equally sanguine about my first glimpse of the way the two departments approached problems. We in marketing wrote proposals, made suggestions, and looked for broad formal approval before moving ahead one step at a time. Our engineers made quick data-based decisions and implemented them. If data supported a particular option, they rationalized, it was the right choice to make. Data didn't lie. If the numbers said changing A to B would improve product X, why not do it now? This mindset drove much of the urgency at Google. Engineers knew how to make things better, and every hour, every minute, every second we delayed improvements, users had to endure sub-optimal interactions with our site. That was unacceptable.

I would discover, however, that data does lie. Sometimes the method of collecting it is flawed, sometimes it's misinterpreted, and sometimes it provides only part of the answer. Take the change to Verdana. While the new font looked great on certain PCs and certain browsers, it rendered horribly on others, most notably those used by America Online customers — essentially making Google unusable for millions of people. Marissa and the engineers hadn't checked it on that platform. That problem was quickly corrected, but even though I supported the move to a sans-serif font, I was left with a healthy skepticism about the ability of numbers to tell the whole story, a loss of faith that I alone appeared to experience within Google's kabala of data-based divinity.

"We Accept You"

TGIF was the four-thirty Friday afternoon meeting at which new Googlers (or "Nooglers," as I would dub them) introduced themselves and the founders shared the important news of the week. When I arrived for my debut, the entire company was gathered in the hallway outside Larry and Sergey's office, leaning against walls, sitting on rubber balls, and sprawling on the floor. Urs's dog Yoshka sniffed at Susan's newborn son, who was asleep in his car seat in front of a wall of Sony monitors stacked in their shipping cases.

Larry, dressed in black slacks and a long-sleeved, dark blue shirt but-

toned to the collar, stepped to the front of the crowd. He carried himself
as if his armature ran on a woefully underpowered processor — stiff,
awkward moves and self-conscious grins — as if he reminded himself to
smile and then manually executed the command set to make it happen.
Lift the edges of your mouth. Stretch your lips back. Crinkle your eyes.
It made him seem painfully self-conscious. I found myself rooting for
him to compile successfully, though sometimes he got stuck halfway
through a sequence and stood leaning to one side with a half-grin fro-
zen on his face. Sergey was more fluid, athletic, acrobatic. Bouncy, even.
He laughed easily and seemed to always have an eye out for a railing he
could vault or a rafter beam he could pull himself up on.

When my turn came to talk about what made me interesting, I hesitated. "Well . . . , I lived in Siberia for six months and, uh, I like to
doodle in meetings."

Everyone politely applauded, but I wondered again what exactly I
had gotten myself into. I had made a career commitment, and my future success rested in large part on the gray matter behind these happy,
shiny faces. I prayed that they had a better idea of what they were doing
than I did.

Larry ran through a presentation he and Sergey had made to the
board of directors and rattled off a few announcements. Then we broke
for beer and cake in honor of those with birthdays that week. For better
or worse, I was officially a Googler. Gabba gabba hey.

TGIF was miles from the formality of meetings at my former places
of employment, where the emphasis lay on keeping key financial information out of the hands of staffers who might wield it in future contract
negotiations. Here we had seen the exact same slides the top executives
had presented to our board. I couldn't believe that all this information
was thrown out to every employee, as if at Google we occupied an alternate universe of kibbutz-like communalism. Despite the transparency
of our accounting, I was troubled by my lack of insight into our business model and our competitive environment. I knew exactly how we
were doing financially, but I didn't have a clue about what was going on.

CHAPTER 3

A World without Form

I WOULD NEVER UNDERSTAND this new world until I was fully grounded in search technology. Craig Silverstein volunteered to school me and a handful of other nontechnical staff with a lunchtime talk he called "Google 7A: Search for non-majors." Craig, a former Stanford grad student with an impish grin and a sense of humor dry to the point of sere, liked to say he was employee 1.5, officially added to the payroll between Larry and Sergey when the company incorporated. Craig also provided our daily bread, wandering the halls on random afternoons wearing a beatific smile and announcing in an interrogatory falsetto, "Breaaddd?" Googlers would scramble from their cubicles to partake of the air-filled, nutrition-free loaf he had just taken from Google's breadmaking machine.

We gathered in the Ping-Pong room, which housed the dark green game table formerly in Susan's garage. The net was down, perhaps knocked over by one of our venture capitalists to clear a place for his laptop during the board meeting the day before. Craig began his lecture as we munched on red licorice and bowls of M&Ms.

"A search engine has three components," he began, writing on the whiteboard beneath a header that read "The Life of a Query."

"First, we have to collect information about what pages exist on the web, which we do through a process called crawling. Our spidering software, which we call Googlebot, jumps from link to link gathering

URLs [web addresses] and data on the content that lives at each one. The crawl usually takes about a month, and once it's completed, we have a big bag of stuff that needs to be sorted into a usable list. That's called indexing."

I wrote "crawling" and "indexing" in my lab book and put boxes around them. Next I connected the boxes and turned them into a pair of Ben Franklin–style glasses, with a spider hanging from a thread where the nose would be.

"Once we have an index," Craig continued, "we assign a rank to each page based on its importance with our PageRank algorithm. PageRank is Google's secret sauce."

"Secret sauce?" I leaned forward to learn what we had that was better than all the other search engines that our founders seemed so quick to dismiss.

"PageRank looks at all the pages on the web and assigns a value to them based on who else links to them. The more credible the sites linking to them, the higher the PageRank. That's the first half of the recipe."

I wrote "PageRank" under the Ben Franklin spectacles and drew an oval around it. It looked a little like a clown mouth, so I sketched a skull around it and added some Bozo hair on the sides.

"The second half is how we determine which results are most relevant to the specific query we've received. Most of our competitors look at basic stuff like how many times a word appears on a page. We look at what we know about how sites use that term on their pages. What words appear next to it? Is it in bold type or a different font? How does the term appear in links pointing to those pages? That link analysis is really important. The words in the link pointing to a page are called anchor text."

A chain grew from a corner of my clown's mouth and fell to the bottom of the page, where an anchor suddenly appeared surrounded by grinning fish with barracuda teeth.

"How well we match the query determines our search quality," Craig went on, "which is not an exact science, since evaluating whether a query is a good match is somewhat subjective. If you searched for 'jaguar,' did you mean the car or the cat or the football team? Sometimes it's difficult to disambiguate a query like that."

I wrote down "disambiguate," and said it silently to myself three times so it would become my word. And I drew something that looked vaguely like a spotted jungle cat chasing the fish around the anchor, then added bubbles since he was underwater.

"Once we determine the order of the pages we want to show, we need to serve the results back to the user who submitted the query. That's where gwiss comes in." As he said "gwiss," Craig wrote "GWS" on the whiteboard. Beneath it he wrote "Google Web Server." "Gwiss is the software that actually interacts with users when they submit a query and when we serve results back to them. When we want to update how Google looks to users, we need to push out a new gwiss to implement those changes."

I couldn't think of what a gwiss might look like, so I sketched some Swiss cheese behind the clown head. By the time Craig had finished, I had a broader understanding of the way Google worked and a bizarre doodle to add to my collection of things not to share with my new co-workers.

Later Urs confirmed that Google had kicked butt in search quality even before Larry and Sergey left Stanford in 1998, because link analysis was an alchemist's stone for turning web dross into gold. Google's relevancy lured in early adopters and the media, but behind its beguiling look lay an arthritic infrastructure in danger of collapsing. "The ranking beat AltaVista by a mile," Urs told me, "but it was slow and we couldn't build an index reliably."

The challenge of improving Google's crawling, indexing, and serving systems was what had drawn Urs to the company. He'd figured the project would take about a year and then he'd move back to Europe. "I underestimated how much of a systems problem this whole thing was," he confessed. "We had a university system and we needed to basically rewrite the whole thing from scratch." While Google did a good job with the data it had, it collected far too little and wasn't searching through it fast enough.

Speed or scale. Pick one. When we crawled more web pages, the index got bigger and the pageranker had more data to draw upon, so we could produce more-relevant results. That attracted more users and more searches, so our audience grew. A bigger index, however, required more machines doing more processing, and more processing took more time. Adding users puts more demand on the network, which, as anyone sharing an Internet connection knows, slows things down.

As they did when forced to choose a future for Google as a destination site or a technology provider, Larry and Sergey chose both. Google's quest would be to get faster even as it expanded in all directions. They went looking for others who shared their disdain for the limits imposed by nature's laws.

Urs to Reason Why, Then to Do or Die

"Urs was mostly setting the goals at that time," early engineer Jeff Dean explained to me, "because Larry and Sergey were doing more stuff on the business side. They were more involved in deals and that kind of thing." Larry and Sergey could write code, but it wasn't what they were best at.

"I didn't trust Larry and Sergey as coders," said Craig Silverstein. "I had to deal with their legacy code from the Stanford days and it had a lot of problems. They're research coders: more interested in writing code that works than code that's maintainable." According to Jeff, one of the quirks in the early Stanford version of Google[*] was that when something unusual happened the program would print out an error message without any explanation. The message read simply, "Whoa, horsey!"

As Craig recalls it, "Urs showed up magically with his beard and his dog," as if he were Gandalf the White appearing out of the fog of Fangorn forest to assume the role of head of engineering. Urs did seem to possess a wizard's omniscience as he bound Google's engineers to the task of gathering data from the shadowy corners of the web and feeding it to his army of servers. Perhaps he drew his power from the red socks he wore every day.

Growing up ten miles outside Basel, Switzerland, Urs had considered a career in chemistry, but he found programming more definitive. "You could invent something," he explained, "and then if it didn't work, you could always deduce why. It wasn't random." A thing is right or it's wrong. If it's wrong, there's a reason, so you work on it until it becomes right. Engineers live in a binary world. Sometimes I envied that clarity.

Urs narrowed his focus to computer architecture at university in

---

[*] Scott Hassan and Alan Steremberg both contributed to the coding of Google's original search engine while at Stanford. Hassan later founded eGroups, a company that enabled online mailing lists. Steremberg founded Wunderground, a popular weather information website that Larry and Sergey often looked to for technical inspiration.

Zurich, then trekked off to Stanford for graduate work on "making stuff faster . . . making stuff cheaper." He ended up teaching at UC Santa Barbara and developing the core of the Java Virtual Machine (JVM) at a small startup. I could lie and say I knew what that meant, but it would betray the trust I've established with you as a reader. To Googlers who used their computers for more than checking email, however, having worked on the JVM made Urs some kind of demigod. So Larry and Sergey were thrilled when he said he'd fix Google's systems problem and turn their "student project" into something reasonably stable and scalable.

Infrastructure is just not all that exciting to those outside a small cult of spec heads who willingly cloister themselves to focus on improving systems that — if they work the way they should — are all but invisible. Larry and Sergey were ensconced in the highest order of Google engineers, but they were not acolytes who needed to know where every bit was buried.

Urs cared, though. He cared a great deal.

"Urs was interested in how we got there and not just the result," said Ben Smith, an engineer who worked on GWS. "You increase the cache hit rate by two percent, and you save three hundred machines. That's the stuff he likes. Without Urs, Google's infrastructure wouldn't have lasted two years."

At first I didn't understand how lucky Google had been to bring Urs onboard. To me he was just another engineer scribbling jargon on whiteboards. But in talking with those who worked under him I came to realize that he was, as Deb Kelly, an engineering project manager, called him, "the key."

"He's got the most fabulous command of detail at a broad level of any human being I've ever met," Deb told me. "He had a tremendous amount of the organization in his head." That knowledge earned Urs the trust of Larry and Sergey and enabled him to keep the founders off the backs of the working engineers.

"Once Larry and Sergey needed to attend to other things," said search-quality engineer Ben Gomes, "Urs was the key person on the engineering side. Whenever there was a crisis he was always called in to deal with it himself."

Enough engineers sang his praises that this book could have been written entirely as a hagiography of Saint Urs, Keeper of the Blessed Code. And if they weren't rhapsodizing about Urs's intelligence, his team members were lauding his communications skills, which kept him from seeming arrogant.

"I've seen him walk into a meeting where he had no context," Gomes continued, "and halfway through the meeting, he was asking the most insightful questions. He was able to put together an argument so that it's obvious this is what you should be doing. The founders are dreamers and that's wonderful, but Urs was always the voice of 'the art of the possible.'"

Paul Bucheit, the creator of Gmail, explained to me how that worked in practice. He recalled telling Urs about a problem he had been struggling to solve.

"Larry said we should put it all in memory."

"Yeah," Urs answered in his usual deadpan voice. "Larry has a lot of ideas. You should just keep doing what you're doing."

"That's when I realized," Paul told me, "that you have to be smart enough to not just do what Larry says, if it doesn't make sense in the present." As the man who had to keep Google's wheels on the tracks, Urs understood that better than anyone. His focus prevented the young company from being shunted down sidelines that led nowhere.

Urs's most significant accomplishment, however, was building the team that built Google. "Your greatest impact as an engineer comes through hiring someone who is as good as you or better," he exhorted everyone who would listen, "because over the next year, they double your productivity. There's nothing else you can do to double your productivity. Even if you're a genius, that's extremely unlikely to happen."

Silicon Valley was one huge inflating tech-boom bubble, and plenty of companies awarded BMW signing bonuses to any coder who could fog a mirror. It was Urs's insistence on only hiring engineers at least as qualified as those already at the company that set him apart. "If you have very good people, it gives you a safety net," he believed. "If there's something wrong, they self-correct. You don't have to tell them, 'Hey, pay attention to this.' They feel ownership and fix it before you even knew it was broken."

Two such hires were Jeff Dean and Sanjay Ghemawat. If Urs was Google's architect, Jeff and Sanjay were the master carpenters who raised the roof beams and pounded the nails that held together the load-bearing walls. Wherever problems needed to be solved, "JeffnSanjay" were there* — from devising the Google file system to developing advertising technology, from accelerating machine translation to building break-through tools like MapReduce.†

Jeff pumped out elegant code like a champagne fountain at a wedding. It seemed to pour from him effortlessly in endless streams that flowed together to form sparkling programs that did remarkable things. He once wrote a two-hundred-thousand-line application to help the Centers for Disease Control manage specialized statistics for epidemiologists. It's still in use and garners more peer citations than any of the dozens of patented programs he has produced in a decade at Google. He wrote it as a summer intern in high school.

Tall, gaunt, and a tad taciturn, with angular features that bring to mind Gary Cooper, Jeff had just left the research center at Digital Equipment Corporation (DEC) to start a new job with a promising dot-com when Urs called him in June 1999.

"I wasn't really thinking that he'd change jobs after just three months," said Urs, "but what he said was, 'It's good timing, because I'm bored. I've solved all the technical problems there are to solve at this company, so I'm thinking maybe I made a mistake.'"

Jeff couldn't wait to engage the challenges at Google. He showed up weeks before his official start date, before he'd even left the other company, and wrote code without being on the payroll because he "wanted to hit the ground running."

Two dozen former DEC researchers would follow Jeff to Google. Many, including Sanjay, were encouraged by the knowledge that Jeff was already there. Mindful of Urs's admonition to hire great people, Jeff went after them with every means at his disposal, including placing recruiting ads on Google that appeared whenever someone searched for obscure coding-related keywords like "TLB shootdown" or "lock free synchronization." (After engineer Paul Haahr joined Google, he told Jeff, "Any company that advertises on 'lock free synchronization' is good enough for me.")

While many of those who came from DEC took on major roles — for example, Monika Henzinger became Google's research director and

---

* So much so that their names came to be fused as one in Google conversations and both were named Google Fellows, the company's highest honor.

† MapReduce enabled engineers to write prototype programs much more quickly, accelerating the speed of Google's product development and systems improvements.

Krishna Bharat created Google news — it was system designer Sanjay who perfectly modulated Jeff's irrepressible need to keep dashing forward. Tall and soft-spoken with premature touches of gray, Sanjay walked quietly through the halls projecting an air of unaffected professorial dignity, reminding me of Obi-Wan Kenobi in his later years of wisdom.

Jeff described the stoichiometry of their partnership this way: "Sanjay and I balance each other pretty well, because he tends to be more reserved and analytical and I tend to say, 'Let's do something now. Let's get it done.' Put the two of us together and we go just the right speed."

Ben Gomes put it slightly differently as he explained to me why he was so comfortable working with Sanjay. Sanjay was very, very smart in a way that was systematic and therefore easy to follow, "whereas Jeff was just brilliant." Ben added, "I couldn't learn to be brilliant."

Engineering had speed and direction and was accelerating toward the goal of building a better Google. Those of us in marketing wanted a better Google, too, but we weren't as clear on how to get there.

"Technically, something either works or it doesn't," ops manager Jim Reese once acknowledged. "If our site is up, it's up. With marketing, there's more gray area." That gray area was bounded by a slippery slope, according to our founders, and at the bottom of that slope lay a cesspool of intellectual dishonesty. Over my first few weeks, the marketing group had to sort out priorities and roles, so it's not surprising that Larry and Sergey did not know exactly what we were doing. They gave a few clues to how they felt about marketing in general, though.

"It doesn't have to be true — it's marketing," Sergey joked about our corporate web pages.

"That's because marketing likes to lie," Larry let slip. He smiled when he said it, but I sensed we were being held to account for everything engineers hated about the nonquantifiable world, with its corrupted communications and frequent flyer programs. God help anyone who offered a marketing opinion as if it were a scientific fact.

As a result of Larry and Sergey's skepticism, we in marketing never attained the sense of purpose Urs brought to engineering. Cindy handled PR with surgical precision and Larry and Sergey trusted her judgment, but the founders wanted to wield marketing like a sledge instead of a scalpel. They'd tell her to "press release" things, by which they meant alert the media that we'd made changes no one but engineers would care about. Reporters didn't respond to whistles only dogs could hear. Cindy held off the founders and went about stitching together deeper, long-term relationships, so when we finally had something worthy of an announcement the press would pay attention.

Before a press release could go out, though, Larry insisted on running the draft past everyone in the building.

"I agreed to do it, with reservations," said Cindy. "I definitely never did this at any other company. I did not have that kind of relationship with engineers at Apple because we had layers of organization between marketing and the techies, and I don't think that's unusual. We lived in different buildings, different worlds. I was pleasantly surprised by the tone and quality of the feedback I got from Googlers."

Google was different that way. Even though engineers were kept separate according to the floor plan, email penetrated all corners of the company and communal meals and snack rooms led to plenty of cross-pollination. It was surprising to me, too, how articulate and interesting the techies turned out to be when you got to know them, though as you might expect, coders were sticklers for the rules of grammar.

"Split infinitive," Craig noted about some copy I had written.

"Shouldn't that be 'the' instead of 'a'?" Urs asked about a tagline.

"'This' and 'FAQs' don't agree in number," another engineer admonished me.

I never minded these grammatical suggestions and corrections, which kept me on my toes and made me conscious that someone was paying attention to what I produced. But that didn't mean I embraced every suggestion that came in from would-be marketers in other departments. And there were so, so many of them.

Striking Out

I didn't know anything about Salar Kamangar when he came to me in my first month at Google and asked for help. Someone mentioned he had been an intern. On the basis of that single fact, I underestimated him, as I suspect most people did. Larry and Sergey had hired Salar out of Stanford as Google's ninth employee in the spring of 1999. They tried him out as a temp for a couple of weeks, then put him on the payroll, where his undefined role as savant-at-large grew to encompass every new business challenge the company encountered, from hiring a controller to transferring the company's twenty-five-million-dollar nest egg from one bank to another. He was twenty-two at the time.

Salar was a Porsche packaged as a Dodge Dart. Dark haired with large, limpid brown eyes and a shy, infectious grin, he could have stood in for Sal Mineo in *Rebel without a Cause,* but despite his disarming demeanor, he argued his positions with passion, persuasiveness, and persistence. For a thin man, he was very hard to get around.

Salar's friends had an Internet company that mailed free postcards for users who typed in a message and a recipient's address. Their revenue came from selling ads to be printed on the cards.

"I signed us up for a free trial," Salar informed me. "Could you work with them to make it happen? We can promote it through the Google Friends newsletter."* The postcards seemed like a strange way to market Google, and I wasn't happy that a marketing decision was being made by someone who was not in our department—by someone, in fact, who didn't seem to *have* a department. I didn't want to be overly negative about Salar's idea, though, so I agreed to give it a shot.

Shari suggested we send it out to a professional designer. "Anything that goes to thirty thousand of our most loyal fans should have some serious thought put into it," she insisted. "Especially in the absence of any other Google branding out there."

"Hmmmm," I thought. "This is something I could do myself—a chance to knock an easy one out of the park." Besides, I'd already figured out that Larry and Sergey didn't like spending money on freelancers. I poured my soul into it. I spent hours searching for the perfect stock photos and writing lines that tenuously tied random images to Google products.

The company running the promotion died before any cards could be sent, and I had nothing to show for my efforts but a collection of strained puns. I kicked myself for having made such a marginal project a priority. There must have been more meaningful things to do. Why was I finding it so hard to get into gear?

I felt a strange paralysis induced by infinite possibilities. How many times could I rearrange my desk and make to-do lists? I looked for something familiar to grab onto. My old employer, Knight Ridder, announced they were killing off their online clipping service, NewsHound. Google could snap up the technology, improve it, rebrand it, and re-

---

* A monthly email that alerted users about new Google features.

launch it. A news-alert system seemed like a good fit for Google, since we appeared to be all about providing information to people. I sent a proposal to Larry and Sergey, who thought it would be worth looking into and asked me to set up a meeting. That was more like it — single-handedly bridging the divide between old and new media.

"What exactly would we be buying?" Sergey asked a couple of days before the meeting was to happen.

"We'd be buying their filtering technology," I answered. "We'd have to negotiate separately for the actual news feeds."

"Oh," said Larry. "That's not very interesting."

"Yeah," Sergey agreed. "The news feeds are the interesting part. I'd rather not meet to talk about the other stuff. Let Salar take a look at it and see if it's worth going after the data."

I swung my attention to Salar and tried to salvage something of the original proposal. Sergey wanted news in our index; surely we could work something out? Salar was noncommittal. "I'm not sure this is how we want to add news to the site," he told me after talking with Sergey.

In fact, it wasn't even close. NewsHound was kicked to the curb like a mangy mutt. Larry and Sergey, even without looking at it, knew Google could build a better product in-house. Writing code was easy, so why spend money on some mongrel technology they'd only have to fix? What we really needed was the content, because building an international news organization would be complicated and expensive.

Had NewsHound been a disruptive technology that changed its industry, Larry and Sergey would have wanted not just the code but the Google-caliber engineers behind it. That way, Google would own their future breakthrough ideas as well as the ones they'd already developed. Larry and Sergey didn't like renting intelligence when they could buy it. There are only so many really smart people in the world. Why not collect them all?

Other initiatives I had shepherded also fell foul of the way Google did things. I had been at my job for more than a month and had just one project — the UI guidelines I had worked on with Karen White — that I could point to as an accomplishment. Of sorts.

My strikeouts were piling up. I prayed no one was watching the scoreboard.

CHAPTER 4

Marketing without "Marketing"

W HEN YOU'RE STARTING a company, it's pretty well understood what you need to do," Craig Silverstein assured
me, speaking as an engineer and not a marketer. "You need
to write tools to manage your workflow, you need to write a web server
. . . There are a lot fewer demands on your time, so it's really easy to
crank out a lot of stuff when you're small."

The equivalent for a brand manager would be developing a logo, a
tagline, some market positioning, and a plan for growing market share.
We had a logo and seemed to be doing fine without a tagline, so I decided to focus on positioning and a marketing plan. I wasn't the first to
put effort there.

Scott Epstein, the consultant Google hired in early 1999 to get marketing on track, succeeded in one important area — proving Larry and
Sergey had the same distaste for traditional promotion that a vegan
has for fatback. They rejected his plan to spend millions "building the
brand," and when he slipped away into the night, they asked Cindy to
shoulder responsibility for communications. As a PR person, Cindy
saw the value in building an audience through word of mouth instead
of spreading money like a layer of manure across the advertising waste-
land. Google had a great story to tell, and public relations could harvest
bushels of low-hanging fruit before we shoveled out cash for ads. All
she needed was a little help.

"In late summer '99, we had such a hard time getting anyone to return our calls or to take us seriously," Cindy later recalled. "We did hire one firm, but we had to let them go because they only worked with clients that allowed them to invest, and Larry and Sergey said no.* That set us in the direction of going it alone — hire a small team, build institutional knowledge, and establish direct relationships with the media, analysts, and influencers." But in a classic chicken-and-egg conundrum, the media wouldn't talk to Google, because Google wasn't a company people were talking about.

"I contacted both the *San Francisco Chronicle* and the *Merc*," Cindy said. "I just wanted to get a relationship established. The *Chron* never called me back. I finally got hold of someone on the business desk at the *Merc* who told me they would not be covering Google because our Palo Alto office was 'too far north.'"

Growing by word of mouth suited Larry and Sergey's animosity toward advertising. They scoffed at profligate startups and their Superbowl spots, because TV ads lacked accountability. You could dump millions and not know if you had converted a single viewer into a user. Engineers rebelled against such inefficient excess in the name of "brand building."

"Brand is what's left over when you stop moving forward," was a sentiment engineer Matt Cutts heard expressed in a meeting with Larry and Sergey. It was only when a product stopped working better than the competition that branding became a factor. By then you'd already lost. For a long time, Larry refused to even use the B-word — because "branding" implied that technology alone was insufficient for success.

My marketing plan would change that. Larry and Sergey would see all the ways in which we could get the attention of users and companies and convince them to try Google. I sat staring at my monitor with my feet on my door-desk and my keyboard in my lap and started typing.

"Google's ultimate goal," I wrote, "is to become a mass market search solution, directly serving end users as well as supplying search technology to other destination sites." Then I started laying out the marketing initiatives that would take us there.

---

* Insisting on equity was common practice in Silicon Valley at the time. The landlords at Google's University Avenue office wanted a share of the company, but Larry and Sergey refused them as well.

So, What's the Plan?

My first week, I asked Cindy for a copy of Google's strategic plan. She just looked at me. Google didn't have a strategic plan. Other than the handful of PowerPoint slides used to secure our venture capital, nothing existed in writing about what the company was trying to accomplish. It all resided in the heads of Larry and Sergey, who were never in the mood to discuss it.

I found a copy of the VC presentation, and sure enough, our strategy was right on the opening slide — a *Doonesbury* cartoon in which entrepreneur Bernie says, "Look at the search engine guys. They've got no hard assets, just software that drives everyone crazy. And yet they have market values in the billions! Of course, if someone comes along with a smart search engine, one that actually works, those companies evaporate overnight."

I flipped through the slides, but there wasn't much more than a broad outline of Google's management team, a list of competitors, some market share numbers, a budget, and a slide that read, "What's the secret to Google? 4+ years of R&D at Stanford and Google.com + Highly skilled team." That really cleared things up.

"When I tried to put in more detail, they didn't want to share anything," Salar explained when I asked about the thinking behind the skimpy content. Pulling together the slides had been his first task upon joining the company. Larry and Sergey knew that some of the firms they were pitching already had investments in competing search engines, and they had no intention of giving away their good ideas.

"That made the presentation kind of dry," Salar went on, "so Sergey's solution was to annotate it with clip art the night before our first meeting." I tried to picture the power brokers of Silicon Valley intently pondering an investment of ten million dollars as cheesy money trees and sparkling dollar signs sprouted around Google's potential revenue streams (sales of technology and targeted advertising). Then I imagined their reaction to Google's aggressive traffic projections, which showed the company conducting fifty percent of all Internet searches within two years. Even in Silicon Valley, nobody grew that fast.

In 1999, you would have needed uncanny foresight or powerful pharmaceuticals to envision Google's future success. Or maybe just money to burn. Kleiner Perkins and Sequoia must have had something, because the two VC firms invested twelve and a half million dollars each, leading cynics in the Valley to define "Googling" as "getting funding without a business plan."[*]

The slide deck said nothing about marketing Google, so my plan would start from scratch. I drew a pyramid chart showing a hierarchy of users, with "tech savvy" at the top and "newbies" at the bottom, and outlined a three-phase program to move us through all the stages in between. I asked questions for which we had no answers. What was the size of the tech-savvy market? Had we already won the majority of it? Would we need new products to appeal to less sophisticated users? Research could tell us that, but meanwhile I offered ideas about making proprietary legal databases and domain-registration records searchable and launching a Google Fellows program to reward dedicated users. I felt confident sending the plan to our executive staff. It contained no proposal to spend big on mainstream media and instead emphasized the importance of gathering data. Larry and Sergey seemed to like data.

"Great job," Sergey responded. "This is a good starting place." True, he disputed most of my supporting arguments, but he administered no gut shot that left my plan writhing on the floor spilling its insights. Larry was more reserved, but he liked the questions I was asking and thought the idea of Google Fellows was "cool."[†]

Sergey quibbled with my assertion that speed would not be an important differentiator as everyone moved to broadband connections. "Speed is an issue for me," he said, "and I have a cable modem at home. If search engines were faster and better, they could be integrated into your thought process." He saw Google becoming an invisible component in every user's decision-making, not just a tool for finding a particular fact. Apparently "brain integration" was one of our hitherto undisclosed corporate goals.

He also discounted my conclusion that we needed to add targeted services to steal page views away from the big portals. "Nonfunctionality is a feature," he instructed me. "We don't need to increase page views

---

[*] "Definitely some VC groups had heartache because we had no revenue model and no projects in place for that revenue," said Salar, and "there were definitely some VCs that were less interested because of the valuation we were expecting."

[†] He liked it so much he reserved the honor for exceptional Google staffers rather than well-schooled Google users.

by adding products." Larry and Sergey always thought in terms of scale. Sergey saw that there was a far greater gap between the total numbers of users visiting each portal than there was between the numbers of pages visitors viewed once they were at a portal. The winner in search wasn't going to be the site generating a few extra clicks from the users it already had; it was going to be the site with the most users overall. Google, Sergey had decided, would be the latter.

The Only Way to Win

Having a marketing plan on the way to approval gave me some comfort. No matter how innovative our product was, eventually others would match it. It was the normal course of business. On that day, marketing would be needed to create a clear choice for consumers. On that day, I would step forward and proclaim, "I'm ready to get *up* and do *my* thing."

That day would never come.

It wasn't because Google was lead dog from the get-go and never looked back. "We weren't in the lead," Urs said about the early days. "Google was this tiny company and AltaVista and Inktomi were huge in comparison. Inktomi had a cage in the same data center, twenty times bigger than Google's. Much nicer. They had their logo on the wall. We were a toy company trying to do something new. Our ranking was bet-ter, but we were way slower than Inktomi. We could barely keep up and they had a hundred times the traffic we did."

It's just as well I hadn't realized how fragile Google truly was as I set up the meeting to discuss next steps for my marketing plan. It might have imbued me with false confidence that my proposal held all the answers. Instead, I knew I would have to justify spending on each of the steps I had outlined. I started down the list of reasons we needed to implement the plan and why we needed to do it with some urgency.

"The most important thing to consider," I began, "is that our own internal research shows our competitors are beginning to approach Google's level of quality. In a world where all search engines are equal, we'll need to rely on branding to differentiate us from everyone else."

The room grew quiet.

I looked around nervously. Had I said something wrong? Yes. Not just wrong, but heretical to engineers who believed anything could be improved through iterative application of intelligence. Larry made my apostasy clear.

"If we can't win on quality," he said quietly, "we shouldn't win at all." In his view, winning by marketing alone would be deceitful, because it would mean people had been tricked into using an inferior service against their own best interests. It would be nobler to take arms against our sea of troubles and by opposing, end them.

To Boldly Go Where No One Has Gone Before

The 1999 Google holiday party was a grad student affair with folding chairs and a few dozen folks crammed into a room decorated with whiteboards. Because of problems in the kitchen, the food was late and came out lukewarm. Sergey attempted to address the celebrants by standing atop a red rubber ball five feet in diameter, but he couldn't maintain his balance despite the trapeze classes he was taking at a local circus. He ad-libbed some jokes and made general remarks about things going well, but offered no glowing vision of the future to reassure us that the company would be around for next year's celebration.

Kristen came away more convinced than ever that I had traded our security for some fly-by-night startup that was halfway to shutting down. The ride home was quiet as the kids went offline in the back seat of the Taurus.

"They seem . . . nice," Kristen said, "but do they know what they're doing? It feels kind of disorganized."

"I'm sure things will settle down over time," I murmured over the kids' snores. "They're still putting the company together, so it's a little rough around the edges. It's really not as bad as it looks."

The chaos had already begun to feel normal to me: the jumble of toys, tools, and technology, the roaming dogs dodging electric scooters zipping through the corridors, the micro-kitchen overflowing with free food. I was beginning to see that every aspect of Google's office space had a purpose.

George Salah left Oracle to become Google's facilities manager in 1999 after bonding with Larry and Sergey during a roller hockey game. ("They were much better than I expected for a bunch of engineers," he admitted.) Oracle was an enormously successful international company, so applying their best practices made perfect sense for a young startup. "At Oracle," George noted, "there were standards that I could pull out and say, 'This is what we need to do in Portland.' I said to Larry and Sergey, 'I don't want to re-create the wheel every time. Are you okay with me creating a set of standards?' They looked at me like I was crazy."

"*Absolutely not!*" the founders declared. "We don't want to have *anything* to do with standards. We don't want anything 'standard.'"

"I think that was about the time I began to go bald," George told me, running a hand over his naked pate. "They wanted to be completely different from any company that had come before them. To optimize in every way, shape, and form. I had to throw out everything I had learned in my career and then find vendors and contractors and architects who could begin to understand what the founders wanted — to create the best workplace they possibly could. Not for the sake of aesthetics. It was always function over form."

My colleagues and I, too, were forbidden to do things "the normal and accepted way." As Cindy put it, "Larry and Sergey fundamentally rejected any type of template approaches to marketing Google. At every other company I worked at, when you met with the media you had a set of messages, backed up by a PowerPoint presentation and a leave-behind. You had media training and were prepared with a pat response for any question. Larry and Sergey hated the idea, refused to stick to manufactured messages, did not use presentations, and talked about what they wanted to talk about. The media loved them for it."

My offline marketing colleague Shari was less enamored with our founders' idiosyncratic approach. She hammered Sergey to pay for market research and implored him to bring on an outside agency to develop a promotional campaign. "They just don't get the importance of mass marketing to build the brand," she complained. "They need to trust us to make marketing decisions and let us just do our jobs."

We all wrestled with Google's ambiguous structure. Who were the stakeholders? Who made the final call when we disagreed? Did Larry or Sergey need to approve everything we did? Apparently the company's focus on efficiency didn't extend to decision management.

Confusion about overstepping boundaries was bad enough, but there were worse scenarios than crossing an invisible line. Sometimes a founder put forth "a good idea."

"I have a good idea," Sergey informed Susan Wojcicki a couple of weeks after I started. "Why don't we take the marketing budget and use it to inoculate Chechen refugees against cholera. It will help our brand awareness and we'll get more new people to use Google."

Our company was barely a year old at the time. We had no real revenue. Spending a million dollars of our investors' money on a land war in Asia would indeed be a revolutionary approach to growing market share.

Was Sergey serious? He was. How could I even begin to argue against such a bizarre suggestion? In past jobs, I might have disagreed with colleagues on using radio or TV or debated copy points and tone, but Sergey wasn't even speaking a language I understood.

Looking back a dozen years later, I kind of get Sergey's perspective. Saving lives was a better use of our budget than running ads, which just annoyed people to no effect — and were therefore evil. Why not make a big donation to a humanitarian cause and build awareness by doing good? It had all the classic elements of a Sergey solution: a wildly unconventional approach to a common problem, technology harnessed to improve the human condition, an international scope, and an expectation that the press could be used as a tool to forward our business goals.

Sergey didn't ask Shari or me what we thought of his idea. He knew we would have ridiculed it. Instead, he turned to Susan, one of the few marketers he trusted. She was a member of the inner circle from the University Avenue office, and Google had rented space in her house. Sergey had met her family (he'd later marry her sister), and Susan understood Sergey well enough not to dismiss his outlandish suggestions out of hand. Instead, she went to gather data, which in this case meant asking her mom, a teacher in Palo Alto. As an educator, Susan's mother carried authority with Sergey, and when she confessed to being confused about our plan to support a rebel army in Russia, it took some of the wind out of his sails.

He had a back-up plan, though. "What if we gave out free Google-branded condoms to high-school students?"

Sergey asked Shari and me to investigate other charitable promotions along these lines, and we dutifully did, but it wasn't lost on us that our opinions had only been sought as an afterthought. Susan was part of the marketing group, but Shari and I were supposedly managing it. We felt marginalized. Organizational ambiguity I could handle, but I needed sufficient gravity to show me which way was up and which was down.

We shouldn't do things the way we had in the past. We shouldn't copy other companies. We shouldn't expect to be informed about our strategy, if in fact there was one. We were independent actors, building a cohesive team of nonconformists. I thought I understood: I needed to identify problems and solve them. And so I did.

CHAPTER 5

Giving Process Its Due

J ANUARY 2000. New year. New millennium. New me.

My first month had gotten off to a shaky start, but now I resolved to find solid ground in the primordial ooze of Google's early organization. My first step would be removing an obvious stumbling block between us and success: Google lacked process. We needed a clearly marked path for decision-making about everything from t-shirt design to what product categories we should enter. Fortunately, I was saturated in process implementation, having come from an organization with seven unions, dozens of editors, and an endless appetite for rumination and review. I knew how successful companies set goals, and I would bring the wisdom of the outside world to Google.

"Found a problem," I thought. "Now fix it."

I set up an interdepartmental meeting to address the need for project prioritization and resource allocation. The marketing and business development departments, the two mighty legs upon which the company's future stood, would collaborate to construct a stable platform for growth. My office mate Aydin wanted in. So did Shari and Susan and a couple of others on the business side.

At our first meeting, we brainstormed process structures. We analyzed the competition, our overall market position, and where the industry as a whole was headed. It was a good meeting, a productive meeting, and at its end we were prepared to offer the strategic leadership Google lacked. How much market share could our process-fed Google gain? The world will never know.

Once Larry and Sergey heard that we intended to dictate product plans to engineering, they threw a monkey wrench at us. That wrench was Salar. He didn't kill our committee directly, but it died just the same. Salar said that Larry was fine with answering a list of questions to clarify our corporate strategy, but that product development would remain ad hoc until further notice.

Something must have gotten through, though, because the next day Sergey issued a company-wide manifesto of sorts, listing our top three priorities: "product excellence, user acquisition, and revenue." It wasn't much of an action plan. Nor did it answer broader questions like "How will we ensure user loyalty?" and "What is our market-expansion strategy?"

I stopped asking those questions eventually, as I became convinced our founders intended to pick a path to the future based on gut instinct, then haul ass through a fire swamp of competition with the entire company riding on their backs. Such a strategy required them to hold a degree of certainty in their own abilities.

"They had so much self-confidence that Sergey was convinced he personally could find a cure for AIDS," engineer Chad Lester marveled. And why not? With twenty-five million dollars in the bank, the founders' wild hubris was free to roam the plains. Life gives you few chances to make decisions as if no one else's opinion matters. Google offered just such an opportunity. Venture capitalists John Doerr of Kleiner Perkins and Mike Moritz of Sequoia Capital sat on Google's board,* but the board didn't have control — that belonged to Larry and Sergey. All the board could do was try to guide them.

Larry and Sergey had anointed Cindy VP of corporate marketing and put her in charge of public relations and promotion, but not the development of products. The board wanted a different leader to build that organization — someone with technical savvy, but not an engineer. When engineers drive the gravy train, sometimes they focus on how fast they can go rather than where they're headed.

Larry and Sergey reluctantly agreed to take a look around, though no traditional consumer-marketing person could possibly impress them.

---

* The board comprised Larry, Sergey, and the venture capitalists who had put up the money to get Google off the ground: Doerr, Moritz, and Ram Shriram.

The right candidate would have to be able to communicate with coders, execute quickly, and be very, very smart. And smell nice. Sergey once rejected an applicant in part because "I thought he had kind of a bad body odor."

Jonathan Rosenberg, an executive at Excite@Home, was very, very smart, and the board strongly hinted that he would be the best fit for Google's needs. Jonathan had other ideas and decided to stay at Excite for two more years before claiming the role of Google's vice president of product management. He left behind more than a résumé, though. He convinced Larry and Sergey that there might be a role for a product-management group if, and only if, it didn't usurp the divinely ordained primacy of engineering. God forbid that Google become a marketing-driven company. In marketing-driven companies, researchers identified customer needs and then product managers (PMs)* directed engineers to create products to fill those gaps. I had been taught that was a good thing to do.

"Let's do a gap analysis," I used to say at the *Merc*. "What's the unmet need? Where's the market opportunity? How much share can we gain?" Engineers hate that kind of thinking.

If you're an engineer with a brilliant idea, seeing it dumbed down or abandoned because it doesn't test well is like watching a bully pull the wings off a butterfly. The right thing to do is build it regardless, to prove that you can and because building cool things is — well, you end up with cool things.

Pure-hearted geeks flee the hellish realm of product-driven companies, where soul-sucking suits shuffle after profits instead of perfection and the boss doesn't understand any technology more complicated than a binder clip. There, product management rules, pandering to a public that hasn't a clue about what it really wants, while enslaved engineers make tiny improvements to cruft — crappy products wrapped in promotion and paraded before consumers like lipsticked pigs.

Larry and Sergey would not allow that at Google. Their company would appreciate the inherent beauty of inspired design in breakthrough technologies like a spell checker that recognized a hundred variations of the name "Britney Spears" or a calculator that could convert the speed of light into furlongs per fortnight. For that to happen,

---

* I'll refer to product managers as "PMs" to avoid confusion with project managers. Project managers focused entirely on the logistics required to complete specific tasks. Product managers made more strategic decisions about every aspect of a product's development.

a Google PM would need to be someone smart enough to understand engineers but not intimidate or subordinate them. Someone the founders would feel comfortable having as a direct report. Someone who would stand up to them when need be, but who wouldn't waste their time with trivial concerns.

"I was the first person who wasn't an engineer working with engineering to define the product," Salar recalls. "We decided to call that product management."

Salar's transformation into a one-person department complemented the other process piece that fell into place in January 2000.

"The Internet is under-hyped," John Doerr had declared early in the dot-com boom. Silicon Valley listened, because Doerr's early investments through Kleiner Perkins in winners like Sun, Netscape, Compaq, and Amazon proved his uncanny acumen. Now, as one of our board members, he prescribed the best practices from his portfolio companies to beef up Google's anemic process management and tighten our flabby decision-making.

"We had a marvelous meeting this morning with John Doerr," Cindy said one day. "I was terrifically impressed with the thinking he's trying to instill in our guys."

Doerr's corporate growth regimen comprised a system for setting goals and measuring progress that he called Objectives and Key Results or OKRs. It was far more methodical than the ad hoc list of nebulous goals Sergey had unleashed on us just a week before.

"Objectives," Doerr instructed Larry and Sergey, "should be significant and communicate action. They state what you want to accomplish, while key results detail how you will accomplish those goals." Key results, therefore, should be aggressive, measurable, and time-specific. Doerr warned the founders not to overdo it: five objectives with four key results each should be sufficient.

Larry and Sergey's initial objectives included "move toward market leadership," "best search user experience," "meet or exceed revenue plan," and "improve internal organization." Those broad categories remained for many quarters, but the key results — the steps we would take to achieve them — kept changing, from "distribution deals adding half a million searches per day" to the "launch of Google in ten languages" and "CEO candidate selected."

If I wanted to see webmaster Karen White's priorities, or Cindy's or Larry's, I had only to call up the company phone list on our intranet (nicknamed "MOMA" by Craig Silverstein after the Museum of Modern Art) and click their names. It helped, because in the final days of the quarter everyone rushed to check things off their lists. If someone else's OKRs were contingent on me, I wanted to be forewarned they'd be hunting me down, and I wanted to know that the people whose help I would need to complete my own OKRs were aware of them.

In a company filled with overachievers, I assumed everyone would accomplish all their OKRs. No. It turned out that that would indicate failure. The ideal success rate was seventy percent, which showed we were stretching ourselves. Larry and Sergey assured us that missing OKRs wouldn't factor into performance reviews, because if they did we would take too few risks.

OKRs forced us to reevaluate priorities at least four times a year. If our industry changed or our corporate goals did, we had an obligation to bring out our near-dead initiatives and load them in the tumbrel. At the *Merc,* it had been nearly impossible to stop projects once they started. I had sat on a committee that decided our neighborhood news sections bled cash and should be put down, but for months no one found the will to pull the trigger. Not so at Google. Larry and Sergey expected instantaneous results, and products lived or died based on data, not sentiment.

I had mixed feelings about the efficacy of OKRs as a gauge of progress and individual accomplishment. I could support product launches on my own, because that just entailed writing copy for the website or drafting promotion plans, but I struggled to complete projects requiring engineering resources, like revamping our online store, or refitting a van as a portable wireless-access point (a Larry idea), or launching an affiliate program to pay webmasters to send traffic to our site (also a Larry idea).

As I sat in Cindy's mid-quarter update meetings, I studied my colleagues' reports and the traffic-light-colored circles next to each of their OKRs. Green meant completed or soon to be. Red meant major obstacles or a dead end. PRs' slides always looked like a well-watered fairway. My tech-dependent goals resembled a jaundice victim working on a sunburn. Yet the end result did feel like progress. After the OKRs had been in place a while, I emailed a friend I'd left behind at the *Merc:* "We're suddenly a much more focused company, which makes me think we could actually be on to something here."

Together, U and I Make a Team

"There are contentious issues," I emailed another friend, "but there's no animosity built up around them. Nobody blind-copies anyone and there's not a culture of blame fixation. Corporate politics will undoubtedly come with scale, but for now, folks are too focused on getting things done to cast aspersions."

Egos, yes, we had those in abundance, but we lacked Napoleons building personal empires. Skirmishes sprang from convictions, not power lust, and I saw nothing like the bloody trench warfare I had witnessed at other companies, where heads on pikes decorated fortified domains. Engineering was engineering. Marketing was marketing. It was clear on which side of that line you stood. Unfortunately, my prescience about politics developing with scale didn't take into account the rate of Google's growth. Instead of the years I envisioned, it was just a matter of weeks before the first border guards and checkpoints appeared.

Cindy took the occasion of the new millennium to formalize areas of responsibility within our department, dividing marketing into two groups — one under Shari's direction and one under mine. But it was Salar who erected the first fences along interdepartmental lines.

My effort to instill organizational clarity had been smothered in its cradle, but Salar recognized that uncoordinated decision-making could lead to dissonance, especially with user interface (UI) issues. So he split the baby. Marissa Mayer, who was filling in part-time as a human-computer interactions (HCI) engineer, would develop proposals for the look and feel of the results pages, while Karen and I would oversee content and design of all the other pages on Google.com. Marissa and I could both present homepage modifications, and Larry would make final design decisions on the basis of testing data and his own Larry worldview. The allocation made sense in theory, but as the Catholic Church discovered in 1378, two popes don't make you twice as infallible.

A few days later, Marissa set up a "UI-team" email list for the group that would manicure Google's appearance and shape debate on usability issues. On the list were Karen, Marissa and me, Salar, Shari, and engineers Bay Chang, Krishna Bharat, and Jen McGrath. We would meet weekly to hash out the text describing new services or the color of visited links or the size of the font for the link to our help page. That way Larry could maintain a thirty-thousand-foot view and not get lost in a sandstorm of granular detail.

UI team meetings dragged on for days — or seemed to — in the sterile, airless conference room in which we met. The lights would go down, the projector would go on, and the drone of voices and page design variations would commence. Of course I had opinions about design (everyone did), but after ten minutes debating the exact shade of blue for a three-pixel line on the fourth page of results, I'd be doodling bored skeletons sitting at keyboards in endless cube farms. Human-computer interaction, indeed.

"The table of contents has a hardwired width of six fifty," Bay might say to kick things off. "How about creating another column in the middle, and making it a fixed width?"

"The headings seem to be set farther right on the page than the text," Marissa might jovially rejoin. "Can we fix this with margins or reducing cell padding or cell spacing?"

"You missed a comma after the second item in the series," I'd toss out, just to keep the rollicking good times rolling and oxygen flowing to my frontal lobe.

Mockup wars broke out constantly and quickly escalated, with design ideas expressed as HTML sketches. The projector linked to our laptops fired dozens or even hundreds of layouts at the wall as we fought our way toward the most user-intuitive implementation.

I was handicapped by my degree in English — a burden I alone struggled to bear. It wasn't that I didn't understand basic HTML tags (as a concept, anyway), but my limited knowledge left me unilaterally disarmed. I had brought a cap gun to an Uzi drive-by. As my colleagues furiously revised code on the fly and sent iterations ricocheting, I resorted to paper and color markers to render my ideas. That patronizing chuckle you bestow on toddlers for stick-figure portraits? It became the soundtrack of my presentations.

Sometimes UI team members disagreed, which made it easier to stay awake. Engineering, research, and marketing were all represented, but alliances shifted. I often found myself in concert with Bay, who had written his doctoral dissertation on human-computer interaction, and with Karen, who intuited what might be useful to "normal" people (that is, users who didn't have an advanced technical degree — or, God forbid, even a BA — from Stanford).

I also agreed with Marissa more often than not. She carefully constructed positions based on user test results or data culled from our logs, the automatically generated internal records of users' interactions with our servers. "When Urs put me in charge of UI," she reminded us, "he said we didn't need opinions. We need facts and research to base good UI decisions on."

The problem was that sometimes we had questions the data couldn't answer. Should color bars be used as section headers or only as page titles? Should we use round radio buttons or a pull-down menu? Should we force browsers to display sans-serif text or allow users to override our choices with their own preferred fonts? Divisive issues that could suddenly turn vicious.

"People want to adjust the number of results they see based on the particular search they're conducting. It's query-specific," a debate might begin. And then, "Any idiot can see we must give them that choice on each results page."

"You kludge-riddled broken brainframe!" would come the reply. "Users want to set their number of results and leave it that way forever. The option to change shouldn't be shoved in their face like a smelly sock every time they search."

"You unbuffered buffoon! You understand nothing about online behavior! Have you even read *User-Centered System Design?*"

"No. But I've read your mama's user-centered system design . . ."

Okay, so that never happened. Instead, we looked at what other sites did and hypothesized what would be most effective by drawing on our own experience. Truth could not be objectively and rationally derived until we had actually made a decision and implemented it. When we guessed wrong, usage dropped and user email increased.

"Why can't I change my display font?" people demanded to know. "Isn't this still America?"

Arthur C. Clarke once postulated, "Any sufficiently advanced technology is indistinguishable from magic." Our job on the UI team was to set the stage for the technological marvel that happened whenever someone conducted a search — to make Google's interface supernaturally simple to use. The choices we made may look painfully obvious, but that's a mark of the team's success. We didn't try to distract users with anything showy or ostentatious or follow the portal path of flashing colors, dazzling displays, and other hocus pocus. Instead, we presented a well-thought-out, unsullied space with nothing up its sleeve but an incomparable talent for pulling rabbits out of the black box of the Internet. Assuming, that is, you were looking for rabbits.

The UI team grew quickly. Everyone wanted to touch up Google's public face. We spun off a front-end production group to deal with implementation issues so we could stay focused on overall design philosophy. Schwim set up a UI lab for the front-end team with a dozen different computers and browser configurations and even a WebTV unit so they could avoid a repeat of the AOL-Verdana misstep. Even though we added more engineers, designers, and UI specialists, I remained the only resident writer.

Though I would never get under the hood and retool the code base, my aesthetic suggestions occasionally made it onto the site, and my text decrees increasingly carried the weight of authority. I started to feel a role defining itself around me. I couldn't be a tech leader or a design director. But I could be Google's word guy.

CHAPTER 6

Real Integrity and Thoughts about God

LARRY AND SERGEY were not fond of the mainstay of Internet advertising—rectangular graphics called banners that flashed and screamed for attention in annoying ways—and they wouldn't put them on their Google. In fact, they weren't fond of advertising at all, because they felt taking money for ads provided an incentive to bias search results in the advertisers' favor. Still, they had listed ad sales in their original VC presentation as a possible source of income, and they were willing to consider it—if that could be done in a way that was targeted and useful instead of obnoxious.

Cost containment could only carry us so far. At some point Google would need to start generating revenue to survive. We were selling search services to other companies, which put us in competition with well-established players like Inktomi and AltaVista, and the upside potential didn't look fantastic. While Google was gaining a reputation as a search destination, we had no real standing as a provider of services to large enterprises.

That brought Larry and Sergey back to advertising. The logical course would be to outsource development to someone like DoubleClick, whose core competency was placing ads on websites. We were a search company, after all, not an ad network. Craig Silverstein made that case to Larry and Sergey.

"Why spend all the effort? Why get distracted by trying to make an ad platform?" he asked them.

"None of the existing ad platforms work with the kind of advertising we want to do," they replied. "So we'll have to write our own."

"I thought that was a good argument," Craig told me. "But still it made me sad."

The ads Larry and Sergey wanted to serve were all text, not like the intrusive banners that DoubleClick had helped make ubiquitous across the web. No one in early 2000 thought words alone could be effective compared with the glitz of animated GIFs (image files formatted for display online).

"The DoubleClick people we talked to didn't understand," Urs remembers. "They said, 'We can't serve text ads. You'd have to render the text as a bitmap image and we could serve that.'"

And there was another obstacle.

"They had nothing that allowed you to target to a search," Urs added, "and it was obvious that would be important.* So the question solved itself." Larry and Sergey took comfort from the fact that their old Stanford friends at the weather website Wunderground.com had written their own ad system and found it relatively easy to do.

"Here we were," Susan Wojcicki recalls, "maybe fifty to sixty people, and we were competing already with these huge companies that had much bigger market share in search than we did. And at the same time we were, 'Oh yes, of course, we should build our own advertising system, too.' We wanted to serve ads in every country and have the ads be targeted to every query. And we wanted it to be fast." The company's vision stretched beyond the feasible.

"This was around the time," Susan added, "that Larry decided we should also scan every book in the world." Stretched beyond the feasible by quite a bit.

Jeff Dean began working on systems for managing and serving ad campaigns. He was joined a week later by a recently hired engineer named Howard Gobioff—an iconoclastic thinker and rabid privacy advocate, Howard was a ponytailed, mullet-coiffed Carnegie Mellon PhD and weight-room habitué, equally comfortable sporting a tux, black motorcycle leathers, or a combination of the two. Within days,

---

* Targeting means matching an ad to the trigger that causes it to be displayed: in this case, selecting ads on the basis of the keywords a user enters into Google, so the ads displayed are relevant to the actual results appearing alongside them.

Jeff and Howard had a working prototype. Then they lent a hand to Marissa Mayer, who had been looking at ways to match ads to searches, and quickly knocked out an ad-targeting system.

To test their prototype, Jeff enrolled Google in Amazon's affiliate program. Every time someone clicked on one of our book ads and then bought that book on Amazon, Google would be paid a commission. Jeff dumped a hundred thousand titles into the new system, which began spewing ads across Google's results pages whenever someone searched for a novel or nonfiction work by name. Even though not every ad earned clicks, the system clearly worked. Suddenly Google was generating revenue, albeit modest revenue, from its ad system. No great huzzah went up. No champagne was uncorked. No expectations were raised. There was still work to be done.

There's Something We'd Like to Ad

The Amazon affiliate ads proved the program worked. Now we would try selling ads to companies that didn't have affiliate programs. The ads, appearing as text in boxes at the top of our results pages, would be sold on a cost-per-thousand-impressions (CPM) basis. In other words, advertisers would be charged every time Google displayed their ads (delivered impressions), whether anyone clicked on the ads or not, and the rate charged was based on a thousand showings of the ad. To make the program a real product, however, Google needed to be able to tell advertisers how much inventory was available for them to buy. For example, if an advertiser wanted to show an ad every time someone searched for "titanium golf clubs," we had to figure out how often "titanium golf clubs" showed up in our query stream.

Ed Karrels, who joined Google from SGI, built an inventory-estimation tool to harvest that data from our logs system so we could guarantee the number of ads we would show. Even more impressive to his fellow Googlers, Ed established a thirty-five-mile Friday morning round trip to the nearest Krispy Kreme, where he harvested four dozen donuts, loaded them into his silver Mercedes SLK 230, and drove them at dangerously high speeds back to the office.* Google now had fried dough Fridays and an actual advertising business.

---

* A few months later Krispy Kreme opened its first Peninsula store less than a mile from Google — a good thing because Google's Friday donut consumption quickly rose to eighty dozen.

In January 2000, the Google ad program slid into the open market without so much as a press release to announce it. Cindy thought we should make some waves, but she was overruled, perhaps because Larry and Sergey didn't want to alert the sharks circling startups like ours that fresh meat was swimming in their territorial waters. The percentage of Google results pages that actually displayed our text ads was minuscule, and for years people swore they had never seen an ad on our site. That worried loyal Google users because they didn't understand how we could possibly stay afloat with no revenue stream. Some even offered to send us donations. We politely declined.

Of course, we tested the ads. Marissa, Bay Chang, and Jen McGrath conducted a usability session at a Stanford computer lab.

"I dunno. It seems kind of unethical," one of the participants suggested. "I thought it was a search result. With banner ads, you know that they're paid for."

Well, that was unexpected. Text ads were less ethical than obnoxious blinking banners?

"Shouldn't we test banners and text ads to see which users prefer?" I asked when I heard the feedback. "What's our long-term view on banners anyway? How much are we leaving on the table by not running them?" My assumption was that because image ads were more intrusive, we would be able to charge a higher rate for them. I was on the wrong side of history, but fortunately Larry and Sergey overruled me. They argued that we could always escalate from text to image ads if need be, but it would be much harder to roll back from image ads to just plain text. Text it would remain — at least it would if the ads were successful, about which I had my doubts. We added color backgrounds to distinguish the ads more clearly from search results, but they still looked to me like a throwback to the pre-Windows days of DOS.

Jeff and Howard never expected their hacked-together system to grow into an economic engine. It was just a prototype to prove we could actually serve ads ourselves. Sales gave engineers information about what advertising they'd sold, and the engineers input each ad by hand. The system wrote directly to the database and there was no way to back it up. The gross inefficiency of this manual system bothered Larry. Once it was up, however, no one wanted to take it down.

"The targeting stuff ended up not working so well," Jeff Dean admitted recently, "but we used the core ad-serving systems for many, many years. The nugget of that original design is still in there."

Engineers Ed Karrels, Radhika Malpani, Matt Cutts, Howard Gobioff, and Chad Lester took over as keepers of the advertising flame. They would develop the features demanded by clients and keep the limping system from collapsing under its own weight. Jane Manning joined the group as a project manager and became the port through which the sales team channeled customer requirements. All of the sales team, that is, except for Bart.

Bart Woytowicz, a six-foot-six retired semi-pro international basketball player and bon vivant, headed sales operations. He liked to talk directly to engineers, and the engineers liked talking to him since he was the end user of the code they were writing. Besides, Bart always could be counted on to lighten the mood, as he once did at Halloween by wearing a leather S&M mask and a baseball uniform and claiming to be San Francisco Giants player "Barry Bondage." Bart didn't feel obligated to beat up the engineers about deadlines and deliverables. That was the project manager's job. He did, however, assure them of something they already suspected: the flat-rate CPM pricing we offered advertisers was a dying business model.

The market was shifting to "cost per click" (CPC) pricing. With CPC, advertisers paid for ads only when users actually clicked on them. It was the way our competitor GoTo worked. In GoTo's model, the price paid for each click was determined by a real-time auction, and those advertisers willing to pay the highest CPC won the most prominent positions on the page.

The GoTo model was innovative but flawed. It encouraged advertisers to bid high, but not to target their advertising only to relevant keywords. An attorney representing asbestos victims in a class-action lawsuit, for example, for whom each new client might be worth tens of thousands of dollars, could bid high for dozens of unrelated keywords to blanket results pages with his asbestos ads. ("Mesothelioma" was for a time the most expensive keyword you could buy on Google.) Ninety-nine percent of the ads would be ignored, but the lawyer wouldn't care, because most of that exposure cost nothing. Those off-target, high-bid ads, however, bumped other, more relevant ads to less prominent positions where they'd be clicked on less often. Since GoTo only got paid when the ads were clicked, that would be money out of their pocket. GoTo instituted a manual review process to ensure that advertisers only bought keywords relevant to what they were selling, but they were fighting a losing battle.

Larry recognized that the bidding aspect of the GoTo system had value. The flaws, though, he didn't know how to fix, and he remained skeptical that we needed a CPC pricing model to compete at all. If we did, we certainly didn't want an imperfect system to deliver it. It was hard to believe GoTo would be very successful anyway — their results were nowhere near as good as Google's. Larry put off dealing with the question. For now, anyway, Google had more important things to worry about.

A Real Ethical Dilemma

Having banned banners, we looked for other sources of revenue to supplement our plain text ads. A company called RealNames fit into that plan, but not comfortably.

Foremost among the moneymaking strategies our competitors employed in early 2000 was pay-for-placement, the practice of allowing advertisers to pay a fee to receive a more prominent position in organic search results.[*] GoTo's model was entirely pay-for-placement since it blatantly sold the top position to the highest bidder. Other sites simply included listings in the body of their search results without identifying that money had changed hands to put them there.

Pay-for-placement made Larry angry. It was unethical to confuse users about what was objectively useful and what showed up because someone paid to jump to the front of the line. Besides, it ruined a good algorithm. If you were generating useful results, why intentionally corrupt them with less valuable data? In the paper they had written together as grad students at Stanford, Larry and Sergey had identified pay-for-placement as "more insidious than advertising, because it is not clear who 'deserves' to be there, and who is willing to pay money to be listed."[†]

The problem with religious principles is that believers employ different standards of orthodoxy. For us, RealNames was the shibboleth that

---

[*] Besides "organic," names that have been applied to search results generated entirely by computer programs include: "algorithmic," "natural," and "objective."

[†] From Brin and Page, "The Anatomy of a Large-Scale Hypertextual Web Search Engine," Appendix A.

separated purists from pragmatists. RealNames sold keywords to companies and then worked with search engines to make sure that links to their clients' homepages showed up at the top of search results. For example, Ford might buy the keyword "Ford Explorer" to ensure that searchers for that term would see a link to Ford's own Explorer page. If we didn't already display that page as our first result, RealNames would pay us to include the link above and separate from our results. MSN, AltaVista, and Go.com were doing it, but we struggled with how to display RealNames links while making it clear they were neither Google-generated results nor paid advertisements.

"I feel as though we've sold out with this RealNames thing," engineer Paul Bucheit complained to a large group of Googlers including Larry and Sergey. "RealNames is a real source of junk and I think it is only going to get worse." Paul cared deeply about engineering quality and about ethics and especially about the intersection of the two. He summed up his attitude some time later with the phrase "Don't be evil." It caught on.

"This is even worse than auctioning off results," Paul complained. "Just for fun, I registered the RealNames keyword 'Craig Barrett.' Now when you search for 'Craig Barrett' on Google, the top result links to my hideous little web page." I tried it and found myself staring at a glittering pink screen full of animated unicorns and rainbows. At the time, Craig Barrett was the CEO of Intel.

It had never even occurred to me that search engines had integrity to protect. An Internet search engine was just a business, after all, not a public watchdog. Yet the RealNames debate took me right back to 1998 and the boardroom of the *Mercury News*. I had developed guidelines for accepting advertising on Siliconvalley.com, and the publisher grilled me on every worst-case scenario. "Will Microsoft be able to buy ads next to coverage of their antitrust trial?" he asked. "People will think we've compromised our editorial objectivity." It took weeks to iron out all the permutations to his satisfaction.

In Google's initial implementation in early 2000, we displayed only a small "RN" next to each RealNames result. That didn't test well. Or rather, it tested too well. In usability groups, Stanford students thought that the RealNames link was an extra-special search result that we gave prominence because of its superiority to the rest of the dreck we'd found.

Omid Kordestani was our VP of business development and responsible for Google's revenue generation. He started off defending the RealNames deal, but just when I expected him to dismiss all the research conclusions as flawed, he said something odd: "There should absolutely be no reason for Google to sell out its quality, even for great revenue."

What? A business guy turning down money already in hand? That kind of blew my mind. Who was this "salesman" who could see past his commission checks?

In the spring of 1999, Larry and Sergey had hired Omid — a Stanford MBA and a former Netscape exec — as Google's eleventh employee. His black Armani suit slimmed his silhouette, despite the travel weight he packed as a souvenir of globe-hopping sales calls. He smiled often and laughed easily. He listened when other people talked. I worried that he was too nice to be our dealmaker. Where was the forced sincerity I saw modeled in professional selling seminars? Where the thrashing, slashing, primordial-reptile-brained need to crush, devour, and destroy our competitors? Omid crushed you with kindness and devoured only desserts. Over time, Google ate away his extra pounds, but not the cuddly-teddy-bear persona, which masked an extremely intelligent and analytical mind. Omid could see where deal terms would settle and would shepherd both sides to that resolution point without snapping at their heels along the way — though he did on occasion unleash others who were perfectly willing to bare their fangs.

"When RealNames results are bad, they're really bad," Sergey noted, "but that doesn't mean we shouldn't have them. We should clearly differentiate them from Google results so that users can tell they're paid for."

Larry didn't want to change anything. "I don't think it's a problem if people confuse RealNames with our search results," he said. "If the result is better, they should probably click on the RealNames link. As long as it's clear to someone that it isn't exactly like a search result, that seems fine to me." Besides, he didn't want to give RealNames any free branding by identifying links with the RealNames term "Internet keyword." It could help them grow into a competitor.

"Slightly better for business, slightly worse for UI," Larry acknowledged. Most likely, he thought, RealNames wouldn't survive the year anyway. Society would be better served if we used their capital to improve Google before they lost it to bankruptcy.

It surprised me that Larry took the issue so casually. He seemed to be backtracking on the notion of keeping our integrity intact. Fortunately, someone was willing to point out the danger.

"I couldn't disagree more," said Urs. "While a relatively mild form, it's still a paid placement, and making it look like an 'objective' result is deceptive. The *New York Times* didn't become a leading newspaper by blurring the distinction between paid ads and independent news."

It was Marissa who found a solution. She examined how other search sites implemented RealNames results and concluded that our UI didn't meet the same standards. She sent around mockups that more clearly separated RealNames listings from our search results, and Larry selected one. The partnership lasted twelve months, and a year after we ended it, RealNames was no longer in business.

Once the issue had been resolved, I reflected on what I had seen. At the *Mercury News,* approvals took months and required written proposals in scheduled meetings. Opinions were formally presented, debated, evaluated, and carefully revised. At Google, quick mockups ruled, data persuaded, and decisions were made in hours. Yet Google was no less intent on setting an industry standard for incorruptibility. I embraced the notion that speed need not be the enemy of ethics. And I began to view competitors who took payment for placement in their results as duplicitous — if not outright evil.

The Nine Billion Names of G.O.D.

My corporate branding experience had not been an asset so far, but with the imminent launch of our first major product since the search engine, I prayed that would change. G.O.D. would provide. And by G.O.D., I meant the Google Open Directory.

Based on Netscape's Open Directory project, G.O.D. would siphon users from Yahoo, though it would have been impolitic to admit that publicly in January 2000. We wanted to maintain our friendly relationship with Yahoo — they owned the galaxy in which we were but a small rising star. Mostly, though, G.O.D. was an annoying, if necessary, distraction.

"Everyone should just use search," Larry complained. Directories were dead. To find something in a directory, you had to understand the structure of the categories within it and then drill down through layer after layer to the hidden pool of knowledge you sought. With search, you just threw everything into a big ol' sloppy data bucket and fished out answers using words describing what you wanted to find. It didn't matter where your data swam, because a good search engine would catch it, review it, rank it, and serve it to you before your fingers stopped twitching from clicking the mouse. Search? Efficient. Directories? Not.

People, though — irrational, illogical, and idiosyncratic as they are — sometimes preferred to troll the data themselves instead of dispatching a helpful search engine with an enormous net. Perhaps they wanted to see what other information fell into the same category. Perhaps they felt more comfortable worming out the perfect little fact or file or figure for themselves. If people insisted on wasting time with a data-retrieval method other than search, Google would oblige by offering an alternative — a far less useful alternative, but an alternative nonetheless.

We couldn't incorporate the best-known directory into Google, because it belonged to Yahoo. So Google hooked up with the Open Directory, a project under the stewardship of Netscape (and its parent AOL). Thousands of volunteers reviewed websites, then added them to the appropriate directory categories. That human involvement also offended search purists. Who could be trusted to categorize sites accurately? Even if a semi-intelligent agent looked at every site, figured out what it was about, then slotted it into its appropriate cubbyhole, there was no chance a manual operation could keep up with the Internet's growth. Robotic software tirelessly scouring websites at the speed of light — that was the future.

Once Google had found a directory, we couldn't just duct tape it onto the search engine. You don't put a rust-stained camper shell on a Ferrari. So Paul Bucheit added a search component to our version of the Open Directory. Now people who insisted on browsing for information could at least use search to get to the appropriate category to browse. It was an ugly baby, but it was our ugly baby.

Now our ugly baby needed a name.

Product naming is a tricky process. Do you give a product a new name that suggests it's completely separate from your core business? Do you incorporate your primary brand name to show that it's equal to, but distinct from, your existing product? Or do you simply use a generic term to describe it so that it becomes just another service you offer, rather than a distinct product that stands alone?

"Let's label it with a lower-case *d* and make it a feature," I said to

Salar. "And let's use that as the model for future product launches. We want all our brand equity to reside in the Google name, not in each sub-product." I sketched out a brand architecture showing Google in a separate box at the top, with "directory" and other potential services in smaller boxes underneath. "That makes Google more powerful as a primary brand," I explained, "so it can add credibility to any new service we introduce."

Salar agreed. "Let's stay with this strategy as we build out the information types accessible from our site," he said, "like Google images. We'll brand them as extensions of Google's service rather than new products." That decision, which took a few minutes to make, ensured that all of our engineers' awe-inducing achievements would accrue to the benefit of the Google name, rather than be parsed out to a hundred different product lines.

I look back on that as a quarter-hour well spent.

A brand is the sum of all the "touch points" you have with a product or service — your interactions, your impressions, your expectations, your unplanned casual encounters. Brand managers strive to make those touch points consistent. An obsessive brand manager at Google would have reviewed every pixel on our web page, every punctuation mark in our customer emails, every word in our sales literature, and every note of our switchboard's hold music. That's pretty much what I did. It absorbed an inordinate amount of energy, and I knew I couldn't apply myself at that level to managing a thousand Google sub-brands.

"Why don't we create a thousand Google sub-brands?" Sergey asked me a short time later. "That way we can give users all the things they like about our competitors, except with really good search results. We could do a sweepstakes site like iWon or a portal site or natural language–style queries, only with Google on the back end running the actual searches."

His logic appeared sound: if you could get all the benefits offered by competitors *plus* a search engine that actually worked, why would you use anyone else? I pointed out that with our limited resources, promoting a dozen or a hundred other brands would be counterproductive. Unless he wanted to hire more brand managers? Sergey backed down, but he revisited the idea anytime a competitor appeared to be gaining market share with search technology inferior to ours.

The Google directory service never proved a great success. We prominently displayed it on the homepage as a dark green link, then demoted it to a tab above the search box. It never drew much usage. You can still find it in the cutout bin of discounted and little-used services listed on the More Google Products page.

That's another nice thing about keeping features from becoming "real" products. Nobody misses them when they're gone.

Let a Hundred Banners Bloom

Legend has it that Google grew entirely by word of mouth. That's not quite true. We didn't mind running online ads; we just didn't want to pay for them. We established barter arrangements with Netscape and Go2Net, so we—I—needed to come up with banner ads to run on their sites. We had a few banners that a freelance agency had created before I came onboard. One featured a scary-looking voodoo doll and a disclaimer that Google employed no black magic to get results. It felt off target.

Shari didn't want us to be embarrassed by our first public marketing campaign. She carefully laid out a plan, a budget, and a schedule for developing our banner ads. We would do market research, analyze it, hire a hungry young agency for under a hundred thousand dollars, write a creative brief, get sign-off on the mockups, go into production, and then launch the ads—all within seven weeks. It was a breakneck, hurry-up, no-huddle timetable, but given Google's penchant for speed, Shari felt emboldened to rush the process. The ads would be ready practically overnight by traditional marketing standards.

Sergey also wanted the ads overnight, but he applied an even more traditional standard: he gave us twenty-four hours. He agreed that the voodoo ads had not been ideal, but he wasn't convinced that our promotion needed to be part of some big brand-identity initiative. If we wanted new ads, that was fine with him.

"How many can you have by tomorrow?" Sergey looked at me when he said it, since I was the online marketing manager. "Why don't you start with a hundred banners? That should give us enough genetic diversity that we can see what's effective and what's not. Then throw out the losers and come up with a hundred more like the ones that work." I had read *Ogilvy on Advertising* to prepare for my career. Sergey had read *On the Origin of Species*.

We didn't need to hire an agency, Sergey argued. After all, Google had a bunch of marketing people, and if we couldn't write code, certainly we could write ads. And then we could optimize the images and animate the GIFs. That wasn't coding, that was just formatting. "Why don't you just teach yourself Photoshop and the HTML you need?" he asked. I had been working on my software skills, but I had a long way to go to meet Google's exacting standards. Sergey reluctantly agreed to let me hire a freelance designer, but he wasn't happy about spending money on contractors.

Cindy dropped heavy hints that Sergey had begun doubting the wisdom of hiring marketing staff, since apparently we couldn't actually do anything for ourselves. "You need to recalibrate, Doug," she counseled me privately. "You need to stop worrying about potential problems and obstacles and just figure out how to get things done." The incompletes on my Google transcript apparently hadn't gone completely unnoticed. If I couldn't get these ads produced quickly, my days at Google would be numbered, and the number was going to be a very small one.

The "hundred banners assignment" became an inflection point for me. I threw myself at the task, spewing out every idea that crossed by mind onto a yellow legal pad. I brought in John O'Neill — a gifted copywriter with a sardonic streak and a fondness for Abba — to help develop concepts.

"Our founders still get carded," one of my animated ads began. "Our Ops guy is a brain surgeon," said the next panel. "Our chef cooked for the Grateful Dead," it continued. "No wonder we search differently."

It was John, though, who came up with Sergey's favorite line. "The last unbastardized search engine," he wrote. Sergey had a fondness for the word "bastard."

When the mockups of the first ads came back from our freelance artist, the company toasted them with an email flame circle, scorching them from all sides. Most of the comments centered on issues of aesthetics and were easily accommodated with minor changes. Sergey had only one strong objection. The artist had illustrated the line "They really, really like us" with a stock photo showing a stereotypical movie star in dark glasses and head scarf, holding a long cigarette holder. Sergey hated everything about the image, from the artificiality of the obnoxious Hollywood personality to the way the picture promoted smoking.

Larry was even more blunt. "I won't run cigarette ads," he declared.

Feedback trickled in for days. Sergey didn't like a particular shade of green we had used. Cindy thought an ad looked too much like a competitor's. One model was too young. Another too old. I unleashed Sergey's own logic like a sheep dog to contain the flock of ad hoc critics.

"It's unlikely we'll ever come up with fifty ads that all of us like," I pointed out. "And there's no guarantee that if we do, they will be the ads that our users also like. That's why we're testing these."

"Very good point," Sergey agreed. "We don't need everyone to be happy." But still the critiquing continued unabated.

"Too slow."

"Too many stripes."

"Too many words."

After another week of flung arrows, Sergey weighed in again.

"We should try a bunch of these out," he said, "and see how they per-form. We're wasting time by not running them and getting the ultimate feedback — clickthrough. Just run them. It's not a TV campaign. Run the hundred banners, see how they do, and then revise them."

I was glad Sergey had spoken. It was time for the banner bus to leave the depot.

That's when Shari, the offline brand manager, threw herself under it. "Sergey," she said, "I agree they don't all have to be perfect, but we risk hurting our brand if we don't set a quality standard. This is why compa-nies hire experienced marketing people. Please . . . trust our judgment."

Now I was caught between Shari, whose professional opinion I val-ued, and Sergey, who was advocating for my right to test ideas in the marketplace. I made the quick changes I agreed with and gave a green light to the rest.

The trades had been negotiated. The creative work was done. All that remained was placing our ads on partners' web pages and seeing what worked best. That's when I learned that every dot-com didn't run like Google. The people our partners put in charge of managing their advertising inventory were intentionally recalcitrant or unintentionally incompetent, or both. One site wouldn't commit to dates for delivering the impressions promised in the contract we had just signed. Another refused to return repeated calls and email messages. Even Netscape couldn't confirm they had actually run any of the millions of ads they were supposed to have delivered for us.

When the ads did run, the results were disappointing. I wasn't ex-pecting much because I had seen clickthrough rates (CTRs) dropping across the web.* Only zero-point-five percent of those viewing on-line ads had been clicking on them when I left the *Merc*. I assumed the rate had continued to decline. So when our ads started running, I was skeptical they'd reach the three percent CTR Sergey had set as a goal. They didn't. Most of our banners pulled less than three-tenths of a percent — a disaster in Sergey's eyes. He demanded we stop the ads immediately because he felt we were wasting our inventory. In his view, we should substitute new creative for any ad performing at under one percent once we had shown it five thousand times. Given that we had tens of millions of impressions to use up, that would have meant creating and managing thousands of banner ads, since even successful ads would "burn out" over time as they became overexposed.

Moreover, I didn't trust the numbers our partners gave us. Netscape claimed one ad had a 476 percent CTR, which, being impossible, skewed the metrics for our entire campaign. I asked our own logs-analysis team to verify the traffic our ads actually drove, but no one had time to hand-code our banners to make that possible.

Each day I would gather the reports for every ad we had run on every partner site, plug them into a spreadsheet, and hand-deliver printouts to Larry and Sergey. I'd highlight the best performers and let them know which ads we'd be rotating in or out. The association with actual data seemed to improve my standing in the eyes of our founders. They scanned every cell in the spreadsheet and asked me why certain ads were up or down or performed differently on different sites. I didn't always have the answers, but I could point to the numbers and speculate. I became a convert to the power of data persuasiveness and swore I would make all my future arguments only when I could back them up with real-world metrics.

With attention now focused on the ads' performance instead of my own, the pressure from above eased somewhat. We had created our first hundred ads quickly and cheaply and the production costs were going down. Our most effective ads featured nothing more than a white background, a search box, a logo, and some text ("The answer's in here"; "Who are you looking for?"), and webmaster Karen and Wacom† wonder Dennis Hwang could crank those out in fifteen minutes. I had actu-

---

* Research firm Millward Brown published a study in 1998 saying CTRs were averaging less than one percent.

† Wacom is the maker of a stylus and sketch pad that hook up to a computer to enable freehand drawing.

ally accomplished something to justify my existence in the eyes of our engineering overlords.

The shelves in my cupboard of confidence were no longer empty but for crumbs and cobwebs. Still, each night as I tucked my ego tight behind shuttered lids, I could just make out the sounds of a grindstone rubbing against a metal blade, slow muffled footsteps, and the whistle of an ax falling toward a wooden block.

It kept me on my toes.

CHAPTER 7

A Healthy Appetite
for Insecurity

WHAT DID IT feel like — the experience of coming to work at Google when it was fewer than sixty people? Let me give you a few impressions. Before I started at Google, I had never said any of the following on the job:

"Yes, I see the eight shelves of programming books. Where do we keep the dictionaries? No, I can't just print out the words as I look them up online."

"Is it a good idea to have all those bikes leaning against the fire door?"

"Sorry. I was aiming for Salar. Did I get the printer? Super soakers are really inaccurate at more than five feet."

"Who do I ask if I have questions about Windows? No one? Really?"

"Wow, Larry. Who trashed your office? Well, it's just that . . . uh, never mind."

"Wouldn't it be easier to buy rollerblade wheels that are already assembled?"

"Is there any way to set the sauna for more than half an hour?"

"Is it okay to go into the women's locker room to steal some towels?"

"Oh, sorry. Didn't realize anyone was napping in here."

"See, you knock down more garbage cans if you bounce the ball instead of just rolling it straight at them."

"It's in the area behind the coffee-can pyramid, right across from where the Big Wheel is usually parked."

"I tried to book ninety minutes, but the schedule was full. So I only got an hour. Could you focus on legs and feet? I think I pulled something running this morning."

Insecure in the Knowledge
Your Contribution Matters

I needed to stretch. I'd been staring at my screen for two hours thinking up new banner ads, responding to users, and working on an "email-a-friend" program that Sergey thought had the potential to go viral.

"Your user name is not valid," I wrote for one of the program's error messages. "It may have a bad character. That's not a reflection on you." I was getting a little pixel punch-drunk and it was affecting my judgment.

I left my cubicle in the marketing pod and meandered off in search of glucose and caffeine. Google was growing. The company was still contained in a single building when the millennium began, but the offices lining the outer edges of the Googleplex had all been occupied.

One day a crew of Samoans, their thick biceps shrink-wrapped in coconut-leaf tattoos, arrived to fill the open space with cubicles. The area was now partitioned by a maze of cheaply acquired, mismatched fabric panels, the flotsam and jetsam of the dot-coms that had suddenly started sinking all around us. Fast-food toys, manipulative puzzles, empty soda cans, and geek-chic objets d'Nerf feathered the work nests. Ratty couches shambled through open areas and settled on brightly colored crop circles cut into the carpeting, offering lumpy, coffee-stained comfort and filling in for laundry hampers. I brought in a couple of four-foot-high inflatable dinosaurs and left them to graze on the new flooring.

Walking the gray-padded arroyos, I glimpsed many heads silhouetted by code-filled screens. It may sound deadly dull, but there was an energy to the place — conveyed in quiet conversations, snatches of laughter, the squeak of dry-erase markers on rolling whiteboards, exercise balls bouncing, and electric scooters humming down hallways.

Yoshka ambled past, ears flapping, collar jingling. Someone flopped on a couch, took off his skates, and dropped them on the floor. Someone ground coffee beans for an afternoon espresso. A pool cue slapped a cue ball. It passed the aggression on, smacking an eight ball loitering in its path and sending it into the deep funk of a faux leather pocket.

I sensed the tension of potential — building and bound only by time — like the feeling of crossing the tracks in front of an idling train. Great efforts were being made, and the energy they required rippled outward seeking physical release.

Sometimes that physical release took an intimate form behind closed doors with a willing partner.

We had a crash cot in a windowless nap room for those who had reached the edge of endurable fatigue and lurched beyond it. One afternoon a staffer peeked in and found two engineers on the bed, engaged in an act of noncomputational parallel processing. It was decided that the space — once sanitized — could be put to better use as an office. No punishments were administered, no stern policy reminders sent out. Those who might have cast stones couldn't find adequate purchase on the moral high ground, and so unofficial UI experimentation continued, just later at night and relocated to offices lit only by passion and the glow of multiple monitor screens. "Hormones were flying and not everyone remembered to lock their doors," recalls HR manager Heather Carnes.

Larry and Sergey encouraged everyone to channel their excess energy into roller hockey instead. Any employee who signed up was issued a free NHL jersey emblazoned with his or her name and Google's logo. Hockey provided yet another metric by which Googlers could be evaluated.

"There is no better way to get to know someone," George Salah, a regular participant, believed. "To have their true colors come out, play sports with them. You get to see how aggressive they are, if they're ruthless or not, if they're capable of giving a hundred and ten percent." As a result, no one held back when fighting the founders for the puck. In fact, the harder you played, the more respect you earned. It was not uncommon to see blood and bruises when the games ended.

I never strapped on skates and joined Google's Thursday parking-lot hockey game, but I wasn't immune to the competitive intensity driving the company. I found my outlet in the rowing machine shoehorned into a corner of the rec room that engineer Ray Sidney had cobbled together. I'd drop into the gym between meetings, sit on the sliding seat, strap my sandaled feet into the footrests, and breathe deeply. I'd reflect on the electronic cholesterol clogging my inbox, the uninvited additions to my work queue, or some viewpoint variance I'd had with a colleague. I'd grip the padded pull bar, close my eyes, and jerk with all my might, sending my stationary craft slicing outward to placid waters far from the source of my current distress.

It wasn't approved form, but I wasn't trying to win a regatta. My goal was to generate the maximum number of ergs in the minimum amount of time, to best the score posted on the "Google Rowing Club" whiteboard resting against the wall. Claiming the title "best" in any category at Google took on added significance given the capabilities of those with whom we worked.

At age forty-one, I had much to prove. Sometimes it took me a little while to parse a TLA everyone else seemed to know.[*] I voiced objections based on "irrelevant" experience gained over a twenty-year career. I drove a station wagon that smelled like baby wipes and spit-up. I didn't want the unripened grads with whom I shared the locker room to assume I was slowing down physically or mentally.

One afternoon the receptionist called me.

"Doug, can you come downstairs? Sergey asked if you could load his scuba gear in the car. He said you're the strongest guy here."

"Sure," I replied. Halfway to the lobby, I slowed down. Then I stopped. The founder of the company wanted me to do his scutwork. That couldn't be good, could it? But Sergey felt I was uniquely qualified. That was a plus, right? I was glad to be singled out, but embarrassed about the reason for it. Was I that in need of recognition?

Google's obsession with metrics was forcing me to take stock of my own capabilities. What did I bring to the table? What were my limits? How did I compare? Insecurity was a game all Googlers could play, especially about intellectual inferiority. Everyone but a handful felt they were bringing down the curve. I began to realize how closely self-doubt was linked to ambition and how adeptly Google leveraged the latter to inflate the former — urging us to pull ever harder to advance not just ourselves but the company as a whole.

Toward the end of my Google run, a newly hired senior manager put into words what I had discovered long before. "Let's face it, Doug," he confided, "Google hires really bright, insecure people and then applies sufficient pressure that no matter how hard they work, they're never able to consider themselves successful. Look at all the kids in my group

---

[*] A Silicon Valley joke: TLA stands for "three-letter acronym."

who work absurd hours and still feel they're not keeping up with everyone else."

I had to agree that fear of inadequacy was a useful lever for prying the
last erg of productivity out of dedicated employees. Everyone wanted to
prove they belonged among the elite club of Google contributors. The
manager who articulated that theory, though, considered himself too
secure to play that game. Which may be why he lasted less than a year
at Google.

Keeping It Clean

Google's embrace of "organized chaos" extended to our workspace,
which might charitably have been called a mess, or less charitably, a
pigsty.

The locker room had come with showers and saunas. The odor we
added ourselves: a pungent mix of soiled jerseys, scuffed knee pads,
muddy pucks and headless hockey sticks, grip tape adhesive, deodor-
ant dispensers, ripped underwear, and expired aftershave. Google soon
provided towel service and installed low-energy Swedish washing machines that took a week to spin through a single cycle — introducing a
ripe finishing note of undone laundry, abandoned athletic socks, and
mildewed terry cloth. Imagine a geek fraternity claiming squatters'
rights in an insurance office.

The one area in which hygiene was fastidiously maintained was engineering. Not the engineers' physical space — they were apparently all
feral children — but their operating principles.

Urs insisted on adopting the best practices he had seen in more industrial settings to things like source control and compiler warnings.
"We'd make sure the compiler actually failed if it had a warning, so you
couldn't ignore it," he told me. He formalized the most important elements into a style guide, which became a mandate enforced by Craig
Silverstein.

"I had no desire for a style guide," Craig noted, "but Urs was really
insistent."

The biggest question was which programming language to use. Craig
wanted to use C. Urs preferred C++. Urs prevailed, but he agreed to restrict Google coders "from using the bad parts of C++."

"What are the bad parts of C++?" I once asked Craig.

"Most of it," he said with a straight face.

Craig believed Google would need an integrating force to prevent redundant or conflicting efforts, maintain standards, help set priorities, and provide feedback during performance reviews. He made it his goal to be that force, to be "the one who knew what was going on everywhere."

"Until we were about a hundred people," he recalls, "I'd go around and talk to everyone. I'd say, 'How's your work going? Do you need any help?' Some people got really upset about that. 'This guy keeps bothering me. What's he doing?' Urs had to take me aside and tell me to stop." Craig realized that "they didn't need someone to pay that close attention. Everyone was still just one degree away. They knew who to talk to. There was very good communication."

The one thing that did need a high level of attention was the code itself. To look for potential problems, Craig started scanning every automatic alert generated whenever someone checked in a codebase change — no matter how minor. But a lone proofreader couldn't keep up with the growth of engineering's output. So Urs instituted a formal code-review process.

"You get to pick one good engineering practice to be your cultural touchstone," Craig said, "and for us it was code reviews." To initiate a review, a coder would send out a pointer to an online design document. Anyone could respond with comments, but an official reviewer had to sign off on the actual code.

The benefit was obvious. "Finding problems in the beginning," engineer Ron Dolin explained, "was a hundred times more efficient than finding them later on."

Still, as Google grew, not all the programmers subscribed to the idea that their code needed proofing or that it was their responsibility to look over other people's work. As Craig explained it, "We put a process in place to prevent submitting code without review, unless you lied."

To get around the process, people would perform cursory reviews. "I'd send out a big, giant piece of code," Craig said, "and they'd send back, 'Looks good.' I suspect there's more that could have been said about that code."

When new employees started, Craig reviewed their code himself, inculcating them into the system of collaborative authoring. Some people

hated it. "Paul Bucheit hated it," recalls Craig. "Noam[*] hated it. But
Paul ended up doing a lot of code reviews on his own and being really supportive of that methodology. Noam thought it was a waste of
time — he's like Larry and Sergey, a research developer. He'd say, 'I'm
spending more time reviewing this code than I spent writing it — how
is that a good use of anyone's time?'"

Sanjay Ghemawat did not hate code reviews. Though he had come
out of a research lab where looking over others' shoulders was considered intrusive, if not inappropriate, he immediately saw the value of
input from an intelligent reviewer. The code reviews enforced cross-
pollination of ideas while elevating standards for what was acceptable.
"At one extreme," Sanjay recognized, "you could say, 'Okay, just make
sure it obeys the style guide,' which was pretty mechanical. My take
was different. You needed to see if you could convince yourself that
it was actually going to work, that it didn't have corner cases or problems — that it would be easy to understand. I think it worked out really
well."

Ben Gomes praised Sanjay's code and his systematic approach to
growing the code base: "It set a tone for the rest of the code that was
written." But he joked that Sanjay maintained unreasonable standards.

"He couldn't stand the fact that I didn't use white space properly. At
a code review, he'd put his cursor below the end of everything and say,
'There's white space there. Why is there white space there?'"

Sanjay laughed when I asked him about that.

"I just did it a little bit to wind Ben up. I wanted to be able to come
back to it in a couple of years, having basically forgotten everything we
were thinking about when we wrote it, and still understand it. If all this
bad formatting is getting in the way, it's something to fix."

Because Urs promoted team engineering to break complex problems
into solvable pieces, code reviews were essential to ensure the pieces
would fit together when reassembled. The system gave engineers in-
dependence but kept them from wandering too far from the standards
unifying the codebase.

"A good team is ultimately what makes or breaks the problem," Urs
explained years later. "If the team isn't the right one, they make little
mistakes that erode the solution and in the end, you don't know what
mistake you made, but it doesn't work. You need the control every day,

---

[*] Noam Shazeer wrote Google's spell-checking software and designed its calculator function.

every week. A new person will make little tiny judgment calls and not realize the cumulative effect. So after a few months you have actually destroyed the idea while you made no recognizable mistake. It was a sequence of small things."

A Day in the Life

Engineering had its discipline and routines — I had mine.

I began arriving earlier. Much earlier.

I'd tiptoe out of the house before six, start my car, and pull out of the driveway without turning on the headlights. Our bedroom faced the street, our blinds were broken, and Kristen was not a morning person. When I hit Highway 85, I'd crank up the heat and the radio and roll down the windows. By the time I arrived at the darkened Googleplex I was fully awake. I'd pull into the spot closest to the door and turn on my brights to see if the neighborhood skunk had camped out on the front steps. My first run-in with him had scared the crap out of me. I'd turn on the office lights and the copy machines before heading to the locker room.

Google's building stood adjacent to a wetlands preserve on the edge of the San Francisco Bay. Jogging trails lined with white, yellow, purple, and pink wildflowers stretched for miles north and south, from the blimp hangars at Moffett Field along a jetty and over small hillocks to the Palo Alto airport. Hawks floated overhead and herons waded through the ponds. Raccoons, rabbits, and wildlife-watching retirees shared the dirt paths with swarms of gnats and a powerful ebb-tide aroma. I'd stretch against the front steps, start my DiscMan, and trudge slowly across the asphalt toward the Bay.

By eight a.m., I could run a couple of miles, have a sauna, shower, read the paper, eat a bowl of cereal, and still be practically alone in the building as I began cleaning out the barnacles that had attached themselves to my inbox overnight. Having unscrewed the fluorescent bulbs above my desk, I used the warmer glow of my desk lamp for illumination until the sun was high enough to come tripping through the windows. I'd plug in my headphones; crank up my homegrown hash of Yo Yo Ma, Otis Spann, and Ozomatli; and begin banging keys in a state of complete Zen-like absorption.

It felt good to be alive.

The euphoria usually passed by ten o'clock, when the drip of incoming email turned into a raging torrent and the daily meetings began. I shuffled from talks about new search features to UI discussions to product-roadmap updates. Google's clock ran on tech-company hours, which began no earlier than ten a.m. and ended when the following dawn poked the engineers in the eyes with rosy red fingers. At seven or eight in the evening, I drove home to tuck the kids into bed before logging in remotely to write copy and put out any fires that had started in the hour I'd been offline.

Any illusion of work/life balance was sucked from beneath me like beach sand in the retreating tide preceding a tsunami. Kristen wasn't thrilled, but she understood I had to get "the startup thing" out of my system. She kept the kids fed, clothed, homework-compliant, and off the drugs.

To preserve some connection with my offspring, I'd take an hour on Fridays to volunteer in their classes at school. No one at Google had a problem with that because, in theory, I had near autonomy over my schedule.

"As long as you get your work done," Cindy reminded me. Since the work was never ending and never defined from day to day, it was never "done." I did manage to keep most of my Saturdays after the CableFest relatively free, though that simply meant I hadn't planned to do any work until Sunday afternoon, when I'd need to gear up again for Monday. It wasn't unusual to get an urgent email or phone call that drew me back into productivity mode for an hour here or there on Saturday or Sunday morning.

"Do you want to go to Daddy's office?" I'd ask my tween-age sons when I had to go in to the Plex on weekends. The answer was always yes. The office was so much more fun than home, which was tragically sugar-free and devoid of video games, bouncy balls, and air hockey. I set them up with the Dreamcast game console in the conference room and carefully wrote my phone extension in big block numbers on a whiteboard. They didn't seem to mind loading paper cups with malt balls, M&Ms, and Twizzlers, then sitting in front of the screen slurping root beer, but I knew in my heart I should be outside with them throwing a ball or building something splintery out of plywood and two-by-fours. If nothing else, I was giving them a horribly warped view of what "going to work" actually meant.

I wasn't trying to impress the boss with my diligence. I was merely

trying to keep up. Many of my overcaffeinated twenty-something colleagues had relocated from outside the Bay Area. They had no local
friends, no attachments, no relatives, and often no TVs to distract
them. They had Google.

On the off chance an employee might succumb to the allure of
some idyllic "real life," Google encased us in a cocoon of essential services — on-site haircuts, on-site car washes, on-site dentist and doctor, free massages, free snacks, free lunch, free dinner, gaming groups,
movie nights, wine and beer clubs, tech talks and lectures by globally
recognized speakers. And everywhere you turned, intelligent compan-
ionship. If the city of Mountain View had not zoned our building non-
residential, many Googlers would have given up their apartments to
establish a Plex Biosphere.

George Salah and the facilities team gave the lobby a makeover: two
bright-red couches with fuzzy rounded edges on either side of a surf-
board-shaped glass coffee table, a few large ferns, a mirror, and some
lava lamps. They covered the elevator doors with primary-colored me-
tallic rectangles, installed a cooler for Naked juice drinks, and hung
a neon version of the Google logo in the stairway like the welcoming
sign of an all-night diner. Googlers draped themselves over the couches
to read the paper or bounced on balls while knocking back Mighty
Mangos and chatting with the receptionist. It was our communal living
room and our airlock to the outside world.

It wasn't always treated with respect. An engineer eventually broke
the glowing neon Google sign while trying to see if he could kick a
three-foot rubber ball all the way to the second floor from the lobby.
"Why didn't they have a note on it saying, 'Don't kick balls around
this'?" he groused afterwards.

Sergey decided we needed a piano to add a touch of class to the lobby
and instructed George to buy a disklavier that could play by itself when
staffers weren't around to tickle its keys.

One night around two a.m., I heard the piano suddenly start playing
at high volume. Going downstairs from my office to shut it off, I saw
Salar sitting at the keyboard in the half-light, ripping through a Chopin
scherzo and filling the small space with his frenetic finger work. I stood
and watched as he flawlessly hammered out notes, the sound crashing
against the walls, the windows, the furniture, as if it needed to break
free and soar across the moonlit wetlands just outside our door. The
piece felt familiar to me. Then I realized that it wasn't the melody but

the tempo — the mad racing pace, the unrelenting forward momentum — that I knew all too well. It felt like Google chasing opportunity through the night.

De-Stressing Developments

"Come in," said Babette. She was sitting at her computer looking at her calendar. "Take off as much clothing as you're comfortable with and lie face down." She stood up and stepped toward the door. "I'll be right back."

The office door with the sign "Googlers massaged here" looked like any other in the Plex, but it was the only one behind which it was officially okay to be naked. (Google's official office dress code was "You must wear clothes.") On one wall was a large print of *Squares with Concentric Circles* by Kandinsky. On another was an anatomical chart of the human muscle system. The large window overlooking the industrial park was draped with a beige sheet. Protean organic shapes swam languorously inside a yellow lava lamp glowing from the floor.

I'd never been naked in an office before. It felt weird, as if I were exposing a part of me that didn't belong to the company and inviting them to lay their hands on it. Just another case of Google breaking down the wall between my life at work and my sense of my private self.* Yet the massages were one of the best parts of working at the company. Google's high energy and even higher expectations lent my bottled-up stress its own unique flavor, and the supply never seemed to run dry. Massage was the best way to relieve my knotted shoulders and knitted brow and to reduce the torque spinning my teeth against each other like millstones as I slept.

Larry and Sergey had bestowed upon us Bonnie Dawson and Babette Villasenor to smooth the kinks in necks craned over monitors and the aches in fingers that clawed at computer keys like Gollum scrabbling for the ring of Sauron. Not that the founders possessed special immunity to tension. Their names could often be found filling the boxes of the online massage schedule, and it was prudent to check carefully before

---

*I felt this even more strongly the first time I visited the Google doctor, for whom the company had converted an office into a full examining room. It's unsettling to walk past the cubicles of your coworkers on your way to a physical.

calling a meeting you expected them to attend, lest you be preempted by their need to be kneaded.

Larry once blew off a meeting I had scheduled weeks before because a massage slot suddenly opened up. "You understand, don't you?" he asked apologetically. Actually, I did.

The free massages didn't last long. Demand quickly exceeded supply, even when the company started charging a nominal amount. To manage the backlog, limits were placed on how far in advance massages could be booked, and the appointment calendar was opened at random times to ensure that day and night workers had equal access. Automated Japanese massage chairs installed in the lobby did nothing to prevent the development of a gray market for massage coupons. In Google's shadow economy, the certificates — originally offered as tokens of appreciation or awards for extraordinary work — were repurposed as bribes for equipment or technical services or even drink tickets at company parties.

If the massage table wasn't available to depress beta-wave activity, there was always the blue room.

"I think we're at an impasse," I told Salar when we butted heads on a branding issue neither of us would concede. "I'll meet you in the blue room in fifteen minutes to decide this once and for all." When he showed up, I handed him a Dreamcast controller, took one for myself, and loaded the *Soul Calibur* disc. For the next ten minutes we battled onscreen as two mythic warriors intent only on the other's destruction. I handily put him in his place, proving the superiority of my marketing sensibility and my manual dexterity. To his credit, Salar recovered from the crushing defeat, racking up a number of accomplishments at Google only slightly less impressive than the slide kick I used to knock him out of the ring in game three.

Ben Smith,[*] Ray Sidney, Bogdan Cocosel, and John Bauer also had the skill to kill and swaggered and swore and vowed vengeance when forced by crashing servers to abandon play just because Google was in a tailspin somewhere.

"We're down? Where? The East Coast? All right, just a minute, it's four a.m. there. No one will notice while I finish this round."

The games became so rowdy that play was forbidden during daylight

---

[*] Smith was unbeatable. He once challenged me to a game in which he used only his toes to operate the controller. He won, literally hands down.

hours, giving rise to email challenges that flew all through the night, often consisting of no more than the simple subject line "My soul still burns."

Cosmic Charlie, How Do You Do?

"No thanks," I told Charlie Ayers. "I don't eat that."

"That's because your mama never made them like this," Charlie replied, leaning across the steaming trays with the grinning confidence of a used-car salesman. "Most people overcook lima beans until they're gray and mealy. You have to serve them fresh and green."

"Um. Okay," I said, putting five lima beans on my plate.

"And try this," Charlie said, sweeping his hand over a tray overloaded with gold-encrusted chicken parts as if it were a cherry Thunderbird driven only by a Baptist widow to Sunday prayer meetings. "You know where I got the recipe for this? I got this recipe from Elvis Presley's personal chef. This is the exact same Southern-fried chicken the King and Colonel Tom Parker used to eat. Tell me that's not the best damn chicken you ever tasted."

While I wrestled with where I fit in the company, Charlie Ayers had no doubt about where he belonged: in the kitchen. Charlie was the chef Larry and Sergey had hired the week I came onboard. He had immediately begun converting the downstairs dining area into a working café (he corrected anyone déclassé enough to call it a cafeteria). In his oft-voiced professional opinion, the facilities were deplorably inadequate for what he wanted to do: re-create the healthy organic menu he had served while catering for concert promoter Bill Graham Presents. While we eventually shorthanded Charlie's story to "former chef for the Grateful Dead," he always made it clear that the Dead had never hired him; he had just prepared meals for them on occasion. "It wasn't the stuff I was feeding him that killed him," Charlie protested when staffers made cracks about Jerry Garcia's heft and untimely demise.

With sixty-plus Googlers to feed — most of them young with the caloric intake of orcas — Charlie sweated through daily lunch and dinner with only sous chef Jim Glass and a couple of kitchen staffers to help prep and clean up.

"Goddamn the oven," Charlie could be heard to mutter. "Goddamn the refrigerator. Goddamn the dishwasher." The catechism continued, embracing the serving line, the layout of the room, the sinks, the suppliers, and his skinflint bosses, Larry and Sergey. Charlie cursed the uncaring employees — fresh from college food services — who took more than they could eat or brought guests in unannounced, nullifying his careful menu math. And through it all, he delivered one incredible meal after another.

Charlie made everything on the premises except for the bread, which was dropped off outside the kitchen each morning in gray bins marked bread only — not for garbage. He selected his ingredients with a bias toward organically grown produce from local farms, and he railed against processed foods like the creamy gelatin-filled yogurt I preferred to the lumpy organic style he insisted was healthier. Compared with the *Merc*'s Front Page Café, with its limp greens and greasy grilled cheese, Charlie presided over a gastronomical nirvana.

He'd tantalize us each morning with an email outlining his plans for ravishing our taste buds, an email that included a different menu every day, like this one:

Soups: Cream of Asparagus, Savory Mushroom & Lentil

Salads: Thai Noodle, Old-Fashioned Potato Salad, Carrot Dill, Organic Mixed Greens

Entrees: Roasted Turkey Breast with Miso Turkey Gravy and Cornbread Stuffing, Braised Tofu & Eggplant over Brown Rice*

Sides: Candied Yams, Green Beans

Desserts: Apple Pie, Blueberry Tarts, Cherry Pie, Creamy Rice Pudding

Once marketing moved downstairs to the cubicles adjacent to the café, I could see the lunch line begin to form shortly before noon. I always dropped whatever I was doing to be near the front.

"Wait for the bell!" Charlie spat at us if we pushed too far into the café before he was ready. If things weren't going well in the kitchen, it was dangerous to get too close.

---

* Charlie always offered at least one vegetarian option for the main entrée.

"Watch out. Hot soup!" he'd yell, pushing through anyone blocking his access, giant steaming tureen held high. Charlie dashed about, paring knife in hand, madly slicing and dicing last-minute garnishes and loading the breadbaskets, his temper flaring like the gas burners under a fatty stir-fry. Only when everything was in its place would he ring the little hotel check-in bell on the counter signifying that it was safe to begin. The chain gang would shuffle past, serving itself salads and a main course before ambling toward the desserts and the drink cooler. Still, it was better to risk Charlie's wrath than to miss a favorite entrée or some special chocolate confection whipped up in limited quantities. Ops — ever optimizing performance — installed a webcam over the door for a live feed of kitchen conditions, line length, and the intensity of Charlie's agitation.

The six-foot folding tables at which we sat were straight from an office supply store and surrounded by the cheap metal chairs they bring out for overflow crowds at church services and funerals. The implicit protocol was to take the first available seat next to whatever engineer or salesperson or facilities staffer happened to be the last one seated, and then engage them in conversation. Sometimes the resulting dialogues were peppered with German or Chinese or with the equally incomprehensible acronym-laced geek-speak. I feasted on critiques of competitors' releases and detailed descriptions of the esoteric elements of GWS, accompanied by diagrams inked out on paper napkins. I asked naive questions and got sophisticated answers about our technology and our industry, a process that was part of Larry and Sergey's calculus behind offering employees free food in the first place.

Much has been written about Google's free meal plan (one estimate put the cost at seventy-two million dollars per year),[*] but the basics of the program were simple: lunch and dinner were free, and we could eat as much as we liked from our first day with the company until our last. Like most Googlers, I spent less than half an hour at lunch and, if on deadline, would just retreat with a plate to my desk. Without the café, I would have lost twenty minutes getting to a restaurant, half an hour eating, and another twenty minutes getting back. I would have stopped thinking about Google as soon as I cleared the front door so I could focus on consuming fatty, salt-saturated foods on my way to increased

---

[*] Vasanth Sridharan at Businessinsider.com, April 23, 2008.

sick days and a premature death. Looked at that way, the policy made sense to me.

Charlie did have a budget, however, and given his complaints about its limitations, everyone was shocked the day he served lobster for lunch.

"Don't worry," Charlie assured the crowd, "I got a special deal because they only had one claw." No one dared ask where he had shopped for one-clawed lobsters. Perhaps they got in too deep with loan sharks. They tasted great. That was all we had to know.

Besides, Charlie made sure nothing went to waste. "In the early days, Charlie used to call me down to eat *all* the leftovers," engineer Chad Lester fondly recollects. "At the very beginning I could sometimes do it. I'd eat my normal lunch and wait for everyone else to eat what they wanted. Then around two-thirty, I'd be hungry again. If I didn't show, Charlie would come get me, and I would eat everything that remained."

"Once I ate an extra nine pork chops," Chad recalled with a happy smile. "Another time Charlie gave me a mixing bowl full of ice cream, whipped cream, nuts, candy, and chocolate sauce. It must have weighed a couple pounds. That was insane."

Great food also had the ability to attract great talent.

"I don't know what to do," senior engineer Luiz Barroso moaned to Jeff Dean the night he had to decide whether to join VMWare or Google. "I've made these lists. I've assigned points to all the pros and cons, and it's tied at 112 to 112."

Jeff knew that the day of Luiz's interview at Google, Charlie had served crème brûlée for lunch. "Did you factor in the crème brûlée?" he asked. "Because I know you really like crème brûlée."

"Oh no! I didn't consider that," Luiz admitted. The next morning he accepted Google's offer.

It wasn't just a nice gesture to treat job candidates to a decent meal, it was part necessity and part test of temperament. Since interviews stretched into daylong affairs, it was important to give applicants enough nutrition to sustain them. We could easily spot the aspirants — they'd be sitting out on the deck sweating in navy blue suits while all around them Googlers in shorts and sandals chatted and chewed. Any Googler who happened to be within earshot could pepper candidates with questions, and the answers could influence a hiring decision as much as anything in the formal interview process. Giving off a "Googley" vibe mattered.

I never knew whom I might bump into while waiting for a fresh platter of polenta to be put out. At first, celebrity drop-ins tended to be tech
luminaries like pundit Esther Dyson, Sun superstar Kim Polese, or the
chairman of Intel, but as Google's fame grew, you were just as likely to
run into Nobel laureates and internationally known politicians, people
like Muhammad Yunus, Queen Noor, Bill Clinton, or Jimmy Carter,
pushing trays along the aluminum rails under Charlie's watchful eye
as the Grateful Dead wailed from wall-mounted speakers. Journalists
from Japan and France stood in the middle of the café pointing cameras
and murmuring in their native tongues as print reporters from *Time*
and *Fortune* and *BusinessWeek* huddled with Larry or Sergey to chew
on chicken sandwiches and ruminate on the future of search. The café
took on a circus quality and lost some of the intimacy of the first few
months. But the food always brought me back.

Blending equal parts fanaticism, ego, and artistic temperament,
Charlie served up a mélange of exotic tastes mixed with intelligent
discourse and the fellowship of shared interests. He was a blur in the
kitchen, throwing inadequate resources at impossible demands, with
sweat beading his brow and food stains augmenting the all-over tie-dye
of his custom-made apron. The lesson of the data center applied to the
kitchen as well: cheap production units pushed to their limits offered
superior performance. Individual servers, whether of web pages or of
steamed broccoli, might give out, but the system wasn't truly broken as
long as it kept delivering results. To their undying credit, Charlie, Jim,
and the rest of the Google kitchen crew never experienced a catastrophic
failure. Day after day after day, they fed us — their infrastructure running on elbow grease, ingenuity, and heart. It was a very Googley way
to be.

CHAPTER 8

Cheap Bastards Who
Can't Take a Joke

H OW MANY GOOGLERS does it take to screw in a light bulb?"
Sergey asked the UI team in late February 2000. His complaint
was about browser buttons — a trivial bit of code that allowed
users to add Google search links to their web-surfing software. We were
debating names and design details by email, and the list of people involved had grown to ten, including Urs and Cindy. Sergey found that
ridiculous.

"If we continue to do all of our work at this kind of pace," he observed, "I find it highly unlikely we will meet any significant number of
our goals." Instead of exhaustive user testing and internal deliberations,
he argued, "We should just put up the service and test it when we get
a chance. Don't forget, we can change it at the drop of a hat — or we
should be able to."

Sergey's perspective on "launch first, iterate later," was nothing if not
consistent. "I don't think we should have *any* meetings about a project
like this," he said, "or *any* group emails except the one to users announcing the launch. Having everyone involved in every issue is not a good
use of anyone's time."

Sergey wanted one person to take charge: Salar. As product manager
(PM), Salar could talk to Karen to set up the web page, to Marissa or
Bay to check on the UI, and to me for branding, then work with an en-

gineer to make changes if necessary. Salar had no training as a PM — no ivy-covered MBA, no internship at an overpriced consulting firm, no career spent hauling himself one rung at a time up a corporate ladder. But Sergey thought he was bright enough to figure it out. Sergey felt the same way about Susan, who soon left marketing to take on a role similar to Salar's. More important, Larry and Sergey trusted them not to get in the way of what the engineers wanted to do.

Larry officially anointed himself chief of products in March 2000, taking charge of the entity coalescing around the kernel of product management. He would oversee any project requiring engineering resources — the "Googlettes" hatching all around the building — including the directory and WAP (Wireless Application Protocol) search for cell phones. Larry decreed a meeting be established at which views would be heard from all corners of the Plex, disagreements would be aired, and edicts would be issued. He dubbed it "product review." Google had birthed a process.

Product review met in Larry and Sergey's office. I arrived early to get a seat on the black pleather couch. Otherwise, I'd have had to balance my laptop while sitting on a three-foot rubber ball. A large metal exoskeleton — the prototype for Larry's book-scanning project — held a camera and an array of lights pointing down at the coffee table in front of me. Karen White, Marissa Mayer, Jen McGrath from the front-end team, and Craig Silverstein worked around it, connecting cables to a projector so we could display mockups against the office wall.

Sergey leaned back in his desk chair across from us, reading and eating a sandwich. It was hard to tell if he was paying attention.

Marissa set the agenda, determining which products to discuss and who should be at the meeting to present the case for or against proposed changes. Marissa was twenty-four. A slim, blond Wisconsinite, she was well versed in UI issues and she never met a problem she didn't try to fix — immediately. Her mind worked so quickly that her buffer overflowed, filling all available conversational space with a flurry of words. She would download what she was thinking, punctuate it with an ellipsis laugh, and then preemptively address all objections or alternative viewpoints that could conceivably be expressed. It took me a while to get used to, even though I had dwelt among New Yorkers.

Marissa took the role of product review gatekeeper as seriously as an

embassy guard in a hostile nation. She ardently argued her views about
the best way to help Google prosper while protecting the inner sanctum
from antagonistic ideas. Over the months to come, as she began casting
a larger shadow on both the product-development process and Larry's
personal life, she would iris down the exposure others had to the chief
of products. We were, of course, free to talk with Larry outside product
review, but since the meeting was now the place where decisions were
officially made, those conversations could easily be viewed as redundant and a waste of Larry's time.

No one wanted to waste Larry's time.

Larry himself remained unassuming about his new role. He sat at his
desk at the far end of the cramped office, glancing up from his array of
computer monitors when we presented something of interest to him.
"How does Yahoo handle that?" he might ask, sending us on a round-
the-web sightseeing tour to learn if someone else had already solved
our particular problem. When we presented competing views, Larry
would call for the data supporting each side, then offer his Solomonic
verdict.

And when Larry was done, he was done. "I don't want to talk about
this anymore. It's not worth discussing. Just do it."

Larry (Sergey, too) ended discussions abruptly when he saw time
being wasted on something he had already decided. He hated rehash-
ing arguments and bringing irrelevant people up to speed. Mostly, he
couldn't abide having to explain the obvious. Sometimes all it took was
a look. Project manager Deb Kelly proposed a new method for putting
content online and ran it by Larry. "He did the eyebrow thing," she later
recalled, arching one eyebrow like Spock. "And he didn't even give me
a reason. He was just basically — 'No.' It was clear that it was a stupid
idea."

It didn't take long for me to have my own first brush with Larry's
debate-killing decisiveness. Larry wanted to relabel the "cache" link on
our results pages to read "show matches."* Clicking the link would still
take users to a cached version of the page, but it would now highlight
words on that page matching the user's query. I found the name change
confusing and felt sure our users would too. It was a wording issue.

---

* A cached page is a copy that Google stores in its index when it crawls the web. It's not the live
page hosted on the site itself, but more like a photo Google takes for reference. Because the cached
page is hosted by Google, it's available even if the original site goes down or the content of the page
changes.

That was my domain. I voiced my objections at the UI meeting and won agreement that we wouldn't make the change without at least testing it first.

The next morning I woke to find "show matches" had replaced "cache" on all our results pages.

"The UI team does not have control over these decisions," Bay Chang reminded me when I asked what had happened. "Larry wanted 'show matches.'" Larry had stopped Marissa as she headed home, and together they had decided to implement the edit.

"I carefully considered all the feedback," Larry said when I confronted him. "And I don't want this to be discussed endlessly. There are a lot of more important things for us to do. We've already repeated all the arguments, which means it's time for a decision."

I had thought that decision time had passed during our UI team meeting.

"Why did Google stop showing cached pages?" asked the first user complaint we received.

"I loved the cached pages! Why are they gone?" demanded a dozen others. It wasn't the End of Days, but given how few people actually used the feature, it qualified as a minor plague. Most alarming, reporters complained to Cindy and passed along notes they were getting from their readers. A week later we changed the label back to "cached" and I plotted three new data points on my Google graph:

Nothing was final until Larry said it was.
Larry communicated directly to the people who could implement his decisions.
Larry erased what he had etched in stone if the walls crumbled around him.

The third point was the most important lesson to me, because undoing things done wrong would be the crux of my own Jericho moments at Google.

The first of those moments started as a joke.

Are You Kidding Me?

It was the middle of March. Time to put away the space heater and break out the cargo shorts and sandals. April was right around the corner. My first April at Google. My first April first. My first opportunity to undertake the torqued brain aerobics and flop-sweat composition that I came to know as the Google April Fools' joke.

April Fools' Day would become a perennial black hole in my calendar, a gravity well into which my attention would be sucked from increasingly great distances in time. Sergey, on the other hand, loved April Fools'. His sense of humor didn't stop at the boundaries of good taste, and when it came to April Fools', he dynamited decorum and put moderation to the torch. The cruelest month, indeed.

I was headed into Charlie's Café when I ran into Sergey. The day was warm and my mood was full of springtime. Charlie had made my favorite apple galette for dessert. As I pushed my tray through the line I chatted with Sergey about the possibility of doing something fun for April Fools'. He lit up and encouraged me to go for it. That afternoon I sent him a press release announcing that Google had patented an "alpha-numeric system" that eliminated the letters Q, Z, and C. They were redundant and increased page-load times. Sergey granted it was amusing but, he informed me, unnecessary. Susan would head up our April Fools' effort. If I had other ideas, I should coordinate them with her.

Ouch. That hurt. Funny stuff on the homepage felt awfully like online branding to me. I went back to the drawing board.

"Let's see. The message should be positive. Improbable, but not obviously impossible. Hmm. What if Google were so good it delivered results before you even searched?"

Thirty seconds later, I was typing a description of "Ante-Temporal search," a breakthrough development that anticipated user requests. The tone was heavily geekish, but Susan liked it. Sergey thought it was overdone (akin to the pope saying you're overly religious), but encouragingly, he said it had potential. "Maybe you could make it more like this site I saw about kitty porn?" he asked.

Sergey asked Susan to include engineer and bodily-function satirist Ray Sidney in our discussions to make sure the joke ended up with plenty of funny and sufficient tech cred. I dragged Ray and Paul Bucheit into a conference room to brainfart jokes. In that redolent atmosphere, Ray pinned the name "MentalPlex" on our new mind-reading technology. That settled, I hashed out the text for a link on the homepage, a dozen error messages that would be displayed randomly if someone entered a query in the MentalPlex search box, and an FAQ explaining how to visualize a search so MentalPlex could detect it.

Q: I am unable to visualize clicking and have to use my finger to activate the mouse.

A: Click visualization takes practice. Try pushing the mouse button with your eyebrow, then gradually increase the distance between your eye and the mouse.

Marissa pointed out that with our newly launched foreign-language interfaces, we could extend the joke beyond English. "One of the error messages should say that MentalPlex has detected foreign thoughts," she suggested, "and then we can translate the interface text on the results page into German."

In what would become an April Fools' tradition, our webmaster Karen White worked at warp speed right up to the deadline to get the final images and copy in place. We wanted maximum exposure in all time zones, so we would send MentalPlex out at eight p.m. on March 31 and keep it on the site throughout the following day.

Karen pushed the last of the files at 7:55 on Friday night. Soon Google users would see a spinning cartoon spiral on our homepage inviting them to try MentalPlex. I was relieved we'd made the deadline. I was also terrified.

Humor is subjective. Done poorly, it just comes across as pathetic. I didn't want my first attempt at instilling personality into our brand to be branded lame by the digerati, but I also didn't want it to be so much of an in-joke that only geeks would get it. It would be bad enough to tell a joke to millions of people and have no one laugh, but if MentalPlex bombed, I was sure Sergey would just hand all future fun stuff to engineers, condemning me to write product spec sheets and error messages for all eternity.

As soon as Karen hit Submit on the push, I started compulsively refreshing my inbox to check for feedback from users. I had a sense that my entire career was resting on whether or not I had nailed the punch line for this one stupid joke, which felt weaker and more juvenile by the minute.

At 8:01 the first email arrived. "Google is great!" was the header. The user liked the way we played with our homepage. More emails started trickling in. People were surprised. They didn't think search engines had a sense of humor. They liked it. They were ☺. LOL. ROFL. ROFLMAO. They really, really liked it. I let the glow of their adoration wash over me from the screen of my laptop. There were a few confused souls who didn't get it at all, and some who felt we should forget comedy and stick to searching, and a handful who threatened to leave if we put graphics on our homepage permanently. One guy who said he was "incipiently epileptic" believed our spinning spiral graphic could induce seizures. But these sour notes were drowned by the chorus of hosannas sounding steadily over the next few hours. It was a love fest of praise and joy and Lo! Was that inaudible rhythm the music of the spheres thrumming softly in the heavens?

"Turn it off. It thinks I'm German." The off-key refrain caught my ear.

"I found MentalPlex mildly amusing, but the different languages on the results page make it harder to use. The joke gets old very quickly."

Discordant voices sang about confusion and annoyance. They swelled from a hoarse whisper to a shrill harangue to a roaring cacophony of insistent outrage that could not be ignored. By ten p.m., it was painfully clear that for many in Google's global audience, jokes about Germany and mind control were just not funny. I emailed Susan, who was still at the office monitoring feedback, and suggested we get rid of the German message. She had already identified the problem and called Sergey. He okayed removing the German error message and the linked results page. Okay. A minor hitch resolved.

Except, it was Friday night. All the engineering staff were with Sergey, washing away the week's woes at Zibbibos, a trendy restaurant twenty minutes away in downtown Palo Alto. No one in the office was authorized to make the change. I sat at home watching more and more messages complaining about Germans, German thoughts, and German jokes drop into my mailbox and explode. Little ice balls formed on the back of my neck, then rolled down my spine.

A half hour passed. Then another. We were taking a pounding on email. Finally, the offensive German ground to a halt. Thanks to some anonymous engineer, no more unwanted German results confused our users. Now our unwanted results were in Portuguese. The engineers thought the joke was just too funny to eliminate entirely, so they simply shifted the interface to another language. Users didn't like German? Fine, we'll give them something else.

"*No! No! No!*" I told them. The problem wasn't the language; it was how hard the foreign interface made it to use our results. We were breaking our brand, and instead of repairing the cracks they found it more amusing to watch our equity pour onto the floor. I had lived through PR crises before, and this one was becoming a *sabakova kashmar.**

Complaints kept coming. Though the tone was less virulent than when the German text was up, users were still unhappy they couldn't navigate the site easily. We were breaking a cardinal rule by making it difficult for them to get to information they sought. One user lamented that our little joke was costing her money — a professional researcher, she could no longer use Google to do her job.

I had worked at big companies long enough that I hesitated to escalate the problem to our top executive. But I had worked at Google long enough not to be intimidated by an org chart. I called Sergey. It was hard to hear over the background noise of rowdy engineers in a crowded restaurant, but I could tell he was surprised when I insisted we drop all the foreign-language results.

I was pooping the party, but Sergey reluctantly agreed, most likely so he could rejoin the festivities without fear of another interruption.

It took forever to reach Susan, and it was midnight before all the foreign-language text was stripped off the site.

"A not-insignificant fraction of our users are complete idiots," groused one engineer, "if they can't figure out how to use our site, just because it's all in Portuguese." Google had clearly crossed the gap from serving the tech elite to playing in the mainstream market — an online segment he knew to be densely populated with the clueless.

"I'm more worried that we got spooked by a little negative feedback," said Howard, the iconoclastic easy-riding engineer. "We backed off the playfulness that's an important part of Google. We watered down our April Fools' joke to make it less invasive. I guess that's what happens as we grow up — we become a more conservative company." He did not see that as a positive development.

Sergey tacitly agreed that the problem was not on our end. German results were quite funny. Besides, far more user feedback about MentalPlex was positive than negative.

At two a.m. I crawled into bed. I dreamed a monochrome dream about Germans and Lisbon and a police captain who looked at me quizzically and asked, "Shut it down? But everyone is having such a good time!"

The next morning I felt emotionally hung over. I had launched a joke

---

* A term I picked up during my six-month stay in Siberia. It means "a dog's nightmare."

that worked. MentalPlex perfectly fit Google's unconventional and just-a-bit geeky style. Sergey had been right all along — it was okay to play with our brand. But the mistake of translating the results interface embarrassed me. I worried that it didn't embarrass any of my colleagues.

Why had it required so much effort to make a change once complaints started coming in? Why had the decision been made to switch to Portuguese? Who had made that decision anyway? What was my role as brand manager, if not to manage the brand? I now understood where true power resided at Google. It lived in the keyboards of those authorized to push a new GWS, to actually check in the code that drove the site. Those engineers were the ultimate gatekeepers. Even when I had a green light to move a project down the tracks, someone with a different idea and a hand on the switch could change our course in the middle of the night — leaving me to awaken a hundred miles away from where I'd thought I'd be when I went to bed. MentalPlex had almost derailed us.

As soon as I got to work on Monday, I wrote up a postmortem memo to keep it from happening again. I included all the data I could glean from the six hundred email responses we had received. Seventy percent liked MentalPlex. Most of the rest complained about the translation of the interface into another language. My note codified the lesson that we should never, ever intentionally make it harder for people to search. I drafted a letter of apology to users who had complained and offered to send them free Google t-shirts. The nightmare was over. We had taken our lumps and learned from our mistake, and now we could roll on.

Not necessarily so, Marissa argued.

"The problem is not that we translated the interface into German," she said, "but that we called attention to the change by including a 'tip' about MentalPlex detecting German thoughts." In her view, if we had just put a disclaimer on the page that it was a joke, no one would have been upset.

"Most people would likely not have even noticed the translation without the tip," another engineer agreed. "Only the navigational text on the page was rendered in German — the web results themselves were still in English."

How could users not notice, I wondered, that all the text except the actual results was no longer in English? And adding a line at the bottom explaining it was all in jest would not only have failed to solve that problem, it would have been an admission that the joke was too weak to sustain itself. Jonathan Swift rarely used asterisks to explain he was being satiric.

Marissa and I never saw eye-to-eye on MentalPlex. She questioned my categorization of the user feedback even when I sent the original emails to her. I had cut-and-dried, irrefutable, objective facts at my disposal, yet we fundamentally disagreed on how to interpret the data. I wasn't interested in placing blame, but I did want to make sure we learned from our mistake and didn't repeat it. To do that, we had to reach consensus on what the mistake had been.

Omid Kordestani, the head of our sales and business development group, offered his opinion. "Really amateurish!" he complained. He meant MentalPlex from start to finish. Omid hadn't seen MentalPlex coming, and when it smacked him in the face on April 1, he was furious. Calm, smiling, even-keeled Omid derided our joke as likely to alienate the very advertisers his team had been working so hard to befriend. And had we even considered international users who simply wouldn't get our all-American attempt at humor?

"I hope we never repeat it," he admonished us. "Thank God this happened on a Friday night." There was only one silver lining Omid could see. Portal sites like Yahoo, who thought we might compete with them, would no longer worry about us. We clearly wouldn't be stealing their users with this kind of immature grab-ass idiocy. We weren't a Stanford dorm-room project anymore, Omid reminded us. We were running a serious business, and this came off like a beer-fueled freshman prank. I think he flashed back to his days at Netscape — a company high on its own hubris until a giant jackboot ground its face into reality.

"Not to worry, Omid," Sergey offered reassuringly. "We do foolhardy things from time to time, but not at random, and they usually have positive results."*

I pointed Omid to all the positive feedback from our users, but Cindy let me know I had blown it big time. Omid was a stakeholder and should have been in the loop. Another lesson learned the hard way. If nothing else, I consoled myself, at least this would give impetus to a more formal sign-off process. That would reel in the late-night GWS pushers and stop their off-key improvisations. As if.

---

* Sergey may have been referring to his own April Fools' joke, an all-staff memo announcing that the board had raised Google's stock price from $1.20 to $4.01, which led one employee to borrow money to buy his shares. The fact that Sergey sent his note on March 31 made it all the funnier — to him, anyway.

Though no one else seemed to take a lesson from the MentalPlex mishap, I found an epiphany in the dust of the dying hubbub. I could build Google's brand from inside the product. I didn't need to rely on banner ads or postcard programs. Google's personality would shine through in the way we — the way I — talked with users. I could try anything, because the only ones looking over my shoulder were two guys noticeably lacking inhibitions. It was a liberating moment.

I owned Google's words. Now I would give them a voice.

Disorienting in the Extreme

Google time folded in on itself like a tempered samurai sword. So much activity took place simultaneously that the linear narrative of this book flattens the immersive 3D experience into an unrecognizable shape. Maybe if you tear out the pages, throw them in the air, and read from them randomly as they flutter down around you, you'll get a better feel for what it was like. I'd been at the company five months, and every hour of every day another neural pathway in my brain uprooted itself and traced a new route to an unexpected destination.

"I've drafted some lines we could put on the homepage," I told Larry and Sergey at a product review. "They should drive repeat traffic by reaffirming our quality to first-time users. Here's the list."

Sergey didn't look up from the new phone he appeared to be breaking into pieces.

"How are you defining first-time users?" Larry asked. "What if they have cookies turned off?" He glanced at the dozen rows of my text the projector pinned neatly against the screen. "Why don't you use the testimonial quote from *Time* magazine?" he asked before I could answer his first question. "I don't think any of these are going to be very effective."

Sergey raised his head to stare at Larry, who raised an eyebrow in response and spoke.

"You need to make these much more compelling. Like, 'If you printed out all the data Google searches, the stack of pages would reach from here to the moon.'"

Sergey smiled and leaned farther back in his chair.

"No," he said.

Larry's eyebrow shot up again and hovered at its apex.

"What we need to do," Sergey went on, "is test things that are totally random to see what has the biggest effect." His eyebrow called Larry's and raised it a quarter inch.

They stared silently at each other for a moment, their eyebrows dancing a pas de deux in a closed loop of telepathic communication. I sometimes thought I grokked Larry or understood where Sergey was coming from. Observing them together, though, was like trying to catch a glimpse of light in the thin patch of space between twin neutron stars. There was enormous energy being exchanged, but at a spectrum range I could not detect.

Sergey returned his attention to the disassembled phone. "You know what we should do?" he asked his lap. "We should make the homepage hot pink and see how many people come back."

Larry's face lit up as if all the eyebrow bouncing had earned him a free ball and a bonus round.

I smiled too, but when I stopped, they didn't. A doubt crept in. They weren't . . . they couldn't be . . . surely they didn't mean that as a serious suggestion? I began the long trip from incredulity to denial to sputtering refutation based on logic, only to be sent packing until I could come up with a data-based argument proving their idea lacked merit.

Staking out extreme positions and making staffers fight their way to a safe haven of sanity seemed to amuse our founders. They got to watch forehead veins throb and palms drip sweat as PMs, ops people, and engineers probed carefully, attempting to keep a grip on logic while cutting through a thicket of distractions to defuse explosive ideas.

"Google was the first company I worked at where I had that experience," project manager Deb Kelly recalls. "Where you're thinking, 'That's nuts. That's crazy. That's dumb,' and then thinking about it for a while and going, 'Actually, that might be really, really smart — hard, but really, really smart.'"

The madness was not without method. Not only did Larry and Sergey's hyperbolic proposals force us to reason more tightly, but starting at the ideological antipodes exploited the full value of the intelligence in the room. After Larry or Sergey made one of their outrageous suggestions, nothing that followed would seem inconceivable. To sort the improbable from the impossible, we needed to pay attention and to argue facts, not suppositions or conventions. If we began with only "acceptable" solutions that had been tried before, we would never uncover the state-changing breakthroughs that destroyed worlds and raised new ones from their rubble.

Urs understood this better than most. "Larry and Sergey had an expectation that things would be watered down along the way," he explained. "Starting with something that's more ambitious will get you something that's reasonable. But if you don't put the goal post way out there, people are already taking fewer risks and are less ambitious about how big the idea should be."

It was another reason Google valued intelligence over experience. "In the best case," Urs said, "you had someone who was very excited and didn't know what was impossible and got really far. The big question was always, 'Can you do it cheaply enough for this to actually be affordable?' Maybe, but without trying it and measuring and doing the next iteration, you're not going to find out."

I felt sorry for new Googlers who stepped into the reality abattoir for the first time and looked around the room with naked-at-school-nightmare eyes, trying to see if this was some cruel initiation rite. If you were a goal-oriented, eager-to-please new staffer, what did you say when Sergey insisted, "We should really forget about [whatever topic was under discussion] and focus on building space tethers?"*

Meetings weren't the only place ideas went to die. If the founders didn't like a proposal, they might consign it to what PR director David Krane called the "dead letter office": "You'd ship something into the ether and there was no response. That was your way of knowing you'd probably missed."

It didn't help that when Larry and Sergey did respond to our ideas, their responses were often ambiguous. "If they liked something they'd say, 'It doesn't seem too sucky,'" recalls facilities manager George Salah. "When they pushed back on something, they'd say, 'Hmmmm, that seems suboptimal' or use some technical way of saying something between yes and no. They never gave a clear decision."

When I took copy to Sergey for approval, he would say, "It's cute. I like it" or "No. That's not very Googley."

Once I spent days with my team developing a full rationale for an ad campaign, based on what we understood about the target audience and

---

* Deb Kelly looks back on this as a way "to get all the ideas out there. Why not outsource it to Mars? Anything is possible." She ruefully admits, "I could never talk about space tethers very convincingly."

their motivations. Sergey glanced at the layouts, frowned, and said, "I think you need to think about it some more."

"Is it the concept you don't like? The art? The wording?" I asked, looking for something more definitive so we could eliminate what was offensive. He simply shook his head and turned back to his monitor.

"Think about it some more," he repeated infuriatingly.

Eventually I concluded that because Sergey was an engineer, he wanted our ads to depict an idealized world in which everything was optimized, including the people. I discovered that he disliked images that didn't fit a classical notion of beauty and thus could be seen as outliers in the data set of fully realized human potential. One trade ad for our advertising program included a picture of a sweaty sumo wrestler. Sergey wrinkled his nose when we showed it to him. "I don't think we should run ads with unattractive people in them. Our ads should always be aesthetically pleasing so people will think happy thoughts when they think of Google."

Devin Ivester, who left his own ad agency to join us as a creative-team leader,[*] remembers another such occasion, when he showed Sergey an ad with an exhausted man asleep on a couch, surrounded by books, notes, and papers. Sergey's response was, "No, we can't use that guy. He's ugly."

"You don't mean ugly, right?" Devin asked, somewhat taken aback.

"Well, no, but he's obviously not organized. He's just not a good person."

"How is he not a good person?"

"Well, look at him. He's just asleep on a couch."

"But if you read the headline, he's asleep because he's actually been working all night. He's almost tireless, but at some point he's had to give up."

"Well, obviously, he's disorganized then — if he can't keep up with his workload."

The lesson for Devin was that "Sergey had a very Disney-like idea of what we should show in our ads. It didn't have to be so real life. It was his idea of the perfect Googler and how people should be."

Perhaps because they viewed the world through a polarizing filter

---

[*] Devin was one of the few hires who made it through Google's screening process without a college degree, an accomplishment he attributes in part to his ability to quickly brainstorm ideas in his interview and in part to the fact that he let Sergey know that he "didn't have a big book of rules to apply to our brand."

of "ideal" and "suboptimal" (or "good" and "evil," if you will) and were so confident about which position they occupied in this binary system, our founders displayed a fondness for hyperbolic vilification of those who disagreed with them. In almost every meeting, they would unleash a one-word imprecation to sum up any and all who stood in the way of their master plans.

"Bastards!" Sergey would mutter if a competitor signed a client we were pursuing.

"Bastards!" Larry would exclaim when a blogger raised concerns about user privacy.

"Bastards!" they would say about the press, the politicians, or the befuddled users who couldn't grasp the obvious superiority of the technology behind Google's products.

It was a little intimidating until you got used to it, but it wasn't long before "bastards" became corporate nomenclature for any individual or institution that didn't see things the Google way. Ratings services undercounted our traffic? Bastards! Hard-drive vendors refused to cut deals below wholesale cost? Bastards! It became so prevalent that someone proposed that Sergey's five-word acceptance speech for an online award should be "The Webbys are for bastards."

Things could have been worse. In fact, they could have been far worse.

I rarely heard profanity in the halls of the Googleplex, where raised voices raised eyebrows. People could be infuriating, but the approved response was to bludgeon them with facts until they succumbed to superior logic. Not that Larry and Sergey couldn't be caustic, even to each other. David Krane, who traveled extensively with the founders, sums up their relationship this way: "Those guys had a communications channel that was very direct, very open. When there was tension, it was when they were fighting over data. They would be downright rude to each other, confidently dismissing ideas as stupid or naive or calling each other bastards. But no one would pout."

It didn't take long to figure out that Larry and Sergey wanted to optimize the organization until it was as efficient as its technology. Anything that increased costs or reduced productivity added friction and slowed our progress. Ideally, we would churn out perfect products while incurring no expense. That was impossible, of course, but it didn't stop us from trying.

Free Is Too Much

"I negotiated a really great deal for this data," I bragged to Sergey as I presented a spreadsheet showing all the countries for which we would get traffic rankings once our research contract was signed. "They offered twenty percent off at first, but I hammered them down to half."

Sergey poked and sniffed at the spreadsheet as if looking for chunks of meat in a vegetable stew.

"I don't think this is going to be very useful data," he told me. "They don't have much experience in these markets, and they're trying to expand their customer base. Having Google as a client would give them some great credibility." I knew what came next. It was as inevitable as rain after a carwash. "They should really pay us," Sergey said.

"They should pay us" was the starting position for any negotiation with a vendor. As Google grew in prominence, the benefit of being tied to our rising star increased exponentially — at least in Larry's and Sergey's minds. As our brand value approached infinity, our costs should go to zero. To the founders, winning a deep discount wasn't a victory; it was an admission of failure to get something for free. Their high expectations for low prices became a self-fulfilling prophecy, because I dreaded bringing them any proposal that shaved only ten or fifteen percent off the rack rate. "Never pay retail" was a Google core value. I was lucky, though. Marketing didn't buy services every day, so I didn't spend all my time beating suppliers into submission. It was different for facilities.

By late spring of 2000, Google's rate of growth was accelerating on all fronts. Traffic was building, our advertising had caught on, and so many dot-com refugees claimed space in the Plex that the walls bulged every time someone exhaled. Lines began forming outside the men's room, leading an engineer to install a "take a number" machine next to the stalls. In oversaturated offices, the person closest to the door had to stand up when an office mate wanted to leave or enter. Corridors were so choked with desks and power cords and boxed computer components that a stroll down the hall felt like a tour of Akihabara.

"We took a building that supposedly had a capacity of 220 and packed it with 298 people," George Salah confided when no fire marshal could hear him.

Engineers Howard Gobioff and Ben Smith complained to eStaff (the

executive staff) that lack of room was poor for morale and adversely affected productivity. In the midst of a hiring frenzy, they were conducting phone interviews in the stairwells and out on the grass because all
the conference rooms and private offices now housed multiple full-time
occupants. Cubes for two people held four workstations, and whenever
employees were out of the building for more than a day, newly hired
engineers would appropriate their spaces. Worst of all, work teams were
split up and located in different parts of the building, hindering communication.

Larry and Sergey gave George the okay to acquire more space. Sergey
helpfully advised him that SGI's office six blocks away looked "nice." It
was a joke. SGI's world headquarters complex had four massive buildings, each of which dwarfed ours.

"In April 2000, an office building across from us came available,"
George recalls. "They wanted $8.00 per square foot and we were paying
just over $2.50. I said to Larry and Sergey, 'This is a ridiculous price. I
don't think we should even bother with it.' They said, 'No, let's put in an
offer.'"

George saw trouble brewing. The Silicon Valley vacancy rate was
parked at one percent, and landlords saw no need to negotiate. "We're
going to have to deal with this guy again," he warned them. "He owns all
of Mountain View. We don't want to get on his bad side. Let's not place
an offer."

That only made Larry and Sergey more eager. "No, no. Put in an offer," they insisted. "A lowball offer. Let's offer $6.45 per square foot."

George called a broker. The broker called back. "The landlord
screamed at the broker," George remembers. "'How *dare you* send me
this offer? You know better than this. Don't bring me this kind of stupid
offer. And tell them it's *now* $8.25!' And he slams down the phone. So
we didn't get the building."

Two weeks later the dot-com fever broke and the real estate frenzy
passed like a kidney stone. Suddenly everything was fluid. George sub-
let space in that same building for $3.50 per square foot, and a year later
he leased a completely furnished building nearby for forty-five cents a
square foot.

It became a pattern. Just at the brink of disastrous overcrowding — or
perhaps a few weeks after — George acquired more space at fire-sale
prices and the Pacific Islanders reappeared with hammers and rails.
Google swallowed every adjacent building on the Pac-Man path lead-

ing straight to the SGI complex. Three years later, in 2003, we gobbled that too.

Whenever Google expanded, new cubicle configurations appeared. There were half-height cubes, three-quarter-height cubes, cubes with cut-out pass-through windows, and cube suites with courtyards for couches or dogs. Larry and Sergey wanted to optimize the tradeoff between productivity and rent. What would happen if you put three people in a space designed for two? How about five? How many interns could you line up along rickety tables in a busy hallway? What if you made a fishbowl with glass walls all around and put four engineers inside it? Would they get more done? Less? Would ideas breed in captivity? They conducted the servers-and-corkboard experiment with bodies and fabric walls — rearranging the elements to yield the greatest computational output while generating the least amount of heat. Things could always be more efficient and cost less, in either time or money.

And that's where Gerald Aigner came in.

Gerald was the flaming sword of frugality wielded by the lords of Google — a cost-cutting obsidian blade with an Austrian accent and close-cropped blond hair. Blue-white sparks glinted from his angular glasses and lit his Jack Nicholson smile, and the air crackled when it squeezed into the furrows of his brow. Before meeting with Gerald, I checked my shoes for rubber soles and whispered thanks that I wasn't across a negotiating table from him. There are still parts manufacturers who shudder and blink uncontrollably at the invocation of his name. After doing a deal with Gerald, one vendor refused to talk to Google again unless we agreed to their price up front, without any discussion. "You're too hard to deal with and we won't make any money," they complained.

"Gerald is probably the most difficult person on the planet to please," George confirmed. "He wants everything for nothing, has to have it faster than it can be delivered, and it has to be to his exact specifications, which can be unrealistic and just bizarre."

Jeff Dean heard Gerald put competing vendors on the phone together and make them beat each other's bids, fight-club style, until only one was left standing — offering a price Gerald was willing to pay.

When Google needed data-center capacity in Ireland, Gerald went to all three major facilities in Dublin and pitted them against one another to win the business. Who was most willing to undercut the competition to become Google's premier partner? Who was willing to sacrifice the

most to win a foothold for future business? Only after he had brow-
beaten them all into deep concessions did he sign a contract — with
each of them. He needed all the capacity he could buy, but there was no
advantage in revealing that in advance.

"The man had a penchant for cheap," recalls hardware designer Will
Whitted, who worked closely with Gerald. "I loved him dearly for that.
Anytime you told him the cost of anything, it was too much. The guy
made me absolutely nuts, but he was almost always right. Brilliant guy."

"This is ridiculous," Gerald said about the cost of the boxes encasing
our servers. "We shouldn't pay three hundred dollars for a piece of sheet
metal." He convinced Urs to get rid of the boxes and go with an open
design based on the bread racks he had seen in Charlie's kitchen. The
lack of a case made everything far easier to service.

"There wasn't any part that I couldn't change in under thirty seconds," Whitted remarked about his implementation of Gerald's idea.
"That allowed us to have far fewer data-center technicians. The average
in the U.S. is one tech per thirty machines. Google was running three
thousand machines per tech because there was no box."

Gerald's expertise extended from the lowest level of the hardware
to the software that ran on it, enabling him to identify savings others
couldn't see. Despite that according to Whitted, "Gerald was hugely
afraid of electricity. He was sure if he touched a thing with five volts on
it he was going to be electrocuted."

"That never happened," Gerald insisted. He disputes most of the
stories his former colleagues tell about him. He denies that a vendor
dumped boxes of computer parts in our parking lot and just drove off
when he realized he had sold them to us below his own cost. Bogdan
Cocosel, who worked with Gerald on hardware, assured me that it did
happen and that when they were tested, only half of the machines
worked. Fortunately, Gerald had such a deep understanding of hardware that he knew how to salvage even problem parts.

There were other bargains to be had. When Google needed data-
center space in Atlanta, Gerald approached the recently bankrupted
company Cable and Wireless. He bought eighty million dollars' worth
of equipment from them for a million and a half. He admitted to me
that a ninety-five percent discount was a reasonably good deal.

Gerald dealt with numerous bankrupt data centers, though not all of
them had reached that point before taking on Google's business. Exodus
and GlobalCenter both hosted Google servers before sinking together

under a sea of red ink. MCI WorldCom went out of business before they could sign their pending contract with Google. Gerald denies that he single-handedly drove data centers out of business. "The dot-com bubble burst. They had built all these data centers and couldn't fill them. They didn't realize they were in the real estate business." Besides, he explained, "I don't think I was a great negotiator. I only got eighty to ninety percent off list."

Urs gives him more credit than that: "Gerald understood the cost of ownership. Often, people didn't know what they were signing on the other side and were guaranteed to lose money. They should have known that power costs money and you can't just give it away. Or you do it once, but you don't do it twice — and they let us do it multiple times."

Gerald made a point of knowing everything about the companies with which he was negotiating, from their cost structures and breakeven points to the tariffs on their power bills. He knew what data centers had to pay for electricity even if they didn't, and he used that knowledge to Google's benefit. Other Googlers took advantage of Gerald's abilities to smooth over their own mistakes.

"I'm in front, cabling some of the machines to the switches," Jim Reese told me about a visit to Google's data center, "and all of a sudden I hear 'Zzzzt! Ahhhh!' I walk back and Harry [another early engineer] is just standing there, kind of dazed. We had fried the entire rack — all the RAM. RAM was difficult to get and very expensive, and we didn't have credit — I would drive down to Exodus with a half-million-dollar check in my hand so they'd offload the servers from the truck. We had Gerald convince the vendor the RAM was defective — because how could all three hundred and twenty sticks of RAM not work — right? So they replaced it all and sent it back to their manufacturer."

When I asked, Gerald disputed this account as well. There's something about him, though, that spawns such tales, perhaps because, as Urs described him, Gerald was "a very intense guy": "Sometimes people felt that he was angry, and he was just so energized about the problem that it appeared he was physically struggling with things." Because Urs felt Gerald was "an incredibly good match to what we needed," he protected him.

"Urs shielded me from Larry and Sergey," Gerald claimed. "I had a pretty good life because I could do what I wanted to do." Eventually he decided he wanted to live that good life in Europe, giving rise to one last — possibly true — story to add to the canon of Gerald legendry.

"When Gerald wanted to work in the Swiss office," Jeff Dean heard, "he somehow managed to get a Canton outside Zurich to change their tax laws for options. It's unclear if they did it for him, but it certainly would have applied to him."

To me, Gerald represented the unattainable ideal of bargaining savvy. When I brought in contracts, still wet with red ink bleeding from the slaughtered profit margins of vanquished vendors, Sergey sniffed, "These terms don't look very favorable. Maybe we should have Gerald talk to them." In his suggestion I heard, "Summon the Prince of Deepest Discounts! Let him pick the carcass clean and suck the bones of their marrow!" Perhaps my fears were exaggerated, but I knew Gerald, if set loose on my deal, would dash any hope of future favors from my supplier. The specter spurred me to put the screws in, which often was enough to sufficiently improve the terms. The sales reps I dealt with will never know the kindness I did them by squeezing them as hard as I could.

Think big. Stay flexible. Embrace data. Be efficient and economical in the extreme. I was mapping Google's unique terrain and starting to feel less like a toddler lost in the wilderness and more like an intrepid explorer boldly exploring *terra incognita*. I kept my eyes open and took one step after another in a direction I hoped was forward.

Examining My Options

Serious men wearing jackets (but no ties) were gathering in the I'm Feeling Lucky Lounge — our largest conference room. I watched the shadow army of laptop-toting factotums come and go, speaking in dry cellular whispers. Inside, I imagined our directors laying out visions, making revisions, moving, acting, arguing, and trying to keep their egos in check. Hours later they would emerge as the factotums checked their Palm Pilots and scuttled off to fetch their cars. At that point, I would start scanning my email very carefully.

I never dealt with our board face-to-face, but I always read the notes distributed after their meetings. Why? Well, of course I wanted to know about major shifts in our strategy, and announcements about significant executive hires, and . . . Ah, hell. Mostly because the board set the price of our stock.

Maybe this would be a good time to talk about money.

Almost no one talked about money at Google. It was an easy topic to avoid because nobody at the company had money to speak of. There may have been one or two people who left other startups with spending cash, but if they were rich enough to retire, they hid it well. What we did have was wealth potential.

I mentioned that in coming to Google I took a twenty-five-thousand-dollar pay cut. That did not help my cash flow, but at dot-coms stock options carried more weight than salary. Each option locked in the purchase price for a single share of stock, set at the stock's value the day the option was granted (the "strike price"). Even if the shares' price had skyrocketed by the time I actually exercised my option and bought the stock, I would still pay only the strike price, guaranteeing me a hefty profit. Companies usually offered their first hires significant numbers of shares but got stingier as the company grew. The earlier one joined, the greater the risk. The more risk, the greater the potential reward. Buy low, sell extremely high, retire young.

Stock options could compress the distance between a life of daily toil and one of affluent ease to the width of a sidewalk crack. I had seen friends and neighbors step across, buying mansions and taking charter-jet vacations, while my kids shared a room and were lucky to get day passes to Raging Waters. Why them? Why not me?

The truth is, most people in Silicon Valley worked hard, made smart decisions, and yet never passed that threshold. Randomness played too big a role. Or call it luck. I wasn't an entrepreneur or a brilliant scientist. I needed to jump on someone else's bandwagon and pray it didn't wind up in a ditch.

"We're prepared to offer you a salary only slightly lower than what you're making now," the hiring manager across the table from me at Yahoo had said, "and" — he paused dramatically — "*one thousand* stock options." I wasn't blown away. Yahoo's stock was already at fifty dollars a share. If it went to a hundred, I would make fifty thousand dollars. But if the stock dropped and never reached fifty again, my options would be "underwater" and hold no value.

For tax reasons, it's advisable to buy your options at the time they're issued, which would have meant putting fifty thousand dollars of my own money on the table: fifty thousand dollars I would never see again if the company took a dive. Plenty of dot-coms did go under in the big bust the following year, leaving little in their wake but suburban bathrooms wallpapered with worthless stock certificates. And even though I would be putting out the money up front, I wouldn't actually take ownership of the options immediately. I would take possession or "vest" on a schedule that began with a "cliff" of one year, meaning that not one share would actually belong to me until I had completed twelve months at the company. Then I would earn the rest of my shares month by month over the next three years, at which point I would be fully vested. Until the company went public, however, I couldn't sell the stock to anyone but the issuer.[*]

When I read my offer letter from Google, I thought there must be a typo. I was prepared for the pay cut, but the comma was in the wrong place on the number of options granted. It was an order of magnitude larger than I expected. Google was offering me a large stake, but I would have to bet it all on the company moving into the black. If Google did well, so would I. Salary? That was just a free drink and a complimentary crab cake while I waited for the roulette wheel to stop spinning and my chips to come in.

I've never been a numbers guy, but no matter how I did the math, the results looked pretty good. The board would meet within a month to approve stock grants to new employees and set the price at which my shares would be valued. I had decided to buy the options to avoid the tax penalty and now I waited to find out what I would have to pay for them.

The email headlined "Strike price" pinged into my mailbox. I opened it. The board had approved my offer at a share price of twenty. Twenty cents. It felt a little high, given the company's lack of revenue or a proven business model, but not unreasonable. Unfortunately, I was broke. Even at twenty cents a share, I couldn't afford to buy my options. My capital was tied up in a significant stake I'd taken in plush toys and flame-retardant pajamas. I would have to borrow money from my parents.

Kristen considered my decision on its merits.

"You want to borrow money?" she lovingly inquired. "To buy worthless shares of a company that doesn't have any revenue? Are you out of

---

[*] Some Googlers celebrated their fourth anniversary by wearing a vest to work. Others quit. One engineer with thousands of vested options left the company in anticipation of a quick IPO and a shower of gold. Instead, the company didn't go public until more than a year later, by which time he was whiling away his days surfing the net, living off his girlfriend, and subsisting on ramen noodles.

your mind? Can't you buy the shares later? Will you get the money back if they go out of business? You know, the car keeps stalling and we need a sewer line cleanout." Then she said, "Fine. Do what you want. Are you sure you really want to do this?"

My parents were equally skeptical, but they were my parents. They dug deep into their retirement savings to lend me the money, though I'm sure they believed it would go flush, right down the toilet.

So I bought the shares and waited and watched each month as they ticked up a few pennies at the board meetings. It was all play money since there was no way to cash out. Yet I found it hard to resist calculating my worth, even if it was imaginary. I never spoke of it at work. It was very bad form to discuss compensation within the company. We were all there for the love of technology and to radically improve the world. Really, we were. Seriously. Mostly.

One month the board met and raised the stock a dime. Suddenly I could repair the backyard fence or re-pipe the bathroom. I couldn't actually do it, because the money existed only as a line item in some accountants' spreadsheet. But in theory, at least, I was becoming increasingly comfortable.

Affiliated with Failure

Personal finance was off limits at the office, but we talked freely about how to spend the company's money.

"All we need now," I informed Cindy after Larry and Sergey had given our marketing plan tentative approval, "is a budget." Shari and I started drafting one. A department of half a dozen people could never implement all the programs outlined in our blueprint, so Shari planned to hire a promotion agency. She had talked with one that recommended we build campaigns around a "Google Challenge" and a "Google Scavenger Hunt." The concepts made me squirm. They seemed old school. A taste test? A scavenger hunt? Would we do clip-and-save coupons too?

"Larry and Sergey are intrigued by ideas like painting the Google logo on rooftops along the flight path to the airport," Cindy said. "Outrageous stuff. They want to project the Google logo on the moon."

Shari would have to wrestle with that — I was busy figuring out Larry's proposed affiliate program. Affiliate programs were all the rage among online retailers like Amazon. Amazon encouraged other sites to put up links pointing to a particular book or video or CD they had for sale. Users who clicked on that link would be transferred to Amazon, along with information about the site that had sent them. If the users ended up buying something, Amazon would pay a bounty to the referring website. That made sense. A referring agent should be paid a commission when a sale is made. But we weren't selling anything. Our search service was free.

"I don't get this," I told Shari. "we're paying people to use a free product? Won't people just abuse it?" We would get more users, but we'd also end up paying people who just clicked on the links they had put on their own websites. I didn't think it would work, but I looked into it anyway, expecting we would eventually bury the whole program under a rock.

The first back-of-the-envelope budget calculation Shari and I did suggested six million dollars would fund all of our marketing initiatives. We went back and carefully reviewed all the variables, including efficiencies we could realize by doing work in-house. We ended up doubling it. Twelve million dollars was dangerously close to the number that Scott Epstein, the interim VP of marketing, had mentioned just before he headed out the door. Still, it was far less than Shari had spent in prior jobs, and Cindy assured us it was a reasonable amount for establishing a global brand. So we built an elaborate spreadsheet justifying the need to spend most of the cash we had in the bank on promotional activities.

We sliced, diced, and fluffed the numbers every way we could, showing how many impressions we'd generate and how many visitors we'd convert into regular users. Our arguments were clear, compelling, and fact-based. We gave the twelve-million-dollar figure to our controller, who tossed it in with all the other finance numbers to be scrubbed by the board of directors. Cindy would present our case.

"I'll never forget," said Cindy of that fateful board meeting, "John Doerr saying to me, 'Would you rather spend ten million dollars on marketing or on machines?' And I said, 'Machines,' and he said, 'All right then.' And I was dismissed. I was so pissed at Larry and Sergey for leading me to slaughter, not saying a word during the presentation. I'm sure they knew what the sentiment of the board would be. Why we had to go through this exercise I'll never know."

When the scrubbing was done, our marketing budget had shrunk by two-thirds and most of what remained was allocated to the affiliate program, which, Larry let us know with some heat, had already taken far too long to put into place.

I wasn't entirely surprised at the cuts. It was one thing to approve abstract ideas, but committing real dollars to implementing a plan was quite another. Larry and Sergey expected us to execute everything we had proposed; they just didn't want us to spend any money doing it. As for the affiliate program, I had been trying to figure out the best way to give it life despite my desire to see it die. One useful big-company lesson I retained was to always make the boss's idea a priority, even if it's patently unreasonable.

The Netscapees (as former Netscape employees are called) in our business-development department were ironing out the wrinkles with BeFree, our affiliate-program management company. I expected it to take weeks for such a complex deal to be completed. It was close to New Year's, and nobody did serious business around the holidays. Larry did. He wanted the program launched immediately. Cindy sent me a note at four in the morning explaining this very succinctly. Every passing minute we did not have an affiliate program in place was an affront to Larry, and that got back to Cindy. When Cindy couldn't sleep, I had nightmares. And when I had nightmares, I grumbled to my wife.

"Haven't we earned some slack? I mean, things are going pretty well overall, considering most of the marketing group is so new. We've already developed a marketing plan and a budget . . ."

"Wait, didn't you tell me the budget was cut?" Kristen asked, just to prove she didn't always ignore me when I talked about work.

"I set up a committee to prioritize projects," I said, ignoring her.

"Oh. So they decided not to kill your committee after all?" Now she was toying with me.

"I worked with engineering on measuring traffic! I collected user testimonials! I put together UI guidelines!"

"I'm sure the engineers really appreciated that," she said in the soothing tone she used on the children. Clearly I would have to stop sharing so many of my frustrations with her.

It did feel as if we had digested huge projects during a period most companies spent eating down the leftovers from their Christmas parties. And not just systems stuff. We'd also begun updating the Google corporate pages, run focus groups with an outside research firm, redesigned our corporate stationery, and printed sales collateral. We'd even managed some guerrilla marketing at MacWorld in San Francisco, where we showed up at dawn to hand out thousands of Google-branded luggage tags before Apple's goon squad chased us away for lack of a permit.

"Luggage tags are the key to Google's growth," Sergey had dryly remarked when I pointed out that Apple-related searches on Google went up noticeably, if not significantly, in the weeks that followed.

All that effort without any inkling of what our overall company priorities or strategy might be. I began to suspect that my new employer's expectations were always going to exceed my capacity by at least thirty percent.

The affiliate program launched in early 2000, less than a month after the contract was signed with BeFree. It was a time suck from day one. Tens of thousands of affiliates signed up to be paid for sending a search or two a day our way. Most of the traffic came from a handful of large sites and a swarm of dishonest spammers. It wasn't hard to put a Google search box on a web page and then write a program to keep entering searches into it. Each week we prepared a list of cheaters we needed to block, but it was the legitimate low earners who ate up most of my time. They clamored for their two-dollar checks as if nothing else stood between them and the soup kitchen.

We started off paying three cents for each search sent our way, then cut it back to a penny. Traffic instantly plateaued. I never felt the expense and the hassle were worth the trickle of new users we were attracting, but Larry believed acquiring new users this way cost less than finding them through online advertising. Susan took control of the program a few weeks later, since she managed our other search-technology products. Secretly I celebrated having an albatross off my neck, and took some solace from the fact that even in Susan's more willing hands our affiliate network never contributed to the bottom line. A year after its launch, Susan asked me to write a letter telling our affiliates we were killing the program.

That was one of the rare occasions when I felt we made an avoidable error. As Susan conceded years later, "In the scope of things, it wasn't the right program for us to be running." The time and money could have been put to better use, though perhaps this was only obvious to me because the time and money belonged to my department. Larry saw staff productivity as infinitely expandable, and one more program to manage could hardly be considered an obstacle. If the affiliate program interfered with other responsibilities, then we would just work harder and longer. We were blessed with boundless opportunity, so our output would need to grow without limit.

When we pulled the plug, it didn't matter that Larry had originally been a proponent of the program. The financial data didn't support it, so we took it out back, put a stake through its heart, and buried it deep in the field of failed ideas.

CHAPTER 9

Wang Dang Doodle — Good Enough Is Good Enough

IT WAS HARD to let go of the absolutes I had clung to so tightly over a long career of managing brands. Sergey tried to help me by prying tenets from my rigid belief system and beating me over the head with them. Case in point, the daily affirmation I chanted to our logo's inviolate purity.

This is our logo.

It looks like this.

If it looks like this, it's our logo.

Because our logo looks like this.

One of the convictions I'd brought with me to Google, based on the two books I had read about branding, was that you needed to present your company's graphic signature in a monomaniacally consistent manner — to pound it into the public consciousness with a thousand tiny taps, each one exactly the same as the one before.

So when Sergey reminded me that he wanted us to play with Google's signature homepage graphic, I put my foot down. Remember, this was not merely the most prominent placement of our logo; it was the only placement of our logo. We weren't advertising on TV or on billboards or in print. The logo floating in all that white space was it. And though we had millions of users, we were hardly so well known that we could assume people already had our brandmark burned into their brains.

Sergey didn't see the big deal. He had changed the logo twice during Google's infancy, adding a clip-art turkey on Thanksgiving in 1998 and putting up a Burning Man* cartoon when the staff took off to explore nakedness in the Nevada desert. But now Google was a real company, I reminded him. Real companies don't do that.

Even as we argued, Sergey enlisted webmaster Karen White to resurrect the turkey for Thanksgiving, create a holiday snowman in December, and festoon the logo with a hat and confetti for New Year's 2000.

"What about aliens?" he asked. "Let's put aliens on the homepage. We'll change it every day. It will be like a comic strip that people come back to read."

I tried not to be condescending as I explained again why it was bad branding. I gave him my spiel about consistency of messaging and uniform touchpoints and assured him it wasn't just my opinion; it was the consensus of marketing professionals worldwide. Manipulating one's logo was identity dilutionary.

I knew I had finally convinced him when he stopped asking me about it.

I was wrong. Sergey wasn't convinced; he just didn't like repeating himself. So he turned to Susan instead. Susan didn't argue; she started looking for an artist to execute Sergey's vision. She found illustrator Ian Marsden and put him to work. In May 2000, Ian created the first Google Doodle.† It featured — surprise, surprise — aliens making off with our logo.

NYU professor Ken Perlin created a bouncing heart applet for Valentine's Day and a bouncing-bunny game for Easter. Larry showed his gratitude with an offer of Google stock sufficient to make the code Ken sent us, line for line, quite possibly the most expensive ever written.

Our users loved the randomness of the logo artwork and sent us dozens of appreciative emails. Google's brilliant strategy of humanizing an otherwise sterile interface with cute little cartoon creatures was an

---

* An annual gathering of thousands of free spirits who — often clad in little more than bandannas and body paint — celebrate technology and creativity by assembling unique structures and burning them to the ground.

† "Google Doodle" originally referred to a multipart logo that changed each day to tell a story, though people now refer to even a single altered homepage logo as a Doodle.

enormous hit—and as the company's online brand manager, the person responsible for building Google's awareness and brand equity, I had opposed it as adamantly as I could. Yes, if it had been left to me, there would be no Google Doodles at all; just our cold stiff logo lying in state, wrapped in a sheet of pristine white pixels.

It was so blindingly obvious (to me) that I was right, yet I was so clearly wrong. Google did that to you—made you challenge all your assumptions and experience-based beliefs until you began to wonder if up was really up, or if it might not actually be a different kind of down.

Why Wrong Was Right

Larry's Rules of Order:

- Don't delegate: Do everything you can yourself to make things go faster.
- Don't get in the way if you're not adding value. Let the people actually doing the work talk to each other while you go do something else. Don't be a bureaucrat.
- Ideas are more important than age. Just because someone is junior doesn't mean they don't deserve respect and cooperation.
- The worst thing you can do is stop someone from doing something by saying, "No. Period." If you say no, you have to help them find a better way to get it done.

Larry wouldn't enunciate this brief set of principles until 2004. Even if I'd had them on day one, it would have taken a while to reprogram my operating system to accept them. I happened to be really good at saying no.

All my previous jobs had inculcated in me the conviction that bad ideas, like termites, must be exterminated before they could gnaw away at our core business. If a proposal didn't arrive chained to a rock-solid guarantee of success reinforced with a five-year projection, breakeven points, and upward-trending arrows, it was a bad idea.

At the *Merc* I learned that the presumptive answer was always no, as in "If no one in authority tells you to do it, don't." At Google that answer was supposed to be yes. You should take initiative, though it was never clear how far you could go on your own.

Larry and Sergey had never worked in a company where they were taught otherwise — say a company that had been recording past events on the pulped remains of dead trees for a century and a half. So I needed to stop saying "Here's my concern," and start saying "Here's what you need to do to make that happen."

Sergey gave me an opportunity when he dynamited the dam of my resistance and homepage logos came pouring through. If I couldn't stop them, at least I could divert them from sweeping away the brand equity we had already built.

Karen White was the webmaster, and the webmaster had responsibility for the homepage. The webmaster also constituted one-half of the online brand group reporting to me. Karen would decorate the logos when we didn't have outside help.

About the time Ian Marsden's first Doodle ran, Karen hired an intern to help with updating the website. The intern, Dennis Hwang, was majoring in art and computer science and had helped with graphics for the gator-gone-wild horror flick *Lake Placid* ("You'll never know what bit you"). During his interview Dennis mentioned that on his last job he had volunteered to work thirty-hour weekend shifts without pay. That got our attention. And he could draw. Over the next year, we gave Dennis responsibility for decorating the logo and we stopped using contractors. Why pay for milk when you own a cow?

"Hey, tomorrow is election day! What are we doing for a logo?" a curious engineer would ask Karen or Dennis or me over dinner.

"Oh, something really cool. You'll see," we would answer. Then we would go back to our cubes and discuss whether we actually were going to do a logo for election day. For the first couple of years, that was the carefully structured process by which we instigated homepage alterations. If we decided to go ahead, Dennis would get to work, churning out one idea after another. Dennis never slept. In the still of the night, his stylus danced over the drawing pad connected to his computer, and by the time the morning dawned, a new logo was ready to adorn the site.

One of the few decorations we actually planned in advance was Mother's Day 2000. To prove that Google wasn't composed entirely of metal and wiring attached to positronic brains, I suggested we collect photos of moms from our coworkers and arrange them around the old poem spelling out "What Mother Means to Me." Straight out of the Hallmark emotional-manipulation handbook. We were so inundated with fan mail I became verklempt.

"Your mothers must be *so* proud," a user told us. "I want my son to work at Google."

We received more letters of praise when we did the same thing the following year, but we also received pointed questions about why there weren't any African-American moms depicted. We answered that not all staff members were represented — but it was the last time our mothers put in an appearance.

Sometimes the artwork itself misfired. "Why do you have a turkey, a turtle, and a thermometer on your logo?" users asked when Dennis celebrated the Japanese holiday Shichi-Go-San with a crane, a turtle, and a traditional candy bag.

"Why does King Neptune have a boner?" Several users noted an unfortunate tenting in Poseidon's toga during a logo series Dennis did for the Olympics that featured figures from Greek mythology.

"Your anti-Christian political correctness is showing." "Your hemisphericentric world view is apparent." We heard both these complaints about the snowy "winter holiday" scenes we ran instead of Christmas-specific artwork. Australians in particular wanted to make it very plain to us that December is the middle of their summer and hence winter scenes on our homepage made us look uninformed, uncaring, or both.

"Where's your patriotism?" other users demanded. "You celebrate Chinese New Year, but not [pick one]: Memorial Day, Veterans Day, D-Day, V-J Day, Presidents' Day." We wanted the logos to be unpredictable and special, but eventually they took on a life of their own with a complicated set of rules governing what we would commemorate and whom we would honor. That came later. For the first couple of years, Dennis and Karen and I had free rein to pick and choose, which is why Korean Liberation Day made the list twice before Australia Day. Yo, Dennis — represent, Seoul brother.

Good Enough Is Good Enough

"Do you know what our greatest corporate expense is?" Sergey asked at TGIF. The assembled Googlers looked up from their laptops. Everyone wanted the chance to be right in front of others.

"Health insurance!" shouted an engineer. "Salaries!" "Servers!" "Taxes!" "Electricity!" "Charlie's grocery bills!" rejoined others.

"No," said Sergey, shaking his head solemnly. "Opportunity cost."

Products we weren't launching and deals we weren't doing threatened our economic stability far more than any single line item in the budget. We were falling behind even as we leapt ahead. Success was spilling through our fingers. This was Sergey's rallying cry to redouble our efforts. I heard it, but sometimes I had a hard time answering.

After six months on the job, I had plenty on my plate, and I swept away my daily tasks like an umpire brushing away the dust of a homebound slide. Big amorphous projects, though, like reorganizing all the corporate information pages or developing a banner-ad strategy for our trade partners, I just couldn't find time to complete.

If I wasn't responding to coworker requests, sitting in meetings, or flicking my mouse at emails infesting my inbox, I was being seduced by the rustle of M&Ms each time someone dipped a scoop into the bin across the hall. Kitchen aromas suffused my senses until I was compelled to pore over the lunch menu and plan my noon repast. There was always someone up for after-dinner *Soul Calibur* in the Blue Room, and the sauna beckoned when the pressure got intense — I could think about all the tasks piling up on my desk as freshly made Italian coffee dripped out of my pores.

At the *Merc,* I had never felt a pang when making personal calls on my office phone, because, I mean, just look at the dearth of perks they offered. A discounted subscription to our own newspaper? Gee. Thanks. At Google, I was in worker's paradise, but I felt I didn't deserve it. I was putting in way more hours than I had at the *Merc,* but it never seemed enough to justify the bounty the company was bestowing upon me. As dot-coms slipped into insolvency all around us, I was constantly reminded how lucky I was, not only to have a job, but to have such a great job. Survivor's guilt tormented me. Yes, I was cranking out great volumes of material, but I wasn't pushing us quickly enough toward a global marketing strategy. Cindy knew it. She made it clear she wanted more urgency, more big ideas, more leadership from me. She was right: I could, I *should* do more. My days stretched longer. I hung around in the dark (but hardly empty) Googleplex forcing myself to *be productive.* Was I the only one feeling this insecure?

"I don't know if I can last here a year," search-quality guru Ben Gomes thought to himself after starting his first hard assignment. "I hope I can make it. I want to reach my vesting cliff." Gomes survived. "A few months later I started working on ranking," he recalls. "I was here till four a.m. and coming back at ten in the morning. My entire life was here. It was *great*. I really enjoyed it."*

The hours and the intensity fostered a sense of camaraderie among the night shift, especially when Larry and Sergey held court in their offices. They were so much easier to spot in the moonlight, stripped of the protective cover provided by blocked-out calendars. Meetings devoured daylight, but seven p.m. opened broad vistas of uninterrupted uptime. I could brew a fifth cup of coffee and face down the monstrosities lurking in forsaken corners of my to-do list. But first . . .

"Daddy? When are you coming home, Daddy?" one of the kids would croon as soon as I called the house. "I miss you and I want to see you." Kristen wasn't above fighting dirty in the war for my attention. "I love you Daaaddy."

How could I blame her? While I snuggled in the bosom of my new Google family, she picked up the parental duties I shirked. Playing pattycake, making macaroni, kissing boo-boos, and keeping the roof securely fastened on our little bungalow next door to a guy doing home-based auto repairs. All while lecturing local college students on Russian avant-garde cinema and Persian poetry of the thirteenth century.

My previous jobs had been in public broadcasting and newspapers, both infamous for obscenely inflated compensation packages, so money was never an issue unless we needed to buy something. Kristen didn't play the martyr, though I could discern her doubts.

"He was just ready to try something new," I heard her tell a friend on the phone. "It's Google. No. Goo-gle. Gooooo-gle. Like a baby sucking a pacifier. Yes, it's a real company. Well, not as real as the newspaper was . . ."

The feeling that I was failing at home while underachieving in a spectacular way at work shook me. There were so many things I *could* be doing better in both places that I started parsing my schedule into thirty-second segments and communicating in sentence fragments.

"Adam! Out of bed, dressed, and ready to go in ninety seconds." Adam was eleven. "Nathaniel. Bathroom? Socks and shoes in the car. Pants too." Nathaniel was six. "Avalon. Diapee?" Avalon was one.

---

* Hardware designer Will Whitted once complained, "I hate it when I tell Urs I'm working twenty-four hours a day, and he says, 'Well, I guess you'll have to work nights, too.'"

Surprisingly, children are not onboard with that mode of interaction. I had to force myself to remember that the goal of being a father is not to download a set of instructions, check for understanding, and then move on to the next task on an endless list.

Meanwhile, status requests showed up in my inbox at midnight asking about assignments handed out five hours earlier. Instant messages arrived minutes later.

"Just wondering. Where are you with the text for the browser buttons? We need to check in the code in an hour."

If one task fell behind schedule, the project circling behind would sink lower and lower until it slid to a fiery end on a foam-covered runway. I wanted to take the time to do everything right — polish the prose and perfect the text, double-check the targeting, and drop it precisely on the intended audience. The engineers wanted to shove stuff out the window when it was still a mile away from where it should be.

"Good enough is good enough" was the standard Urs set for engineering. In those five words he encapsulated a philosophy for solving problems, cutting through complexity, and embracing failure. It should be stitched into the fabric of every cubicle at Google. It drove Google's software development, the heart and soul of the company's technology.

"When you have a list that's longer than you can deal with, you have to prioritize," Urs instructed us. "If you give a project a quick improvement that gets you eighty percent of the way to solving the problem, you haven't solved it, but it drops below the line versus one you haven't worked on at all." And then he put his finger on the crux of my conflicts with engineering. "Once a problem falls below the line you should work on something else, even though it's not finished."

How the hell could I stop working on something when it wasn't finished? The whole world would see scratches in our metal-flake paint and dings in the door panels of our corporate identity. The shame!

"Even if something starts big, it decays in importance as you work on it because you fix some parts of it," Urs informed me. "At some point all the problems above the line that are really important are being worked on. That is my definition of success: if you do a good job hiring, you get the luxury of actually doing it right and the luxury of going far beyond what you 'need to do.'"*

I touched on the importance of hiring back in the Introduction,

---

* Urs claims this inflection point happened for Google sometime in 2003.

and I'll touch on it again in the pages that follow. Urs made it clear that adding talented staff cured everything but male-pattern baldness. Larry and Sergey agreed — as long as the new staffers' talents lay in the technical realm. I was able to hire a marketing coordinator, but for a long time the only bodies added to Cindy's group worked on public relations. That meant I had plenty to do updating the content of our website while overseeing our ad partnerships, affiliate program, and user-support service.

Larry and Sergey wanted to keep Google's ratio of engineers to non-engineers at fifty-fifty, but in the dot-com feeding frenzy the pickings were slim. And hiring was the one area in which Urs would accept nothing less than perfection. "In April 2000," he told me, we didn't make a single offer. Our plan was to hire three to four people per month. We asked, 'Did we make a mistake? Maybe we're too tough? We can't succeed if we don't get people in.' We looked at all of them and said, 'No, actually, this was the right decision.'"

Fortunately (for almost no one but Google), the dot-com bubble burst the following month. Coders suddenly warmed up to cold calls from recruiters, and Urs began collecting résumés that matched the profile of a good Google engineer.

"Nobody had experience with search engines," Urs recalls. "What was most important was what else they had done, how good they were technically, and how quickly they could learn." He dictated a mantra to Google's HR staff: "Hire ability over experience."* Brilliant generalists could reprogram themselves like stem cells within the corporate body: they would solve a problem, then morph and move on to attack the next challenge.

"The key thing," Urs said, "was that they be able to independently make progress, because there wasn't much room for babysitting. They had to have good judgment about whether to coordinate or not."

Google generalists needed a firm grasp, not just of coding, but of the hardware and performance issues essential to scaling the search engine. Most recent computer science grads didn't have that breadth of knowledge, but Urs and the founders remained adamant that offers be extended only to those who could retool quickly. "It was too

---

* A handful of true search scientists — most notably Amit Singhal and Monika Henzinger — did join the company early on, but they were exceptions. Google also hired specialists to build Windows apps and to manage its Oracle database when Larry became convinced auditors would not certify a financial system we built ourselves.

hard to predict where the next fire would be," Urs explained. "If you only know how to do *A* and it turns out the company moves in a way that *A* isn't important anymore, you have an intrinsic reaction to argue that we *must* do *A*. If you're a generalist, you're much less threatened by that. Instead, it's, 'Fine. Great. Here's something else to do that's exciting!'"

That expectation applied to everyone at Google. I was to identify key issues, then solve them or learn how to solve them. Saying "I can't do that, because I don't know how" revealed a deficiency of initiative, flexibility, and perhaps even IQ. It was a shock to my sense of the way an office operated. I'd worked mainly in union shops, where grievances were filed if you tried to do a task that "belonged" to someone else. I once flicked the wall switch in an empty TV studio and was scolded because studio lights could only be turned on by a member of NABET. When I worked at ad agencies, media buyers didn't write copy, copywriters didn't talk to clients, account people didn't buy TV time. It would have violated the natural order.

Matt Cutts, who carved out a niche attacking the porn and spam that degraded search results, summed up our staffing philosophy this way: "It works pretty well if you hire really smart people who are flexible and can get things done. Then just throw them into the deep end of the pool."

What you had studied in school wasn't relevant. What you had been doing at your previous job didn't matter. Once you waded into Google's sea of needs, someone tossed you a project and you were expected to grab it. Either you learned how to swim with it or it sank you.

It Goes without Saying

Even though Urs had an unhealthy fixation on hiring, he seemed like an upright guy who thought beyond the black and white of "Can we do it?" to the murkier question "Should we do it, just because we can?" I was impressed with the stand he took on RealNames, but I didn't realize that his fundamentalist views on absolute honesty had a dark side, one that seeped into the company culture and cast a shadow over working collaboratively.

"Urs was rather sparse with his praise," as systems guy Ben Smith diplomatically put it. Smith* wasn't much of a talker himself. Not aggressively reticent, just coolly laconic. A world-class Ultimate Frisbee player, Smith had the intensity of athletic confidence wrapped around an intellect capable of solving Google's most intransigent grit-in-the-gears software problems. Steve McQueen with a PhD, maybe.

"I had written up detailed instructions," Smith told me about a piece of notoriously unreliable software he had been up all night trying to fix. "I explained to Urs before I left, 'Here's what we've done. Here's how it's running. Here are the things to look at. Here's what's going to go wrong if it goes wrong, and here are ten steps you need to do to turn it off.' I was driving home, listening to *Morning Edition,* and I get a call from Urs. 'It broke like you said it would,' he says. 'I fixed it. Good work.' It was like, 'Your directions worked. Thank you for not completely screwing us over.'"

"Urs was people-challenged in just the funniest way," engineer Ron Dolin confirmed. "He didn't give compliments. If you were doing a good job, that's enough said. But some of us — especially the ones who were not the supermen of the company — could have used a little encouragement here or there."

So why was Urs so parsimonious with his accolades? Is it just that engineers are tight-lipped? "I don't think there's an engineering aversion to praise," Urs replied when I asked about our compliment-free culture. "It's one of my biggest management problems. Myself, I don't need effusive praise. I didn't grow up like that and it doesn't come naturally."

The language barrier contributed to Urs's reticence to laud his team. "'Good' in German really means 'good,'" he explained. "Here it means 'not really that good, but not bad yet.' In German, you wouldn't say 'excellent' almost ever. You'd say 'very good,' because the highest mark at school was 'very good.' That's the best there is. 'Excellent' maybe means Olympic caliber. Not what normal people would achieve. That was always a little bit of a challenge."

Urs not only had trouble giving compliments, he had a hard time accepting them as well. "My advisor at Stanford would tell me that things were 'great,'" he once confided with a grimace, "and I knew it wasn't all great and I had trouble understanding. In Switzerland, you'd say, 'This is bad, and this is bad, and this is bad. And why did you do this? This is

---

* Google hired a bushel of Bens. I'll refer to each by his last name so you can keep them straight.

not going to work.' And here it's like, 'Do you think that . . . maybe you could . . . ?'"

Urs acknowledged to me that his attitude created problems. "I'm not really proud of that," he said, "because we had really excellent people. It's easy to forget, because there are problems everywhere, and obviously you focus on problems, because that's what needs to be fixed, right? But that can come across as 'everything's bad,' right? When in fact things are great." And then, because, after all, he was Urs, he added, "Except there still are problems."

The tone set by Urs in engineering was the tone for all of Google. The company stacked its payroll with high achievers unaccustomed to going unacknowledged, and despite the stock options and the free food, they often felt underappreciated. At the same time, many felt unsure of their own contributions or where they stood in relation to their peers.

For my own ego nourishment, I deciphered different types of feedback I received and developed an interpretative scale of success. Ordered from "Can I double-check your SAT scores?" to "I don't think that would have occurred to me," it went like this:

It's a waste of time.

It's not worth talking about.

It doesn't offend me.

It will do until we can fix it.

It seems reasonable.

It seems sensible.

It's kind of interesting.

I also developed a personal theory about why encouragement to improve productivity came easily but effusive praise proved elusive. It wasn't that people didn't expect and appreciate exceptional performance, or that coworkers and managers were too envious to note a job well done. Just the opposite. If you assumed all your colleagues were at Google because of their skill and intelligence, calling attention to their success might be insulting — as if you were surprised that they had done what was expected.

I took some comfort from that notion, specious though it may have been, because I didn't want to dwell on the alternative possibility — that I was hearing so little praise because no one thought I actually deserved it.

What? Me Worry?

The fear of falling behind churned my stomach and tattered my sleep. Not so for Urs. Despite the massive load Larry and Sergey had placed on his shoulders, at the end of a full day he could let things be. "I've always had the ability to accept that there's stuff that I can't deal with right now," he said. "And I don't feel bad about it because I know I made the best use of my time. People are going to laugh when they hear this, but it's actually easier for me to accept failure or imperfection than for other people — if it's there for a good reason."

I always questioned my allocation of time and how I set priorities. Looking over my shoulder, Cindy did too. A bike-to-work-day flyer got the same attention as a vital piece of a product launch. Once I latched onto a project, I forced myself to stay with it until every preposition was assigned an object and every participle properly tucked in. I sometimes struggled with a single word choice for an hour and then spent days defending it. Intense focus. Willful execution. Methodical progress. Long periods lost wandering in the trees.

Urs would take a step back, squint to obscure the details, and take in the larger picture. He understood the minutiae, but he was self-disciplined enough not to obsess on them, which freed him to paint in large sweeping strokes. As he put it, "You have to say both emotionally and intellectually, 'I can only work so many hours. The best I can do is make good use of these hours and prioritize the right way so I spend my time on the things that are most important.' Then if I see something below the line that is broken and I can fix it, it's important *not* to try to fix it. Because you're going to hurt yourself. Either personally — because you add another hour and that's not sustainable — or you're going to hurt something that's above the line that's not getting the hours that it should."

What did that look like in practice?

"Screw quality," Urs instructed one development team, urging them on to an earlier launch date. "Screw anything you can screw." Adopting that mindset might have reduced my intake of antacids.

I concluded that Larry and Sergey trusted Urs because they shared his preference for quick fixes over long-term solutions. They, too, gladly sacrificed perfection on the altar of expediency.

"Larry and I would differ on how important it was to fix problems so they never recurred," Craig Silverstein recalls. "Larry was usually in favor of patching things up and dealing with them later, and I was always in favor of fixing them right. His take was, put out the fires faster and then you can spend time on the other things."

When duplicate results began showing up in searches, for example, Craig wanted to completely restructure the software to eliminate the problem. "No," Larry overruled him. "We can just make it work better in this system."

"Then it will be really fragile, and I guarantee the time will come when it breaks and will be harder to fix," Craig warned. But, of course, Larry won and Craig patched the system instead of replacing it. "I was wrong," Craig said later. "It never ended up being a problem again, and as far as I know, we're still using that same technique to deal with it."

Urs did his best to institutionalize his prioritization strategy among Google's engineers. He set up formal project reviews every couple of weeks, to force people to pay attention to the most urgent issues and to identify obstacles that might impede progress. "Sometimes people try to solve the problem," he explained, "instead of immediately escalating it and saying, 'Please help me get rid of this problem.'"

"It was pretty obvious what to do," Sanjay Ghemawat told me about his first few months on the job. "I could see the problems in the infrastructure around me. So a lot of it was finding the biggest pain point and working on that." Once the agony had been reduced to a dull throbbing, it was time to move on to the next source of irritation.

A potential drawback with Urs's notion of "self-correcting" engineers was that too many people might unwittingly work separately on the same problem. That didn't happen at first.

"There were maybe two or three people per project," recalls Jeff Dean, "so there were only like twenty pockets, and at that point you say, 'I know what those twenty are doing.'"

As Google grew, though, the company instituted an automated weekly update system. Engineers used it to file brief online "snippets" describing the areas in which they were working. The system compiled all the snippets into a single list, which it emailed out to everyone who cared. Though many engineers didn't make the filing deadline each week or ignored the process, Larry and Sergey rolled it out to other departments, including marketing. That was pretty typical. Engineering would create some new technology and try it out, then share it with everyone else to get the whole company aligned around the same set of productivity tools.

That we used the same systems as engineering, however, did not mean we were equal partners in the product-development process. "Never, ever, *ever* delay the launch of a product just for a marketing issue," Cindy warned us. It was the third rail of company politics. We could not fall behind or fail to deliver. If my piece of a project wasn't completely up to my standards and the launch date was at hand, I would have to dump all the loose screws into the box, solder it shut, and hand it off to the engineers impatiently waiting for it. And then move on.

A day would come — or at least a moment — when it would be appropriate to stop and drink the decaf, reflect on what we had accomplished, and contemplate what lay ahead. This was not that moment. "There's plenty of time," Cindy reminded us on numerous occasions, "to rest when we die."

CHAPTER 10

Rugged Individualists
with a Taste for Porn

THE MARKETING PLAN I had drafted drifted along without a budget for implementation, so Shari and I salvaged the elements we could execute ourselves. My situation wasn't completely untenable. Most of my proposals entailed online promotions that didn't require hard dollars for the purchase of media or materials. If need be, I could barter search services for banner-ad space on other sites.

Shari didn't have as many options. She became increasingly frustrated with her inability to convince Larry and Sergey to spend money on offline customer acquisition. When she requested outside resources, the answer was "Why don't you do it yourself? It's not that hard." In Google's culture, when you ran into a wall, you built a ladder. If there was a moat beyond the wall, you made a boat. If there was a crocodile in the moat, you fed it one of your arms and used the other to paddle across. The takeaway was "Take responsibility. Do something."

So Shari did. She went shopping for an outside agency to create the offline promotion she had been planning. She didn't have much luck. "We were disappointed at how close-minded Larry and Sergey were," her first choice admonished her. "We don't trust Larry, so you'd have to pay us in advance."

Larry and Sergey didn't disguise their antipathy toward ad agencies and the industry to which they belonged. They were disgusted by the sea of self-congratulatory awards and the bad math and the pseudoscientific jargon used to proclaim advertising's effectiveness. Larry even hated the stiff black cardboard that agencies used to present creative campaigns — each concept perfectly center-mounted to convey greater gravitas. To Larry, a good idea was self-evident, even if scrawled on a wrinkled napkin in blotchy ballpoint. Ad agencies, he hinted, were full of bumbling simpletons and evil dissemblers.

When Shari located a promotion agency willing to take our account, she acted boldly. She signed a contract and put them to work. When Larry and Sergey found out, they made it clear that when they urged us to "do something," they meant "do something that doesn't cost Google money." And that wasn't the worst of it.

Google didn't acknowledge outside firms that served the company — not even for client references. As the company grew in size and stature, suppliers begged for permission to announce their ties to us, often offering steep discounts if they could just display Google's logo on their client lists. Almost always we said no. We spent valuable time evaluating vendors. Why spare our competitors the same hardship by tipping them off that we had found a company worthy of our business? It would be far better if our competition made its own choices, and, perhaps, chose badly.

That's why I was amazed to read in *Advertising Age* that we had signed an agency to handle our five-million-dollar promotion account. No one had authorized the article or known it was coming. The agency had taken the initiative to place it and to exaggerate the facts. It was not the kind of creative effort we wanted from them. All of Larry and Sergey's hot buttons were mashed at once — strongly and repeatedly — and Shari suddenly had a crisis on her hands.

I empathized with her and wanted to help, but there wasn't much I could do to sway our founders toward acceptance of our new partners. Shari would have to convince them on her own.

And the Winner Is . . .

Each morning I scanned the press for signs that the tectonics of our industry had shifted overnight. Who had been acquired? Who had a new alliance? Whom did we need to fear? Sitting in my cube thumbing

through the May 2000 issue of the magazine *Upside*,* I found an in-
depth analysis of the search space. I scanned it eagerly to see how things
were viewed from outside the Plex. Reading the article, I learned that
our focus on search was outdated and our strategy was doomed.

"In the early days, search was the marquee item and major driver of
traffic on our site," Excite's director of search told *Upside*, ". . . but now
it is one of many services." Google just had search. Well, search and a
directory. Did that constitute "many services"?

"What's missing from search is the context," said Peter Kui at Disney's
Go.com.† He added, "You only get that by being part of the entertainment business . . . There will be niche search players. Some will come at
it from a technology standpoint, but we take the larger view." A technology standpoint offered an insufficiently large view? Should we also be
working a Mickey Mouse angle?

AltaVista would face a serious channel-conflict challenge, *Upside*
predicted, because it was peddling its technology to other portals while
maintaining a consumer site of its own. Well, at least someone wasn't
doing better than we were. Wait. Wasn't that *our* strategy?

Inktomi, *Upside* noted approvingly, was "the only major search engine to focus exclusively on providing search technology to other sites."
Inktomi had Yahoo as a client. They had AOL. Now they had Microsoft.
Despite all that fabulous success, however, Inktomi had lost $2.4 mil-
lion in their fourth quarter. They had exclusive deals with the three biggest sites on the Internet and were still losing money? That didn't bode
well for a company just getting into the business.

Ask Jeeves offered a "natural language" interface they claimed could
answer questions written in plain English. They also had a spiffy cartoon butler for a logo and a big marketing budget. I had tested Jeeves and
found their branding much better than their search results. Evidently
they reached the same conclusion, because they bought the up-and-
coming search company Direct Hit in early 2000. Direct Hit was pretty
good, though when I asked Larry if it was a threat, he replied, "Any
technology can do a good job with a hundred thousand queries a day.
It's a lot harder to do it with a hundred million."

Still, good technology combined with strong brand awareness could

---

* John Ince, "Inside Search Engines," *Upside,* May 2000.

† Go.com grew out of the merger of Infoseek and Disney's online unit and featured content from
Disney and ABC properties.

make Ask Jeeves a search juggernaut. And wasn't it always the butler who turned out to be the bad guy?

Finally, *Upside* turned to upstart Google, noting, "In terms of pure technology, Google is getting the best reviews."

"Google is a shining example of superior technology actually drawing traffic on the Internet rather than marketing," analyst Danny Sullivan pointed out, explaining why Google had grown to more than ten million searches a day in just over two years.

Not that it would help, *Upside* opined, since "the company seems to give such short shrift to the more mundane aspects of developing corporate strategy, penetrating new markets, and creating revenue. Nor does anyone in [the] Googleplex have a clear timetable for when Google will turn search technology into profit." Yeah, I was kind of wondering about that myself.

The article's conclusion implied that Ask Jeeves would ultimately pull ahead, because it "has a clear sense of direction and is staking out an important niche [that] has great potential as a tool for customer service." Google, it suggested, might be an acquisition target for AltaVista.

As I finished reading, I realized that I had allowed myself to inhale the air of inevitability settling around our office like a tule fog. People were putting in long hours, our technology clearly worked, and revenue continued to grow. How could things go wrong? Yet, for all the confidence I felt inside the Googleplex, there was a world of doubt outside our doors. Established players had more polished brands, greater market share, and better business strategies. Google's only asset was a reasonably good tool for finding information.

Search, however, would surprise the skeptics. Technology not only mattered; it mattered in a way that was immediately and completely obvious. People searched with a purpose: to find a particular item of information that they needed. A site that obscured its search box behind a wall of links and paid promotions was as useful as a box of crayons for filling in a crossword puzzle. Distracting and fun to play with — but not practical for the task at hand.

Google's founders believed down to their DNA that simplicity was a benefit. They pared Google to its essentials for one reason: as insatiable consumers of data, they used it themselves. To them, Google was a tool, nothing more. A hammer that did one thing really, really well. "Context" didn't make the hammer work better. Neither did a cartoon butler.

In 2000, only a handful of people saw the value of pure search clearly, and many of them already worked at Google. Quietly, steadily, and without even a hint to their colleagues down the hall, the engineers were building a plan to share their vision of a perfect hammer with a much wider audience.

Because, they knew, the world was full of nails.

How Larry and Sergey Role

Larry and Sergey, for all their opacity and their antipathy toward traditional thinkers, were easy to approach and easy to like. That was fortunate, since once I had tossed them the keys to my future, they had slipped behind the wheel of my psyche and taken it careering over bumpy back roads and slick mountain switchbacks. My ego struggled to keep a grip. They were twenty-six years old, but not the first successful young people to pass through my career. At the *Merc* I had met with Elon Musk of Zip2, who sold his startup for $300 million at age twenty-eight before helping to found a new venture called PayPal. Successful young technology executives were the crabgrass of the Valley, popping up everywhere and self-confidently calling attention to their greenness as they choked out the existing paradigm in one field after another.

Annie, my boss at the *Merc*, was a decade younger than I was, yet she taught me how to respectfully disagree with superiors in the face of catastrophic decisions. I was sure Larry and Sergey would act diplomatically with their superiors — if they ever met any. Backers read a lack of deference to others among Silicon Valley entrepreneurs as confidence and disapproved when one of our candidates seemed "too much in awe of authority." That observation was never made about our founders, who paid deference only to data.

As the progenitors of a golden goose that had sprung from their own minds, Larry and Sergey had no obligation to kowtow to anyone. They treated the Queen of England as an equal and Benazir Bhutto as a friend. When they wanted business advice, they called Jeff Bezos or Warren Buffett. They spoke bluntly to industry leaders they felt weren't getting what was self-evident to them, chastised vendors, and ignored or badgered staff members who disagreed with their ideas, even if those staffers had more experience or more advanced degrees.* They weren't intentionally rude so much as constantly impatient to keep things moving along the path that sometimes only they could see.

Even before they had the funds to start a company, "the Google guys" antagonized potential investors with their aggressive style. They gave no quarter and left none on the table. They insisted that Kleiner Perkins and Sequoia invest together or not at all, because it was to Google's advantage to have both of the Valley's premier VC firms backing them. Our founders set the terms of the valuation according to what they saw as the potential of the technology they had created, not according to the accumulated acumen of the men who had funded Yahoo, eBay, Sun, and Amazon. Neither Larry nor Sergey had been to business school or run a large corporation, but Larry had studied more than two hundred business books to prepare for his role running Google as a competitive entity. He trusted his own synthesis of what he had read as much as anything he might have picked up in a classroom.

Self-aggrandizement often accompanies a sense of personal infallibility, but Larry and Sergey rarely displayed signs of undue self-importance. They didn't scream at people or make grand pronouncements or believe the inflated claims about Google in the press. In fact, any hint of puffery in presentations would engender a rapid-fire request to "just get to the data."

They did have healthy egos, of course, and as their reputations grew apace with the company, they even joked about the enlarged magazine covers the PR department hung in the halls featuring their oversized portraits. Larry claimed the display didn't prove the company was promulgating a cult of personality — at least, not yet.

"When we have statues," he warned, "then you should worry."

MISC Communications

Given their habit of abruptly cutting off debate, I was surprised at how much Larry and Sergey valued others' opinions. We had no shortage of those. Googlers shared their views willingly. Aggressively, even.

---

* Larry and Sergey took leaves from their Stanford PhD programs to start Google, to the chagrin of their professorial parents. Sergey mentioned that his mom would greet good news about Google with the question "So will you be able to finish your degree now?"

Call it "crowd-sourcing" or "illumination through alternative insights," asking what other Googlers thought was fundamental to the way Google worked. After all, Googlers had been poked, prodded, and sniffed before gaining a desk in the Plex, so anyone wearing a badge was clearly one of the clueful. It didn't matter if an idea came from someone fresh out of college or a veteran VP of engineering; it would stand or fall on its own merits rather than on the status of the person putting it forward. Even a lowly marketer could make suggestions and expect them to be considered.

"Larry and Sergey were up for honest intellectual debate," Salar told me, "and so they wanted to hear ideas. If you had a strongly felt view . . . even if they didn't agree with it, they wanted to debate it."

Input from outside the Googleplex? That didn't carry the same cachet. As I saw with the April Fools' feedback, we discounted user dissatisfaction unless it could be clearly demonstrated to cause significant shifts in actual behavior. Our arrogance ultimately became a nasty undertone in conversations about Google taking place in the press and among those trying to do business with us, but I rarely saw it expressed by Googlers toward their own colleagues.

When Googlers did engage in blatant opinioneering, they did it on Googlers-MISC,* the Las Vegas of mailing lists, where nothing was out of bounds. On MISC, Googlers offered theories about proving $P = NP$ and the best way to levitate frogs. They debated the brand of bottled water Charlie should stock in the micro-kitchens, a discussion encompassing total dissolved solids, bottle size, and the health benefits of naturally occurring uranium. After a week of this, Charlie's patience wore thin enough that he threatened to pull all the bottles and let the staff drink pond water.

I started a rancorous MISC thread by suggesting we eliminate the free donuts Ed Karrels delivered on Fridays in favor of fresh bagels. That one bounced around for years. A request with the subject line "Your mother doesn't work here," asking that Googlers do more to clean up after themselves, set off an explosion of self-righteous rage about the value of engineering time, the role of women in the postfeminist workplace, and the second floor's desperate, heartbreaking, and absolute need for more flatware. That lasted almost as long as the discussion about the corrupted physics in *Star Wars: The Phantom Menace*.

---

* For "miscellaneous." MISC was open to any Googler who had the patience to read it.

MISC was where I went to take the pulse of Google's culture, and by all signs, that culture was vibrant, diverse, and occasionally obsessive.

The Perpetual "Why?"

The mental image of engineers I carried into the Googleplex was one of introverted nerds with retarded social skills and skin that never experienced direct exposure to sunlight. I anticipated they would be easily cowed by strong personalities with loud voices and authoritative manners. Not that I would necessarily fall into that category, but after seven years working with acid-tongued inquisitorial journalists arguing points ad absurdum, I expected things at Google to be easier. I thought the most forceful pushback would come from the springs in my keyboard as I typed directives into my computer.

I discovered that the hardest-bitten investigative reporter is more easily appeased than the mellowest engineer riding a Prozac high. Engineers don't accept intuition, aren't swayed by emotion, refuse to surrender to rhetoric, and can't let anything imperfect pass by without comment. Engineers never stop asking "Why?" until they get an answer they consider demonstrably, provably, irrefutably true.

As Craig Silverstein explained it to me, "It's not an engineering personality to keep quiet when you feel things are going wrong . . . and being intimidated by people is not very productive."

"Google engineers were so strong-willed," agreed Matt Cutts, "that sometimes if we thought that Larry and Sergey were wrong, we just ignored them."

Many Google employees lacked nonacademic work experience. They had never tasted the lash of a manager's reproach or the sting of a colleague's rebuke, so their impulse to jump over fences and spread the wild oats of their wisdom remained unneutered.

"They would fight over everything," according to HR manager Heather Cairns, who often dealt with their issues related to job benefits. "'Why should I sign this? I'm not gonna sign it.' They challenged the most mundane things — minutiae — even though it was a benefit for them."

Project manager Deb Kelly, who got a steady stream of unsolicited feedback, wondered about those who offered advice, "Why are you weighing in? I'm not even sure I've met you yet."

This state of perpetual "Why?" occasionally annoyed even other engineers. Hardware designer Will Whitted found the ever-inquisitive commentariat a pain: "It may have been powerfully important in getting Google to work, but it pissed me off a lot. Because they were really, really bright and had been successful in one thing, they thought they automatically knew everything else. So they could tell me how to do thermal design and they could tell me what size screws to use. They honestly thought it would make things right or they thought the thing I was doing was incorrect and would make things bad."

Emerging unscathed from this idea melee required access to information about the company's inner workings. At first this information floated freely, permeating Google like radio waves. You just had to know what frequencies to tune in to. I took to poring over engineering's weekly snippets and diving deep into MOMA, our intranet. I paid attention at TGIF and eavesdropped on tablemates at lunch. No one consciously tried to limit data flow, but we lacked a formal clearinghouse for updates on company initiatives.

Larry's product-review meetings created a central information nexus. I could sit on the black couch, plug directly into Larry's head, and get root-level access to all that I needed to know. Nothing helped me do my job better than downloading directly from Google's wellspring of strategic direction. Cool draughts of clear vision washed away ambiguity about user interfaces, product features, and competitive positioning. I basked in my unobstructed view of the deliberations driving our company's creation, blissfully unaware that I would soon be banished from this information Eden and forced to forage for the info bits that I had come to rely upon to do my job.

Yes, I'm Saying No

With everyone expressing opinions about everything, I had to speak louder and more insistently lest my voice be lost in the din. Apparently other people felt the same way. We held robust dialogues.

When I needed to advance an argument, whether about the name for a new product or the wording of a promotional line on the homepage, I began by building alliances. I put Salar near the top of my list of draft picks, because he and others who had joined Google before the move to

Mountain View* held sway in the decision-making process. Any of us could talk to the founders and have our opinions considered, but their voices were the first to be sought and the loudest to be heard. When one of this inner circle diametrically opposed my position, earning the counterbalancing support of another became essential.

Most flare-ups quickly damped to a simmer, the heat dissipated through flames on topic-specific email lists, the private clubs where Googlers could assemble to gnaw their own intestines. Particularly hot issues, however, might engulf the full Googlers list, which went to every inbox in the company.

"Engineers are argumentative," Urs acknowledged. "You don't want to stop it, but it shouldn't get in the way. At some point we made Googlers a moderated list,† just because people weren't thinking that their messages went to three hundred people."

"Googlers had passionate beliefs," remembered Matt Cutts, whose first pass at a porn filter was publicly picked apart on the engineering list. "So two entirely polite, consensus-driven people — you would have to send them on a walk around the block and have them work it out, because they both believed so strongly."

Matt believed the head-butting over issues outsiders wouldn't care about — if they even noticed them — wasn't about turf or politics. It was about determining what was best for users. The question, then, was who best represented the voice of those users within Google.

I thought I did.

I read users' email to us. I wrote the words that spoke to them from our site. I had spent decades in direct contact with customers of all kinds who didn't understand how to use any device with more than two knobs and a button. In UI team meetings and product reviews, it was easy for me to see which changes could cause confusion, because those changes confused me. I might not have been a digital everyman, but I was better cast in that role than my colleagues who could name a half dozen open-source operating systems and considered them all superior to Windows.

Marissa Mayer also strove to channel the concerns of users, refer-

* Susan Wojcicki, Marissa Mayer, Jeff Dean, Salar Kamangar, and Urs Hölzle were among this group.
† Meaning that posts had to be approved by a designated moderator before they went out to everyone.

encing her mom in the Midwest as someone to keep in mind when introducing features or rearranging the interface. It was natural that Marissa's role as the interim UI engineer would lead her to safeguard user interests, and she did so with intensity. Her enthusiasm and intelligence carried her opinions as a kind of rolling assault. If you weren't initially overwhelmed, she launched wave after wave of data, ideas, and arguments like landing craft at Normandy.

In a data-driven company, numbers are a big stick to wield, and Marissa cited stats that convinced her she was empirically correct. But while I had seen the power of quantitative analysis to persuade, I had never fully climbed aboard the data train. As a result, we didn't always agree.

If I lacked the numerological faith of my colleagues, I did share some of their characteristics: a focus that detected subatomic flaws, an inability to ignore inconvenient truths, and an obdurate unwillingness to cede my position until completely overrun. I stood up for what I believed, even when my only support was the gates of Hell pushing into my back.

I come from a stiff-necked people.

I often yielded on issues of design — or at least funneled my views through Karen, who had complete credibility as an impartial webmaster — but my disagreements with Marissa about wording and tone grew deeper after the MentalPlex April Fools' contretemps.

Many Googlers believed they spoke the tongue of the "average user" with native fluency, not realizing how thick a geek accent they brought to conversations about privacy or customer communications. What would users like? What would they find intrusive? Offensive? Why would anyone be upset by that? We all quoted the gospel of efficiency and swore to put our users first.

Whatever the nature of our opposing views, our culture urged quick resolution. Googlers wanted to get things done. Sanjay described engineers' approach to disputes this way: "We said, we can keep on discussing this for a long time and try to get agreement or we can just go ahead and do at least the part we know."

Complete buy-in wasn't a requirement. If there were holdouts, Urs would call a meeting and announce, "Okay, fine, we've argued for a week. There are no new insights being produced. Let's do the pros and cons and make a decision and move on. Because it's time to move on."

Larry was the only one who could play that role when it came to

interdepartmental divergences, and given Cindy's directive not to delay
product launches for marketing reasons, there was some risk in defending a branding perspective past a certain point. I had trouble seeing that
point. When my lack of a self-preservation instinct became apparent,
others sought my help in elevating issues to upper management. Would
I forward concerns about our poor translation quality? Would I put the
brakes on an off-strategy plan regarding Japan? Would I throw my body
in front of a badly timed product launch?

Yes.

Yes.

Yes, I would.

The Sweet Taste of Porn

Larry and Sergey randomly fixated on details that caught their attention, such as the exact shade of yellow paint to be applied to the Google
Search Appliance (our "search engine in a box" for corporate intranets)
or the wording of their biographies on the website, but mostly they set
up a management infrastructure, wrote a few rules, and let the system
run. Each new layer of process would require compiling time and slow
things down, so they promulgated a laissez-faire style that largely left
employees to their own devices.

Total autonomy was a satisfactory state for most engineers. "Larry
and Sergey went to meetings every week, sat in back, and listened to
people talking about things," Matt Cutts later recalled. "They'd give us
room to decide whatever we thought was the most important thing to
work on." Which isn't to say that the founders didn't express their own
strongly held beliefs. "If something didn't match their intuitions," Matt
added, "they fought until they had good data or a good reason to believe or had seen a particular person be right a few times. Then they'd
be willing to trust that person's judgment."

Matt earned his own chunk of autonomy by taking on one of the
company's dirtiest jobs. He'd been at Google a month or two when project manager Deb Kelly stopped by his cubicle with a question.

"Hey, Matt. How do you feel about porn?"

"That depends," Matt replied. "Why are you asking?"

Deb needed someone to work on a filter to screen out "adult" content, which by definition meant being exposed to the seamiest parts of

the web. Matt agreed to tackle the job, thinking it would take only a couple of weeks. Instead, it was three months before he had a prototype ready to test. To give it a thorough vetting would require conducting more searches than Matt had time to do himself, so in May 2000 he sent out a call to his fellow Googlers for help.

No one responded.

"It's weird," Matt said to his wife that evening. "You'd think people would take advantage of an officially sanctioned opportunity to look for porn."

His wife thought it might just be a matter of the proper motivation. "Why don't I make cookies," she suggested, "and people will get a little reward."

The next day Matt reiterated his need for help but augmented it with an offer of free "porn cookies" for everyone who participated. Search for porn, get a cookie. I was one of those who couldn't resist such a come-on. Over the next few hours I learned several new words and new meanings for some I thought I already knew.

Porn is a cutthroat business that often leads in the exploitation of new technology. Working on what would be dubbed SafeSearch, Matt became aware of a new problem for Google. Spam. Spammers attempted to game the system and thereby win a higher ranking in search results than they deserved. Matt came to think of spammers as "black hats" who placed invisible white text on a white background, stuffed their pages full of keywords, and employed a wide range of sophisticated and devious means to deceive Google's search bot.

"Once you start to see spam, the curse is, you'll see it everywhere," Matt told me. He was offended by spammers' unethical behavior and continued thinking about the problem even after he finished his filter and began working on Google's advertising system. Larry and Sergey thought spam was a non-issue, because they were confident Google's PageRank algorithm would sort the wheat from the chaff.

"It took quite a while for Google to wake up to fact that while Page-Rank was very spam resistant, it wasn't a hundred percent perfect," Matt noted. He took the initiative to sound the alarm. Although it was no longer his area of responsibility and not an area of concern to management, he asked to work on fighting spam. "One thing I learned at Google," he said to me, "is that you make your own cred. If you propose your own initiative, you're much more likely to do it than if you sit around and wait for someone to say, 'What do you want to do with your life?'"

Within days, Matt connected with the group of eight engineers focused on overall search quality, including Jeff, Sanjay, and Amit Singhal. They invited him to join them around the Ping-Pong table and delve into the deepest aspects of Google's core technology. Matt became privy to Google's secret sauce, the weighting factors that determined whether a website was near the top of the first results page or buried somewhere on page thirty.

Matt always struck me as a pillar of moral rectitude, a keeper of the faith in algorithmic integrity, and an adamant protector of Google's purity — our own avuncular Elliot Ness, bringing to account those who parasitically thrived by bootlegging traffic. As a University of Kentucky student, Matt had enrolled in a co-op program through the Department of Defense and ended up spending a few semesters at the National Security Agency. That internship was great fodder for the conspiracy theorists monitoring Google. Matt's "secret" government tie made their tin hats stand at full attention, because they assumed Matt still served as a conduit between big government and big search.* In truth, Matt was one of the least "spooky" guys I knew at Google.

Because he understood the innermost details of Google's ranking calculations, Matt was outraged when a webmaster bulletin board speculated in 2001 that Google was manipulating results to increase sales of our advertising. If a business didn't show up near the top of our results, they alleged, it would have to buy ads to have a presence on the first page users saw after a search. The rumor wasn't surprising, given the practices of most search engines at the time. The Federal Trade Commission had called out eight of Google's competitors for blurring the lines between paid placement, advertising, and algorithmically produced results. Matt again took the initiative to address a problem others didn't immediately see. He went to PR manager David Krane.

"So . . . while I'm compiling," he asked Krane, "would it be okay if I stopped by this forum and debunked misconceptions?" Krane reported to Cindy, and Cindy had read the *Cluetrain Manifesto* — a guide advo-

---

* Matt dressed as a trench-coated spy for the office Halloween party the same year I went as FBI deputy director Skinner from *The X-Files*. A photo of us somehow ended up on Slashdot, where posters seriously pondered the implications of government agents appearing at an official Google function.

cating that companies speak directly and plainly to the public instead of engaging in Velveeta-smooth, committee-processed, content-lite corporate blandishments. Cindy had made sure everyone else in marketing read it as well. Krane gave Matt carte blanche to speak freely on the company's behalf, without running his posts by PR.

"GoogleGuy" was born.

Matt's nom de plume became an authoritative voice in the webmaster community and a trusted source of information from inside Google. GoogleGuy corrected misinformation, killed rumors, and explained why Google did things that seemed off kilter to outsiders.

Initiative crossed with autonomy provided unforeseen benefits in unexpected areas. Unexpected challenges as well. Other engineers also sought to speak in unvarnished language on Google's behalf without formal endorsement by Cindy's minions — or even our awareness.

Ray Sidney comes to mind.

The Ray Way

Ray, Google employee number six, embodied the cult of individual authority. His "dude"-infused speech and ribald and unpredictable passions obscured an education earned at Caltech, Harvard, and MIT. Ray was our first line of defense against webmasters who pummeled Google with automated queries. Webmasters and SEOs* wanted to make sure their sites showed up near the top of Google results and so used monitoring software to conduct repeated automatic searches for keywords important to them. In periods of high volume, automated queries slowed down Google for everyone, which is why we considered them a violation of our terms of service.†

Ray took unauthorized automated queries very personally. If he could figure out the spammer's email address, he sent a terse cease-and-desist warning. If he couldn't find an email address, he blocked the spammer's IP (internet protocol) address — the unique number assigned to a computer connected to the Internet — from accessing Google altogether.

No one was immune. When a user left a book on the Enter key and

---

* Search engine optimizers: consultants who help clients obtain higher ranking in search-engine results.

† According to Matt Cutts, at one point automated queries from Web Position Gold — software used by SEOs — accounted for four percent of all queries Google received.

sent the same query to Google thirty-nine thousand times, Ray cut off access for everyone at that address. The query was "This is the CIA," and it came from that agency's headquarters in Langley, Virginia. Another user searched for "net oil importers" over and over and over again. Ray got annoyed and shut off the State Department as well.

If Ray couldn't identify a specific IP address, he contacted the spammer's Internet service provider (ISP) and asked that they track down the offender themselves and sever his access to Google. If the ISP refused to play along, Ray upped the ante — he blocked access to Google from all of the ISP's addresses. That usually got their attention. It was how Ray shut down access to Google for most of France. The French ISP definitely noticed, all the more so because at the time they were negotiating to become one of our larger customers.

Ray didn't hate the French. He did the same thing to the Germans. Also to a major American ISP, though he did post a note to their customers who complained. "The short story here," he wrote, "is that some user at your ISP was abusing Google. We were unfortunately unable to turn off access just for this evil individual. Since your ISP didn't respond to us, we had no choice but to shut off access to Google from a large number of IP addresses."

Cindy was, as she put it, "displeased" when she read Ray's note reprinted in a headline article on CNET describing Google's rude treatment of users. She "suggested" that I take over user communication related to service interruptions and "work with" Ray to smooth out the rougher edges in his correspondence. It was hard for me to keep up, because Ray was all about initiative. He was not part of the company's business-development team according to the org chart, but he never let reporting lines fence him in.

"Well, to be blunt," Ray told a partner who wanted to renew a deal for Google technology, "it's clear to us what you get out of our relationship, but it's far from clear to us that we get anything out of it. Given that, it seems like poor business practice for us to continue with it. So, unless I'm missing some key observation here, please stop performing Google searches immediately."

Many things made Ray wroth. He sent out long notes to all Googlers demanding we clean up the kitchens, the locker rooms, our interviewing techniques, our security practices, our personal habits, and our grammar. He also urged us to recycle our trash at every opportunity. Once a burr got under his saddle, he didn't wait for it to work itself out. "Can we please, please, please finally just end our relationship with these leeches?" he begged of Larry Page when another partner continued to annoy him. "If only to make me happy?"

Impulsive and opinionated, Ray will always personify for me Google's engineering id, a lone cowboy patrolling the electronic frontier in shocking-pink shorts, facing down the black hats and making them blink, then riding off into a sunset that was only half as colorful as he was.

A single engineer holding that kind of power speaks to the assumptions inherent in Google's culture. Individuals were considered capable of weighing the effects of their actions and presumed to have the best interests of the company (and Google's users) at heart. We were encouraged to act on those interests without hesitation. Spend time doing, not deciding.

Of all the elements of "big-company thinking" I had to unlearn, that was one of the hardest. I constantly sought reassurance that I was empowered to move to the next step, only to be asked, "Why haven't you finished that already?" The upside of this philosophy is that Google did things quickly, most of which turned out to be positive. The downside is that individual Googlers sometimes misinterpreted exactly how much power they possessed and when it was okay to use it.

Shari had discovered the downside the hard way. She had reached the breaking point with Larry and Sergey. They weren't supporting her work with the promotion agency, and without outside help, she couldn't move forward. She threw up her hands in frustration, and while they were up, she tossed in the towel.

At her farewell party at a local Mexican restaurant, I said goodbye to the one other person at Google who completely understood the practice of branding for customer acquisition. Google didn't do that kind of marketing. The company rejected any attempt to graft traditional practices onto its new breed of business.

Over salsa and Dos Equis toasts, I resolved that I would remain open to new ideas and new approaches. I would make it work. I would prove to myself and to my ever-adaptable colleagues that this old Doug could still learn new tricks.

PART II

GOOGLE GROWS AND FINDS ITS VOICE

Beyond a startup.
Not yet a search behemoth.
Google's awkward phase.

CHAPTER 11

Liftoff

WHILE I HAD been trying to figure out what to do next, the engineers had been killing themselves to do the big, hard, complicated things that absolutely needed to be done. Their yearlong effort would come to fruition just about the time I started to get my bearings.

The engineering story began in June 1999 — before I had even heard of Google. Jim Reese, the neurosurgeon turned sysadmin, had just been hired. On his first day, he arrived at eight a.m. and worked straight through for fourteen hours. The next day he came in a little later — about ten a.m. — to add backup servers to Google's intranet and to handle networking issues in the Plex. He left the office around four for an early dinner on his way to Exodus, Google's data center, where he stayed until five in the morning. He did the same the next day, and again every day that week, including Saturday and Sunday. His task, assigned by Larry without explanation, was to install two thousand new servers and bring them online.

That many computers wouldn't fit in the cage Google owned at the time, so Jim needed to arrange for additional space at the data center. "I worked as hard as I could," he said, "negotiating with facilities at Exodus. In 1999, cage space was hard to come by and Exodus was pretty full." Partly that was because of companies like eBay, whose cage was near Google's. "They had a cage ten or twenty times our size and they had perhaps eighty computers in it," Jim recalls, "whereas we had eighty computers in one rack." There were nine racks crowded into Google's cage — but, as Jim and his new associate Schwim realized when they looked closely, it wasn't at capacity.

"If we move every cabinet on this side of the cage three inches, we'll have exactly enough room to fit in another rack," Schwim pointed out, turning sideways to squeeze down the aisle. "The only problem is, there's no way to roll a rack through here. We'll have to take off the side cage wall." They called the facilities manager, described what they wanted, and left for lunch.

When they came back, the black chain-link fencing that had protected the side of Google's space had been unbolted and removed. Jim and Schwim slid the rack in, cabled the computers, connected them to the main switch with fiber, and flipped the switch. Everything lit up the way it was supposed to. Jim double-checked the connections at the back of the rack as Schwim stood at the front typing in commands to monitor its progress.

"It's a go!" Jim heard Schwim announce from the front of the rack.

"The next thing I knew," Jim recalls, "I'm sitting on my butt on the floor of the data center."

"We just lost the rack!" Schwim yelled. "What's going on?" He stepped around to the back and found Jim on his back, groggily rubbing the crown of his head, a two-hundred-pound metal crossbeam, smeared with blood, lying beside him where it had fallen from the top of the cage.

"Uh . . . ," said Jim, shakily pointing upward toward a batch of severed cables that had lain in the beam's path, "we're going to need more fiber."

"You're the only neurosurgeon around," replied Schwim, assessing the situation with both concern and an engineer's practicality. "Do you think you can fix yourself?"

The facilities team, for reasons known only to them, had unscrewed the support for the crossbeam while removing the wall. In Jim's professional medical opinion, the beam would have done him considerably more damage if it had landed a couple of inches to either side. "They were very, very, very kind to us after that," he said about the Exodus crew.

Jim finally found some unoccupied space in a corner of the building and Exodus agreed to throw fence walls around it. He spent the better part of June and July installing two thousand brand-new computers into the cage. The machines didn't always work. They were built quickly and with parts purchased at very reasonable prices. "For some racks," Jim recalls, "we got fifty-six out of eighty working, so we'd spend a week installing these machines and then another week repairing the ones that didn't install."

Eventually Larry let Jim in on why his work was so urgent. Google had signed a deal with Netscape to be their fall-through search engine. If Netscape users couldn't find what they wanted using Netscape's open directory, they would be able to search from the directory page using Google. So Google needed more computing power to handle the potential traffic.

Jim load-tested Google's capacity as he added machines — checking to see that it could handle the increased traffic and any occasional spikes that might occur. "In general," he told me, "you like to see two times capacity. For peaks, you like to see four times capacity. Netscape anticipated a one-point-seven-times increase over existing Google traffic, so I tested it. At nearly five times, we were completely in the clear."

It wasn't easy. Jim and Schwim were still at the data center installing machines the night of June 24. Netscape would announce the deal and start directing traffic to Google the morning of June 25. Schwim worked until two a.m., when the cumulative lack of sleep caught up with him and he went home to crash.

Fortunately, Jim had recruited another tech guy to help them over the finish line. Though it had been a while since Sergey had dirtied his hands installing machines, he stayed at the data center with Jim until five a.m. "He didn't know all the technical details of how the routing went," Jim remembered, "but he was in there crawling under the floorboards, running cables, and hooking up switches."

For Jim it was the culmination of weeks of exhausting physical labor, and when he finally dragged himself off to bed it was with a sense of accomplishment. Google had averted a potential disaster by tripling its capacity in record time.

An hour later, his phone rang. It was Sergey. "Get in here right away. We're melting down."

Netscape's press release had hit the newswires at six a.m. West Coast time. Within seconds Google's traffic had increased not the expected one-point-seven times, but sevenfold. The servers couldn't handle the load. Sergey and Jim rushed back to Exodus and began desperately throwing the last batch of machines they had into racks and hooking them up.

Meanwhile they did everything they could to clear away extraneous demands on Google's infrastructure. They stopped the crawler from adding websites to Google's index and reallocated those machines to serving results. It helped, but not enough. Response times had slowed perceptibly, and some users got no results at all. Google's most important launch to date teetered on the brink of becoming an epic pooch-screwing.

The atmosphere in the office Craig Silverstein shared with Amit Patel was grim as Larry and Sergey, Urs, and the rest of Google's engineers reviewed their options. Netscape was not a small partner like their first client, VMWare. If this relationship went down the tubes, everyone would know and Google's tech reputation would be toast. They could think of only one way to increase capacity to handle Netscape's users.

"Shut off queries to Google.com," Larry instructed the team.

For the next couple of hours, anyone who went to Google.com saw a static page explaining that Google was down. Every computer and every bit of bandwidth Google had at its command was serving results to Netscape users. Larry and Sergey were risking their own site's reputation to maintain credibility as a reliable technology partner.

By lunchtime, traffic had subsided enough that Larry and Sergey gave the okay to turn Google.com back on. Schwim and Jim returned to Exodus to finish installing the last of the servers, and within four hours they had brought an additional three hundred machines online, ending the immediate crisis.

As Jim and Schwim left the controlled environment of the data center and headed out into the warm evening air, they received another call. Netscape's engineering team was at the Tied House Brewery in Mountain View, celebrating the partnership, and they wanted Google's tech team to join them.

"They threw us a great post-launch party," Jim remembers. "And the thing that came up over and over again was, 'I can't believe you guys shut down your own site just to serve our traffic.'" The Googlers in attendance noted well that their sacrifice had paid off handsomely.

The deal with Netscape promised to blossom into a beautiful friendship. Google gained not only trust, but also access to a whole new set of data in Netscape's query stream — data we could analyze and compare with our own traffic. Most important, the company's first major crisis battle-hardened it. Larry and Sergey would never again underestimate the challenges of occupying new territory. Though it seemed epic at the time, the battle of Netscape would go down as a minor skirmish once Google fully engaged the major players in the war for search supremacy.

That day was coming.

What's Going Down?

A little after midnight one Saturday night in the fall of 1999, Jim's phone interrupted his sleep again. Again it was Sergey.

"The site's down. What's up?" he wanted to know.

"Not me," Jim replied with a yawn. "You woke me."

A circuit breaker at Exodus had flipped, taking down Google's main switch, an inexpensive little piece of Hewlett-Packard hardware through which all of Google's traffic flowed. Exodus had set up the switch before Google moved the first racks into its cage, and had done it in a hurry. The device had been placed on the floor under one of the racks and was cabled in such a way that it had to stay there. It was known to all the techs by the designation "Switch on the ground." There was no backup, and when it crashed Google went offline until someone did something about it.

"Sergey had been at a party. He came home and noticed we were down," recalls Jim, who logged in, figured out the problem, and had Exodus turn the circuit on again. Google was offline for about half an hour.

"We should probably be monitoring our site, huh?" said Sergey when Jim called to let him know it was back up.

Jim spent the rest of Saturday night and Sunday morning writing a script to monitor Google. His script checked the site every five seconds to make sure it was operational and called a phone number if something went wrong. The next week everyone in operations got a pager.

Google had gone dark for a second time, but no tempers flared and no heads rolled. "If Larry and Sergey were upset about anything," Jim told me, "it was, Why didn't any of us think of that? We're a bunch of bright people here and none of us even thought to monitor our own site."

The pager alert system created problems of its own. "Claus,"* a logs engineer, was one of the first to be hooked up, and he watched carefully as our traffic numbers kept redlining, threatening to crash the logs system. The logs were money — we billed advertisers on the basis of the data they contained — so he set up his own scripts to crunch the numbers and to call his pager when they were done. That happened about three times an hour, every hour, all day long. According to engineer Chad Lester, Claus "kept Google alive in the early days. He'd be sleeping at his desk in twenty-minute intervals between pages. One month he got a pager bill in the thousands of dollars."

Google renegotiated its pager service contract but never compromised on-site reliability again. Google.com would stay online, no matter what.

Here Comes You-Know-Who

During the spring of 2000, I didn't sense any great strain in the fabric of the company as I grew accustomed to its rhythms. The basic elements had coalesced: a physical plant, a core engineering team, finance and HR staff, and even marketing in support of a product for which the demand seemed insatiable. The coming months would be about holding on. A previously unmet need was rushing headlong toward the provider of a free solution — bucking our audience numbers higher and higher with each lunge forward. On May 8, 2000, Google's traffic topped eight million searches a day. Two weeks later, it was nine million. In theory, we could grow forever, but each bounding leap threatened to bring our ride to an abrupt and messy end because we couldn't add capacity fast enough.

The biggest jump lay just weeks ahead. No one spoke about it, but as I stood in line at the café, debating what I could actually eat from Charlie's Appalachian Day menu (pickled pigs feet, okra consommé, free-range pork rinds, moon pies with mayonnaise, and Twinkie cheez-

---

* He prefers I not use his real name.

dogs), it seemed there were more than the usual number of empty seats. The few engineers I did glimpse hurriedly filled their trays and headed back to their desks wearing stress and fatigue like battle-tattered hockey jerseys.

Rumors and whispers about a big hairy deal had been spreading over the cables and through the cubicles, but no one would confirm whose business we were attempting to capture.

Urs knew. He rode herd on his ops team to build capacity in the data-center cages as fast as humanly possible. We would need every server we could cobble together to feed the ravenous behemoth we hoped to contain there.

We were going after Yahoo.

Inktomi's contract to supply search results to Yahoo was up for renewal in June 2000, and Yahoo did not intend to extend the partnership, a fact they were hiding from the world at large. They wanted Google to provide the fall-through search on their site, just as we did for Netscape. If users couldn't find what they wanted in Yahoo's directory, they would use Google to search the web.

Why the shift? Inktomi saw portal search as an unprofitable sideline — they focused on providing search services for the internal networks of large enterprises — so they didn't feel the need to push themselves on Yahoo's behalf. That opened the door for Google. Larry and Sergey dug deep to offer favorable financial terms,[*] and it didn't hurt that the Stanford guys running Yahoo and the Stanford guys running Google had common ground, or that Omid Kordestani knew Udi Manber — the top search guy at Yahoo — or that Google and Yahoo shared a board member in Mike Moritz of Sequoia Capital, a communication channel that smoothed the progress of the deal.

Google also promised dramatic improvements in search quality. Google's technology had surpassed Inktomi's and would continue to do so, because Google did care, truly and deeply, about consumer search. Google, however, wasn't the only contender pushing for a seat at the table to eat Inktomi's lunch.

"FAST[†] was a scare for a while in early 2000," Urs admitted. "They came out with a large index and they were pretty fast. They were not bad quality-wise, but they had real trouble keeping their index fresh.

---

[*] Including warrants for millions of shares of Google stock once the company went public.

[†] FAST Search and Transfer was a Norwegian search company. Microsoft bought it in 2008.

Maybe they were trying to do too many things. By 2001 we felt we were clearly better than Inktomi results-wise, clearly better than AltaVista, clearly better than FAST. We had the best search engine."

And what about Google's comparative quality the year before, when Netscape had become a partner? "Netscape was kind of crazy to switch their search to us," Urs confessed. He believed they made the change "in part because they didn't care about search that much . . . It was a cost center."

Not to mention that Omid Kordestani happened to be an excellent salesperson. "Omid could type in 'IBM' on Google and type in 'IBM' on AltaVista," Urs recalls, "and say 'Hey look, aren't our results better?' That was the level of sophistication. Our search was good, but our coverage was bad. You had all kinds of queries where we didn't have the page and AltaVista or Inktomi had it. People's expectations were just low."

That wasn't the case with Yahoo, where Udi Manber, a search specialist, was chief scientist.* "Udi wrote the contract," Urs told me, "so he paid attention to the important things." Manber would settle for nothing less than the best that Google could produce, which he knew to be more than what the search engine was offering at the time.

Larry and Sergey committed to Yahoo that Google would make numerous improvements in a matter of weeks: to set up two new data centers — including one on the East Coast — to freshen the index by crawling more frequently, to reduce spam in results, and to meet strict limits on latency, the time between the search being entered and the results being delivered. Each of these promises would require enormous effort to fulfill, but if all were met, Google would give Yahoo users a visibly better search experience.

Better, but not the best. "What was important," Urs confided to me, "was that if you syndicated something and you had your own property, you wanted to make sure that over time you could innovate and actually have something better than Yahoo search powered by Google. And that was Google search, unrestricted by commercial agreement."

Had the company bitten off more than it could chew? Yahoo's traffic dwarfed Google's,[†] and the moment Inktomi stopped answering Yahoo

---

* Manber became a VP of engineering at Google in early 2006.

† Yahoo had 48.6 million unique visitors in April 2000, making it number two overall in the Media Metrix rankings for that month, behind only AOL. Google, with slightly more than three million unique visitors, wasn't even in the top one hundred.

queries, Google would need to respond to each and every one of them quickly and correctly. With the capacity we had in place at the time, it would be like hooking a garden hose to a fire hydrant.

"Operationally it was a large buildup," Urs said, "so we needed to get lots of servers." Five thousand, to be exact, each of which required hand assembly. The new data centers that would hold them had yet to be identified or prepped for occupancy. New networking systems would have to be developed to ensure queries went to the right place and results were identical regardless of where the responding machine resided.

The Google operations team[*] worked with the contractor, Rackable Systems,[†] building the machines from parts Gerald supplied. A "bat cave" was set up between Charlie's café and the marketing department for the ops staff to test and burn in servers before shipping them off to the East Coast. The loaded racks were large and heavy but fragile. Google tried renting a truck and having ops move the racks themselves, but one fell over in transit and almost crushed a technician. The decision was made to splurge on professionals. That didn't stop the ops guys from tossing hundreds of thousands of dollars' worth of RAM into their cars and driving it all over town.

Once all the racks were ready, they needed to be moved cross-country practically overnight. Christopher Bosch hired a truck to drive non-stop to the new data center in Virginia. It would leave the highway only to change drivers en route, and once it reached the data center, the racks would roll out the back and directly into the new server farm.

Serving capacity was just the first item on a very long checklist, and in some ways the easiest. The pressure to build quickly was enormous, but at least with hardware the task was clearly defined, the process known, and the progress clearly measurable. Adding hardware to add capacity would not solve Google's problems by itself, however, even without the Yahoo deal.

"Our traffic was increasing eight percent a week for a long time," said Jeff Dean. "Any time you have that rate of growth, you basically

---

[*] Keith Kleiner, Shawn Simpson, Frank Cusack, Marc Felton, Gabe Osterland, and Dave McKay with assistance from Jim Reese and Larry Schwimmer, plus Christopher Bosch, who moved into the role of Gerald's apprentice for negotiating purchases.

[†] Rackable Systems grew so quickly on Google's business that it went public in 2005. In 2009 it bought the last remnants of SGI (also known as Silicon Graphics), the company whose former headquarters Google now occupies.

have to make software improvements continuously because you can't get the hardware deployed fast enough. They were working as hard as they could, but if you add four percent machines per week, and you've got eight percent growth, that's not good. So we continuously worked on improving our serving system and looked at alternative designs for pieces of it to get more throughput." That kind of software required creativity and design breakthroughs that could not be scheduled in the same way as a server assembly line.

"It was actually good for us," said Urs, who believed contractual obligations to continually refresh the index and meet latency guarantees made Google "a more grown-up company" by forcing it to closely monitor its own progress. "We always wanted to be fast, but the contract said, 'The maximum one-hour latency is this.'* You had to start measuring it. Once you can measure it, it's much easier to set goals and say, 'Can we make this ten percent better by next month?' So a lot of these things started then."

Last Crawl

Along with speed and capacity, Google had promised Yahoo fresher results. A seemingly reasonable offer, except that in March 2000 Google's crawler was crippled and barely running. The Googlebot software would stumble around the web gathering URLs, lose its equilibrium, then crash to a halt. The engineers would restart it and the same thing would happen. Try again. Crash. Google hadn't built a new index in four months—approximately the time I had been at the company, though I never pointed out that coincidence to anyone.

Creating an index required weeks of collecting information about what websites existed and what they contained, data that then had to be compiled into a usable list of URLs that could be ranked and presented as search results when someone submitted a query. Most users assumed that when they typed in a search term the results reflected the exact state of the web at the time they hit Enter, so they were puzzled and sometimes angry when they didn't find the very latest news and information. When an index hadn't been updated for more than a month, it became noticeably stale and user dissatisfaction increased. Google's in-

---

* The average delay in returning results over any given hour.

dex wasn't just stale, it was covered in mold. Without a working crawler, Google would violate its contract with Yahoo, and more important, Google.com would become increasingly useless.

"It wasn't really very tolerant of machine failures," Jeff Dean recalls about the crawler — "a half-working mess of Python scripts" — written before he joined the company.* "So when a machine failed in the middle of a crawl, it just ended. Well, that crawl was useless. Let's just start it over again. So you'd crawl for ten days and then the machine would die. Oh well. Throw it away. Start over. That was kind of painful." As Jeff put it, the backup plan was "Oh, shit. Let's try that again."

Unfortunately, the more the index grew, the more machines it needed to run, and the more machines that ran, the more likely it was that one or more would fail,† especially since Google hadn't ponied up for the kind of hardware that gave warnings when it had problems.

"Our machines didn't have parity," noted Jeff. Parity could tell you if a computer's memory was randomly flipping bits in ways it shouldn't. "Parity memory was for high-end servers, and non-parity memory was what the cheap unwashed masses bought. The problem was, if you had a lot of data and you'd say, 'Sort it,' it ended up mostly sorted. And if you sorted it again, it ended up mostly sorted a different way." As a result, Google's engineers had to build data structures that were resilient in the face of what Ben Gomes called "adversarial memory."

"For a while I had all these bugs because the machines were crappy," Gomes told me. "I was writing this code — one of my first big projects out of school — and it was crashing all the time. I was sitting in this room with people I really respected, Jeff and Sanjay and Urs, and Jeff said, 'The pieces are mostly working, but the pageranker keeps crashing,' and I wanted to sink into the ground. I stayed up for nights on end trying to figure out *why* was it crashing? Finally I checked this one thing I had set to zero and I looked at it and it was at four. And I thought, 'Not my bug.' After that I felt a lot better."

Finally, in March 2000, a new crawl hobbled to the finish line — with, according to Gomes, "a lot of pain." "The March index was the last gasp of the old crawler, but it had so many bugs in it, it was impossible to push it out." That index came to be known internally as the "MarIndex,"

---

* Python is a high-level programming language.

† Five thousand machines running for twenty-four hours was the equivalent of almost fourteen years of computing time. The likelihood of one or more machines failing during that much activity was high.

denoting both the month it was created and the quality of its content. Larry and Sergey declared a state of emergency and, as they would time and again when events threatened to overwhelm the company, convened a war room. Jeff Dean, Sanjay Ghemawat, Craig Silverstein, Bogdan Cocosel, and Georges Harik moved their computers into the yellow conference room to bang their brains against the problem. By early April they had patched the index to the point that it could be sent to the servers, but it limped and lurched every step of the way.

The old crawler would never be able to jump through Yahoo's hoops.

1B Wannabe

Urs recognized from the beginning that before Google could make a quantum leap to a higher state it would have to correct the mistakes of the past — especially the creaking codebase underlying the main systems. "We've fixed some of the problems," he noted after putting out the fires immediately threatening to consume Google the day he first walked in the door, "but we should really restart completely from scratch." That was a risky thing to do, because it required using resources that were in short supply to fix something that wasn't yet broken. Most companies would put off such a complex task until a time they were less overcommitted.

"This wasn't the burning problem of the day," Urs told me. "The site wasn't down because of it; it was just a productivity problem. If you stayed in the old, messy world too long, your effectiveness would continue to go down." He gave the green light in the fall of 1999 to create a new codebase called Google Two. New systems would run on Google Two, and the original codebase would be phased out. Jeff and Craig started working on it, but writing new infrastructure took time — and time refused to stand still, even for the engineers at Google.

In the months that followed, ballooning traffic increased the pressure at every point, and as Urs had predicted, cracks appeared in the lines of the original Stanford code.

Sitting in the hot tub at Squaw Valley Resort during the company's annual ski trip, two months before the March index meltdown, Craig suggested to Jeff that they write an entirely new crawler and indexer for Google Two. It would be cleaner than replacing the old ones bit by bit. Jeff saw the logic in that. The MarIndex suddenly gave that project urgency. Joined by Sanjay and Ben Gomes, they ripped out Google's aging guts and replaced them with a streamlined block of high-efficiency algorithms.

The team didn't know Yahoo was floating out there, nibbling on Omid's line, or that when he landed the contract in May, they would have only a month to complete their work. The new systems would have to be completely stable under triple the highest load Google had ever handled. They would need to distribute queries to thousands of servers in multiple data centers and automatically balance the flux of traffic on the basis of machine availability. The engineers couldn't shut off Google while they tested the system, and they couldn't drop a single Yahoo query once the deal was done. Google embraced risk, but sensible, talented engineers could infer that this indicated a company-wide death wish. So many ways to go so horribly wrong. Urs evaluated the situation and his team's capabilities and decided they needed more of a challenge.

The great white whale of search in early 2000 was an index of a billion URLs. No one had come within sight of anything close, but Urs set out to harpoon just such a beast with Google's shiny new crawler. While only half the pages in the index would be fully indexed (meaning the crawler would examine their full content, not just identify the URL at which the content lived), it would still overshadow Inktomi, which claimed to have crawled 110 million full pages. A billion URLs were not required for the Yahoo deal, but to the crawl team, the "1B" index held epic significance. It would catapult Google into the undisputed lead as the builder of the best, most scalable search technology in the world.

"In search," Urs believed, "the discussion was really, How can we outdistance our current system and make it look laughable? That's the best definition of success: if a new system comes out and everyone says, 'Wow, I can't believe we put up with the old thing because it was so primitive and limited compared to this.'"

"Urs just said, 'We will have a 1B index,'" recalls Ben Gomes, "and it seemed like crazy talk." Gomes knew that increasing Google's size by that amount required more than slight improvements in current methods. "My advisor had a saying," he told me. "'An order of magnitude is qualitative, not quantitative.' When you go up by an order of magnitude, the problem is different enough that it demands different solutions. It's discontinuous."

Given the two equally impossible tasks — meeting Yahoo's requirements and creating the world's first billion-URL index—Larry and Sergey doubled down. Google would do both and do them at the same time. Google would begin answering Yahoo queries on Monday, July 3, leaving the Fourth of July holiday to repair any major disasters that might occur. It was a one-day margin of error in which to parse convoluted code, find bugs, squash them, and, if necessary, restart a system that had never dealt with the load it would now be called upon to carry twenty-four hours a day, seven days a week.

Before You Can Run, You Have to Crawl

Late on an April evening in the Googleplex, a steady clicking sound filled the space between the fabric walls, echoing the spring rain tapping against the windows. In his office, Jeff Dean stood looking over the shoulder of Sanjay Ghemawat, suggesting code variations as Sanjay typed and lines of text scrolled off his screen like the stairs of an ascending escalator.

Craig Silverstein drifted in, twisting a purple and black toy spider in his hands. Craig looked over Sanjay's other shoulder and set the spider down to point to a command about which he had a question. Jeff answered and Craig, satisfied, left. The spider remained—forsaken, but not alone. A block puzzle held together by an elastic band and a grip strengthener lay nearby, visible testaments to Craig's recurring visits. Ben Gomes stood in the hall, tossing beanbags into the air and catching some of them. Juggling rejuvenated him after hours of screen time and broke up the crusty patches that formed over his creativity. Inside the "Ben Pen," the office he shared with Ben Polk and Ben Smith,* the soundtrack of the 1986 film *The Mission*, a tale of pride and the struggle for redemption, swelled to a crescendo.

They were babysitting the crawl.

The engineers took turns monitoring the crawl's progress to make sure it didn't fail because of a single machine running amok. Urs had finally confided in his team why he was pushing so hard for so much new code. Everyone now knew the Yahoo deal was real and the deadline

---

* Googlers would shout "Ben!" just to watch all three heads prairie dog at once, though the Bens soon acquired a Nerf machine gun to discourage interruptions.

firm. Intensity set around the engineering group, a hardening cement of stress and pressure that grew firmer with each passing hour.

Even the implacable JeffnSanjay were not immune to its effects. "It was only a few months after I joined," recalls Sanjay, "and it was one of the most stressful times working at Google. We saw the deal and we knew when we had to get things done. We could do the math."

Sanjay worked on the new indexing system, which would be tested for the first time with the April index. Instead of taking three or four months, the index would have to be finished in one. "When something failed, we were on it," he told me. "People would just wake up every few hours and see if anything bad had happened, and then go fix it. The working style was long hours, constant attention, and quickly fixing things as they went bad."

Jeff remembers this entire period as the most demanding of his decade at Google: "From March 2000 to the end of 2001 was just frantically spent redesigning our systems and trying out different ideas on a very short time scale. The difficulty was the product of several different dimensions. How many queries do you have? How big is your index? How often do you want to update your index?"

The Bens provided a perfect barometer for reading the state of the software development. As each shouldered his part of the load, signs of the pressure he was under increased. Gomes was first, because he was helping JeffnSanjay with the code for the actual crawler and indexer and updating the pageranker. Polk was next as he worked with Bogdan to push the index out to the data centers.

"That was a pretty tricky business," Gomes recalls, "because you had to copy onto machines that were currently serving the traffic and then at some point arrange for the flipover to take place. The new index was almost always larger and more complex, and you were never sure what would go wrong at a flip." Something almost always blew up. Gomes once started to explain the process to a colleague: "If things go well . . ." Then he paused and asked, "Why the hell am I saying, 'If things go well'?"

Ben Smith owned the front-end infrastructure that enabled Google to serve the index to Yahoo. Smith and Craig Silverstein were the experts on the Google Web Server (GWS), the system that actually communicated directly with users. This put Smith in the role of riding herd over latency problems.

"It was the most miserable couple of months in my life," Smith said about the Yahoo buildup. "I'd be driving home with the sun coming up. I'd get four hours of sleep and then head back to work."

Every neck felt the hot breath of failure, and every throat tasted the bile waiting to erupt if they fell behind schedule. Though not all felt it with the same intensity. "I wasn't too worried about it," Urs told me. "What we promised Yahoo was a lot smaller than our goal in terms of coverage [the 1B index]. The scary things were the reliability parts, not the quality. They can't measure quality."

Urs knew that ultimately it was just a business deal and that Yahoo had the upper hand. "If Yahoo wanted to walk away," he conceded, "they could walk away. They didn't even need a pretext. It was a pretty one-sided contract."

Google would be taking a calculated risk by giving Yahoo guarantees, but Urs made that calculation and felt comfortable enough with the odds that he slept easy at night. "We promised ninety-nine-point-five percent uptime," he said, "and we weren't reeeeaaallllly quite there. So you look at the penalties and say, fine, if it occasionally happens, then we'll pay some of these penalties. Hopefully in a good partnership, people are going to be rewarding you for seriously trying. And we were definitely *seriously* trying."

The End of "The"

So what did all this effort produce?

"Mostly," Jeff said, "we wanted to get many more queries per second served out of these machines. One of the big things we did was completely change the index format to make it much more compact."

In layman's terms, Google's index was full of spaces that didn't need to be there — it fit the data like baggy pants in constant danger of hitting the ground. Google wasted precious time searching empty pockets to find the bits it needed. One of JeffnSanjay's innovations was to shove most occurrences of a particular word into a single block in the database. Kind of like putting all your nickels in one pocket, dimes in another, so if you see a nickel, you know not to waste time searching through that pocket for a dime. The software searching the index could tell quickly from the block header that it didn't need anything in that block and skip ahead, which made each machine faster.

"We improved that," Jeff said, "and we added skip tables to skip even larger chunks than just blocks." The goal was to minimize the number of times Google read each hard drive, because physically moving a head across a disk is far, far slower than doing things within an electronic circuit. JeffnSanjay rewrote the disk-scheduling systems to give each disk its own set of code. That cut search times by thirty to forty percent. A thirty-percent improvement was like running a four-minute mile in under three. A stunning accomplishment. But it wasn't enough.

So Jeff and Sanjay got rid of "the."

"The" is the most common word in English and conveys little useful information. JeffnSanjay decided to ignore it, freeing up one percent of the space being used by the index. The only downside? It became infinitely harder to find information about the eighties alternative rock band "The The." Engineering lives and dies by its tradeoffs.

To keep the failure of a single machine from corrupting the data and requiring a restart of the entire crawl, the war room team implemented checkpointing, which saved the state of the crawl so that if things blew up they could go back to the last checkpoint instead of starting over from the beginning.

With the hardware on its way to the data centers and the crawler, the indexer, the ranker, and the serving side progressing, only one issue remained. Yahoo wanted its search results to appear current, so it insisted that at least part of its index be updated on a daily basis.

Think of a card shark at a blackjack table. She carefully arranges the cards to ensure that everyone gets a good hand, but not as good as hers. She starts dealing around the table. Now imagine her trying to add new cards to the deck in her hand as she deals, improving all the results, including her own. It was that kind of problem.

Google's PageRank algorithm required a full day and a half to score an index. Adding additional information every twenty-four hours meant the pageranker would have to run faster, while integrating the new data in all the appropriate places. "It is a much harder problem to update an index every day than it is to have a static index," Jeff explained. "There are many more moving pieces to deal with."

Jeff was maxed out. Sanjay was overloaded. Ben Gomes had a full plate. Developing an incremental indexing system could take a dedicated team of programmers years, and there were only weeks before the contract went into effect. Larry and Sergey, understanding the desperate need, threw the resource floodgates open and gave Urs carte blanche to do what was needed. Never one to waste an opportunity, Urs went all out. He hired a guy.

"I had no experience with crawls," Anurag Acharya recalls, "and Google didn't tell people what they would be working on." Urs had sung his siren song at perfect pitch and persuaded his former UC Santa Barbara colleague to abandon academia for Silicon Valley.

On his first day, Anurag focused on part of the indexing system. That same evening, Urs stopped by for a chat about his next assignment.

"I'll take a look at the logs," Anurag suggested, "and see what problems there might be."

"Why don't you do incremental indexing for a while," Urs casually replied, "and then we'll see?"

"I say 'Yeah,'" Anurag told me about that conversation, "like I know what doing incremental indexing really means. So there went the next five months."

Google didn't haze newbies, but Anurag must have felt as if he'd been led blindfolded into a room full of drunken frat boys with wooden paddles. He was hit with the complex issues of how to crawl additional sites, rank them appropriately, and then integrate them seamlessly into the existing index.

"I don't think I was brought in specifically for the index," he said. "It just happened. I showed up at that point, and at that point, those were the problems."

"Anurag started and a couple of us in the company knew him," said Ben Smith, who had been Anurag's student at UCSB, "and he basically just disappeared. He wouldn't come down to lunch. He was always in his office. He was there late for two months. What is up with this guy? And then Urs called me into his office and said, 'This is what's coming. Soon. Can you help him out?' Okay. Now I understood why."

Smith knew exactly what he was getting into. The first time Urs had asked him to take on incremental indexing had been almost a year earlier, on his first day as an intern at Google. Smith had refused. "I said," he told me with a laugh, "'That's way too big for a summer project, nobody really knows how to do that. I don't wanna tackle that.'" Now he and Anurag would have to figure it out in a matter of weeks.

Smith had already sped up Google's response rate by improving the search engine's ability to cache queries. The first time someone searched for "hotels in Madrid," Google searched the entire index, then stored the query and the results it had found. The next time someone searched for "hotels in Madrid," Smith's code delivered the same results from memory, without having to search the index. Instead of accessing hundreds of machines, a cached query used only one—an enormous reduction in the cost of search. Unfortunately for Smith, the new incremental index threatened to undo his work, because a continuously refreshed index would quickly make cached queries obsolete.

"Anurag cranked maybe six to eight weeks and he had something that kinda worked," recalls Smith. "He wrote a new server called 'the mixer,' which hid the fact that we were talking to two different indices [a daily index and the main index] and mixed them together."*

"Anurag and I were very stressed," Smith went on. "For whatever reason, we had to keep it quiet." They couldn't talk about what they were doing or why they were in the office every night after even the vampire coders had gone home. "Many, many days, we'd leave somewhere between three and five a.m. That was the time when Anurag and I could try to plug in our new system, because that was when Google had the least amount of search traffic. There were a lot of days where it was, 'Let's turn it on and see how it works,' because we didn't really know. The mixer would talk to the cache and the mixer would talk to the incremental. And sometimes the mixer would melt down and sometimes the incremental would melt down, because it didn't have enough capacity, and we'd say, 'Okay. Why? What happened and how do you fix it?'"

The hours and the stress shaved tolerances among the engineers until little remained to insulate their frustrations from the friction of the outside world.

"For a large fraction of my career here," Smith explained to me, "I worked on infrastructure or on the serving side. Larry seemed much more interested in the product aspect of things. He wasn't interested in the infrastructure side of the Yahoo deal—he didn't even know what was going on regarding it. I remember one time he wandered into my office and made some crack like 'You need to relax more,' and I just chewed him out."

Because the 1B index devoured almost all the available machines, only a few hundred remained for the incremental team to use. Even if ops could have built them faster, there were no data centers in which to

---

* Anurag worked with Howard Gobioff to integrate the incremental index with the new crawler and with Smith on integrating it with the serving system.

put them. The team struggled on as the last days of May passed and July loomed over the horizon like the Imperial death star.

Yahoogle

The final deadline was a week away.

The machines were built, the data centers filled. The crawler had worked. The indexer had worked. The pageranker had worked. Google had identified a billion URLs and now could search them. We had the superior technology. The Yahoo deal proved we had the business smarts to go with it. It was time to take our light from under its bushel and show it to the world.

At 2:59 a.m. on Monday, June 26, 2000, Cindy sat in her office, her fingers poised on the keyboard, waiting to hit Send. On her screen was a press release announcing that Google was now the largest search engine on the planet. A minute later, just in time to feed the gaping morning news maw on the East Coast, the message was on its way. Cindy gave the business and technology editors an hour to digest that tantalizing morsel, then served the pièce de résistance: a brief announcement that Google had signed a contract to replace Inktomi as the search technology provider for Yahoo. It was the biggest accomplishment in our company's short life.

The experts were underwhelmed.

"Analysts agreed that the announcement may have hurt Inktomi's pride," CNET reported, "but they said the implications for its revenues and profitability are mild . . . That side of its business is a money loser that has increasingly played second fiddle to its exploding networking-services division. The search market in general, meanwhile, remains a low-margin, commodity business . . . Dick Pierce, Inktomi's chief operating officer, said . . . losing the portal as a search licensing partner . . . will have 'little impact with respect to profitability.'"

Wall Street didn't buy the expert view. In fact, it sold heavily. By the end of the day, Inktomi's share price had fallen eighteen percent. This despite the fact that Yahoo had thrown Inktomi a bone, naming them a "corporate search" partner for an initiative launched the same day — because everyone knew the real money in search was on the corporate side.

With impeccable timing, I had planned my first vacation to coincide with the most momentous week in Google's history. Sunday night I had trouble falling asleep in our Lake Tahoe hotel, and on Monday I was up early flipping through the cable channels looking for news about the blockbuster Yahoogle deal as my family snuggled under their blankets. Much to my surprise, it wasn't the lead story on any of the major networks and, unbelievably, it didn't make headlines in the Tuesday papers. The *San Francisco Chronicle* had a brief mention in the business section and the *Mercury News* had slightly more, yet even that thin coverage signified that things had changed. Up to that point, the mainstream media had portrayed Google as another quirky startup and California cultural oddity, with an emphasis on the wacky ways of western entrepreneurs. Now, however, Google was a business-section item, suggesting that the company should be taken seriously as a corporate entity.

We didn't care what the press said. We knew it was a major win. The Googlers at the Plex celebrated accordingly. On Monday Charlie and his crew prepared a luau lunch and served it up al fresco. The grass was green and freshly mown, the food hot and plentiful, and the spirits high. Music filled the air and margaritas sloshed in paper cups hoisted in salute as Larry and Sergey, wearing plastic leis, introduced Yahoo co-founder David Filo. Filo eschewed the customary rhetorical pats on the back in favor of a brief speech that boiled down to, "Thank you. We have a lot to do. You should really get back to work." Perhaps his absent partner, Jerry Yang, was the party guy.

Susan Wojcicki handed out t-shirts she had secretly ordered proclaiming "Google and Yahoo got lucky" — Google's first official commemorative garment. If you want to make a killing trading tech stocks, find a friend in the t-shirt business between San Francisco and San Jose and ask to be alerted any time a rush order gets placed. Conventional wisdom in Silicon Valley states, "If it's not on a t-shirt, it didn't really happen."

Copy That, Good Buddy

Saturday, July 1. Google was serving the 1B index to all its own users from a new West Coast data center. All that remained was to load a copy of the index into the new data center in Virginia and the old one at Exodus. The Virginia transmission went smoothly, but when ops tried sending a copy to Exodus, it failed. The connection between the data centers couldn't be established, so the data couldn't be sent. Without a copy of the index, the third data center would be useless and Google would be unprepared to handle Yahoo's queries, which were due to start flooding in within forty-eight hours.

Jim, Schwim, and Zain Kahn piled into Jim's ten-year-old Volvo station wagon and sped off to check it out. The network line between the data centers hadn't gone live yet. Instead of relying on outsiders to activate the cable, they opted for a backup system known among technicians as "sneakerware."

"We just ripped out the eighty machines that had the index," recalls Schwim, who helped load the machines that held Google's future into the Volvo. The techs climbed in with the hard drives and drove them to Exodus, where they piled them on the floor of the already overcrowded cage. "We stacked up eighty machines on the ground, with nothing around them, not even cabinets, and we plugged them into these ridiculous power strips so we could copy the index off. You have to imagine someone working at Inktomi thinking, we have this beautiful cage and there's a pile of . . . 'bleep,' and *they* got the contract?" As one of the ops guys remarked to me later, "Never underestimate the bandwidth of a truck full of hard drives."

While Inktomi's cage may have been beautiful, it wasn't completely secure. Google didn't have enough outlets to plug in all their machines, so Zain crawled under the raised floor and snaked out an unused cable from the Inktomi side of the fence. It would have been the ultimate indignity had anyone from Yahoo's jilted partner been around to witness it, but to Google, it was just an opportunity to improvise.

The Wake of the Flood

Early on the morning of Sunday, July 2, Howard Gobioff turned his black Honda Nighthawk into the Google parking lot, killed the motor, pulled off his helmet, shook loose his ponytail, and climbed the stairs. Inside, Romanian roller-hockey enforcer Bogdan Cocosel had been up all night as the push propagated the new index to the thousands of servers in all the data centers. Bogdan nursed the system and, when it appeared to hiccup, cursed it with enthusiasm. Howard sat at the terminal to relieve him.

To those inside the Googleplex, it was a glorious new dawn. There was no going back now. Howard watched as the index skated along the ragged edge of disk capacity. The push held throughout the day, and by the next morning the billion-URL index at last stood locked and loaded and ready to serve. Yahoo would initiate the switchover at eight p.m.

Monday, July 3, 7:45 p.m. The team floated in and around Urs Hölzle's office, anticipating the opening of the spillway and the rush of the incoming torrent of queries into Google's query stream.

Eight p.m. came, but the flood did not appear. Not even a trickle came through. There were no queries from Yahoo being passed to Google. Had Yahoo reconsidered? Had Inktomi somehow sabotaged the deal? Urs called Udi. Yes, it was supposed to have happened at eight p.m. Unfortunately, Yahoo was having problems reconfiguring the DNS (domain name server) that would tell the queries to go to Google instead of Inktomi. No one at Yahoo had changed a DNS entry in quite some time and they had forgotten how to do it.

"You should be seeing it now," Udi told Urs.

"Hmmm . . . No."

"Now?"

"Still no. Try changing your DNS expiration time."

A pause.

"How about now?"

Yahoo's traffic came sweeping into Google's data centers and Google itself seemed to swell in magnitude, to be lifted on a crest of queries to the upper tier of online search companies. A loud pop was heard and a cheer went up from the assembled Googlers. Someone had uncorked a single bottle of Dom Perignon and was passing around cups with a sip for each of the dozens of people on hand.

Urs was even more succinct than his Yahoo counterpart had been. "To something!" he said, raising his glass.

The engineers downed their champagne in a gulp and dug into the bag of Big Macs Craig Silverstein had brought in from McDonald's. They wiped their greasy fingers on their jeans and then went home to sleep for many hours. The changeover passed flawlessly. Not a single query was lost. Yahoo had licensed only a portion of Google's full data set, a distinction that would probably make no difference to most Yahoo searchers but meant that Google.com retained absolute superiority.

The only nagging question had been whether the 1B index would cross the finish line with the incremental index running alongside it. It didn't. The incremental solution would continue to elude the Sisyphean efforts of the engineers for months to come. Google satisfied Yahoo with assurances that the incremental index would be completed quickly and that until it was, the new indexer would enable monthly updates to ensure freshness.

The Yahoo deal ended all my concerns about Google's future. We had momentum on our side and no visible obstacles in sight. If we could take Yahoo from Inktomi, who would stop us? I allowed myself to believe that I just might be living a Silicon Valley success story.

I called my mom and dad to tell them the news, since I wasn't sure the Internet had made it as far as Jacksonville. I hinted I might be able to pay back the money I had borrowed to buy my stock options. Not anytime soon, mind you, but someday.

All in the Family

My part in the Google-Yahoo tango played out weeks prior to the actual announcement. Omid wanted to cozy up to Yahoo by buying advertising from them as a gesture of good faith, so I scheduled the hundred banner ads I had created to run on their site. Sergey insisted I get the best return on our investment, even though he knew the ultimate goal was fostering good will. He directed me to buy untargeted run-of-site ads because they were cheaper than Yahoo's premium-content channels and because they gave us branding exposure even if nobody clicked on them. Did I mention they were also cheaper?

Yahoo, too, wanted to get the most out of our overture of friendship and resisted when I tried to negotiate lower rates for our buy. It was a difficult conversation in which I had to reconcile Sergey's deal-making directive to maximize value with our larger diplomatic goal of making Yahoo happy. I didn't want to push too hard, yet I felt an obligation not to roll over and accept whatever Yahoo felt they could get away with charging us. No matter what I negotiated, I knew Sergey would think we were paying too much. Then I discovered another complicating factor. The Yahoo sales rep assigned our account was married to David Krane, who had just been hired as Google's PR manager.

David was not the only Google executive in a mixed marriage, that is, one with a spouse working at a potential competitor. He wasn't even the only employee in the marketing department who had married outside the faith.

Let me give you an example of how convoluted and semi-incestuous Silicon Valley gets. We used the company eGroups to mass-mail our Google Friends newsletter to users, because Larry's brother, Carl, was one of eGroups' founders. Larry had done the configuration for the original eGroups server himself, and for a while the company's computational heart had lived under his desk. The same week we announced our deal with Yahoo, Yahoo announced they were buying eGroups for $428 million (Yahoo has been very kind to the Page family). With the integration of eGroups into Yahoo Groups, we began experiencing problems with our newsletter, from formatting issues to administrative headaches. Luckily, one of the software engineers absorbed into Yahoo with eGroups also had a connection to Google marketing. He was Cindy's husband. When our situation was dire and normal channels of communication failed, Cindy's "special friend" could usually help us get our problems addressed.

Silicon Valley is a Petri dish filled with amoeba-like corporations absorbing and digesting smaller technology firms, only to find themselves absorbed or growing large enough to split off their own subsidiaries. Employers have a penchant for hiring from the same pool of candidates over and over again, so everyone ends up working with everyone else at some point, or at least working for the same companies. Job-hopping is encouraged—no, expected—since no one place could possibly be interesting and innovative enough for an entire career. That's why the question Sergey asked when he interviewed me for the job was not "Why do you want to leave the *Mercury News?*" but "Why did you wait so long?"

No wonder social networking took root here; we're one big interconnected family whose members are always happy to find out how we're related to one another. "He's a first employer once removed on the Intel side." "She used to be my assistant at Sun, but she left me for some hot new startup over in Cupertino." A surprising number of tech workers have friends and lovers with whom they share intimacy but not the details of their office lives.

Google was no more immune to the lure of fraternization within the building than it was to relationships that crossed competitive lines. There were romances. There were marriages. On occasion, there were affairs. My sense is that the number of these dalliances was not out of line with a normal distribution in a population the size of Google's, especially one as densely populated with energetic young overachievers. It would be indiscreet for me to go into the details of people's private lives beyond what the participants have acknowledged publicly — and it would also be largely irrelevant, since office relationships had little effect on the course of the company. Usually, anyway. I did detect the tidal force of one pairing tugging at my ability to get my job done.

Larry and Sergey's insistence on seeing performance metrics for marketing redoubled with the addition of our ad buy on Yahoo. They began a drumbeat of demands for better measurement of our customer-acquisition techniques. What about the promotional text on our homepage? Which messages converted the most newbies to regular users? Testimonials? Promises? Comparisons? How many ads did they click? How many searches did they do?

The only way to answer these questions was to generate the homepage dynamically — essentially to implement code that would give us the ability to deliver variant versions of the homepage to users who came to our site. That would enable us to show different users different text and then track what they did after they saw it.

Larry gave me the task of writing the text to be displayed in April 2000 and assigned the coding of the dynamic homepage to Marissa. A logs team would generate the report on how many new users came back. While it took me a long time to get signoff on the homepage messages I wrote, dynamic homepage generation proved even more elusive. Soon every conversation I had with Larry turned into an inquisition about the conversion-rate test.

"Doug, when are we going to see those numbers?" he'd ask me. "We're wasting money because we're not effectively using our most powerful promotional medium."

The conversion-rate test was one of my main OKRs (Objectives and Key Results), and each time I had to tell Larry I had no data, a bit more of my credibility crumbled. I used every method at my disposal to jump-start the project, but I simply couldn't get the priority moved high enough. The only one who could move things along was Marissa, and it had been announced at TGIF that she and Larry were now a couple. Finally, in late August, I trudged upstairs to camp outside Larry's office.

I waited until he was alone, then entered and closed the door behind me.

"Larry, I've begged, cajoled, and demanded," I said, "but the dynamic homepage code still hasn't been implemented so we can test conversion rates. Can you recommend some other approach?" I was frustrated and nervous and didn't hide it very well. I was admitting I couldn't get something done. At Google, that was not a career-enhancing move. And I felt uncomfortable telling the company president that the obstacle in my way was the engineer he was dating. Larry listened quietly to my concerns.

"Don't worry, Doug," he reassured me with a broad smile. "We'll work something out." Then he put his hand on my shoulder, gave it a gentle shake, and guided me to the door. It was a strange moment for me. Larry's earnestness emanated in waves, as if he wanted to let me know that he understood the unspoken dilemma I faced, that he and I were all right and that the situation would be all right, and that he would take care of things. I went back to my desk unsure what to do next. What if other issues came up with Marissa? I could already see that we had differing perspectives about our brand. Would I have to go to Larry for resolution each time we disagreed?

Coincidentally or not, within days the dynamic homepage coding was completed. In theory, anyway. We still needed a script so webmaster Karen could run the program on her Windows machine. That took several more weeks. Then the logs team had problems extracting the user data we needed. The first actual report wasn't ready until November.

I never believed that my engineering colleagues were intentionally neglecting my number one priority. Any of a thousand projects competing for their attention could legitimately take precedence over a marketing request. And as hard as Larry and Sergey rode marketing, they rode the engineers harder. The founders were engineers, after all, and they understood what engineers could do. They just didn't understand why our engineers weren't doing it faster, and they let them know so.

The feedback to our group was more ambiguous.

"Marketing should be less risk averse," Larry said.

"And more creative," Sergey added.

"And more productive," they concluded.

Cindy kept us informed when marketing's inability to make things happen was a topic for discussion at the executive level. It seemed to come up frequently.

"Don't let anything hold you up for eventual delivery," Cindy wrote in my six-month review. "Figure out the fastest way to get it done. And don't let your signature high standards slip!"

"Absolutely," I assured her. But without engineering support, some things just weren't going to happen, and support from engineering only came when a project was endorsed by Larry or Sergey. Negotiating personal relationships to gain their blessing added a complicating factor.

Google was a company that enforced closeness more than most, from overpopulated workspaces to shared meals to all-company ski trips to constant electronic accessibility twenty-four hours a day, seven days a week. We saw a lot of one another and often became good friends — but close quarters also drove people apart. Peccadilloes and idiosyncrasies became inescapable irritants. Privacy was hard to come by, and personal hygiene took on added importance. There were undercurrents of annoyance and avoidance and sometimes overt expressions of exasperation as the pressure to perform intensified. In the midst of all that, people fell in love and out of love, formed lifelong bonds and ended their marriages. For some, Google became more a lifestyle than an employer.

I liked coming to work. I liked my job. I liked the challenges. I liked the energy, and I liked my coworkers — with whom I was spending more hours than with my family. But for me the Googleplex was just a place to get things done. I was a forty-one-year-old man, married, with three kids, two cars, a cat, and a mortgage. I already had a home.

CHAPTER 12

Fun and Names

ERGEY SAT WITH Susan in the front of the aluminum canoe I was steering down the Russian River in Sonoma County. It was September 2000, and I was using all the navigational skills I had picked up at sleep-away camp to keep us clear of rocks and overhanging branches. Around us other Googlers fired super soakers and shouted gleefully when someone ran aground or capsized.

"Paddle closer to Larry's canoe," Sergey urged me as he stripped off his shirt and positioned himself near the side. In an instant, he was out of the canoe and swimming toward his co-founder, grabbing for the gunwale of his boat — splashing and rocking it as if to tip it over — before heading off to attack one of the other engineers.

When we reached the last sandbar two hours later, Larry was waiting to take his revenge. While I pulled the canoe up onto the beach, he came running toward us through the shallow water.

"Hah," I thought. "Sergey's going down."

I was caught totally by surprise when Larry bypassed Sergey and tackled me instead, sending me sprawling into the water. I had never been subjected to a physical attack by a manager before. It was the kind of rambunctious roughhousing I associated with adolescent boys. I came out of the water smiling. The canoe trip was intended to forge closer ties among Googlers and to break us out of our crusty cubicle-enclosed lives. It was company-mandated fun, but it was fun.

I may have given the impression to this point that Google was a relentless pressure cooker in which we gave every ounce of sweat and passion to advance the greater good envisioned by our brilliant, demanding founders. That's pretty accurate. A very pregnant project manager — overcome by exhaustion — apologized to me for not answering an email I sent her after midnight. She shamefacedly admitted she had fallen asleep. However, Google was also a great place to hang out, filled with interesting people who were physically active and quick of wit.

"I want Urs for my boat," engineer John Bauer punned when we were choosing canoe-trip buddies. "I can't row without him."

"Unfortunately the root is defunct now," Jeremy Chau nerdily joked about a tree that fell in the parking lot. "Should we take a look at the log?"

We held an employee contest to guess the first day we would do a hundred million searches, with the winner riding away on a new electric scooter. We had a spring-cleaning ice-cream social and a flood of geeky jokes. ("How many Microsoft engineers does it take to change a light bulb?" "None. They just declare Darkness™ the standard.")

When Karen took a vacation, we ordered a thousand plastic playground balls and filled her cube with them. They were still being thrown from office to office and rolling around under desks a year later.

For Mardi Gras, Charlie adorned the café with beads and cooked little plastic babies into king cakes. On Cinco de Mayo we tasted crawfish and sweet potato tamales washed down with horchata and sweet sangria.

For Halloween we had blood-clot punch with life-sized baby dolls floating in the bowl (Charlie had a fetish for food garnished with infants) and a parade of tasteless costumes including choirboys with sinner priests, bloodied plane-wreck casualties, and oozing shark-bite victims — and those were just the outfits worn by our not-so-politically-correct HR manager, Heather.

And we had groupies. Tourists in Linux t-shirts took souvenir photos under the Google sign by our front door — proof that Yahoo had put us on the map and that our brand was striking a chord deeper than that of a typical tech company.

It seemed I merely had to stand up and walk a few paces away from my chair in any direction to experience something new and entertaining.

"Cock rings? I overheard one sales rep ask another as I passed her cube. "How many of those do we have? And vibrators? How many can we come up with for that?"

"There must be a supply cabinet I don't know about," I thought. "Or perhaps I forgot to sign up for the mailing list about after-work parties."

Adult services advertisers, I learned when I asked, were among our earliest customers. They needed to know how many ad impressions we could deliver targeted to the words that defined their businesses. The sales reps had been checking the "inventory" of projected searches for those keywords. Google was not the place to work if you had delicate sensibilities.

The lighter moments helped make the load bearable, but it was the boldness of our business initiatives that really got my blood flowing and kept me from feeling trapped in a thankless grind. I never knew when some fastball would smack me in the head and reset my thinking yet again.

Say What You Will

"What the hell are you thinking?" I asked Larry when he explained his idea for a new do-it-yourself advertising system.

The engineers had continued to innovate on our initial CPM ad system, beginning with placing ads on the right-hand side of search results in addition to those at the top of the page. The next step, Larry informed us, would be a feature that made it possible for anyone to create right-hand-side ads and post them live on Google within minutes. We would have guidelines and terms and conditions, but we would start running ads before verifying they were in compliance. In effect, anyone with a valid credit card could make an ad that said anything.

Anyone. Anything.

"How in the world is our brand going to survive racist, pornographic, and defamatory ads?" I protested. "They're bound to show up on our results pages. Do we want our brand to be associated with hate speech and worse? I have a very bad feeling about this."

Larry's decision to let user-created ads go live on our site without review convinced me he occupied some alternative and severely distorted reality. To allow the publication of unscreened ads was a classic marketing crisis in the making. Any fool could see that. Evidently, I was that fool.

Others shared my incredulity. One engineer was so appalled by the plan that he considered writing a letter to the VCs on the board informing them we were about to lose all the money they had invested in us. Chad Lester — the omnivore engineer — however, celebrated our founder's risk tolerance.

"I was excited about it," Chad told me after the fact. "It was like high school and TP-ing someone's house. Why not try it and see what happens?"

I'd seen managers build consensus before moving ahead with unpopular decisions, and I knew bosses who dipped their toes in untested waters, fully prepared to pull out quickly if the temperature rose above or dropped below their comfort level. This was a different kind of leadership. Larry was so suffused with conviction that he simply brushed aside opposition and ran toward risk without fear or hesitation. He was absolutely convinced that unfiltered ads were the right thing to do.

In retrospect, Larry's and Chad's zeal may reflect the difference in our stages of life. I was a middle-aged father with a lot to lose if Google died on the vine. Chad and Larry were just beginning their careers. They could afford to flame out in Silicon Valley, where bold failures earn more respect than incremental success.

Not all mid-life guys are too conservative to survive startups, but to be successful you have to love uncertainty the way Chad loved pork chops. You need enormous reserves of energy to undertake everything thrown your way — along with the confidence to bounce back each time you fall off the high wire and hit the ground hard. I had moved to Nagoya before I could speak Japanese and to Novosibirsk without a word of Russian. I'd jumped from a steady job at the *Merc* to an unsecured position in an unknown company without a safety net. I didn't fear the unknown. Neither did I want to see my brave new world implode because of reckless, ill-considered decisions. I found it increasingly difficult to judge what fell into that category.

There were people my age at Google when I joined and people older than me within a few months. Hardware designer Will Whitted had been fifty-four when he started, and he saw no gap between his thought process and that of his younger colleagues. "I think that I think younger, which probably means more irresponsibly, than most people do," he confessed. "There were people at Google who had the opposite problem — who were a little younger than me, but perceived by people who mattered to be old-thinking. To be slow and overly conservative, and it got them in trouble."

Those who succeeded, as I was trying to do, needed to be open to new ideas regardless of their source or seeming defiance of logic.

It's hard to accept that everything you know is wrong, or at least needs to be proved right all over again. Larry's decision to run unscreened ads opened the scab over my opposition to messing with our logo. It tested my resolve to adopt a wide perspective — to see the panorama of opportunity opening for us, rather than the walls fencing us in. If Google were filled only with people who shared a "big-company" perspective on reducing risks, we would never reap the rare fruits that flourished only in environmental extremes.

The First Family of Online Advertising

Larry had decided. We would launch our new do-it-yourself ad program in late 2000. Now we began debating what to call it. "AdsToo" was engineering's working name (it was version two of the ads system and engineers are very literal people). No one wanted that to become the permanent moniker.

Since no one person or department owned product identity, the process got messy. Larry wanted a name that didn't sound funny if you said it five times fast. Omid wanted separation between the Google name and the name of the ad product (so no "Googlads"). Those were the only guidelines. Suggestions flew in from all quarters, each beloved by its originator and endorsed by odd lots of others.

Salar supported "PrestoAds" before deciding it was too seventies. He switched his allegiance to "Self-serve Ads," which clearly described the product's unique feature.

"AdsDirect" had Susan's support.

I proposed "GIDYAP" (Google's Interactive Do-It-Yourself Ad Program). Everyone immediately barfed all over it. I tried "BuyWords" next: a play on "bywords" (words to live by) and "buy words." The sales team allowed that they could dance to that, and Bart agreed the name was catchy. Larry gave it his blessing.

"All done," I thought, once again mistaking consensus for final approval.

Then the lobbying began.

Salar pointed out that the keyword-targeting concept was relatively new and we wanted a name that made clear how it worked. BuyWords might imply that we were selling placement in our actual search results, rather than just ads next to the results. Still, he liked BuyWords better than AdsDirect, which I argued was too generic and evocative of old-fashioned direct mail.

Susan countered that "AdsDirect" reminded users they didn't need a middleman to create or place their ads and thus suggested the benefit of a discounted price.

Cindy expressed a slight preference for BuyWords, because she viewed it as a way to engage the press on our refusal to sell placement in results. But she could live with DirectAds too.

Once again we were at an impasse. I went home that night and spent an hour generating more names while my boys did their homework and Kristen gave the baby a bath. In the morning I sent out a new list of possibilities.

"Promote Control."

"Ad-O-Mat."

"Ad Commander."

"Impulse Ads."

I didn't love any of them, but I did feel pretty good about the last name on my list: "AdWords."

"It's new! And improved!" I shilled. "It's like BuyWords without the Buy! It also sounds like Edwards, which is a big plus in my book."

Salar liked AdWords better than BuyWords. Omid liked it. Bart liked it. Larry liked it.

Sergey cast the final vote. He informed the engineering team that our new system would be called "AdWords." He neglected to tell me — or anyone else in marketing — about his decision. It's hard to imagine such an oversight at a brand-driven company like Procter & Gamble. From an engineer's perspective, however, the name question only needed to be resolved so the proper string of characters could be entered into the program before the "code freeze," at which point no major changes were allowed. The marketing stuff that went along with establishing a brand was secondary and could be dealt with once the program had been locked down. It was Jen McGrath of the front-end team who let me know that my family's name would live forever, enshrined in Google's revenue stream.

Lobsters and Porn, Redux

AdWords had a long way to go before it could go out to the public. The engineers wrestled with the software that would actually place the ads and charge for them. The UI team worked with Salar to finalize the interface advertisers would navigate to create and activate their campaigns. PR would introduce AdWords to the press. I owned the language we used to explain it directly to our users. There was a great deal to explain. We needed an FAQ, error messages, terms and conditions, customer service emails, and sales materials. And engineering kept changing things in the weeks leading up to the launch. Many long nights ensued.

I didn't mind at all, because AdWords added another dimension to my role. I was not just building Google's brand but also our bottom line. From that point on, I wrote almost all of the words that appeared on our website aimed at either consumers or clients. I began envisioning myself as the human interface between the company and the people who used our products. It may have gone to my head a bit. If I was going to be the voice of Google, Google's voice would sound like me. I terrorized colleagues with imperious screeds about tone, style, and the overuse of capitalization and exclamation marks. Engineers viewed letter size and punctuation as knobs they could twist to raise excitement in otherwise uninspired writing — LOOK! THIS MUST BE IMPORTANT! I emphatically told them that most exclamation marks were completely superfluous! Unless they were writing about Dick and Jane! And Spot!

It all got done.

AdWords launched quietly in a beta test version late on September 27, 2000. Two hours later, Lively Lobsters in Kingston, Rhode Island, signed on as the first customer (keyword: lobster) with an eighty-three-dollar ad buy. Ryan Bartholomew, Lively Lobster's owner, ad manager, and sole employee, quickly figured out that AdWords would be an easy way to make money from other sites' affiliate programs. He placed

AdWords ads for books on Amazon.com, as Jeff Dean had done with his first Google ad system, and earned a commission that more than covered his costs. He found adult-site affiliate programs to be especially lucrative. According to Bartholomew, he grew his affiliate optimization empire to a sixteen-person business that placed more than twelve million dollars in ads on Google over the next decade.

Lobsters and porn. From its very first customer, AdWords proved its versatility and potential as a moneymaking tool. Twenty other customers signed on in the next two days, and with them came new issues we hadn't considered. Someone wanted to use "Google" as a keyword trigger to display an ad. Was that okay? Jane Manning, the project manager, decided it set a bad precedent, and we disallowed it. Should we treat ads targeting the trademarks of other companies the same way? An engineer suggested we forbid any trademark targeting, but how, then, I wondered, would you handle words like "staples," which is both a company name and a generic term? Larry and Sergey decided not to restrict others' trademarks, but the issue would eventually go to the courts, who at the time of this writing have sided with Google. That was part of the excitement of working for a company unrestrained by precedent. We improvised as we went along and watched as the rest of the world caught up.

AdWords formally launched on October 23, 2000, and accelerated past the outer moons of Jupiter on its way to some distant galaxy made entirely of money. No PR crisis ensued. If inappropriate ads did run, no one noticed because they were merely wet spots within an ocean of searches. Still, we instituted a limit to ensure ads were reviewed before we delivered too many impressions, and we hired a temp to check each new ad by hand.

Would Google never tire of succeeding with big ideas that I found patently ludicrous? It was starting to make me feel like a crotchety geezer yelling at kids to get off his lawn.

Laughing at Our Mistakes

I had christened AdWords with my own name. Next I worked on giving it my own voice. Emboldened by the feedback on MentalPlex and my growing confidence as Google's word guy, I started gently introducing bits of humor where they weren't specifically called for.

"Okay, we've got a problem here," I wrote for an error message. "Not only did something not work right with our software, it went so spectacularly wrong that our automatic report generator can't begin to describe it for our engineering group. You can help." I went on to suggest that users email us details including their horoscope signs.

"Sorry, something didn't work correctly," another message read. "If we knew exactly what the problem was, we would tell you instead of giving you this useless error message. Actually, if we knew, we would most likely have fixed it already. Rest assured. A report will soon be in the hands or our engineering team detailing the bad thing that happened here."

When the AdWords team not only raised no objections but thanked me profusely, I rejoiced. I no longer worked at a company where everyone wanted a cut at neutering my language. My colleagues didn't know "professional" marketers would assume user ignorance, target the lowest common denominator, and eschew polysyllabic words. I wasn't about to tell them. Besides, they were focused on the code swimming across their screens. Words not preceded by a command prompt were insignificant.

I began writing copy for the site as if the person reading it were a friend. I added Simpsons references to our FAQs, made puns in our newsletter, and, after engineer Amit Patel confessed a love of prosimians and their googley eyes, started including lemurs in all my examples. ("I don't want anyone to know I'm into lemur racing. Is my information private?") It made my job a lot more fun, but also made it clear that an actual human being had touched the page the user was reading.

"Sometimes we have to shut the service down to implement improvements," I wrote about an unstable product launch. "Sometimes it decides on its own to break for a nice pot of Earl Grey and some fresh silicon wafers."

I found out humor wasn't so funny when it came time to translate our FAQs into languages in which the jokes didn't work. Or when a joke wore out from overexposure. The error message I wrote for orkut, our experiment in social networking, quickly grew tired as the service crashed time and again.[*]

"Bad, bad server," it said. "No donut for you. We're sorry, the orkut

---

[*] For more on orkut, see Chapter 25.

.com server has acted out in an unexpected way. We apologize for the inconvenience and our server's lack of consideration for others."

I thought I had written an amusing tribute to an obscure half-remembered cartoon, but the page became the focus of intense user frustration. A Google search for "bad, bad server" still brings up close to ten thousand results, most of them rants about connectivity problems.

Despite the occasional misfire, I knew I had found my stride. I was increasingly aware that Google was developing a voice and increasingly confident in my ability to speak with it, not just to users, but to those working inside the Googleplex as well.

In November 2000, almost a year to the day after I started at Google, I wrote two lines that defined for me exactly what Google should be as a new kind of corporate entity — two lines that distilled the essence of the company I wanted to be part of and believed I had joined. It was the click of a tumbler falling into place, securing my role and locking in the sound of Google's voice once and for all. It was good timing, because Google was adding new people every day. They brought fresh energy and ideas, but with new blood the complexion of the company couldn't help changing.

CHAPTER 13

Not the Usual Yada Yada

I WAS AT LUNCH," said Allegra Tudisco, the new marketing coordinator I'd hired in September, "and I introduced myself to everyone at the table. They all gave me their names except this one guy, who seemed kind of shy. I asked him who he was and he said his name was Larry, so I asked him what he did. And he said he was Larry Page, the CEO. I had no idea."

Google had reached a cultural milestone. The company had grown so large that Larry and Sergey no longer had time to interview each hire personally. That proved a problem for Larry a week later when he visited our new nine-person office in New York. They refused to let him in because they didn't believe he was who he claimed to be.

Mostly, however, the growth meant we had more going on. More work on infrastructure, more deals in negotiation, more salespeople calling on clients, and more products in development. One of those products was a toolbar that tucked a search box right into users' browsers, enabling them to conduct Google searches without going to Google .com. The product had been worked on by Joel Spolsky, a contract developer, based on prototypes developed by my UI team colleague Bay Chang. Googler David Watson created the first working version, and Eric Fredricksen finalized the software we actually launched. Larry was very keen to get it out the door.

The Google toolbar came with more than just a search box. It had "advanced features." One displayed a green bar with a relative length approximating the PageRank of the web page the user was visiting. PageRank was Google's assessment of the importance of a page, determined by looking at the importance of the sites that linked to it. So, knowing a page's PageRank could give you a feel for whether or not Google viewed a site as reliable. It was just the sort of geeky feature engineers loved, because it provided an objective data point from which to form an opinion. All happiness and joy. Except that when the "advanced features" were activated, they also gave Google a look at every page a user viewed.

To tell you the PageRank of a site, Google needed to know what site you were visiting. The Toolbar sent that data back to Google if you let it, and Google would show you the green bar. The key was "if you let it," because you could also download a version of the toolbar that would not send any data back to Google. The user could make the choice, though Larry and the engineering team believed — and hoped — that most people wouldn't pass up the advanced features just because Google might learn their surfing habits. We're talking free extra data here. While knowing the PageRank of a page might have only nominal value to users, knowing the sites users visited would be tremendously valuable to Google. The PageRank indicator provided a justification for gathering it.

I thought it was an enormous privacy tradeoff. I knew we planned to anonymize the data and wouldn't match the list of visited sites to a user's identity. Still, it felt creepy to me and I figured I wouldn't be the only one. So how to inform users without scaring them off?

If we said that turning on advanced features showed Google every web page a user visited, many people would never download any version of the software. That would be a disaster. The Toolbar was a secret weapon in our war against Microsoft. By embedding the Toolbar in the browser, Google opened another front in the battle for unfiltered access to users. Bill Gates wanted complete control over the PC experience, and rumors abounded that the next version of Windows would incorporate a search box right on the desktop. We needed to make sure Google's search box didn't become an obsolete relic. To do that, we would turn Microsoft's strength to our advantage and pit one group within the Redmond-based company against another.

If the Google toolbar became so popular that people downloaded

Internet Explorer just to run it, then the browser gang within Microsoft might defend us when the Windows mafia inevitably tried to snuff us out. In the meantime, we would piggyback on the world's most popular web browser to gain millions of users.

The wording users saw when downloading the Google toolbar had to be subtle and assuage their concerns while downplaying the risks. We could just bury it in the EULA (end user licensing agreement) in tiny type and no one would be the wiser. Almost nobody reads the legalese terms of use before installing software. Knowing that, I considered long and hard and came up with an appropriately nuanced response — the two lines I referred to earlier.

"PLEASE READ THIS CAREFULLY," I wrote on the first line in large bold red letters. On a separate line beneath it, also red and bolded, came the words "IT'S NOT THE USUAL YADA YADA." The text that followed was equally subtle: "By using the Advanced Features version of the Google toolbar, you may be sending information about the sites you visit to Google."

That seemed to cover it.

Maybe I had been drinking the Google Kool-Aid too long, but I believed that telling our users explicitly what we were up to and giving them the power to decide if they wanted to play along was the right thing to do. I didn't want to leave the information lying about where they might stumble across it — I wanted to set it as tablets before their eyes, scribed in burning letters a hundred feet high.

There was a less altruistic reason as well. I thought we could forestall future criticism and distrust if we were forthright about our actions. That would spare me, as the person responsible for user communication, a great deal of pain.

Yes, I expected we would scare off some potential users, but those who did sign up would completely understand the tradeoff they were making. I believed the value of the Toolbar would become so obvious to them that they would evangelize to others. Eventually even those who had been hesitant at first would become convinced.

Bay, our UI guru, worried the language would frighten away too many users unnecessarily, though he didn't insist we change it. Eric, the Toolbar's creator, expressed concerns as well, but agreed that talking to people about privacy up front would reassure them nothing sinister lurked in the shadows.

I felt the truth of that deep in my soul. Those two sentences sparked an epiphany in me, that we could be the company that never tried to sneak an unpleasant truth past its customers. The company that always went overboard to be completely transparent about its actions. The company that did no evil. I would advocate as strongly as I could that we engage the issue of privacy and educate our users about exactly what information we collected. Surely that aligned with our core values.

When the Google toolbar launched in November 2000, the installer included the language as I had written it, bold red font and all. The page users saw after installing the Toolbar also called attention to the information collected and offered links to Google's privacy policy and instructions on how to disable the reporting function. People noticed.

Instead of a hue and cry there was a yawning silence. When users emailed us with concerns, we politely quoted the language on the installation page and reiterated that we had fully described all the options available to them. When the issue bubbled up on message boards, users who had already downloaded the Toolbar pointed to the bright red message and asked what more a person could want regarding notification. Those who downloaded the Toolbar with advanced features made a fully informed choice. Carnegie Mellon professor Randy Pausch confirmed it with a user study that led him to conclude, "The red Yada Yada message definitely works: it catches users' attention, and in a positive way."

For years, people talked about Google as a brand that could push hard against edges Microsoft could never approach without setting off alarms. The Yada Yada message was a big part of that.

News organizations from CNET to *MIT Technology Review* to *USA Today* and the *Washington Post* referred to Google's disclosure language in articles about the company and users' privacy, always giving Google the benefit of the doubt because it so clearly went out of its way to inform users about its intentions.

I believed that we had discovered the golden rule of user communication, and the cynical marketer in me rejoiced. We could defuse any controversial issue by rolling out our secret weapon: a brilliant and devious strategy that happened to be built on absolute honesty. It really was the best policy.

I may have taken that policy too far. With each new product we introduced, I refused to support grudging admissions about things users might have some interest in knowing. I demanded in-your-face, ki-mono-wide-open, wart-revealing, naked-before-the-eyes-of-God, full-frontal fact-flashing. I had been converted like Paul on the road to Da-mascus by the lightning bolt our bold red letters had deflected from our young brand. The more you informed people, the more they trusted you not to abuse them. Just as with MentalPlex, the lesson seemed as clear and sharp as shattered crystal. Yet, once again, others considered the same data and saw things in a different light. The issue of user pri-vacy wouldn't arise again for months, but it would never cease to come back, no matter how many times we ignored it.

De Parvis Grandis

"This is version X.X of the Google toolbar," I wrote. "Earlier versions, if they exist, retain only sentimental value. Such is the transience of material things." Eric, the Toolbar engineer, was pleased. He had ex-pected something more traditional for the text users and checked to see if they were up to date with the latest software. He soon added his own personal signature to the information box: "De parvis grandis a cervus erit" (Small things make a big pile).

It didn't always go so smoothly when I wrote copy at engineering's request. For example, we went back and forth on the text to display when users rolled their cursors over the "I'm Feeling Lucky" button on the homepage.

That button was an anomaly. If users clicked on it after typing a term in the search box, instead of seeing a full page of search results they would go directly to the one that would have been first on the list. Larry and Sergey were so confident in their technology that they thought the first result would provide adequate information for the majority of searches. Unfortunately, most of our users had no clue what the "I'm Feeling Lucky" button did. They let us know, however, that they liked seeing the phrase on the homepage and liked the self-assured attitude it implied. So we kept it — a small triumph for sentiment and brand building over cold, unemotional efficiency.[*]

In December 2000, I proposed "Go to the highest-ranked result" as

---

[*] We once calculated that serving the extra text characters for "I'm Feeling Lucky" billions of times cost Google millions of dollars each year in bandwidth usage and lost revenue: if users go directly to someone else's website, they bypass the ads on Google's results pages.

the text explaining "I'm Feeling Lucky." Bay liked the way that emphasized our quality. Salar liked that it educated users about our unique
method of ordering pages. Marissa thought it stank. Literally.

"Rank is a harsh-sounding word that has an alternate definition of
'bad smelling,'" she pointed out. She preferred "Go to the first result,"
because she wasn't sure users thought about search results as being
"ranked." They more likely thought of them as "scored" or "ordered."
You say tomato, I say tomahto. We ended up not implementing any
rollover text at all.

I received similar pushback when I sent text to Schwim in ops for the
automatic reply our system emailed to anyone who wrote us. He sent it
back. With edits.

Schwim viewed himself as a sort of catcher in the rye, the last pair
of hands to touch our outbound communications, and he took seriously his self-assigned duty to keep Google's brand from tumbling into
the bottomless pit of mediocrity. He rewrote copy if it didn't meet the
standards he felt Google should maintain. When a glaring typo myste-
riously appeared overnight in an outbound email I had written, I confronted him. It hadn't been his fault. Another engineer had requested a
change and introduced the error in the text. I had been copied in their
online discussion, but hadn't replied, perhaps because the conversation
took place at one-thirty in the morning.

Years later, Schwim explained. "We had a major product launch," he
reminded me. "We weren't going home. We weren't going to bed. We
wanted to give feedback and there wasn't anyone around, because surprisingly, you were sleeping." He meant it facetiously, but it was also
true. The engineers weren't terribly sympathetic to the fact that I had
a family at home and a life outside the office. Or that my day started at
six a.m. while theirs ended then. Either you were available when they
needed you or you weren't — in which case they would use their best
judgment and move ahead. Nothing could stand in the way of the company's progress.

Maybe that's why Cindy kept my promotion to marketing director
a secret, telling only those within our group. I'm sure it was a tough
sell to Larry and Sergey to add a layer of management to the organization, even though December 2000 marked our first profitable month.
What message would a director-level position in marketing send to the
rest of the company? Would it indicate that marketing was gaining importance? I was doing my job and what was left of Shari's, but I wasn't

writing code. I chose to view the promotion as a positive step. I had created a brand tone and put our external promotions in order. I was now the voice of Google. Cindy, at least, felt that was worthy of some recognition. As 2001 began, I looked forward to a new year of interacting with our users. My new challenge would be finding a way to answer the many, many questions they were starting to ask us.

CHAPTER 14

Googlebombs and Mail Fail

THE YAHOO DEAL turbo-charged Google's growth. Claus in our logs group carefully and scientifically plotted our traffic in crayon on a three-foot-tall roll of paper taped to one of the hallway walls. Significant milestones were precisely noted, with different colors signifying the components of our audience (searches on Google .com vs. searches on our partner sites like Netscape and Yahoo). Light-green foothills rolled in front of jagged dark-green peaks, beyond which could be spied a towering orange mountain range that stood in front of purple Alps majestically overshadowing all the others. The summits represented Mondays, and the valleys on either side reflected the weekend dips in our traffic.

Googlers annotated the chart with their own hire dates and other events of significance (such as the founding of the Google wine club). Celebrity-guest signatures appeared with regularity. Al Gore was there. Jimmy Carter. Chris Martin from Coldplay and his girlfriend Gwyneth Paltrow. Claus quickly decreased the scale of the graph so that three hundred thousand searches no longer appeared as a hill reaching halfway up the page. That mark now represented three million searches. Within months, he recalibrated so that the same height equaled thirty million searches. And still the mountains grew until they scraped the top of the chart.

Schwim sent out emails announcing major increments in the number of searches per day on Google.com, which started at around four million when I was hired in late 1999. Less than a month later that number, not including partners, was more than five million. Two months later we crossed eight million, and by the middle of September 2000 we were conducting a million searches an hour. Ninety days after that, it was a thousand searches per second. Claus added taller pieces of paper to the side of the graph as the volume of our traffic marched inexorably upward and to the right.

Operations had shifted into high gear on machine construction for the Yahoo deal, and now the production pedal was nailed to the floor. Fleets of computers provided enough capacity that a whole data center could be taken offline without bringing down Google or its partners. When a new index was built, the techs copied all the files to one data center and then moved on to update the next one. That caused some weirdness in our results.

"For about a week each month," Matt Cutts recalls, "depending on randomness and chance, you'd either go to the old data center or a new data center." If your search was routed to a data center that hadn't been updated and then you did the same search again at one that had, your results would appear to jump around, as if they were dancing. The "Google Dance" became an event of great concern to those who cared about their ranking in search results. On the WebmasterWorld website, commenters named each index switchover as if it were a hurricane, and the outcome could be equally devastating for any business whose website dropped off the first page of results. For Google, the switchover was not just about adding more data to the index. It was a time to tweak the ranking algorithms as well.

Google's focus moved back and forth from search quality to infrastructure. The initial innovation of PageRank at Stanford improved search relevance. The systems work in early 2000 led to the billion-URL index and faster response rates. In 2001, the pendulum swung back to search quality.

"Larry used to say, 'Search is too cheap,'" Urs told me. "The cost per query is really too low. Given the revenue we have, we should be able to do much more." Spending money to improve search quality would create a perceptible gap between Google's results and those of our competitors, enabling us to build a brand based on quality. Other search companies would have to invest at an equal or greater rate just to catch up. We would launch an arms race and spend our opponents into bankruptcy.

"Raising the cost of search will in fact increase the profit," Urs believed. "Your top line is going to go up much faster than your bottom line, and your margin is really very large."

Larry and Sergey wanted a focus on efficiency, but they also wanted to find out how much better Google could get if we threw twice as many machines at the problem of search quality. So they tried an experiment.

"In 2001," Sanjay recalls, "I was sitting in Larry's office and he just said, 'Here are three thousand machines. You guys figure out something to do with that.' It wasn't like we just happened to have all these spare machines lying around. It was driven by the need to figure out how to use lots of computation to do interesting things." That was just the beginning.

"There was an intent to send a signal," Urs confirmed. "Let's assume machines are plentiful — what could we do?" The three thousand machines were followed by ten thousand more, all allocated to improving search quality. Jeff, Sanjay, and Amit Singhal[*] focused all that computational power into an explosion of innovation that greatly improved Google's ability to return relevant results. One key to better results, according to Jeff, was "being much more careful about how we handled anchor text."

The more pages in an index, the more information there was about who linked to whom. And just as important to Google, the more information there was about what those links said. The wording of an actual hyperlink is the anchor text. Associating anchor text with the content of the page it pointed to turned out to be enormously helpful. For example, some links to the University of California at Berkeley contained its Spanish name or synonyms like "Cal" or "Bears." Sometimes, however, relying too heavily on anchor text caused problems.

"Some anchor text was good and some was not so good," Jeff explained. "The query 'cold lemon soufflé' used to bring up MapQuest's homepage." One website used that exact phrase in a link to MapQuest, and Google gave the association too much weight. Another example was "more evil than Satan." In 1999 that search brought up Microsoft's

---

[*] Amit Singhal joined in December 2000 and led the effort to improve Google's search quality.

homepage.* Sergey instructed Cindy to tell reporters it was the result of an "anomaly caused by quantum fluctuations in web space," a nonsense phrase that was repeated verbatim in stories purporting to explain the glitch.

Sometimes deceptive link language was intentional. Webmasters realized they could affect the ranking of results for certain search terms by intentionally pointing to pages with very specific anchor text, a trick that came to be known as "Googlebombing." The Googlebomb that caused me the biggest headache was "dumb motherfucker." Around the time of the 2000 presidential election, conducting a search for what we euphemistically called "DMF" brought up an online store selling George Bush campaign merchandise. As the person responsible for customer service, I held up the umbrella as crap rained down on us from outraged supporters of the president. I got in touch with the Bush website people and explained that it was not an intentional slight by Google. Then I drafted a message saying the same thing for our customer service representatives to use as a reply to users. The best reply, though, came from someone already familiar with the issue.

A couple of months after the Supreme Court ended the 2000 election, Eric Schmidt invited his friend Al Gore to speak at Google about the campaign, the Internet, the environment, and whatever else Gore wanted to talk about.

Gore zipped into TGIF on one of our many electric scooters. "I just rode in from Washington," he said to approving laughs as he dismounted and took the microphone. "You may know me as the man who used to be 'the next president of the United States,'" he joked, garnering thunderous applause. When question time came, a Googler asked Gore if he was familiar with the Bush Googlebomb. He was.

"So what's your opinion about it?" came the follow-up question.

Gore paused and looked around a bit, as if checking for camera crews or reporters. There weren't any, though the room was packed with Googlers sitting in folding chairs and standing on cubicle desks to get a better look.

"Well," he said at last, with a completely neutral expression, "I do believe you might have discovered artificial intelligence."

---

* In 2004 a query on Microsoft's "improved" MSN search engine for "more evil than Satan" brought up both Google and Microsoft, but a search for "evil corporation" went directly to Microsoft's own homepage.

Users would orchestrate many more Googlebombs in the years to come, from "French military victories," which led to a fake Google error page that read, "Your search — 'French military victories' — did not match any documents. Did you mean French military *defeats?*" to "out of touch management," which, immediately before Google's IPO, directed users to the page on Google.com featuring profiles of our own executive team. That alone should prove to cynics that Google does not manipulate its search results or inject bias on a case-by-case basis.

Wait a Minute Mr. Postman

Each time a Googlebomb detonated it blew my schedule to hell. I'd have to drop everything to smother the flame wars that might damage our brand. User support cast ominous shadows across my world, but the poor grunt who faced the unending deluge of incoming missives was our sole customer service rep, Max Erdstein.

Fresh out of Stanford with a degree in history, Max had offered to do whatever needed to be done at Google, which initially meant working on writing projects like the Google Friends newsletter and responding to user email. After Cindy restructured the marketing group, Max moved into my world, dragging behind him responsibility for Google's rickety user-support department, which at the time consisted of Max, a laptop, and an off-the-shelf copy of Microsoft Outlook.

Max never envisioned customer service becoming an omnivorous blob consuming all his time, but soon he found himself responding robotically to more than a thousand emails a day from users around the world. Crushed under the load, he could do little more than succinctly reply, "Thanks! Keep on Googlin!" Non-English emails presented the biggest problem. We had no idea if people wanted to praise us or harangue us. We tried using off-the-web translation software, but it left us more confused than when we began.

Meanwhile, there were rumblings from sales VP Omid that supporting advertisers and search-services customers should be a higher priority. Could Max help with that, too? After all, unlike users, these people were actually paying us. Max was emptying an ocean with a teaspoon. As the backlog of unanswered emails began to swell, Sergey offered a useful perspective. "Why do we need to answer user email anyway?" he wanted to know.

To Sergey's thinking, responding to user questions was inefficient. If they wrote us about problems with Google, that was useful information to have. We should note the problems and fix them. That would make the users happier than if we wasted time explaining to them that we were working on the bugs. If users sent us compliments, we didn't need to write back because they already liked us. So really, wouldn't it be better not to respond at all? Or at best, maybe write some code to generate random replies that would be fine in most cases?

Given their lack of concern about unanswered email, the founders were not sympathetic to Max's distress over the monotonous and unfulfilling nature of his work. Besides, when Google started, Larry and Sergey had answered all the email themselves, and written the code, and designed the logo, and handled press inquiries. We had more resources now, so how could anyone complain, given that we all had such small shards of responsibility in the wake of the big bang that was Google's conversion from a two-person project to a full-fledged corporation?

Eventually I realized that the answer, as always, was in the data. In the spring of 2000, I had Max start quantifying how many emails per day he received and responded to. I plotted the data on a chart and estimated Max's maximum capacity, then extrapolated how many Max-equivalents we would need to answer all email within forty-eight hours of receiving it. The data clearly showed that we would require at least one more Max as well as better tools for managing the email itself.

Reluctantly, and under pressure from Omid, eStaff gave us a green light to hire another customer service representative (CSR) and to buy an electronic customer-relationship-management (CRM) system. I immediately began the search for both, a task that took on increased urgency that summer, when Max moved into his new role helping advertisers generate better returns from their AdWords campaigns. The sales team nicknamed him "The Maximizer."

I had tried contractors even before Max left, but the generic office temps who showed up couldn't grasp the subtleties of search protocols or master the intricacies of our epistolary style. Max trolled Stanford's campus networks and landed a couple of prize candidates, including Anna Linderum, an international student who donated her time because we couldn't legally pay her, and Rob Rakove, a poly sci major. They quickly mastered the art of providing intelligent answers to befuddled users.

Meanwhile, after five months of rejecting applicants, I hired Denise

Griffin in October 2000 to fill the role of full-time CSR. Surprisingly few candidates had the temperament and writing skills necessary to represent Google with the grace and grammar the job required. Denise had the requisite ability, a Berkeley degree, and community service experience that Sergey found appealing.

The day Denise started we were three thousand emails behind. Issues kept popping up like the methane fires dotting the grass-covered landfill down the street. A porn star desperately needed us to remove her home phone number from our index. History buffs claiming Israel had sunk a U.S. warship in 1967 objected to being classified as a hate group in our directory. Turks were outraged by an ad about genocide targeted to the keyword "Turkey." And those were the minor complaints. We were reaching the limits of what our Outlook software could handle, and user questions were becoming more complex and time-consuming to answer.

Our email output slowed from Sergey's remembered (and perhaps unconsciously optimized) personal response rate of one per minute to a more languid pace of one every three minutes. Of course, Denise and Rob couldn't pull answers out of their heads as Sergey had, but in his eyes that didn't excuse lower productivity. Then Cindy found some week-old unanswered emails that could have resulted in negative press.

"The situation is getting out of control," she warned me. "You need to get it in hand."

You know that dream where you're trying to run away from some menacing figure and your legs turn into melted marshmallows? I felt my feet mired in the sticky mess of text that was our user base asking for help.

I went back to the only solution that ever worked. I argued the numbers with Salar and convinced him to support a push for another CSR for our group. Omid put in a separate request for a service person for advertising clients. With two additional staffers, we would be able to make progress for at least a couple of months, until the volume of mail doubled again. Prompted by Salar, Sergey agreed to let us hire another CSR. *One* CSR, that is, to handle both the user support and advertising jobs. It wouldn't be enough, but it was better than nothing.

Since so much incoming mail was not in English, I sent out a note asking Googlers to list their language abilities in hopes of tapping in-house translation skills.

The languages spoken by staff included Arabic, Chinese, Hindi,

Indonesian, Japanese, Hebrew, Romanian, and Swedish, but that didn't help me. Engineers didn't have the time or inclination to sift through foreign-language spam all day looking for urgent messages. We needed better technology to sort the mail, store common responses, and send bulk replies, but choosing the right customer-relationship-management (CRM) software required engineering skill to evaluate the efficiency and security of the code we'd be installing. Engineering project manager Mieke Bloomfield agreed to help me separate the good bits from the bad.

Mieke and I quickly learned that Google's trivial needs didn't impress big CRM firms. They focused on companies managing extensive sales operations and providing product support for thousands of paying customers. We didn't need to identify potential big spenders, and we had no desire to create buyer profiles. We just wanted a tool that could track basic metrics around volume and response rates. And we didn't want to spend a ton of money. Unfortunately, it was a seller's market.

Kana, which Wall Street dubbed the leader in the CRM space, had just split its stock at an adjusted high of about fifteen hundred dollars a share. Wall Street believed CRM tools were as essential to the web economy as shovels at a gold rush, and their sellers priced them accordingly. The cheapest solution from Kana's rival eGain cost more than a hundred thousand dollars. Larry and Sergey would have preferred to write our replies longhand with quill pens rather than sink that amount into someone else's code. Nor were the vendors willing to bend very far to accommodate a small startup like ours. Any features we wanted to add could only be considered during their regular development cycle and would be incorporated only if they were beneficial for their other, more significant clients.

So we looked at second-tier firms that offered stripped-down versions we could strip down even further. After evaluating a half dozen, we settled on a year-old company I'll call "Miasma" that offered what we needed: a simple solution to routing mail, a way to store a list of responses, and support for some foreign languages. Miasma proposed to give us five seats (that is, individual user licenses) plus a one-year maintenance contract and installation at a total cost of thirty-five thousand dollars, plus travel expenses for their technicians to come and plug everything in. I thought that was relatively reasonable.

"The technology's okay, I guess," Sergey told me after seeing a live demo, "but they should pay us to implement it. They need reference clients, and we're growing very quickly. They could learn a lot from watching how our usage changes. And make sure to get two extra licenses for Larry and me. They should throw those in for free because it doesn't cost them anything and we'd be good test users."

Miasma wouldn't pay us, but they did cut their price almost in half, including five seat licenses and the cost of traveling out to install their product, contingent on our willingness to act as a reference for them (evidently Sergey's logic was not entirely unconvincing). We scheduled an install date and awaited the arrival of the technology that would simplify our lives.

Miasma's techs worked industriously to get the software up and running while training us to write rules for routing mail to the proper queues and for forwarding messages to our staff "experts" for translation or sales follow-up. Everything was going according to plan, and though we were falling even further behind during the transition period, I was confident we had put into place a scalable solution to a growing problem. We said goodbye to the install team, certain that we would be caught up on our email in no time.

The problems at first were minor. Our engineering "experts" couldn't read our rich-text-formatted attachments on their Linux-based machines, so they couldn't help us answer technical questions. Some of the routing rules were unpredictable, and everyone who contacted us received multiple automated responses. Then, one day, a help request I sent to Miasma's own corporate mail system bounced back as undeliverable. That seemed a touch foreboding.

Miasma's staffers were eager to help when we finally got in touch with them, and we continued plugging in patches as needs arose. They fixed reporting so we could see how far behind we were and gave us access to the system remotely via the Internet. We added RAM to the server sitting under Denise's desk and learned how to restart it when it froze, as it did frequently. Though Miasma improved our organization of email, it ran slowly and required repeated manual intervention. With the new technology completely installed, we weren't responding to users any more quickly than we had been before.

We fell further and further behind. I checked the queue one day and saw we had more than ten thousand unanswered emails. Miasma's tech staff came back to tweak and tune and reboot the server, but — after months of fits and starts — we gave up. We declared email bankruptcy, archived the unanswered mail, and started over with a blank slate. We were able to normalize our system after a few months, but we never approached the level of rapid response we had envisioned. Each week as I reported our anemic numbers, I felt the pressure to make things work better.

If Max had been able to answer x number of emails without Miasma, Salar asked, shouldn't Denise and Rob be able to answer some multiple of x emails with the new tool in place? Why hire more reps if we weren't getting everything out of the people we had? I knew the problem wasn't the people answering the email, it was the increase in complex queries and foreign-language messages and the built-in limitations of the software we were using.

I had put myself in a precarious position. My chosen vendor's product had failed to improve throughput and instead hampered our ability to maintain the level we had achieved previously. It didn't matter that Larry and Sergey had liked the software enough to consider using it for their personal email. It didn't matter that budget constraints precluded a more established supplier. It didn't matter that the vendor seemed committed to whacking the moles as they popped their problematic heads out to taunt us. We were leaking productivity, and it was my mess to clean up.

Denise and Rob worked diligently over long hours to clear our backlog, but if they answered easy questions, the response time for more technical questions grew too long. If they focused on technical questions, overall response rates dropped, because more time was needed to find the answers. Foreign-language email just languished in limbo.

This went on for a full year, with issues popping up and emails flying back and forth to Miasma tech support in India. Finally Miasma announced they would deliver a full upgrade to their software to fix all our problems and make rainbows shine across our network and unicorns dance on our desks. First, though, we needed to walk through the fire of a major assault on user support.

Post Apocalypse

It was November 2000 when I first learned that Google was buying another company. The acquisition, code-named "Yogi," was an online archive of Usenet posts known as Deja News. We would announce the deal the following February.

If you're a Usenet aficionado, you'll probably take issue with what I say about it here, so why not skip the next paragraph and avoid the heartburn? Of course you won't. If you like Usenet, you live for heartburn.

In a nutshell, Usenet is a computer network that preceded the World Wide Web. Founded in 1980, it provided a place for academics and scientists to share information with colleagues by posting messages in newsgroups on an electronic bulletin board. Newsgroups were divided into subject categories such as "comp." for computers or "sci." for science or "rec." for recreation. The name coming after the period indicated the subgroup, as in "sci.research.AIDS." Over time, Usenet devolved from its noble purpose to reflect the common concerns and issues of our times, with groups like "rec.arts.movies.slasher" and an explosion in binary files, which contained encoded software, music, and images since reposted on websites requiring a credit card and proof of age. Moreover, the nature of the dialogue on Usenet changed from dry academic discussions to heated polemics on politics and religion and a multitude of other contentious issues, giving birth to such terms as "flame mail" and "trolling."

Deja News was home to a continuously updated archive of five hundred million of these posts going back to 1995, including such classics as the announcement of AltaVista's launch and the first mention of Google. Unfortunately, Deja News could no longer afford to maintain the service. In fact, it couldn't even provide access to all the data it had archived. Desperate, it came to Google, seeking a way to keep their data from sinking forever into obscurity. Recognizing the value of the content, Larry and Sergey threw them a lifeline, offering to take the archive, clean it up, make it more searchable, and host it going forward. Google already had plans to launch its own Usenet site at groups.google.com, so the timing was fortuitous. Still, it was an act of mercy and everyone involved knew it.

The handoff happened quickly — too quickly for Google to do much more than launch a stopgap service based on a separate, recently acquired archive of Usenet posts, while our engineers organized the Deja data and built a better system to deliver it. The interim site wouldn't contain all the posts back to 1995 as Deja's had: it would only offer posts dating back a year. Users wouldn't be able to browse through different groups (though they could search them) or post new messages. Most significantly, they wouldn't be able to "nuke" or remove posts they had already written, even if they had deleted them previously (Deja had suppressed display of deleted comments, but never actually expunged them from the old database). Some Deja users were about to rediscover the offensive and embarrassing notes they had written while angry or drunk, thought twice about, and destroyed. Or at least believed they had destroyed.

I could smell the crap clouds gathering.

I drafted copy for Deja's former homepage and an FAQ explaining that Google was engaged in "brute force mud-wrestling with gigabytes of unruly data" to reintroduce a new and improved Usenet archive. I made it clear the effort was ongoing and things would get better soon.

On Monday, February 12, 2001, the old Deja.com went away and Google's interim site went live. Within seconds, outrage overflowed from clogged limbic systems across the network and flooded my inbox. User support began responding with the soothing language I had supplied, acknowledging that we had "received a number of questions and comments" and letting our angry customers know that we understood "the inconvenience that this has caused." Cindy assured me the tone was perfect. I had to agree, and as we were both professional word-smiths, I assumed that would be the end of it.

It wasn't. Deja's stung fans reacted as if we'd snatched honeycomb out of their hive with a big hairy bear claw. They swarmed us. Their emails overloaded our fragile CRM system all Monday afternoon and just kept coming. We couldn't answer the specialized questions that related only to Usenet, and our generic responses just agitated users. Our mailboxes filled with mud and fire.

Larry and Sergey were surprised by Deja's ungrateful users. We had rescued a valuable Internet resource from the ash heap of history at our own expense and committed to launching an improved archive with access to far more data than Deja had ever offered. "What's wrong with these people?" they wondered. They wouldn't have to go far to find out; within days, disgruntled Usenetters were literally knocking on Google's front door to complain.

"OK, you guys are in *damage control mode, act like it!!!*" screamed one user. "So far your attitude is real smug." He went on to compare us to Firestone, whose fatally flawed tires were the subject of a safety recall, though as far as I know no one died from lack of access to three-year-old posts in rec.arts.sf.starwars.

Wayne Rosing, our new head of engineering, shook off the assault, saying, "What matters is whether we're doing the right thing, and if people don't understand that now, they will eventually come to understand it."

It was a lesson that would shape Google's attitude toward the public from that point on. Sure, we had upset people with MentalPlex, but at least some of us conceded their kvetching might have had cause. With Deja, we were clearly on the side of the angels. The public just didn't get it. Even when we worked our asses off, spent our own cash, and tried to do something good for them, they bellowed and ranted, bitched and moaned. Since users were being so unreasonable, we could safely ignore their complaints. That suited our founders just fine — they always went with their guts anyway.

I've been asked if Larry and Sergey were truly brilliant. I can't speak to their IQs, but I saw with my own eyes that their vision burned so brightly it scorched everything that stood in its way. The truth was so obvious that they felt no need for the niceties of polite society when bringing their ideas to life. Why slow down to explain when the value of what they were doing was so self-evident that people would eventually see it for themselves?

That attitude was both Google's strength and its Achilles' heel. From launching a better search engine in an overcrowded field to running unscreened text in AdWords, the success of controversial ideas gave momentum to the conviction that initial public opinion was often irrelevant.

By the end of the year we proved our intent had always been honorable, rolling out not just the features users had clamored for but an archive that extended back twenty years instead of just the five Deja had offered.[*] This was almost single-handedly the work of Michael Schmitt, an engineer who took it upon himself to conduct a global search to track down tapes and CD backups of the earliest Usenet posts and the hardware that could read them. He recovered for posterity the first Usenet mention of Microsoft, Tim Berners-Lee's first posted reference to the "World Wide Web," and Marc Andreessen's

---

[*] Though we did kill BigMailBox, Deja's legacy email service, in June 2001, telling its users that "while Google maintained this service during the transition of the Usenet archive from Deja, offering email does not fit our core mission of giving users access to all information online." Well. Not then anyway.

public disclosure of the Mosaic web browser that would become Netscape.

"If there were justice in the world," wrote a formerly disappointed Usenetter, "you guys would be rich and Bill Gates would be standing in line waiting for watery soup." Not that Larry and Sergey needed affirmation that they had made the right call, but still, it was nice to hear.

CHAPTER 15

Managers in Hot Tubs
and in Hot Water

A MONTH AFTER WE bought Deja, a hundred and forty Googlers packed up overnight bags, boarded a fleet of buses, and headed for the hills. It was time for Google's annual ski trip.

The ritual started when Google was just eight people and Larry very cautiously drove a rented van to Lake Tahoe while Sergey, Craig, Ray, and Harry killed time playing logic games in the back and Heather struggled to stay awake. The group saved $2.50 a day by designating Larry the only driver, which was a given anyway because Larry wasn't about to put his life in anyone else's hands.

I didn't go with the group in 2000, even though frequent reminders from Heather made it clear that the ski trip was not optional. The trip was a teambuilding exercise and thus only for staff members. No family. That didn't sit well with Kristen, who had already seen enough at Google to have reservations. The tipping point may have been the day she came to lunch and noticed an attractive twenty-something woman whose thong underwear was all too visible through her sheer harem pants.

"Who's that?" my wife whispered directly in my ear as the woman slid her tray past the entrées toward the desserts.

"Oh, just one of the engineers," I replied. "She rides a motorcycle," I offered helpfully.

So when I let Kristen know that Google required my presence on the slopes at Lake Tahoe for an employee-only bonding trip, what she heard was, "Please stay at home with our three children while I head out with a busload of adrenaline-charged, hormone-drenched post-adolescents for three days of bacchanalian binge-drinking, substance abuse, and room-key swapping."

She got it mostly right. I know, because the next year I convinced her my career would be damaged if I didn't go along. Google paid all our travel expenses, including chartered buses and food and lodging at the elegant Resort at Squaw Creek and gave us each a fifty-dollar stipend to spend on ski lessons. It wouldn't cost me anything, and it was only for a couple of days. Please honey? Please?

We shared accommodations to save money and I roomed with Bay and our newly hired attorney Kulpreet Rana. Bay got the short straw and slept on the floor. While I'm proud to say I was so hopelessly unhip that I missed out on anything more decadent than a late-night soak in an outdoor hot tub with Larry, Salar, Urs, Omid, and a dozen other Googlers, it was clear some of my coworkers were showing less restraint.

I heard tales of excess involving not only recent college graduates but those who theoretically had the years and experience to know better. Many of these tales coincidentally began with a visit to "Charlie's Den" — the room Chef Charlie occupied with Keith from accounting and an SUV load of liquor ferried up from Mountain View. As the trip grew in scale and Charlie's hospitality grew in reputation, the party relocated to an oversized luxury suite and then a meeting room with an open bar sporting seventy-five thousand dollars' worth of booze and an ample supply of other social lubricants. Specialties of the house included herb-infused brownies and dark chocolate Goo Balls.* Out of coincidence, or perhaps the perverse humor of Heather and the HR folks managing the event, Larry's room was usually adjacent to the party plex. One year all the liquor was unloaded into Larry's suite by mistake. Larry didn't drink, though he sometimes carried a thimbleful of beer at parties to put others at ease.

"My mind is money," Larry once explained to Charlie, pointing to a bottle, "and that kills the brain."

---

* Preparation tip: don't cook the flavoring ingredient more than once, as it loses its potency that way. Just mix it with the butter and fold into the chocolate.

"I think he could spare a few brain cells," Charlie told me later.

Other members of the executive staff more willingly sacrificed bits of gray matter, and Charlie made sure their rooms were stocked with their favorite indulgences in case they didn't make it to the party down in the Den.

"It's always cool to see people let loose and have a good time," Charlie observed, confirming the opportunities for staff bonding. "Googlers really let go in ways you wouldn't have seen otherwise." He may have had in mind the toga-wearing ops guys who were only too willing to prove they were unburdened by underwear. Or maybe the sales rep who jumped on the back of another Googler, pulled off her shirt, and began whipping him with it jockey style. Or perhaps the senior manager seen crawling on all fours in the hallway, barking like an inebriated hound.

There was a pajama party with costume prizes. Larry won a bet with Sergey, Salar, and engineer Lori Park that ended with the losers jumping into an icy Lake Tahoe after dinner.

"We tried to re-create Google's 'un-corporation' attitude," Charlie explained to me, "a kind of 'fuck you' to the man, the way Google was saying that same thing to the tech industry as a whole."

Some people who visited Charlie's Den never left, crashing on the floor for the night, though that carried risks of its own, since passing out left one vulnerable to the sophomoric pranks of those still sober enough to stand. Others couldn't remember where they had fallen: one engineer woke up without his clothes and eventually discovered he'd left them at the hot tub. He sheepishly reclaimed them from the front desk. All night long, white-terry-robed figures circulated from room to room, then down to the bar or out to the boulder-shrouded spa, in Lupercalian celebration of the season.

As the company grew in size, more non-engineers participated. Many were female. The Google ski trip came to be known as a great party to crash, with live dance music from bands like the Fabulous Thunderbirds, ample alcohol, and lots of young, unattached people looking to undo the stress of Silicon Valley lives. Uninvited guests were legion.

I uninvited myself after my first trip, and found myself working uninterrupted in the Plex as phones went unanswered all around me. I walked interview candidates down empty hallways and ate pizza I ordered in for the few of us still around. Ski week became my time to clear my inbox and catch up on lagging projects.

By 2007 the size of the company made the annual ski trip impossible, and Google ended it in favor of smaller outings to more family-friendly locales like Disneyland. That was probably a good thing, though I'll always cherish the scars I earned at broomball* and the camaraderie of shared experiences on the slopes and in the lodge. My warm feelings, however, stop at the hot tub and chats by the fireplace, and accordingly may not be as heated as those kindled by some of my friskier colleagues. You'll have to ask them about that.

Surprisingly Good News

"Table! Table! Table!" chanted the crowd at TGIF.

At the front of the room, Omid Kordestani, head of sales, grinned broadly, tugged at the leg of his black Armani slacks, and climbed onto a conference table while holding a microphone in one hand. The crowd erupted in cheers.

"Omid! Omid! Omid!" we chanted.

Omid was very popular at Google. He always came to TGIF prepared with a smile, a joke, and a stack of numbers that led to a very happy conclusion.

As soon as we had an OKR process in place in early 2000, Larry and Sergey gave Omid a goal: he should book half a million dollars in ad revenue by the end of the first quarter. My assumption was that Larry and Sergey wanted to make Omid spontaneously combust. It was, after all, only the first period in which our original advertising program had been active (well before AdWords had launched). Larry and Sergey didn't count toward Omid's goal any leads or promises of revenue that might not materialize; they only cared about actual dollars in the bank. Omid had fewer than a half dozen people in his entire department, and Google was unknown outside Silicon Valley. We had engineering issues and incomplete tools and flaky infrastructure, and our competition was cutting deals at deep discounts.

Still, Omid gave indications that the numbers looked good when he

---

* Hockey played on ice with a tennis ball and short-handled brooms — while wearing street shoes.

presented his updates at our weekly TGIFs. It wasn't until the end of the quarter, however, that we saw just how good-looking the numbers actually were.

Omid stood up and, with classic showman's timing, talked about the difficulty of reaching the team's aggressive goal just months after launching a new product. He showed charts with illegible footnotes and spreadsheets filled with numbers too tiny to read. With all the challenges his team faced, he told us, we had been lucky to secure any new revenue at all. Then, with a grin and a flourish, he revealed that Google had booked six hundred and thirty-six thousand dollars for the quarter. That revenue was already in-house. The sales team had secured more than a million dollars in overall revenue commitments, putting the company on track for a great second quarter as well. The applause was instantaneous and prolonged. Our salespeople, I thought, were amazing.

Three months later, Omid and his team beat their goal again.

The third time around, we started calling Omid a "sandbagger." Sergey mockingly accused him of underestimating what his team could achieve, even though his goal had increased by leaps and bounds each quarter. Omid feigned shock and denied any culpability. We all took up the charge, though some new employees didn't understand why we were harassing the person who had given us such great news. It became a TGIF tradition. In Omid's absence one week, Sergey gave the sales report. He pretended to look over Omid's spreadsheets and materials carefully.

"Let me summarize," he said at last, looking over toward the sales team, imitating Omid. "We're sandbagging." The room cracked up.

The table had its own back story.

When our weekly meeting outgrew the hallway outside Larry and Sergey's office, we relocated to Charlie's café downstairs. The café's acoustics made it hard to hear, so for his presentation, Omid climbed on a chair, then stepped up onto a long lunch table. He had just concluded his remarks when the table gave way. There was a loud crash as the metal legs spontaneously folded and an involuntary "Ohhhhh!" from the crowd as Omid found himself momentarily standing on air. With surprising agility, he executed an acrobatic twist and landed squarely on the toes of his black Italian shoes. The room erupted with applause.

"And he nails the dismount!" I shouted.

After that, chants of "Table! Table!" greeted Omid at every TGIF, and he gamely obliged. Eventually someone placed a burlap bag filled with sand on top of the table, and Omid, impeccably attired, planted his loafers firmly upon it to let us know that yes, despite the overwhelming odds, his heroic sales team had again delivered a record-breaking quarter. For Google's shareholder employees, the story never got old in the telling.

Because Google was so forthcoming with its financial information, not only at TGIF but also on MOMA (the intranet), there was never an inflection point at which we suddenly discovered we possessed wealth beyond our wildest dreams. Anyone could check the revenue and expense figures and do a few projections. One day I calculated our approximate earnings-per-share ratio, then used Yahoo's current multiple to determine what a reasonable stock price might be if the company were being publicly traded. Then I multiplied the number of shares I held by that value.

"It's not real money," I repeated to myself. "It's not real money." We had no CEO. We had no CFO. No one was making plans to go public. I went back to work, but I hummed a happy tune as I did so.

A CEO? Now IPO?

"Schwim? You have a question?" Sergey asked, knowing full well what the question would be.

"Yes," said Schwim, standing up at the front of the TGIF meeting in February 2001. The Nooglers had been introduced. Larry and Sergey had reviewed the news of the week. Omid had completed his slide show. Now it was time for Q and A.

"What's the status of the CEO search?" Schwim wanted to know. It was the same question he asked every week. We all were aware there was a checklist of items to be completed before the company could go public and our stock options would have real value. A CEO was on the list. Also a Chief Financial Officer.

Sergey paused for dramatic effect. "We're making progress," he said with a serious look. It was the same answer he gave every week.

When I joined in 1999, many of us assumed that Google would be public within a year. We weren't obsessed with the idea of an IPO, but it was the height of the dot-com era, and that's what startups did after they'd been around for six months. Larry and Sergey didn't seem in any hurry. They felt no urgency to hire a CEO despite the board's prodding. Sometimes they would make a dismissive remark about a candidate they had interviewed. They didn't give names, just vague disqualifications based on a lack of tech savvy or "Googleyness."

At TGIF on March 23, 2001, Larry and Sergey introduced two Nooglers to the assembled staff: Dirk Aguilar as an international advertising analyst and Eric Schmidt as chairman of Google's board of directors. It was assumed that Eric would be made Google's CEO as soon as he could disentangle himself from his responsibilities as CEO of Novell. I was thrilled, not because I knew Eric and felt he would lead us to search dominance, but because the long wait was finally over. That light we could see at the end of the tunnel was Google's ticker symbol circling the NASDAQ sign in Times Square.*

When I learned that Google had hired a "corporate" CEO, I allowed myself a glimmer of hope. Surely someone who had worked for large, competitive companies like Novell and Sun Microsystems would get the importance of strong marketing. Maybe he would see branding as a powerful tool for claiming market share. Maybe he would want to tell the Google story in new and creative ways around the world. Maybe he would feed Cindy's anemic staff, build my spindly budget, and transform our ninety-seven-pound department into a five-hundred-pound gorilla. Maybe he would cure lepers and help the blind to see. Who knew? I did. Larry and Sergey would never hire someone like that.

"I don't believe in trade shows," Eric informed Cindy and me at a get-acquainted meeting he set up shortly after coming onboard. There was a new sheriff in town and our days of profligate spending and freewheeling excess had ended. Eric's ideas about marketing mirrored those of our founders, only with a paranoid edge sharpened by experience.

"I've seen how the budgets for industry shows grow and grow," Eric regaled us, "until they're so bloated you're paying for warehouses full of booths and furniture and trucks to haul them around. We're not going to do that."

"We're not going to spend money on mass-media marketing," he continued. "No TV spots or big magazine spreads. And everything you buy needs to be on a purchase order signed off by me personally."

I sat back, stunned by the implication that we were an overweight

* Bart Woytowicz, the advertising operations manager, inevitably asked at TGIF how close we were to an IPO. He appeared at the 2003 Halloween party wearing only a barrel to signify the poverty inflicted on him by Google's arthritic grip on the process of becoming a public company.

cost center that needed to be taught self-discipline. We had never done a trade show. We had one booth — a crappy pop-up frame that traveled around in a tube with pictures we stuck on using Velcro. We hadn't done any mass-market advertising, other than banner trades and our buy on Yahoo. Eric obviously didn't know anything about our marketing department, but had come in swinging his big stick to knock us down to size. Stunned, I was, but not surprised. As our new CEO, Eric wanted to control costs and to lay down the law his first day in Dodge. And I also wasn't surprised that Larry and Sergey hadn't bothered telling him our marketing group wasn't like others he might have worked with, or, if they had, that he hadn't believed them.

We nodded our heads and interjected where we could, muttering amens and hosannas when he let us. He seemed to hear some of it. When we let him know that Google t-shirts were our biggest expense, he smiled approvingly.

"That's fine. Keep doing that. If someone likes our product enough to want to wear our brand, we should do everything we can to make it possible. And it's great for staff morale to have everyone decked out in the company logo." He would soon be signing off on expenditures for preshrunk cotton in the seven-figure range.

Cindy and I agreed we needed to bring Eric up to speed. I drafted a memo laying out our brand strategy and listing our guiding principles:

- PR and word of mouth work better than ads.
- Paid ads work against our brand. Focus on the "joy of discovery."*
- We'll grow faster getting current users to search more than by mass marketing.
- All our promotions must include a way to measure success.
- Product interaction is, and must remain, the primary branding experience.
- User retention efforts should center on improving UI and user support.

---

* I believed users felt a deeper connection if they learned about Google via news reports or friends and thus felt they had discovered it themselves. Paid advertising depersonalized that experience because "the product" was clearly being sold to many people simultaneously. Danny Sullivan, the noted search guru, described it this way in July 2000: "When I speak about search engines to groups and mention Google, something unusual happens to some members of the audience. They smile and nod, in the way you do when you feel like you've found a secret little getaway that no one else knows about. And each time I speak, I see more and more people smiling and nodding this way, pleased to have discovered Google." Danny Sullivan, Searchenginewatch.com/2207571, "The Search Engine Report," July 5, 2000.

I dropped the memo into Eric's inbox and copied Larry and Sergey. The response was deafening, as in, I must have gone deaf because I didn't hear anything. I took that as a good sign. We received no more unsolicited feedback from Eric on how to spend our budget. Apparently he realized that we were doing the right thing. Or, more likely, he figured that if we screwed up, our impact on the company's overall health would amount to little more than a sneeze. Or maybe he was just focused on our number one priority: finding women.

"Larry and Sergey did research," HR senior manager Stacy Sullivan told me, "and they believed that having a good gender mix created a healthier work environment. For the few women that you had, [hiring more women] made their lives so much better. They had a community."

It's true that male-skewed tech companies sometimes devolved into frat-boy funhouses, and I never doubted Larry and Sergey's commitment to hiring technically adept women. However, I often wondered whether the ideal of a "healthier work environment" wasn't driven by our founders' own deeper need to lead lives that contained more than code. At the *Mercury News* we had once run an ad in which we assured readers: "In some parts of the world, the language of love is not Java." Google was not one of those places. Hiring more women would not only forestall a Neanderthal culture, it would increase the odds of socialization and ultimately continuation of the species. Given that Larry and Sergey more or less lived at the office, it hardly surprised anyone that each of them dated members of the staff. It would have been more of a shock if they had actually met women they deemed acceptably intelligent and not recruited them to Google just so they could see them on occasion.

Whatever the rationale, I discovered that the emphasis on gender equality was real.

"Why don't we have Google t-shirts for women?" Sergey demanded of me after a female visitor left the office with our standard extra-large men's t-shirt. He was as upset as I'd ever seen him. When a woman in France chastised him about American companies and their enormously oversized t-shirts that no French woman would wear, he insisted we address the problem once and for all. I ordered women's shirts — more than I thought we could ever give away — but we couldn't keep them in stock. I didn't understand why they were so popular, given our limited female staff, until my cousin thanked me for the one I had sent her and added, "They're quite see-through. Was that intentional?"

Missed Management

I saw Eric often in his first weeks. He seemed to spend much of his time roaming the halls with a bemused look on his face, as if he couldn't believe he'd actually joined this company populated with big rubber balls and lava lamps and scruffy animals sleeping on couches — sometimes with the pets they had brought to work lying next to them.

Usually when I saw Eric he had company. One day it was Governor Howard Dean. More than once it was Al Gore. Gore apparently had plenty of free time on his hands. I ran into him everywhere.

"Good afternoon, Mr. Vice President," I said to the tall man standing at the urinal next to me as I took a break between meetings. That experience pretty much dissipated any residual sense of awe.

When Eric and Al stood outside my office chatting about Gore's interest in creating a new independent TV network, I ever so gently nudged the door closed with my foot. I had work to do.

I wasn't sure about Eric. No one seemed to know what he was doing, since Larry and Sergey were still making all the decisions. Other than the purchase-order edict, we didn't hear much from him for a while, perhaps because he didn't officially add the title CEO until August 2001.

Eric did add transparency to the decision-making process, forcing discussions in public meetings so everyone could see the sausage being made, even if we didn't always like the ingredients stuffed into it.

"In a culture which is consensus driven," Eric explained to reporter Fred Vogelstein in November 2005, "the trick is to have everybody participating in the decision and make sure everybody has been heard."* That wasn't true at Google before Eric came onboard. As one drifting into a more distant orbit around the stars of our universe, I appreciated Eric's efforts to shed light on a process that all too often took everything in and let nothing out. That support for transparency led me to view him as an ally, a friend of marketing, and a voice of reason.

A month before Eric could implement his ideas as CEO, Google's top-down decision-making reached its peak — and its nadir. Larry decided that July to reorganize the engineering group. It didn't go well.

---

* Fred Vogelstein, Wired.com, April 9, 2007; http://www.wired.com/epicenter/2007/04/my_other_interv/.

Our founders cut bureaucracy the way they cut costs — with a cleaver instead of a paring knife.

Larry trusted his newly minted product managers (PMs), Salar and Susan, and the two new hires, John "J.P." Piscitello and Pearl Renaker, who joined them in April 2001. They all reported directly to him. He was less happy about the half-dozen project managers who had been working with engineering for months. Project managers created time-lines, allocated resources, and prodded engineers to ensure products shipped on schedule. They conducted performance reviews and kept people like me from bugging the technical staff with requests that might slow things down. They also acted as a buffer between the engineers and the executives, or as systems engineer Ben Smith described it, "shielded their employees from random shit that came from above." In a company like Google, standing between the founders and the engineers did not earn you a sash and a spot on the homecoming float.

I liked the project managers. More important, I needed them. They were our contacts for any task requiring technical resources, such as evaluating vendors or tracking the performance of our banner ads. The project managers assigned engineers to work with us — engineers who were under great pressure and would not normally consider a market-ing task important enough to add to their to-do lists.

Wayne Rosing joined Google in late 2000, and in January 2001 took over as VP of engineering, replacing Urs Hölzle, who, as the first Google Fellow, went off to solve large-scale operations issues caused by our rapid growth (things like energy consumption and efficiency across hosting centers). Wayne had an avuncular manner and a Charlie Brownish appearance that he subverted by occasionally sporting a di-amond-stud earring or dying his hair bright red. He brought with him decades of experience in running engineering groups, including Sun Microsystems Laboratories, which he had founded. Wayne discovered that Google engineers largely controlled their own destinies, some-times acting on — and sometimes ignoring — priorities that flowed from Larry and Sergey in an ever-shifting spectrum of urgency.

The company grapevine soon grew heavy with rumors that big or-ganizational changes were coming, fermenting the staff, who whispered nervously about layoffs and what that would signify at a company not yet out of its infancy. Still, when Wayne called an all-engineering meet-ing in July 2001 and announced a reorganization, most of the engineers were caught by surprise. So were the project managers, who learned in public that their jobs no longer existed.

When the announcement was made, there was audible grumbling among the assembled engineers. They generally respected the project managers and felt they had a real role to play. And they objected to the idea of anyone's dismissal by public firing squad.

To stave off open revolt, Larry stood at the front of the room and laid out all the things he wasn't happy about in the engineering management system, starting with the idea that non-engineers were supervising those who knew more about the technology than they did. The remarks stung the project managers, some of whom felt it was a personal repudiation, especially since Larry had not raised the issues with them individually in advance of the meeting.

"It sucked," one of the project managers told me later. "I felt humiliated by it. Larry said in front of the company that we didn't need managers, and he talked about what he didn't like about us. He said things that hurt a lot of people."

The grumbling got much louder. "I yelled at Larry," engineer Ron Dolin admitted, "because he said that the managers they were planning to lay off weren't doing a good job. And I said that this was no place to give a performance evaluation. Laying these people off was completely ridiculous, and the nature of the announcement was totally unprofessional."

"I did my best to advise that there is true value in management," Stacy Sullivan recalls, "and you can set a tone by how you manage this. And Eric said, 'Let them try this.' Wayne said, 'Let them try it, it's their company.' It bothered me. We tried to give input — me, Omid, Urs. But in the end, hopefully it was a lesson learned for Larry and Sergey."

The solution that Larry wanted was to have all the engineers report directly to Wayne. While it was positioned as a way of streamlining the engineering structure, most of those I talked with thought it was really about Larry's priorities not being addressed.

"Larry and Sergey had certain things they wanted worked on," Gmail creator Paul Buchheit explained, "and there were these standing groups that were making up their own things and not doing whatever it was Larry and Sergey wanted." For example, Larry wanted to scan books. Many, many books. Every book in the Library of Congress. But no one seemed interested in undertaking such a wildly ambitious project. With the engineers operating as autonomous units under the protection of their project managers, Larry found himself increasingly frustrated.

Howard Gobioff was convinced that "this was about people getting between Larry and Sergey and the engineers. At a time when the organization was small enough that the founders still wanted to be very hands on. It was very badly handled. Most of the engineers were pissed because we liked our managers. They were non-technical, so they lacked delusions that they knew better than we did."

Urs, characteristically, blamed himself. "What caused it was my inexperience at managing," he told me, "and Larry being very good at recognizing the long-term conflict that created." Urs had believed his engineers would cover Google's coding needs, so he probed potential project managers for organizational ability and tested their people skills instead of their technical knowledge.

"So . . . what I underestimated," he went on, "is that managers always make judgment calls. They have to in order to function. If you're in a highly technical area, you can't make good judgment calls if you're not highly technical yourself. We changed at that point our strategy for hiring managers — away from coordination to saying that what matters most is technical leadership."

Larry recognized the problem sooner than Urs did, but neither had the experience to make the transition graceful and painless. Instead, Larry just did what came naturally. The system didn't work, so he rebooted it.

"I can't think of anything that people at Google were ever so upset about — at least in engineering," Paul Bucheit recalled years later. "People had some sense of ownership of the company, that it was this big happy family. And all of a sudden, some of your friends were kicked off the island. You're like, 'This isn't what I thought it was. I thought we were all in it together, and we just decided to get rid of these people.'"

At most companies, the notion of an engineering head having hundreds of direct reports would be ludicrous, but because he believed Google engineers were self-directed, Wayne just did away with the management layer between him and them. He divided the engineers into teams of three, with each team having a technical lead who was an engineer, not someone hired to manage.

The catch was that each team would also have a manager assigned from Larry's new product organization. It was a not-so-subtle introduction of a true product-management system. The project managers who had covered the engineers' backs had been replaced by Larry's trusted lieutenants, who would be looking over their shoulders.

"You could do a lot of stuff with tech leads," search quality expert Ben Gomes explained to me, "because of the people we hired. Anywhere else, having three or four hundred people report to one person would have been insane. Yet it worked reasonably well — for a while. And then at some point it didn't work."

Ultimately, the project managers were spared. Urs absorbed most of them into his operations area. But the angst unleashed by the reorg did not fade quickly.

When the dust settled, all hundred and thirty engineers reported directly to Wayne. The bureaucracy was dead. There was no hierarchy. There were no in-depth performance reviews. Engineers were on their own, independent entities, connected only to the other members of their teams and tenuously tethered by PMs to the central organization. Their direct interaction with Larry happened mainly at product review. Wayne took to holding weekly meetings and to walking through the cube farms on a regular basis to ensure that he had face time with individual engineers and that they were able to approach him with issues that concerned them.

It was an engineer's dream come true or a bit of a nightmare, depending on whom you asked. No clueless pointy-haired boss could get in the way and screw things up, but there were no clear signals from above about what was important and what was urgent and what was both. Groups struggled for resources and fought redundancy. Some engineers wanted more feedback on what they were doing and how well they were doing it, and others wondered about opportunities for advancement.

The true significance of the reorg would not be immediately apparent, because shortly after we began rebuilding our world, the rest of the world fell apart.

CHAPTER 16

Is New York Alive?

A S I DROVE to work on September 11, 2001, my mind was on
Ask Jeeves. Late the night before, Larry had sent around a *Wall
Street Journal* article announcing that our competitor was buying Teoma, a promising new search engine. That worried me. The Jeeves
brand was strong, though their search technology couldn't compare to
Google's. If they actually improved it, they might become a formidable
player in the industry.

On the car radio, I heard something about a plane crash in New York
City. I envisioned a Piper Cub that had been sightseeing and gotten too
close to a skyscraper. And then they were talking about another plane.
Another plane had flown into the World Trade Center. Jet planes, filled
with people. The World Trade Center was burning. People were jumping out of windows. Other planes were missing. No one knew what was
going on.

By the time I got to work, the TV was on in the blue conference
room. A couple of engineers sat transfixed, bowls of soggy cereal un-
touched on the table in front of them. I sat down at the table to watch
and didn't move for thirty minutes. "Oh my God," I thought. "Oh my
God." I didn't think much beyond that. It didn't occur to me that there
might be something I could do about what I was seeing. The disaster
was on the other end of the country, three thousand miles away. I never

once considered that I worked for a powerful global information service — that Google could somehow offer assistance.

Sergey walked in. He was frowning and clearly agitated. But his mind
was clear. He saw problems and it never occurred to him that we could
not help — that we *would* not help. He had been having trouble accessing online news organizations. People desperate for information had
besieged them and choked their servers. He directed us all to begin
downloading the HTML for news reports from whatever sources we
could access. He wanted the text and the images too. He had already
spoken to our webmaster Karen and to Craig, one of the few engineers
who could manually push changes out to our website. We would harvest whatever pages we could and host them on Google.com, which was
better able to handle high volumes of traffic than the *New York Times* or
CNN.com.

No one asked whether it was within our legal rights to appropriate
others' content. We didn't debate whether linking to cached news reports fit our brand, our mission, or our role as a search engine. No one
argued that the links would disrupt the aesthetics of our homepage.
People urgently needed information and couldn't get to it. We could
help them. Clearly it was our responsibility to do so.

I realized then how much Sergey saw Google as an extension of
himself. It wasn't an anonymous corporation bound by industry tradi-
tions. He had created it with Larry, and the only rules that applied were
the ones they agreed upon. As William Randolph Hearst and Joseph
Pulitzer had imposed their personalities upon their newspapers, Larry
and Sergey had imprinted Google with more than just lines of code. The
difference, though, was that Google's founders used the power of their
"press" to present not just their own viewpoints, but all viewpoints.

I went back to my desk and checked my inbox. "Is New York alive?"
read the subject line of a note from Chad.

"Oh, Christ," I thought. That's right. Google had an office in midtown Manhattan. Eric Schmidt was supposed to be visiting there that
morning. The answer came back from New York that everyone was
okay. They had evacuated their office near the Empire State Building
when the first plane hit. They were shaken and they were concerned
about friends and family.

My brain finally unfroze, and I thought about what Sergey was trying to do. I realized it would be better to host real news content than

to put up a random collection of bits downloaded from across the web. I contacted Martin Nisenholtz, head of the *New York Times*'s online service, and asked if he wanted Google to host copies of the pages they were posting. Martin was grateful for the offer but, after checking with his webmaster, declined. They thought their servers would be able to bear the load.

Meanwhile, Karen had assembled articles from the *Washington Post* and CNN and put them up on a page at Google.com/currentevents. We needed a pointer from our homepage, so I jotted down a paragraph and gave it to her. It read, "If you are looking for news, you will find the most current information on TV or radio. Many online news services are not available, because of extremely high demand. Below are links to news sites, including cached copies as they appeared earlier today."

I didn't think deeply about the implications of what I had written, which would be picked apart and sniffed at in the months to come as an admission that "new media" had not yet supplanted the old in a time of national crisis. That wasn't my intent, but I knew that our web index was not updated in real time. Searches on Google would fail to bring up any recent news, so the best we could offer users was links to news sites that appeared to be functional plus copies of static reports. It seemed obvious to me that live televised images from New York would be the most informative window on what was happening right at that moment.

The mainstream media, however, were not so quick to write off the power of Google. Within half an hour after the message went up, ABC News had asked for a link to their site. Then came MSNBC. We added them both, and in so doing exceeded the character limit for our HTML table, breaking Google's homepage. Karen and Marissa scrambled to fix it as the mood of the day swung between depression over the events, obsession with garnering every scrap of information, and stress over trying to devise more things we could do quickly to help.

We fed relevant keywords into the advertising system so that searches on topics like "World Trade Center" displayed messages linking to our news page. We prepared a link to the Red Cross to encourage blood donations, then discovered that their site had been overwhelmed and couldn't be accessed. Our engineers ran a special crawl using the new incremental indexing tool we had been building for the Yahoo deal, so searches would bring back up-to-date results from news sites.

We were soon flooded with email from well-meaning users who

wanted Google to help them help others. Most of the mail was about the ad hoc news directory we had created. Requests to be added to the list of links increased with each update we pushed out. A webmaster had a site where people could post messages letting others know they were safe. A Wiccan wanted a pointer to her "online healing book." An old friend at Salon.com wanted a link to their coverage. A British user suggested we add sources outside the United States. I explained to all of them that our mission was not "to replace news services online, but to help people get info they can't get otherwise." Still, the cascade of incoming links became a cataract, roaring in concert with the rush of the news from New York and the Pentagon and Pennsylvania.

I agreed about the value of adding a global perspective, so I asked Googlers what sites they used abroad. They sent back sources in German, Dutch, Swedish, Norwegian, Danish, Romanian, Polish, Spanish, Basque, Ukrainian, Japanese, and Russian. I dutifully checked them all. Unfortunately, I couldn't read any of them, so I had no way to evaluate whether they were espousing extremism in their bold headlines or had bias buried in the tiny type below. I tried to get confirmation from at least two Googlers before passing the sites along to Karen to post. The engineering team sent me a list of the top news sites they were seeing in the search logs — an indication of what sources people around the world were trying to find. If I couldn't get validation from staff, I took search popularity as a vote for legitimacy.

As the changes rolled out throughout the day, user reaction was all over the map. Some praised us for the useful information. Others complained about the wording that directed people to their TVs. Some sniffed that it wasn't our role to act as a news provider. Some warned us that our uncluttered interface had drawn them to us in the first place and threatened to leave if we didn't clean up the homepage and lose the links.

I wondered at the parochialism of these people. Didn't they understand that something extraordinary had occurred, requiring extraordinary measures on our part? To be fair, if Sergey hadn't taken a hammer to the image of a polished and perfect brand I had carried with me to Google, I might have been confused as well. We were a corporation, a legal entity providing a product solely to earn a profit — yet here we were, acting like a well-meaning bystander attempting CPR at a car wreck. Should we maintain professional detachment instead of throwing up hurried HTML that made our homepage a mess?

And then there were those who thought we weren't doing enough. A German user suggested we paint our logo black. Steve Schimmel in our business development group argued that our response lacked a "human side" — that we should put a "message of sorrow" on the homepage. Cindy and I disagreed with both of them. It didn't feel appropriate to jump in so quickly with a condolence message, while news was still pouring out. Would we look insincere? Awkward? Or worse, would we seem to be capitalizing on a national tragedy? I didn't want to make any rash decisions we might later view as ill-conceived. Already I saw disturbing opportunism cropping up around us. One news organization asked to be moved higher on our list while others demanded to know why their competitors appeared and they didn't. The jostling and jockeying for position intensified by the hour.

I shared with Steve my belief that expressing personal grief through our website logo or a homepage message would trivialize an overwhelming tragedy. The wound was too raw for us to give voice to the pain we all felt. What I didn't tell him was that I felt it would be self-aggrandizing, as if Google were saying, "Look at us. Look how important we are. On this day of despair, we're making a statement on our homepage. Isn't that special?"

As usual, Sergey was there to help with my dilemma. "I'd like to put a mourning message on the site," he said. "Offering condolences and a link to more information." Okay then. I drafted the wording and sent it to him, along with my reservations about his timing. He brushed off my concerns and directed me to put up a link the next day, pointing to our expression of sorrow and support.

I went home that evening shaken and depressed. At least I had been able to share in the illusion that I had been doing something useful instead of sitting by and watching impotently.

"So this is how Google handles a crisis," I thought, as I monitored email late into the night. We had no comprehensive plan in place, but there was neither panic nor chaos. In this unique set of circumstances, people did what they did best and thought about how they could do more. We worked through problems, devised solutions, and calmly discussed contentious issues. Ultimately, our leaders made decisions that ended debate and we moved ahead.

The next day did not start well. The *Washington Post* interpreted our message directing users to their TVs to mean Google itself had been unable to handle increased traffic. Users asked why we had not modified our logo to honor those killed, or at least put a flag on our homepage to show solidarity with our countrymen. We changed our logo for less important things. Why not this? I've explained how I felt about a commemorative logo, but I had separate reservations about pasting a flag on the homepage. To me, waving the Stars and Stripes would provide immediate gratification but send the wrong message. I felt physically ill watching my country under attack, but I didn't want Google making a knee-jerk nationalistic gesture just to prove we were loyal Americans. Too many people had claimed moral superiority before 9/11 because they had flags in their hands — even as they acted to promote their own interests.

My dad flew night missions with the OSS over Germany and occupied France during World War II. He taught me that anyone can wave a flag; that the true measure of patriotism is what you actually do when your country needs you. I took that message to heart. Still, we at Google were Americans and we wanted to show our support — and it quickly became obvious that our users, at least those in this country, expected us to do so. I tried to figure out a way to do it appropriately.

Meanwhile, Tim Armstrong, the head of our New York sales team,[*] told us they were planning to reopen Google's midtown office the following day. They had emptied the kitchens and given the food to firefighters and police, but they were anxious to reestablish some sense of routine.

I gave up on work. My heart wasn't in it. I started plugging search terms into Google to see what I could learn about the who and the why of what had happened. What was the significance of the date September 11? I didn't find much. *The Turner Diaries,* a neo-Nazi work of fiction dating from 1978, referred to bombings taking place in Houston on September 11. The Israeli-Palestinian Declaration of Principles was signed on September 13. Tenuous connections at best.

More curious was a September 4 Usenet post archived in Google groups. A writer calling himself "Nostradamus" had written, "Wait 7 days, and then maybe I'll answer this post. You see, I am going away in seven days, and you will not hear from me again." Seven days later was 9/11. Kulpreet, our in-house attorney, informed me that the FBI had already asked about it.

As soon as the names of the suspected terrorists were released, I ran

---

[*] Tim became CEO of AOL in 2009.

them all through Google. Only one returned something interesting. A Palestinian relief organization headquartered in the United States showed up when I searched for Mohamed Atta. However, his name was nowhere to be found on the site. I clicked on Google's cached version of the page, a snapshot of the way the site had looked when we crawled it weeks earlier. That older version of the page referred to several cases the organization had been involved with, including that of a seventeen-year-old Mohamed Atta. Atta had been helped with medical treatment at an American hospital after being admitted with a gunshot wound. I checked the current version of the website again, but Atta's story no longer appeared — and as far as I could tell, his bio was the only one that had been removed. I had no idea how common the name Atta was, and I didn't know if this was the same Mohamed Atta who had been identified as a hijacker, but I wanted to help and the deletion seemed suspicious. Unsure what to do with the information, I consulted Sergey. He told me to pass it on to the FBI.

Sergey, too, had been thinking about how Google might be used to identify the terrorists, but his thinking went deeper than mine. First, he forwarded to Karen and me a Terrorist Activity Information form to post on the site so that users could report tips to the FBI. Then he very quietly asked a small group of us to begin checking our log files.

"Google is big enough at this point that it's entirely possible the terrorists used it to help plan their attack," he pointed out. "We can try to identify them based on intersecting sets of search queries conducted during the period prior to the hijackings." It made sense. While after 9/11 there were many queries about the World Trade Center and the explosive potential of a fully fueled jetliner, it seemed likely there had not been a great number before that date.

A quick note of explanation about what data was in our logs. We did not have personal information about users (names and addresses), but like most websites, Google placed a unique string of numbers on each user's computer when it connected to our site. This string of numbers is known as a cookie. In our logs, all searches were associated with the cookie and the IP address of the computer conducting the search. So if we saw one cookie connected to several searches relating to the bombing, we might be able to identify the user's Internet address. And by looking at other searches he had conducted, we might be able to determine his real-world identity. For example, if the user had searched on his own name (a relatively common occurrence), that search would be connected by his cookie to the other searches he had done.

Sergey compiled a list of words to look for in the logs, including "Boeing," "aviation school," "Logan airport," and "fuel capacity." In a first run, the logs team found about a hundred thousand queries a day that matched some of his criteria. I added a set of terms I derived from searches across message boards where the names of the hijackers had appeared before 9/11, though I realized it was likely those messages were coincidental posts by unfortunate users sharing the hijackers' names.

As far as I know, no one outside Google had requested that we mine the logs, though news reports indicated that the government had installed Carnivore machines (computers that can monitor Internet communications) at a few ISPs to track conversations across the web in real time. Reports also said the government was searching ISP logs for traffic from a specific email address. The Bush administration's interest in Internet chatter had expanded exponentially overnight.

I had no qualms about helping with Sergey's search effort. No one knew if there were other terrorist cells waiting to attack and if so, where they would strike. If we could provide information that might save lives, we had a moral obligation to do so. The cost in terms of potential loss of privacy seemed negligible, given how constrained our parameters were. We would only try to identify individuals who had displayed, before 9/11, a suspicious interest in topics clearly related to the hijackings.

Still, there was no way to avoid the fact that we were trying to sift out specific users on the basis of their searches. If we found them, we would try to determine their personal information from the data about them in our logs. I think about that when I hear debates over Internet privacy. The "Yada Yada" wording I wrote for the Toolbar had been my first encounter with potential issues of user privacy. This was the second. The debate over user data was not one we had actively engaged internally or with our users, and I worried that it would escalate into a potentially devastating communications issue for us. I resolved to find a way to defuse it — once life returned to some semblance of normality.

The search of our logs for the 9/11 terrorists turned up nothing of interest. The closest we came was a cookie that had searched for both "world trade center" and "Egypt air hijack." If the terrorists *had* used Google to plan their attack, they had done so in a way that we couldn't discover.

I turned my attention to our burgeoning News and Resources page, which had grown kudzu-like into a long list of links to news sources and relief organizations. It had been visited more than four hundred thousand times the day after the attacks. My charge was to keep it current, which quickly became a politically sensitive role. One of our VCs asked us to add a donation site run by a company he backed. One of our salespeople had a client that covered technology. News organizations from around the world beseeched us to be added. I had no set criteria by which to determine who was link-worthy and who was not, so I winged it, checking with Cindy on submissions that I felt could go either way or might have PR ramifications. Users requested news sources in the Middle East and Africa. And Canada. I had neglected our neighbors to the north and they felt under-appreciated. I added the CBC and English-language news services from Arab and African sources. I reminded everyone that the page was a temporary service and "not intended to become a permanent feature of our site." They didn't seem to care.

All week, we walked a fine line through a new set of circumstances, unsure of what our next step should be. It was an instance where we couldn't run user testing or rely on data we had in-house. We had to go with our instincts. Eric forbade unnecessary travel, and we cancelled the launch of a group of international Google sites because Afghanistan was one of the included domains. Eric also cautioned us to be particularly sensitive when interacting with angry users, given the tenor of the times. We did not take his warning lightly. One user, irate about the results returned when he searched for his own name, threatened to show up at our office and "do a *Rainbow 6* on Google's front door."* I put our local police in touch with him. Another user, upset about our caching of his copyrighted photos, berated us on the phone with an irrational, profanity-laden tirade. The photos in question were grainy amateur shots of his cat that he had posted online. And so it went. In the days after 9/11, we couldn't write off any threat as coming from just another crackpot.

Meanwhile, I continued to struggle with the tone of our communication to users. On the Monday after 9/11, a Boston University graduate named Alon Cohen emailed us a small image and asked if we would put

---

* *Rainbow 6* was a Tom Clancy novel turned into a videogame featuring a heavily armed paramilitary group.

it on our homepage. It was a red, white, and blue looped ribbon, and it was exactly what I wanted. It wasn't generic, gaudy, or cartoonish, and it didn't shout, "Look at us! We're patriots!" It was simple and tasteful and conveyed respect. I sent it to Karen and asked her opinion. She liked it, so I took it to Larry and Sergey. We posted the ribbon that day — on the homepage — with a link to the condolence message we had put up the week before. Almost immediately an offended user complained because we hadn't used "a real American flag," claiming our ribbon had a "politically correct stench." He was harsher than most, but hardly alone in demanding we display more overt patriotism.

An ad rep in our New York office asked to create Google t-shirts with a stars-and-stripes version of our logo. He wanted to give them to all our clients. His colleagues loved the idea, but it put me once again in the position of saying, "Whoa, Horsey."

"We've been careful with the site itself not to cross the boundary between showing support and calling attention to the fact that we're doing that as a company called Google," I explained in a note to him. "I think this might cross that line by literally wrapping us in the flag." The thought crossed my mind that brand management was all about knowing what you needed to "no." The bigger we grew, the greater the forces buffeting our brand and the more powerful the currents causing us to drift from the anchor of our strategy. Without constant care, the trust we had built with the public would crash against the rocks. I based my decisions on experience, intuition, customer contacts, staff discussions, founder feedback, and my own developing sense of what was "Googley." But I was basically guessing.

On 9/11, the whole world shifted. Old rules no longer applied. Except at Google, where the post-attack anarchy more clearly exposed our normal modus operandi: Larry and Sergey did what they thought was right and the Google brand tagged along for the ride. I ran after our lead-off hitters, always a step slow and a base behind. As soon as I adopted a position I thought they had declared inviolate ("Google only does search"), Larry and Sergey raced on ("Now we do news, too"). I tried pointing us back toward familiar turf by proposing a timeline for phasing out the news page.

"We should return to our normal homepage on Monday, September 24," I recommended. "The longer we wait, the more awkward it will be to remove the ribbon and the link, because when we do, people will say it means we no longer care." The natural flow of news would ebb after the second week, I thought. That was the nature of disasters and the public's attention span. Users would understand our return to business as usual. Besides, we were now crawling news sites on a more frequent basis and including that information in Google searches. We could point people to that service instead.

Larry rejected my plan. Our news search didn't work well enough to use it as a substitute, he said. Sergey believed the United States would attack Afghanistan within a week, and the news page would once again be valuable. Reporters let Cindy know that they loved it, too. And so it stayed, and I went back to tending my little garden of links.

By October 3, it seemed reasonable to start running promotional messages on our homepage again. Promotion lines brought in advertisers and drove use of our services, but we had stopped displaying them on 9/11. If we put the ribbon and the memorial link next to the promotion line, they would look like ads. I recommended that we move them to the bottom of the page, where they would feel slightly asymmetrical and thus temporary, making it easier to remove them in the future. Larry thought it would just make the jobs and corporate info links already at the bottom of the page look 9/11-related too. I was about to respond to his concerns when we started bombing Afghanistan.

Forget the ribbon and the promotion line, Larry commanded. Put up a news headline instead.

"Not so fast," Urs responded. "Are we now a news site? Are we competing with CNN? Why do we have a news headlines on our front page? I can see the point for a one-time event like 9/11, but I don't see the point of doing it now. Can someone explain the rationale?"

The company split on the question. Karen felt it pushed us dangerously close to becoming a portal. Marissa thought we should hold off until we could do news "right" by implementing the automated news service that engineer Krishna Bharat was building. Cindy was still getting smiley-faced comments about the page from her press contacts and wanted to keep it. I argued that portals like Yahoo had dedicated teams that managed news better than Karen and I could do on our own. Our page, to use one of Cindy's favorite phrases that always made me wince, "was Mickey Mouse."

Salar sided with us dissenters. "Do we intend to update the latest news about the war as it goes on?" he asked. "Aren't we setting user expectations and doing a poor job of meeting them?" Salar sounded persuasive, especially when Omid joined our chorus of naysayers. It was a typical Google decision-making episode — input from everywhere thrown into the hopper to be processed by the founders. I tossed in one last point I thought would cinch the deal: only a small percentage of people who saw the news link clicked on it. The use of the valuable homepage space was clearly inefficient.

None of it mattered in the end, because one of the people clicking on the homepage link was Sergey. "As a user, I just want to see what is going on in the world using a few top sites," he told us. "I don't see any rush to get rid of this with U.S. attacks and potential terrorist retaliation."

Sergey found it useful, so it was useful. That was also typical of the way decisions were made. The news link went up and the ribbon came down. For days, then weeks, then months, I cultivated our news page to keep it current — adding links to the Department of Defense, the White House, and breaking news about Pakistan, Afghanistan, anthrax, and the Quran. I checked out African, Asian, and European news reports, the CDC, the FDA, the CIA, and the UN. It made me feel amazingly well informed. I became besotted with my editorial power over a page seen by thousands of people every day. Well, slightly tipsy maybe. It was, after all, just a pile of links, the online equivalent of a mix tape.

One day Cindy asked for the rationale behind which links I accepted and which I rejected. I explained that my decisions were based on the value each site provided to the balance of news already represented. Did it offer a different perspective? Did it reach an audience not already served? How long was its name? Would it fit in the space allocated? Or would it cause my tidy columns to grow raggedy and aesthetically displeasing? In other words, my decisions were completely subjective. Cindy advised me that there were ramifications for the PR team when we left someone out. I needed to be more inclusive and make decisions faster, because reporters who were kept waiting got cranky and their coverage of us might reflect that.

Meanwhile, Krishna had been tinkering with his news-search program, and in November we added a link to a cluster of articles its algorithm selected — the first version of what ultimately became Google News. That day foreshadowed the obsolescence of my hand-picked list of links. Krishna's algorithms could sort much more information, do it much more quickly, and deliver actual stories of relevance instead of pointers to front pages. His breakthrough had the unfortunate side effect of making it harder for newspapers to sell their printed products.

My link-list page would be just the first casualty of the automated aggregation of online news. In mid-2003, we took it down for good.

There was one other coda to 9/11. As we approached the first anniversary of the attacks, we addressed again the charged question of a homepage commemoration of the event. Suggestions poured in. "Fly the flag at half-mast off the letter *L*," a Googler suggested. "Turn the *L* into the Trade Center towers," wrote a user.

Karen, Marissa, Dennis, and I debated a long time before agreeing to keep it simple: we'd put up the same ribbon that we had used before, with the date 9/11/01 beneath it. Nothing more. We'd also only display it to our users in the United States, not those overseas. In preparation for an avalanche of angry email, I drafted responses to the main issues we expected to be raised.

We put up the ribbon and waited. The first email in response surprised me. "Congratulations," it read, "on resisting the pressure to create a special memorial interface. The Internet is full of these special events that are very U.S. focused and simplify the enormity of the events during and after the attacks. Google is obviously created by individuals with a global perspective and a sophisticated understanding of the complexity of the world's current political and cultural problems. By keeping the standard Google interface, you remained intelligently worldly and open, at a time when these characteristics seem tragically rare."

Other users made similar comments. The day passed quietly for us.

Yahoo chose a different path. They rendered their entire homepage in funereal gray and placed in the middle of it a large black box containing these words: "September 11, 2001 — We remember. In tribute to the more than 3,000 lives lost." There was a link labeled "Click here to learn, share and remember."

I appreciated the impulse behind their decision to create a living memorial, but seeing that approach in action confirmed for me the difference between our site and a "traditional" portal site. We were not about content generation, or evoking memories, or creating an atmosphere of mourning. Google's brand was built on simplicity and functionality and we knew enough to stick with it. We acknowledged the anniversary of 9/11 and we provided our usual search service. Our users could direct Google to find the information they wanted to see. We didn't try to tell people how to feel about the occasion or to build an experience for them on the basis of what we thought was most significant.

"I think you articulated the right insight," Marissa agreed. "We as a company have no unique perspective to offer on this tragedy, so while we can recognize and acknowledge it, it doesn't make sense to prepare content about it."

Since those days, Google has developed many more ways to communicate directly with users: numerous official blogs, news feeds, and Google-produced YouTube videos. Our response to 9/11, however, overflowed the banks of our established communication channel and helped establish Google as more than a disinterested corporation. Users could feel the presence of the people beyond the stark white screen of our homepage and see the shadows cast upon it as we scurried about backstage trying to find ways to help. There was no question about our intent, and the constant updates we pushed, while not always professional in appearance, were earnest efforts to go above and beyond the minimum expectations of our service in a time of national need. I think it was one of the company's finest moments. I'm proud to have played a part in it.

PART III

WHERE WE STAND

Google's big ideas.
There are fortunes to be made.
And mistakes as well.

CHAPTER 17

Two Speakers, One Voice

OOGLE WENT THROUGH some rough times in 2001, though the hard work and stress paid off — mostly with more hard work and stress. The company's revenue numbers continued to improve. Traffic was up. The September 11 attacks, though, seeped into everyone's mood.

My own attitude at work was generally positive. I had figured out how to contribute something of at least nominal value, and the variety of tasks requiring my attention ensured I never grew bored. Hours were long and my family rarely seen, but aside from that, life was good. In any decent narrative, however, a certain amount of conflict must occur. I had my share of disputes with Larry and Sergey, but more of my daily friction arose from my fractious relationship with Marissa Mayer.

Marissa and I crossed each other's paths with increasing frequency that year. We'd spend weeks toiling in the product fields in perfect harmony, agreeing on significant projects like RealNames, and then some minor difference of opinion over a word here or there would turn into a flame war that singed every thatched roof in our communal village. Most of our disagreements sprang from a shared desire to do what was best for our users. Their satisfaction was our common deity, but we worshipped in different ways. Those disagreements began to take on more weight as Marissa's role expanded and it became harder to appeal her decisions — especially as she controlled the agenda and attendance list for Larry's product-review meetings, the logical place to hold such discussions. Increasingly, resolutions reached at our UI team meetings were undone at product review, where Marissa was now often the only team member present.

In the late spring of 2001, the UI team debated the color scheme for our expanding product line. Should Google groups be green or orange? What about image search? We sent around mockups to compare implementations. After weeks of discussion, Marissa took her own recommendation directly to product review. She handed down Larry's "final decision" after that meeting, while encouraging us to have a parallel discussion within the UI team.

"Doesn't a final decision negate any parallel discussions?" Karen asked. "I understand the urgency about making these decisions, but since Larry didn't have other pages for comparison, this may have been a rigged vote. We've spent hours on this in UI and it seems that the right thing to do would be to get consensus. Otherwise, why discuss it at all?" Coming from Karen, who always maintained a nonjudgmental tone, the indictment was particularly stinging.

Marissa responded that the timeline had been clear all along and that "forward motion" was needed to stay on track for the release the following week. Since we'd been talking about it for more than a month, it looked to her as if no consensus was reachable and she'd simply gone with what we had.

Marissa's desire to "fix things" as soon as they came to her attention was a common impulse among engineers, and Marissa was unquestionably productive. But where Urs had emphasized the need *not* to do tasks that fell below the priority line, Marissa's focus seemed diffuse. Every problem that came along required her immediate solution, even if it belonged in someone else's realm.

Bay Chang, who was also on the UI team, had done his doctoral dissertation on human-computer interactions (HCI). Yet he recognized that, at some point, creativity entered the equation. When we fell into overthinking a particular question, he bowed out gracefully. "I think maybe I should shut up," he said, "because I've been contributing too much to the design-by-committee on this page. We engineers should probably be involved with designing what components are necessary and how the technical parts of the page work and let the designers do the layout. It's a better division of labor."

I heard in that an endorsement for my own view that human judgment played a role, even in an atmosphere where every breath inhaled stats and exhaled analysis. Marissa tried to base every decision on data and data alone. That was hardly an unreasonable approach, and most Googlers would have supported it. Perhaps I just didn't trust the data I saw.

I had my own idiosyncrasies, of course — obstinacy and self-righteousness among them. The combination did not lead to quick or peaceful resolutions. The more often Marissa and I disagreed, the more I dug in my heels on matters of little consequence, like whether our porn filter screened "adult content" or "mature content."

The question of what to do about Chad was a bigger deal.

On August 1, 2001, I arrived at work to discover that our homepage sported a new feature. There was a link to a page describing the adventures of our beloved leftover-eating engineer, Chad, as he attempted to bicycle from California to Florida. I really liked Chad, and I knew that he was burning off a few pork chops on a cross-country ride that would take him over the Rockies and across the continent. However, for the life of me, I couldn't figure out why we were chronicling his adventures on the homepage of our search engine. Cindy was puzzled as well. And the UI team, including our webmaster Karen, also wondered W, exactly, TF?

"So . . . this page went up on short notice," Marissa explained to us. "Someone came up with the idea at lunch yesterday. Urs presented it to Jen McGrath and me, and we put it in the product review. Larry liked it and informed EStaff. A few hours later it was on the site. Sorry for not giving more notice, but opportunity was short, since his trip is elapsing by the day and we've already missed half of it."

Ah, it was an engineering thing.

"Chad's trip is very cool," Marissa insisted. "We wanted to be supportive and we realized that people might find this of interest." The page included a map showing Chad's general location and offered Google t-shirts to anyone who captured his image and sent the photo to us.

Adding something nonessential to the homepage in the middle of the night struck me as unnecessarily rash. "Given our propensity to test every small modification we make to the UI," I argued in response, "this feels like a fairly significant change to make with no discussion at all. I don't think it's a bad thing to honor Chad or to have a fun promo line on the homepage. But since this particular one involves PR, customer service, and our brand, I wish that Cindy and I had been consulted first. It's unlikely the difference between putting it up last night and this morning would have been significant."

Marissa pointed at Urs and suggested the urgency had been his. There simply hadn't been time to notify the UI team until after the Chad page had already shipped. She agreed the page should have been held until the morning and reminded me that she had worked hard to put the UI team process in place. Still, I bridled at the systemic exclusion of marketing from decisions with obvious brand impact.

In retrospect, I'm not sure that was such a bad thing.

Part of the power of Google's brand was the cluelessly geek chic it projected, as though a site serving millions of users around the globe were being run by a handful of nerds who didn't know any better than to put whatever struck their fancy on the homepage. I think I had a pretty good ear for that nerd voice and was able to channel it into the communications I crafted, but I also know that I always wanted to smooth out the rough edges and make things flow a little more nicely across the screen. It was the English major in me. Sand down too many protruding bits, though, and you end up with a perfect sphere that's not terribly interesting.

So while at the time I was quite perturbed at being usurped, the tension between Marissa and me may actually have resulted in a better brand. A brand that walked a line between overt nerdiness and polished pabulum. We were the yin and the yang: marketing and engineering, glibness and geekspeak, a gracefully arcing comma in a classic Garamond font complementing a rigidly vertical apostrophe in fixed-pitch ASCII.

Okay, so it wasn't a perfect match. There were plenty of occasions when the center did not hold; when we did something I considered tone-deaf or Marissa considered insufficiently Googley. Google was an engineering company. When we did not agree, we usually did what engineering thought best.

One upshot of the bicycle debacle (as I came to think of the Chad contretemps) was that Marissa explicitly agreed that the text on the site was my province, even as she rejected, rewrote, or edited the "final" copy I passed along to be posted. We butted heads frequently over the months and years to come. Sometimes I won and sometimes I lost, but the arguments were always elucidating. And when Marissa and I agreed on the best way to approach a topic or about principles that should not be violated, I felt assured we had captured some essential element of what it meant to be Googley.

Shortly after 9/11, Larry granted Marissa's request to join the product management (PM) team. He put her in charge of the user experience on Google.com — the consumer-facing part of our business and the basis for our brand. Marissa had been acting as the UI lead for some time, but now it was official. Her move to the product side raised some eyebrows, because it meant abdicating her engineering birthright, a sacrifice akin to giving up citizenship in the Roman Empire to become a Thracian slave. It also meant she would be reporting to Larry.

In the end, Marissa's move worked brilliantly for her. Product management gave her a far wider playing field than she ever would have had as an individual contributor in engineering. She became the disciple spreading the word of Larry, a word often passed to her in conversations restricted to the two of them, making it difficult to know where Larry's dictates ended and Marissa's interpretation began. Larry rarely refuted Marissa's directives, though, so eventually we came to believe that the gospel she preached was if not true to its source, at least not antithetical to it.

Cataloging Our Issues

To the casual observer, Project Hedwig was a weird and random product, a tool for searching mail-order catalogs that enabled users to call up images of printed pages online. Enter "blue baby doll t-shirt" and up popped a page from the Gap's merchandise flyer. Not terribly useful, important, or urgently needed. But Hedwig had a secret agenda. Larry wanted to prove it was possible to digitize every page ever printed.

Catalogs were readily available. They cost nothing. They could be easily scanned, since no one cared if they were damaged in the process. And perhaps most important, their publishers wouldn't object to having their copyrighted material reproduced. What merchant would complain about reaching a raft of potential new customers without paying for paper, ink, or a government employee to stuff their mailboxes? That was the theory anyway.

In October 2001, Pearl Renaker, a newly hired PM, began asking Googlers to bring her all the catalogs we received in the mail. Within

a couple of weeks, the engineers had built a prototype for internal testing. The results were less than spectacular. A search for toys yielded no
results for anything I might want to buy my kids. There were, however,
plenty of toys for puppies and very, very naughty grown-ups.

I asked Marissa if there would be a porn filter in place when our catalog search launched, and if so, if it would be on by default. I pictured
kids using catalog search to build their Christmas gift lists, and the
picture was not a pretty one. Google did not automatically turn on its
full-strength SafeSearch filter for normal web searches, but we did use
a milder filter by default for image searches. Marissa and I approached
the issue from different perspectives.

Marissa argued that our handling of objectionable content needed
to be consistent across all the services we offered, and that if users
hadn't turned on the SafeSearch filter for their Google web searches, we
shouldn't assume they would want it on for catalogs. We should honor
the users' preferences, even if the users had done nothing to actively
express them.

Image search, Marissa reminded me, was a special case, because
the odds of getting porn on an average image search were almost seventy percent. She didn't object to turning on that same mild filtering
for catalogs, but it would be an engineering nightmare to have the full
SafeSearch in place for our new service if a user had previously left it off
for regular Google searches.

Her point made total sense from an engineering perspective and
would be logical to a sophisticated user who knew how to turn filters on
or off. As usual, though, I went immediately to the worst-case scenario.
What would happen if we served pictures of dildos to first graders?

Pearl offered a compromise. We would turn SafeSearch on for catalog
search if the user had already activated it for web search. I felt that was
insufficient, but I recognized that the decision belonged in the product
group and I conceded the argument. I was concerned about becoming "the guy who was always concerned," an alarmist doomsayer whose
prophecies were rightly ignored. Not a good fit for a company with an
emphasis on moving boldly ahead as quickly as possible. The first week
of December 2001, Lauren Baptist, the lead engineer, pointed Googlers
to a working prototype.

One of those who looked at it was Schwim, the ops guy who liked to
edit my copy. "I'm flabbergasted this got so close to launching," he told
me. While casually browsing through the catalogs, he had found ample

adult content. A broad group, including engineers, also felt the product wasn't ready for prime time. I let Cindy know that the launch, scheduled for that week, might have hit a snag.

Cindy had been unaware of the filtering issue, but immediately recognized it as a potential PR liability and informed the product team that the risk was unacceptable. Marissa explained again why full filtering couldn't be done, but Cindy remained adamant. Her opinion carried considerable weight, so rather than debate filtering options ad infinitum, the team removed the adult catalogs altogether. That led to deep philosophical discussions about what constituted an "adult" catalog — and to a heightened awareness among all staff about the existence of "anal toys."

Finally, the product launched and all was copacetic. For about a week. Then CNET ran an article that said we would "sell retailers the names and addresses of Google users who request a specific catalog in the mail," and that we had "suggested selling links to product pages on retailers' Web sites."*

Gerald Aigner, our chief frugality officer, was outraged, and complained to the founders that the article implied that we would sell user data and that we put revenue ahead of user interests. "This is a true marketing fiasco," he said. "We basically screwed totally up."

I was just as unhappy about it as Gerald, even though the article was quoting me. Larry had given me specific instructions to add information on our web page directed toward catalog publishers. The copy I wrote said in part, "What are the keywords users enter to find your catalog? How many pages do they typically examine? Google can provide you with information about how your customers use your catalog in ways no other research tool can, all while adhering to the strictest standards of individual user privacy." There were references to ad programs Google was developing and to Google's ability to help generate leads, including "the names and addresses of our users who have specifically requested that your catalog be mailed to them."

We had never telegraphed our product-development plans before, nor given any hint that we might sell user data, even if our users said it was okay to do so. So why do it this time? It was all part of Larry's master plan. If we were explicit about the potential of catalog search for marketers, they might call off their own legal departments when they

---

* Stephanie Olsen, CNET, December 19, 2001, http://news.cnet.com/2100–1023–277198.html.

noticed we hadn't asked permission to include their copyrighted materials.

Larry always thought strategically and never hesitated to make short-term sacrifices to win a more important battle down the road. Trying to pry that strategy out of him was like squeezing water out of a rock, but when he did baptize us with drops of his wisdom or give us insight into his stream of consciousness, I couldn't help marveling at the depth of his thinking and the breadth of his understanding. His pragmatism around user privacy gave me pause, however. I believed absolutely that we would never provide any user's personal data to an outside party, but Larry's willingness to play around the edges of perception made me — dare I say it? — concerned.

Let's Do Launch

Bay Chang was a quiet, good-humored member of our UI team with a floppy mop of jet-black hair that reminded me of the cartoon character George Shrinks. Among the many innovations he introduced at Google was Sparrow, a collaboration tool he had created while still working as a researcher at Xerox PARC. With Sparrow, anyone could edit a web page without knowing HTML. One member of a team could set up a web page and others could make changes to it online, using just their web browsers and a menu on the page. Googlers quickly adopted it to manage all sorts of team projects.

Marissa chose Sparrow as the basis for an online launch calendar in November 2001: our first intranet-based accounting of every project that would ultimately be visible to users. Each project page had toggle switches that needed to be changed from "No" to "OK" before a product was officially ready to launch. I owned the switch labeled "copy." No product was supposed to launch if I hadn't flipped my switch approving all the text appearing within it. I didn't abuse my power to stop the production line, in part because I wasn't convinced anything would actually happen if I pushed my big red button. Once everyone had given approval, a note went out to a Googler mailing list named "Visible Changes." That ensured, in theory at least, that half-baked products would not slip out the door and Googlers would not awaken to find their world radically changed without warning.

Each week Marissa led a meeting to review launch-calendar projects about to become public or stuck in limbo awaiting approval. The
meetings were an extremely effective way to generate buy-in or to force
naysayers to articulate their objections face-to-face with product managers. For all the emphasis on electronic communications at Internet
companies, regular meetings in which people had to explain themselves
to their peers were swords that cut the Gordian knots of bureaucratic
red tape.

If a PM showed up at a meeting without having procured all the
"flipped bits" needed for a launch, Marissa would ask why those approvals were being withheld and what had been done to address out-
standing concerns. People scurried frantically immediately prior to the
meetings, but things got done. Skipping the meeting was not an option
if your approval was the gating factor for a launch or if your product
didn't have all the sign-offs you needed. The minutes were published,
so no one needed to point fingers. It would be obvious who had held up
progress.

Launch calendar grew to include dozens of engineers and PMs, and
Marissa kept the meetings clipping along. I enjoyed going, though (or
perhaps because) meetings were occasionally contentious. On rare occasions a product launched without everyone's okay, but for the most
part you had to win over approvers or expect delays. The people in the
room knew their stuff and, when challenged, fired back with live data
and true passion. There was intellectual satisfaction in finding flaws
in well-constructed logic or uncovering unseen and potentially problematic aspects of new products. If the engineers and PMs were black-
smiths beating code into new plowshares, I was the anvil against which
they hammered. I wanted to ensure that each new product tempered
our brand rather than introducing a weak link into a chain of successes.
I always amped up with a double espresso before taking my seat.

I knew I was playing the role of roadblock, raising red flags left and
right, but my colleagues were driven by youth, enthusiasm, and energy to just do things and damn the consequences. I think we struck a
healthy balance, even as we struck sparks along the way. Marissa made
sure my concerns were given serious consideration, and once they were
answered, I gladly flipped my bit to OK.

Ego eruptions were rare in the meetings, but intensity visibly increased if debate threatened to become delay. When copy was the gat-

ing factor, I made sure that it was done on time or that the reason it wasn't lay with lack of final specifications from engineering or product management. Marketing would not hold up a launch. No one at the table with any sense of self-preservation wanted to violate Larry and Sergey's most sacrosanct commandment: Get it done on time.

CHAPTER 18

Mail Enhancement and Speaking in Tongues

U SER SUPPORT STARTED the year 2001 with eight thousand unanswered emails. Even after the Deja News furor passed, the number again crept up to ten thousand, in part because of an orchestrated campaign to add Catalan to Google's list of interface languages.

Larry and Sergey strongly hinted we should look for an alternative to our customer-relationship management company, Miasma, which continued to hinder rather than enhance productivity. "I don't want to start looking for a new CRM vendor," I warned them, "if we're just going to pick the cheapest one at the end of the road. That's how we got in this situation to begin with. It's better to stay with the devil we know than to start over with a new set of problems."

Miasma had just released a software update. I let their sales rep know that we would order a copy, but that Larry and Sergey wouldn't pay the five-thousand-dollar cost of flying their techs out to install it.

The sales rep was taken aback. "You don't want us to install it? You know, this is a completely new version, not a service pack. It's very complex. We'd strongly recommend against a self-install."

"We have a building full of engineers," I rejoined. "They're confident they can do it themselves. Just send us the disks and the documentation."

"Well, frankly, only one other customer asked to do it themselves and they gave up halfway through. We'll have to pull some documentation together for you."

I wasn't nearly as worried by that as I should have been. I had developed unquestioning faith that there was no task beyond the capabilities of Google engineers. The disks arrived in the mail. The installation did not go as planned.

"We are rapidly approaching a major email meltdown," I advised our executive staff ten days later. The wheels had come off and we were grinding along on sparking rims toward the edge of a very deep canyon. The program kept crashing and the database of incoming emails was leaking bits and bytes at an alarming rate. Miasma's corporate headquarters was not taking our calls, and my sales rep's phone message said she had left the company. It was the email apocalypse.

Two days later, our Miasma server stopped accepting inbound mail.

I accelerated plans to find another email solution, though I had no budget or parameters for the search.

Composing a list of new CRM vendors didn't take long. Fewer than half a dozen major players offered stable, well-tested systems. Google's tech evaluation team would ensure we weren't sold a bill of goods (though they hadn't kept us from choosing Miasma), and Larry had a college friend who would advise us on desirable features. The friend, David Jeske, counseled us on what to ask for, then added that, by the way, he and a buddy were building a CRM product called Trakken — if we were interested. It wasn't really finished yet, but Larry's other Stanford pals at Wunderground.com were using it.

Interested? Interested in an untested CRM product still in development with one tiny client? Created by a company of two people? Sure, that's just what I was looking for — another risky technology with no support and no track record behind it. I thanked David for his help and, because he was a friend of Larry's, assured him we'd be happy to send him our request for proposal.

Meanwhile, our real search was well under way. One vendor couldn't provide any support for non-English email. Another had a terrible UI because it was a first-generation product. A third seemed overpriced and their salesman's aggressive stance made us wary of doing business with them. Only one company offered a reasonable solution, and we began negotiating with them in earnest. With our leading contender scheduled to make a presentation to our finance, operations, and sales departments, I felt confident I could convince Larry and Sergey to loosen the purse strings and do it right this time: spend money for a high-quality, stable system from a respected vendor.

I hoped Larry's friend had taken the hint and forgotten about us. It would be a frosty day in Hades before we'd make the mistake of buying a bargain-basement CRM solution again. No such luck. Jeske came back ready to present his proposal. He emailed us his slides and let us know we should print copies for the attendees and that we would need to set up a projector for his demo. I had to laugh at his chutzpah. I didn't really have the time for what I knew would be a dead end, but a friend of Larry's is a friend of Larry's, so I agreed to give him a half hour. What he showed us was surprisingly well thought out, but still not ready for beta testing. Many of the essential features we required were missing, and the interface lacked the polish of the others we'd seen.

I broke the news to David. "It's a good start, but I'm afraid we need something more developed."

"Not to worry," he said, taking notes on the features we wanted. "I can get these done. How about I come back next week with a new demo?"

It was more like two weeks before we met again. In that time, David and his partner, Brandon Long, had implemented more than thirty feature improvements from our list. It was impressive, but I was far from convinced. I was more worried that David seemed to think he had a shot at winning the contract — I didn't want him complaining to Larry when his hopes were dashed. I decided to head him off at the pass by talking to Larry myself.

"Actually," Larry recommended when I described the situation, "you should hire these guys. They're really smart. They'll work hard to build the product for us, and we can invest in their company."

"Larry," I explained slowly and carefully, "we just went through hell with an undeveloped product. I can't burden my team with another flaky piece of software that will just slow us down. We're close with a real CRM company and should have a proposal in a couple of days. I'll let David down gently."

"No. Really," Larry repeated. "You should hire these guys. Look, they're a small company and they'll be very responsive. We can give them space in the office and they'll live here and build their product to our specs. We'll be their most important client, and we'll benefit from their growth based on our product design ideas. Have Biz Dev negotiate the contract and make sure we get some equity."

I could say I was stunned, outraged, incredulous, but that would be an understatement. I couldn't believe Larry was going cheap again instead of buying reliability. When I informed the other vendors, they thought I was either corrupt or an idiot. One salesman sent blistering emails demanding to talk directly to Eric and our board of directors. "This decision lacks wisdom and foresight," he asserted. "If you are under the impression that you can build an email tool resembling ours in thirty days, you are mistaken. It has taken us four years and twelve hundred customers to get to where we are. To not include us in your plans does not make sense."

That guy was kind of a jerk anyway, so telling him no didn't bother me, but I'd still be cursing Larry's decision today if not for one small thing: Larry was absolutely right. Though we wasted weeks negotiating our investment in Jeske's nascent company NeoTonic (we squeezed just an extra one-tenth of one percent in equity out of them), by the end of October 2001 we had the new Trakken CRM system running in parallel with Miasma. David and Brandon lived in our office and Denise Griffin, our user-support manager, gave them a daily list of desired features and bug fixes. Unlike the big "reliable" company I had wanted to hire, NeoTonic didn't have hundreds of customers using the same product. They didn't release upgrades only twice a year. They fixed things as they came up, in priority order. Within a couple of months we had the CRM system we wanted, built to our specs, fully stable and intuitive to use. We cut our ties with Miasma and never looked back. A year and a half later, we bought the rest of NeoTonic, making its two founders full-time Googlers.

So what did I learn from all this? I learned that obvious solutions are not the only ones and "safe" choices aren't always good choices. I had thought that due diligence meant finding the product most people relied on, then putting pressure on the vendor to cut the price. It never occurred to me to talk to a startup, even though I worked at one. It never occurred to Larry *not* to do that. We had different tolerances for risk and different ideas about what two smart people working alone could accomplish in a complex technical area — and that is why I spent seven years working in mainstream media while Larry found a partner and founded his own company. Two smart guys working on complex technical problems, it turns out, can accomplish a hell of a lot.

Lost in Translation

The "translation console" was an idea, like building our own ad system and hiring the Trakken guys, that originated with Wunderground, the weather site founded by Larry's college friends. It was a tool for translating our site into all the languages scattered over the face of the earth. Marissa was the chief proponent of implementing it at Google, and Ron Garrett was the lead engineer.

The translation console split all the text on Google's pages into single sentences, phrases, or even words to make it easy for volunteers to translate our interface one bit at a time. When users posted multiple correct translations, they earned editorial power to overwrite awkward or incorrect submissions made by others. If it worked, the system would make our site available in hundreds of different languages — a long and arduous task for us to manage alone.

Insofar as we had a clear strategy, a big part of it seemed to be getting other people to do our work for free. Nowadays that's known as "crowdsourcing." We just called it "cutting costs." Self-service AdWords, porn cookies, affiliate programs, viral marketing — all were based on many hands lightening the load and the unbeatable value of unpaid labor. Google parsed all its tough problems into manageable pieces and parceled them out.

Our engineering staff worked in teams of three instead of in large groups assigned to a single massive project. Our hardware employed thousands of small computers working in parallel instead of large mainframes. Our desktops ran on Linux, an open-source operating system cobbled together by volunteers. We sharded databases into smaller segments to make searching them faster. When we finally built a trade show booth, Larry and Sergey made us do it as a design contest for college students. Why settle for one "professional" designer when you can have a hundred students applying their creativity?

This divide-and-conquer approach even informed the basic algorithms running Google search. Rather than basing search results solely on a single source — the content of individual web pages — Google looked at links created by millions of people to determine a site's importance. Sergey called it "the democracy of the web," because each link was a vote cast in favor of a site's credibility. That approach made Google scale better than the competition, because the more the web expanded, the more links Google harvested for its ranking algorithm.

The translation console would be another break-it-into-tiny-pieces solution for the big, bloated mess of multiple languages. Marissa and Ron set up some fun languages Googlers could use to test the system before it went live, including Pig Latin, Klingon, and Elmer Fudd ("I'm Feewing Wucky"). Marissa translated our entire interface into Bork, Bork, Bork, the language of the Swedish Chef from the *Muppet Show*. The first real new interfaces to launch were Afrikaans, Bulgarian, and Catalan, and we formally announced the console to the world on March 27, 2001. Within five months, volunteers had translated Google into sixty-four languages.

That still left a need for translation of our ad products, user-support responses, licensing, and operations. The task of building a globalization group within Google to accomplish these things had been tossed around like a beach ball at a rock concert. Various outside translation agencies billed us enormous amounts for work that sounded awkward to native speakers. No one in the company had any real experience with internationalization (known as "i18n" for short because there are eighteen letters between the word's initial *i* and its final *n*). So, as with user support, this non-engineering function found a home in marketing's realm.

Fortunately, the responsibility came with a "Sergey." To get control of the accelerating hiring within the company, the executive team had decided to allocate positions by department, with each approved job opening represented by a laminated photo of Sergey. The departments had some flexibility in the way they allocated their Sergeys, but when you showed up at the hiring committee, you needed to bring three "enthusiastic endorsements" for your candidate from current Googlers plus a Sergey to trade for the proposed hire. No Sergey, no hire.

It had taken us a while to post our position, interview candidates, and extend an offer, so it was August 2001 before Stephanie Kerebel, a native of France, joined our group as globalization manager. She had years of experience in dealing with professional translators and immediately implemented cost-saving measures, such as paying for translation by the word and not the job. That alone cut our expenses in half.

We had been directing our professional translators to use the console alongside the volunteers, to save time. We needed professionals to help with our most important languages because waiting for volunteers would delay product launches. There was also a risk that volunteers might intentionally sabotage us with bad translations, a risk we were unwilling to take with popular interfaces that might reach millions of users.

Stephanie saw other limitations to our system as well and recommended we supplement it with Trados, the industry standard translation-management software. Trados had a number of features useful to translators, including version control and a customized glossary that increased in scope over time, ensuring consistency across multiple projects and speeding translation while reducing the cost. Professional translators found it helpful, especially those who did not have an easy way to do all their work online. Stephanie announced she was buying a copy of the software for Google.

And so the i18n war began.

Marissa fired the first shot. The ellipsis at the end of "Forse cercavi . . .," our Italian translator's rendering of "I'm feeling lucky," felt awkward to her, so she removed it. She admonished Stephanie to tell our contractors to "pay attention" and not create formatting issues. The head of our Italian office replied that he preferred the original translation: the three dots made the phrase more elegant. I asked Marissa why she had overruled two native speakers and our localization expert. The cork came flying out of the bottle.

Marissa claimed that one of the other engineers thought it looked as if our site had been hacked because the punctuation was unusual. She told me she had delayed pushing out the new Italian interface because of her translation concerns, meaning we had violated the agreement that localization would never delay a launch. And while she was on the subject, Marissa poured out a litany of issues with marketing's i18n approach: the slowness of professional translators, the time required for quality assurance, the resistance of marketing staff and translators to using the translation console. The capper was our decision to buy Trados, which would increase engineering costs because someone would have to insert translations manually. Engineering didn't have time to build Trados features into the translation console as we had requested. Why, Marissa wanted to know, couldn't we just hire people who were not only good translators but also comfortable working in the translation console?

Wayne Rosing, the head of engineering, weighed in with his perspective. He wanted to keep Google's back-end technology as uncomplicated as possible. Google ran faster with fewer systems, and each new technology we introduced slowed our progress like a remora attached to the streamlined body of a great white shark.

I hadn't realized there was contention around our use of Trados or problems with how localization was proceeding. It seemed to me things had improved enormously. Quality was up. Costs were down. I needed more data to support our position, so I talked with the one translator I knew who had the tech chops not to be intimidated by the console or any other online tool.

Dennis Hwang—the same Dennis who drew homepage doodles —had used the translation console to render our interface into Korean. In his opinion, the technology had two major flaws. The most serious was a lack of context. Translators using the console saw one word or phrase at a time, without any awareness of where on a page it might appear. So when a translator saw the word "Bulgarian," he didn't know whether to use the word for a Bulgarian man or the Bulgarian language. And since each piece of text might go to a different translator, there was no continuity in the flow. Once it was reassembled, it often read awkwardly or even nonsensically.

The other problem was that when the console presented a word to be translated, it took the translation and pasted it into exactly the same place the English word had been, and with the exact same formatting. That led to inappropriate bolding, italics, and spacing that could change the sense of a phrase.

I shared Dennis's feedback with Marissa. It was unlikely we'd find translators who were more comfortable with the console than Dennis, and if he felt there were problems, we should probably address them. I was sensitive to burdening engineering, but the primary concern of the marketing group was that the finished translation not embarrass us as we tried to build market share in a new language.

The engineers saw clearly that the problem was the people, not the technology. If we could improve the quality of the translators, we could get by with just the translation console. From my perspective, translators were not engineers and shouldn't have to waste time learning to use software mismatched to the task at hand. Even Marissa admitted having felt frustration while translating our site into Bork, Bork, Bork.

We negotiated a compromise. Work on all but the top eight languages* would be done exclusively by volunteers in the console, while professional translators could use Trados. Those translations would be imported into the console by a yet-to-be-developed automated script. That script remained yet-to-be-developed for years, but the agreement meant we had clear guidelines for moving ahead. The tradeoff was accepting the risk of unprofessional translation in all but a handful of languages. A couple of months later Sergey noticed that a volunteer had used the console to change the Search button on our Russian homepage to say "Click here bitch." Another volunteer changed Google Malta's Search button to a traditional Maltese insult, "Penis in a can."

The word, according to engineering, was that a few bugs remained in the system.

Yet, once again, risk reaped rewards. The willingness to suffer a few quickly eradicated indignities opened up enormous gates to international audience growth. The world tolerated awkward translations and the occasional insult in order to access Google's search technology. It was a reminder that perfecting the polish was not as important as giving people access to the product behind it. The results we returned and the speed with which we returned them were ultimately all that mattered. They were the essence of Google's brand.

Can You CPC Me Now?

Unfortunately, the results we were getting for another part of Google were not proving satisfactory. Our AdWords system kept growing, but we were concerned (and this time it wasn't just me) about the rapid expansion of our competitor GoTo. Their "search results" were actually ads, sold by online auction, with the top listing going to the highest bidder. These ads were distributed across the Internet, and each time someone clicked on one the advertiser paid GoTo, who gave a small percentage to the site on which the ad appeared—the pricing model known as "cost per click" or CPC. It was an innovative approach to monetizing search. In the Googleplex, most of us thought it was a load of crap. GoTo required no algorithms to determine relevance, and it presented paid ads as "objective" search results.

---

* Referred to as "FIGS" for French, Italian, German, and Spanish, and as "CJK" for simplified and traditional Chinese, Japanese, and Korean.

GoTo's rationale was simple: the more someone paid to have an ad show up on searches for a particular keyword, the more relevant that ad was likely to be. Where we had a democracy of the web, GoTo had a dictatorship of the dollar. I found GoTo's auction-based results almost unusable. A significant number of their advertisers bid high for popular, but irrelevant, search terms just to lock in the top position on as many searches as possible. Even when the top result was not pure spam, the whole approach seemed misleading.

Ralph Nader agreed. Nader's group Commercial Alert filed a deceptive-advertising complaint with the Federal Trade Commission (FTC) in July 2001 to stop the practice of "inserting advertisements in search engine results without clear and conspicuous disclosure that the ads are ads [which] may mislead search engine users to believe that search results are based on relevancy alone, not marketing ploys."[*] The complaint called out eight search companies, including AltaVista, AOL, iWon, and Microsoft. Google was not listed among the offenders, but news articles grouped us with companies that had no scruples about crossing the line. That bothered Larry and Sergey a lot.

Larry had thought he was done with ads after AdWords launched in September 2000. Ads were the price we had to pay for building a really cool search engine, but he viewed them as "tainted meat," according to an engineer who was in the ads group at the time. We had made ads better, but GoTo proved we hadn't completely solved the problem. Fortunately for Google, the ads engineers had not been content to leave AdWords alone. They continued to innovate because they saw the danger presented by CPC ads as life-threatening for our company. Fortunately for those engineers, Salar saw it that way too.

---

[*] http://www.commercialalert.org/issues/culture/search-engines/.

CHAPTER 19

The Sell of a New Machine

SALAR FELT HEMMED in. It was early 2001 and he was not getting his way on consumer products. As Larry's first PM, he had helped launch Google news and been involved in the rebirth of Deja.com as Google groups. But there were always too many cooks stirring those pots.

"Everybody had strong opinions about everything," he remembers, "because the consumer product was what we all lived and breathed." I understood that perspective entirely. I kept bumping into concerned parties who wanted to rewrite my copy. Salar decided it would be nice to find some area that fewer people cared about. He settled on ads and began informally working with the ads engineers.

"Larry and Sergey had the strongest views about things on the consumer side," Salar realized. "We all knew that they were less interested in the details on the ads side." Omid, on the other hand, had a deep and abiding interest in ads. As head of sales and business development, he liked having Salar involved and suggested Salar make the arrangement official. Larry agreed and named Salar product manger for ads.

Salar did his best thinking late at night. He walked the bike-lined halls of the Googleplex after dark, thinking about how ads were sold, how they were displayed, and how they could be improved. In the cubicles around him, Matt Cutts and a handful of other engineers[*] worked on maintaining the AdWords system.

Another team focused on ads optimization — a new system to predict which ads users were most likely to click. Predicting user behavior was an enormous technical challenge that required machines to learn in real time and then make educated guesses. Veterans Chad Lester, Ed Karrels, and Howard Gobioff were on that team,[†] along with Noogler Eric Bauer, whose initial project had added a hundred thousand dollars a day to Google's revenue stream by replacing low-performing ads from the original system with the best-performing AdWords ads. Their leader was a redheaded Canadian by the name of Eric Veach, who had come to Google after making fur and smoke look more realistic in movies like *Monsters, Inc.* Eric enjoyed a challenge.

Eric and Salar bounced ideas back and forth from parallel tracks, though their common destination became clear soon enough. Google would need to build an entirely new ad system to replace AdWords. A new system based on cost per click (CPC) instead of cost per thousand impressions (CPM). Remember that with CPM pricing, an advertiser paid a set amount for each thousand times an ad was shown, regardless of how many people actually clicked on it. AdWords offered three CPMs, at ten, twelve, and fifteen dollars. The more you paid, the higher up on the page your ad appeared, which made your ad more likely to be seen and clicked by users. With CPC, an advertiser paid only when someone actually clicked on the ad, regardless of how many times it was displayed.

Advertisers loved CPC, but it scared the bejeezus out of Google executives. Netscape had offered CPC deals, guaranteeing the number of clicks their clients would get over a certain period of time. The numbers had been very large. When the clicks didn't materialize, Netscape had no choice but to keep running more and more ads. And the more ads they ran, the lower the clickthrough rate went, until every page was saturated with banners that were ignored by users. CPC could spawn a whirling, sucking spiral of death.

Salar, though, had seen a great future. He summed it up in one word: "syndication." Salar believed that to truly grow Google's revenue we

---

[*] Other ads team members at various times included Amit Patel, Jeremy Chao, Erann Gatt, Peter Kappler, Radhika Malpani, John Bauer, Zhe Qian, Laurence Gonsalves, and Jane Manning.

[†] Chad named the project "Smart Ad Selection System," which was usually shortened to "SmartASS."

needed to distribute ads on other websites. Advertisers would be unwilling to pay CPM rates to have their ads displayed across a network of sites over which they had little control. They would be much more comfortable if they paid only when people actually clicked on their ads. But if we were going to do CPC, we had to do it differently than GoTo. We had to do it better. The question was how.

The engineering director overseeing the ads team in 2001 was Ross Koningstein. Ross had a PhD in aerospace robotics and notions of his own about how the ads system should develop. He thought we could sell ads CPC, but rank them by CPM. By taking data from the logs files, we could calculate how much revenue each ad actually generated for Google, and display them accordingly. Ross told me that he presented his idea to Larry at a meeting in April 2001, but that Larry was not in the mood to hear it.

Larry only wanted incremental changes to AdWords, according to Ross, not a whole new system, even though the other engineers agreed a new system was needed and were already working to make it so. Besides, Ross said, Larry only wanted to communicate with engineers directly involved in writing the code — and with his handpicked PMs. At the meeting, Larry informed Ross that he was making Salar the lead for ads.

Salar immersed himself in discussions and brainstorming with the engineering team. They shot down most of his ideas, such as selling keywords in bundles, until one night Salar experienced an epiphany. Google could assign a quality score to each ad. "Quality" would be our prediction of how likely a user was to click on an ad. If that score was factored with the amount the advertiser was willing to pay, we could rank ads by their potential for earning money for Google — their effective CPM. Everyone would benefit. The user would see more relevant ads. The advertiser would get more clicks. Google would make more revenue. It was a brilliant idea.

Ross believed he had already suggested something very similar, only to be ignored. According to Eric Veach, a number of people were arriving at the same place independently. "It's kind of an obvious idea," he claimed, though some of the things evident to Eric made my brain ache.* AdWords already prioritized the ads by CPM. If you paid fifteen

---

* Eric once interviewed a job candidate who began explaining the problem at the heart of his doctoral thesis and the way he had arrived at an elegant solution. Before he could describe his breakthrough, Eric asked, "Was it a Hamiltonian system?" The candidate stared at him in awe. That answer had eluded him for months. Eric had deduced it from their five-minute conversation.

dollars, your ad appeared at the top. If you paid less, your ad was lower on the page.

"I know I proposed that at one point," Eric told me about effective CPM ranking. "I said, 'We can prove that it results in the highest expected income if you rank people by their effective CPM,' which essentially means the CPC you charge times the predictive clickthrough rate."

That one idea was worth billions and billions of dollars. So who came up with it? "I think you're going to find very little agreement on that," Eric went on. "It's true that each of us who was involved thinks we contributed. The sum of those numbers adds up to much more than one hundred percent."

But brilliant as the idea was, it wasn't perfect. Two things were still needed. The first was a method for determining the "quality" rating for each ad.

"When Salar was originally talking about multiplying by clickthrough rate," Eric explained, "what he meant was the historical clickthrough rate. If we had shown their ad a thousand times and somebody had clicked on it ten times, they would have had a one percent clickthrough rate." Eric thought that was the wrong approach. "The problem is, that kind of stuff is just, well, garbage really. You have to show a bad ad thousands and thousands and thousands of times to get any good information about how well it's doing."

"The clickthrough rate needed to be a *predictive* thing," Eric insisted. "It needed to be what we thought the chances were of somebody clicking on the ad given all the information we had about the query right then." That required enormous computing sophistication. And secrecy. Eric didn't want advertisers to know how Google was determining the quality of their ads, so that Google could keep refining and improving the algorithms without advertisers' trying to game the system. He insisted that Google retain complete control — that the ranking mechanism remain a black box. He knew that would frustrate and anger advertisers, but it would benefit users, who would see more relevant ads on every page.

While our competitors made trivial adjustments to their ad programs, Eric led an effort to build one of the biggest machine-learning systems in the world — just to improve ad targeting.

The second fix the new system needed was to correct a big problem that GoTo faced. GoTo displayed the price bid by each advertiser, and advertisers kept lowering their bids because they could see they were paying more than they needed to. If the high bid was twenty-five cents per click and the next bid was twenty cents per click, the top bidder was paying four cents too much. A smart advertiser would lower his bid to twenty-one cents.

Salar was intent on getting advertisers to tell us right at the start the maximum amount they were willing to pay for a click. He wanted to charge that full amount, just as Overture did, but he didn't want the advertiser to keep rebidding to lower it.

Eric showed him a solution. "The amount that you bid shouldn't be the amount that you pay," he said. He envisioned an eBay-type auction where the advertiser would pay the minimum amount necessary to win a position in the rankings. Eric had never heard of William Vickrey, the Nobel laureate who had created a "second-price auction" model; he worked out the idea himself. It just made sense to him that instead of charging as much as an advertiser was willing to pay, we should automatically lower the cost to the minimum amount required. Then advertisers would have no incentive to lower their bids, but they would have an incentive to raise them when the bids below theirs increased.

At first, Salar resisted the idea of a second-price auction, because it would confuse advertisers. They would have to trust us to lower their bids, and Salar wasn't sure they would be willing to do that.

Eric saw a fundamental difference between his approach and Salar's. "We both contributed to the design," he said, "but Salar was always looking at the product from the point of view of the advertisers, who he knew were the customers. They wanted transparency. They wanted control. I was looking out for the users."

Eric believed we should only show advertising when it was useful. He refused to put anything into the product that would weaken that principle. He and Salar went back and forth on the auction model and the need for secrecy about ad scoring. Salar was persuasive, but Eric brought an advantage to the debate about how the systems would be configured. "I was in charge of actually building them," he told me, "so as it turns out, I won most of the arguments."

It took both Eric and Salar to convince Larry and Sergey, who still hadn't signed off on offering CPC pricing, let alone on a method for implementing it. Salar explained the advantages for syndication. Eric showed how the auction model fixed GoTo's bid-lowering problem and suggested the changes might protect Google from GoTo's patent claims. Salar argued that different keywords had different values, so a fixed-price model made no sense.

Larry remained unswayed. It was only after Eric pointed out that ad quality and search quality were related — that with the changes we could control the relevance of the ads we displayed and improve the user experience — that he finally consented. As Eric put it, "Larry had always been the biggest champion of getting the best results for users. He was fine with making things tough for advertisers when we needed to."

In the end, Larry and Sergey weren't totally convinced, but they agreed to move ahead. That was not unusual for them. If you brought enough passion and logic to the fight, they'd take a chance that you might be right. Eric assumed they would rake him over the coals if it didn't turn out well, but he was glad to get the chance to move ahead and wasted no time putting together his team. He knew GoTo had a head start and was gaining momentum.

A Friend Accepts an Enemy Overture

Google's first great challenge had been gaining primacy in search. Its second would be winning the war for advertising revenue. Eric and Salar were preparing the company for that battle, but those of us not in the ads group at the time were left in the dark. All we could see was GoTo scoring deals and racking up sales. Not only was GoTo generating revenue, it was running the table, locking up portal sites with multi-year contracts. When our salespeople pitched Google ads to GoTo customers, they came away empty-handed, shaking their heads.

To make it worse, GoTo's sales team kept sending us things, as if we were a potential client. Every week, a new "gift" would arrive. A notepad. A golden egg. A plastic goose that lit up. A hand-delivered pie. Omid would display the latest item at TGIF each week and then send it flying with a kick. Except the pie. I'm pretty sure he ate that.

GoTo's management continued to crow about their successes. In August 2001, one month after Eric's team was given the green light to build a CPC system, a GoTo executive appeared at a Jupiter Research conference and claimed that all search would be paid for in the future. "He said that if users don't like the results, they can keep clicking," a Googler who attended the conference reported back. "It's no problem, since they'll eventually find what they want."

In October 2001, GoTo signed a deal expanding their relationship with Ask Jeeves. They announced proudly that they had attained profitability and that they were changing their name to Overture.

Overture continued the boasting at the Direct Marketing Association conference in Chicago later that month. I was in our small booth off to one side of the large hall, which overflowed with direct-mail houses, list brokers, specialty printers, and foreign governments offering low taxes and cheap labor for call centers. We were handing out magnets and t-shirts and riding our Googlized scooter around the floor promoting a contest for free ads. We stood out from the conservative coat-and-tie crowd, members of which came by to tell us again and again, "I *love* Google!" The only booth generating more interest was staffed by Hooters waitresses handing out free chicken wings as the Bears game played on a big-screen TV.

Overture's chief operating officer, Jaynie Studenmund, gave a speech. She claimed Overture was having a "Barry Bonds year" and acknowledged that Google was "a fine company" and "absolutely in the business of making money off search listings too." She told the crowd that Google "has something called paid placement that's different from Overture's paid placement." She meant the clearly labeled ads next to our search results. I had to restrain myself from heckling her.

Later, Studenmund stopped by our booth with a half dozen of her colleagues in tow. She wanted to chat. Did we think the event was worthwhile? A success? I candidly gave her as much misinformation as I could, and, after helping themselves to our tchotchkes, she and her entourage floated off. They didn't seem too concerned about us. We were just a hungry stray fighting a pack of others to eat the scraps of their success.

Then, on November 13, 2001, Overture dropped a bomb on Google. They were signing a five-month contract with Yahoo to deliver ads targeted to search keywords. Yahoo would keep paying us for our search results, but those results would be monetized by another company. They would skim the cream after we fed the cow and milked it. Larry and Sergey bit their tongues, but they were furious at the setback. They couldn't take it out on Yahoo, which was still our biggest partner, and bad-mouthing Overture would imply that Yahoo had made a mistake. There was no immediate engineering fix to our problem, but that didn't mean we had no way to respond.

We Hold These Truths to Be Self-Evident

While we couldn't talk trash about our competitors, we could use our site to talk directly to our users about the principles that made us unique. I had some thoughts about how to express that.

"Never settle for the best," I wrote, and quoted Larry's vision of the perfect search engine, which would "understand exactly what you mean and give back exactly what you want." Only Google was engaged in an endless struggle for search perfection, I explained — a noble, perhaps quixotic goal that set us apart from portals laden with ancillary services, and from ad networks that put the interests of advertisers ahead of users.

To demonstrate Google's purity of heart, I compiled a list of "Ten Things We've Found to Be True." I tried to distill every interaction I'd had with our engineering team and with Larry and Sergey into discrete nodes that together mapped the attitudes of the company's creative force. I laid them out in priority order:

1. Focus on the user and all else will follow.
2. It's best to do one thing really, really well.
3. Fast is better than slow.
4. Open is better than closed.
5. Democracy on the web works.
6. You don't need to be at your desk to need an answer.
7. You can make money without doing evil.
8. There's always more information out there.
9. The need for information crosses all borders.
10. You don't need a suit to be serious.
11. Great just isn't good enough.

The fourth point stuck in Larry's craw. It described Google's preference for free, community-developed, open-source technology like Linux, which was increasingly viewed as a threat to the dominance of Microsoft's Windows operating system.

"Don't moon the giant," Larry admonished me. Larry, along with

Netscapees like Omid, knew what came from waving red flags at the Beast of Redmond. Netscape had famously "mooned the giant" by boasting that their browser would turn Microsoft Windows into a "mundane collection of not entirely debugged device drivers." Microsoft had responded with their own version of "mooning." They bundled their Internet Explorer browser with Windows to turn Netscape into a barren, lifeless realm by "cutting off their air supply." Google's air supply was still coming through a rather narrow tube, and Microsoft could easily throw kinks into it by making changes to Internet Explorer or focusing on search themselves. I cut out point number four.

That brought the total number down to ten. I had intentionally included eleven because the last point went on to state that we would "always deliver more than expected." I tried to add another point to replace the deleted one, arguing that taking it to eleven would give the list a sort of postmodern, ironic hipness, but the executive staff said to let it go. They were a pretty literal bunch.

They had no objection to the rest, including my favorite, "You don't need a suit to be serious." I hated neckties. I hated ironing shirts.* I hated scratchy trousers and shoes that pinched. I wanted to elevate my sartorial disdain to the level of a corporate value and, God bless Google, they were willing to do it.

Not all items on the list would age equally well. In fact, Google amended it not long ago to make it clear that doing "one thing really, really well" could be extended to cover products like online chat and financial news. I knew that Google would ultimately outgrow search alone, but search was the battle we were fighting at the time and the way our users defined us. Who were we to reject the brand they had created in our name?

Only one point gave me pause: "You can make money without doing evil." It was at the heart of our response to Overture, but I felt uncomfortable talking about our desire not to prosper at the expense of our souls. I thought it could be perceived as naive and would invite criticism every time we didn't live up to our moral code. It also went against another core value, one I hadn't listed: "Underpromise and overdeliver." Up to that point, we had always been careful not to overstate our accomplishments or brag about what we had up our sleeves.

---

* Though, ironically, I was the one who showed Sergey how to press a shirt when he needed to look presentable for an event. We had an ironing board set up next to the massage table. It may be the only time after my interview that I was able to teach him anything useful.

We never boasted about our willingness to sacrifice ourselves to make good things happen for partners, advertisers, or users, and we rarely talked about what we might do for them in the future, but we strove to exceed their expectations. Shutting down Google.com for Netscape had been a prime example. While Larry and Sergey would negotiate every penny out of a potential client's pocket, our goal was to give added value in return. That attitude was uncommon among tech companies. Microsoft, in particular, gained notoriety as the issuer of vast quantities of vaporware, products that they touted as industry standards, but which came to market much later than originally projected, if at all. It's easy to understand why companies did this—it was a way to lay claim to new markets and kept aspiring players from entering them.

We abhorred vaporware. Though recently Google has preannounced products and even whole industries it intends to revolutionize, in its early days the company kept launches secret and downplayed features. We wanted people to discover some things on their own. We'd launch a calculator and let users figure out it could tell them the number of hands in a fathom. We'd launch a spell checker that offered suggestions not just for common nouns but for the names of people in the news.

"Underpromise and overdeliver" became as important a mantra to us as "Don't be evil."

Eventually, users and analysts began speculating about what Google might develop next. Would it be a phone? A travel service? A carbonated beverage? The rumors were rife, and the lack of confirmation or denial from Google gave competitors pause. Google was no longer just a search engine. It was a technology company that solved hard problems. That made the addition of Google's name to any product plausible.

Understating our accomplishments could be frustrating at times, especially for salespeople. AdWords ads got up to fourteen times the clickthrough rate of untargeted banner display ads, but we only let sales reps tell clients they were three times better. We wanted to sound realistic to potential customers and keep our true performance hidden from competitors. If we delivered double or triple what we promised, who would complain?

But there was no way to overdeliver on not being evil—and there were an infinite number of ways to fall short of that goal. Evil, as an operating principle, was a common discussion topic around our cubicles.

In late 2001, in Silicon Valley at least, many saw Microsoft as the primary practitioner of the dark arts in technology, using their monopoly power to corral innovative startups that might turn their Windows cash cow into hamburger helper.

The "Don't be evil" mantra had already taken root within Google when I composed my list of "Ten Things." Paul Bucheit came up with it in 2000 at a "core values" meeting held to codify the way Googlers should act toward one another. It was not intended to regulate our behavior toward non-Googlers, nor were the values supposed to be disseminated outside the company.

According to Amit Patel, Paul became disaffected with all the "corporate"-sounding suggestions his colleagues proposed — things like "Treat each other with respect," "Honor commitments," and "Don't be late for meetings." They were boring, and they were too specific. It was bad coding hygiene to build an itemized list if you could apply a general rule.

"Aren't all of these covered by 'Don't be evil'?" Paul asked.

No one took him seriously. The meeting concluded with a list of eleven core values, which HR asked me to help wordsmith. "Don't be evil" wasn't one of them. The meeting left Amit unsatisfied, and he took it upon himself to proselytize the Word of Paul. Soon, "Don't be evil" began blemishing every markable surface like brown spots on ripening bananas. I had a rolling whiteboard in my cubicle, and one day when I came back from lunch, "Don't be evil" was neatly printed in one of its corners. I saw the phrase scrawled on conference room walls and twirling across laptop screensavers. Others saw it too. I had to assure job applicants, vendors, and visitors that it didn't mean the company was fighting Satanic urges.

It was intimidating to have a corporate commandment stare down at you wherever you went — a dry-erase Jiminy Cricket looking over your shoulder, passing judgment on your every action. That was Amit's intent. Its very simplicity made the phrase unforgettable and gave it the force of an irrevocable law.

"'Don't be evil,'" Paul explained, "is about not taking advantage of people or deceiving them. Anything deceptive is evil. So if we put up search results, move them higher because someone paid us, that's deceptive, that's abusing trust." Paul wanted Google to be the anti-evil company. Amit's marketing campaign sold the staff on formalizing the credo. Once it became a cultural meme, it was impossible to uproot.

The effect was as if Amit had been scribbling with a permanent marker directly into our collective consciousness.

"I also thought it would be a good value because it would be difficult to remove once it was in," Paul admitted. "It wouldn't look too good to get rid of 'Don't be evil.' Besides, Microsoft had a monopoly on evil. We didn't really want to compete."

The idea of not doing evil seeped into conversations as a criterion for evaluating products, services, and life decisions. People brought their own spin to interpreting what it meant:

"If the ads looked more like search results they would generate more revenue. But wouldn't that be evil?"

"Resist evil. Don't make the toolbar less functional to appease Microsoft."

"You took the last éclair and didn't finish it? You are evil incarnate."

"I've noticed that people have this strange definition of evil," Paul observed, "which is 'Anything I don't like.' In my mind, I can not like something, but it can still not be evil." But even strict adherence to Paul's original concern about selling placement in search results put us at odds with our industry. If pay-for-placement was evil, the market was in league with the devil. Overture was growing at an enormous clip and building a sprawling advertising network of sites running their ads.*

When we posted "Ten Things We've Found to Be True" on our website, we earned a handful of kudos from users for our stand in favor of integrity. But that did nothing to slow the growth of Overture, a juggernaut that now threatened to lock up all the advertising dollars flowing to search.

Some Positive Results

Overture's deal with Yahoo seemed to put them out of any competitor's reach. In December 2001, they signed a three-year agreement with Germany's biggest ISP. In January 2002, MSN announced they were testing Overture ads. They were everywhere and they were unstoppable.

---

*Overture reported revenue of $288 million at the end of 2001, up from $103 million in 2000; http://news.cnet.com/2100–1023–962209.html.

Except. Except that by January 2002, Googlers had already been banging away in the Googleplex for almost two months on a working prototype of our new ads system. Just before midnight on November 15 — two days after Overture's Yahoo announcement — Eric Veach had flipped the switch. The prototype had multiple bugs and lacked key features, but it could serve ads sold on a CPC basis through a real-time auction.

While Salar and Berkeley economist Hal Varian refined the bidding system, I thought about how we would sell the system itself. I compiled a spreadsheet comparing it to the original AdWords and to Overture. It looked very compelling on paper, but in reality it wasn't yet ready for public exposure. The gears and wires still showed through some parts of the interface, and some of the steps required to create an ad seemed counterintuitive. Birthed in the middle of the night, the newborn product could not yet survive in the cold competitive world into which it would soon be thrust. It needed to be wrapped in a user-friendly UI and given a name.

This time, the branding went faster. I convinced Salar we needed to make it easy to distinguish the new system from the original while planning for an endgame with just one AdWords system. I proposed "AdWords Select," because it would be easy to drop the "Select" when the original system shut down. He agreed and sold it to Larry and Sergey.

The new interface bothered me more. Overture had a simple three-step process for creating ads, an experience as comfortable and easy as driving a golf cart. AdWords Select was a MiG fighter, loaded with technical terms, incomprehensible gauges and dials, and a long checklist before your ads actually took off. I wanted us to have a shortcut with preset options, but Salar felt the granularity of the system made it powerful and that was its selling point.

Sheryl Sandberg, an economics wunderkind and former chief of staff at the Treasury Department, joined Google the week the new prototype went live. She was immediately handed responsibility for advertising customer support and the team of five people who managed that for Omid. One quit that day. Sheryl also wanted things simplified, but there was no working around Salar, who had developed a deep attachment to the product. Salar obsessed about the UI, the sign-up process, the auction mechanics, even the text of the emails going to users. His power as product manager over everything but the code was absolute. The system's thousand moving parts demanded total focus to keep things moving forward. Decisions had to be made quickly, often at four in the morning. Salar was in his element, running at full capacity and pushing the role of PM to a new and significant place.

Salar asked me for text to explain what set AdWords Select apart in a field dominated by Overture's promise of "pay for performance." Something that would stir the souls of advertisers and compel them to try a new system when Overture already worked well for them. Something in fewer than seven words.

"It's all about results," I suggested. The wording felt right. It emphasized the unequaled quality of our search and the importance of real return on investment. We slathered the tagline liberally over the sales materials we had in preparation. If we were going to win Yahoo and others, we needed to tout our strengths as a provider of both search and revenue.

Word on the street was that Yahoo's trial of Overture was not going well. One of our clients had heard Yahoo complaining about the high level of irrelevancy in Overture's listings. A few days later Overture overhauled their advertiser guidelines and introduced stricter controls on URLs, ad titles, and descriptions. "Given our commitment to providing a world-class search experience," Overture announced, "it's important that we provide highly relevant search results to our users." Evidently some users didn't want to just keep clicking until they found what they were looking for.

Overture's blithe confidence derived from the forty thousand advertisers whose listings appeared across their network of tens of thousands of client sites. Google only sold ads that appeared on Google.com. No matter how big our search engine grew, it could never compete with the reach of a web-wide network.

In January 2002, Omid let slip a hint that things were about to change. "A lot of the companies that we power searches for want us to start syndicating advertisements to them in some sort of revenue share," he told a reporter for Revolutionmagazine.com.[*] "We are looking at that, and it is an area where we may potentially compete with Overture. But it isn't our core business, as we aren't dependant on third-party traffic to generate income."

---

[*] Mark Sweeney, Revolutionmagazine.com, January 23, 2002, www.brandrepublic.com/news/135039.

Omid. What a sandbagger. We already had our first syndication deal signed. Our sales team had inked a contract with Earthlink to supply our original AdWords ads a week earlier. They had been an Overture client until their contract expired, making it our first win in a head-to-head contest. We hadn't even offered them CPC ads. I doubt Overture worried — Earthlink was a trivial account compared to their major partners Yahoo and AOL. But we saw the contract as a very big deal. It proved we could syndicate our ads. Our formerly cold war with Overture began to simmer.

Omid celebrated by telling the entire company to work harder. We needed to increase the revenue per ad we generated to pressure Overture. The more we earned, the more we could offer potential partners in a bidding war for their business. We knew we could improve relevance faster than Overture, because they employed human evaluators to determine ad relevance. People couldn't possibly keep up with a good algorithm.

The Earthlink deal held only one danger for Google — the guarantee of a minimum payment, even if the advertising didn't generate sufficient revenue to cover it. It could turn out like Netscape's CPC death spiral. The exposure was small, but as deals grew bigger and competition more intense, guarantees swelled like great gas-filled dirigibles, casting shadows over our balance sheet. The threat was the "overhang" — the cumulative amount of money guaranteed to all partners. Reduced search volume or quality issues that hurt ad clickthrough rates could spark an explosive expansion of Google's debt and obliterate the company.

Even with Larry and Sergey's high tolerance for risk, no one wanted the company to die under a load of corporate IOUs, especially the new CEO, Eric Schmidt. "Don't make me bankrupt," Sheryl Sandberg recalls Eric telling Salar. "Don't run out of cash."

The guarantees would become a weapon in the battle for syndication market share, as each search superpower tried to bluff the others into spending themselves into economic oblivion.

On February 5, 2002, CNET broke the news that Google had been quietly providing Earthlink with search results and advertising for weeks. It was too late in the day for a market reaction, and the story garnered little attention.

The next morning, Overture's stock tumbled forty-one percent. A day later, Google and Earthlink issued a joint press release announcing that Google would provide search results for Earthlink's network of sites. No mention was made of our syndicating ads for the first time, the shift that changed our industry.

Meanwhile, Overture and a supporting cast of adoring stock analysts downplayed Google's new direction. Safa Rashtchy of US Bancorp Piper Jaffray called the lower stock price a "major buying opportunity" for investors considering Overture. In his view, people were overreacting. Earthlink was an aberration. Its business model didn't apply to the big portal players.

Ted Meisel, Overture's CEO, fired back at us with a press release touting raised expectations for the quarter and stating there would be no "material impact" from the loss of Earthlink as a client. He also announced that the company had extended its relationship with Yahoo to the end of the second quarter of 2002.

Overture's stock recovered over the next few days, in part buoyed by the rosy prognostications of the Wall Street analysts enamored with the company's prospects. Salomon Smith Barney predicted that Earthlink's impact would be minimal since "the major portals can (and do) operate their own CPM-based search advertising models, and they are unlikely to . . . share those economics with Google." Besides, SSB noted, privately held Google was tied to CPM-based ads and couldn't afford to compete for contracts with big guarantees in a cost-per-click, pay-for-performance world.

"You ain't seen nothing yet," Rashtchy crowed to investors a week later. He believed Overture's strong fourth quarter and its deal with MSN had set the table for "huge growth leverage."

Larry and Sergey played it cool. They had a stack of aces up their sleeves. Google would prevail because of the better quality of our search, the greater relevance of our ad matching, and our willingness to commit fearlessly (but prudently) to enormous partner guarantees. And because what everyone else saw as our biggest impediment was actually an enormous advantage: we maintained a site that competed directly with our potential partners. Overture didn't have such a site.

In what Larry termed "the first well thought out article I've seen about Overture," George Mannes of TheStreet.com pointed a sharp stick at Overture's Achilles' heel.* "Compared with traditional media practices," he wrote, "Overture retains an exceptionally large portion of

---

* "Margins may tell Overture Story," TheStreet.com, February 19, 2002.

the money it collects from advertisers." They were keeping forty-nine percent of the revenue from the ads they sold and giving only half to the sites where the ads ran. Traditional media-placement agencies kept only fifteen percent for themselves.

That's where we had them. Overture was entirely dependent on its network for revenue, and if its margins slipped, the company would be in trouble. We kept all the money for the ads we ran on Google.com, and that swelling river of cash subsidized our expansion efforts.

We could give a bigger share of our revenue to our partners. Our costs were low since we had to process the ads to run on Google anyway and additional distribution would be almost entirely added profit. Plus, running our own site gave us an edge in understanding how users responded to keyword-based advertising. Google.com was a living laboratory processing priceless data that revealed what was effective and what was not.

We could — and would — send margins into a nosedive, and that went a long way toward assuaging our partners' concerns about Google as a potential competitor. We were now the good guys, cutting costs for everyone and helping to fill the coffers of search-enabled sites across the web.

The Game Changes

Overture CEO Ted Meisel, interviewed by CNET the day the Mannes article appeared, wasn't concerned about the future of paid search. Portals that had not yet augmented their search results with Overture's paid listings, he told a reporter, had "been essentially providing the largest ad giveaway that I can think of," because they were delivering customers to businesses without monetizing the traffic. Meisel noted that Overture's forecasts for the coming year were based only on extension of the Microsoft deal and added, "We certainly regard AOL and Yahoo as important potential partners, but our business can live without them."

Meisel would have reason to be thankful he had hedged his optimism. On February 19, 2002, we posted a "NEW!" option on the web page describing Google's advertising offerings. CPC-based AdWords Select was live.

Overture's stock dropped ten percent. Safa Rashtchy tried to stem the panic by again beating the "buying opportunity" drum. "Overture has a lock on the major portals," he reiterated. Large partners would never sign with Google as long as we had our own site. Besides, Rashtchy pointed out, Google had only a thousand advertisers using its program. Overture had fifty-four times that.

Merrill Lynch analyst Justin Baldauf concurred, telling CNET, "Because Overture is much bigger than Google, Overture can afford to pay distribution partners more money." He explained that Google couldn't increase distribution without more advertisers and wouldn't get more advertisers until we increased distribution. That may have been true for CPM ads, but the underlying economics for CPC ads were far different. Advertisers paid only for the clicks they received, so the return on investment was almost always positive — search-targeted ads paid for themselves. Therefore the market for our ads was limited only by the advertiser's product inventory and production capabilities. CPC search-targeted ads were like crack for marketers. Advertisers pulled money from other direct-marketing budgets to buy as many relevant keywords as they could. We didn't need to take advertisers away from Overture — the pie was plenty big enough for both of us.

Over the weeks to come, I would check MOMA daily to get an update on the advertisers in our system. The number climbed with the steady speed of a veteran Sherpa. That was encouraging, but what we really needed were distribution partners who would display our ads. Overture had most of the big ones sewn up. But that, we determined, was something we could change.

Grow, Baby, Grow

We continued to bulk up as we prepared for our CPC cage match with Overture. Even marketing was given the okay to add staff, and I suddenly found myself with seven open positions and hundreds of résumés cluttering my inbox. I had no time to read them. The AdWords Select launch ate up chunks of my day, and our new venture into hardware, the Google Search Appliance (GSA), chewed up the rest. Our distributed-computing toolbar nibbled at the edges not already gnawed by catalog search. I had canned responses to feed user support and ongoing scraps with Marissa and Wayne over the translation console. I carried the résumés with me and read them while mopping up the residue of my daughter's stomach flu and while waiting for my endodontist to redo a root canal that had gone painfully wrong.

Still, I got a note from a product manager complaining that I couldn't be too busy to rewrite something a second time because he hadn't seen me in the office at two a.m. I wrote a scathing reply in which I pointed out I had been at work till three a.m. polishing AdWords Select and that, well . . . let's just say it went on for a page and a half of painful detail about his need for urgency and how it related to his management style.

I hit Send and waited for the response. It wasn't long in coming. "Don't send this," Cindy advised me, as I knew she would. I always ran venting tirades by her before sending them to the people who had wronged me. She understood my wrath and sent a curt note on my behalf. I had plenty of wrath to go around during those hectic days, when the smallest bumps threatened to upset my carefully balanced tray of tasks. My buffer, as the engineers sometimes said, was full.

With Google's expansion, the engineers found that they had outgrown the grand experiment begun with the awkward July reorg. In January 2002, Wayne announced that the company's flat structure could not scale much further. Yes, the executives had a clear line of communication to engineering, but Google intended to hire another hundred engineers that year. They couldn't all report to Wayne. The new goal would be to bring the reporting ratio down to thirty-five to one. Senior managers would be hired primarily for their technical skills, not their managerial ability. These new directors would recognize technical talent when they saw it and, when needed, could lend a hand rather than just encouragement.

A month later Jonathan Rosenberg, freed from his prior commitments by the bankruptcy of Excite@Home, joined Google as VP of product management. He formalized the responsibilities of the department Larry had started with Salar and defined the role of product manager. The PMs would work with engineering to design and develop new products and features, handle cross-organizational communication, and determine product road maps.

There would soon be many PMs, with many advanced degrees from the world's top business schools, law schools, and engineering programs. Our cultural evolution would take a giant leap from single-celled amoeba to vertebrate, from anarchy and individual autonomy to the controlled chaos that, at Google, was as close as anything came to a state of order.

Jonathan's new division shoehorned itself into a crack in the org chart between Cindy's corporate marketing group and engineering. When product management had been ad hoc, my colleagues and I had worked directly with engineers to prepare products for launching into the open market. Now PMs would formally coordinate that activity and draw on the PR specialists and brand management (that is, me) as they did on other corporate resources in their tool kit.

As the product-management wedge grew wider with the influx of new hires, resistance to being displaced intensified within Cindy's world. I, for one, was willing to be integrated, but I didn't want to be shoved aside. In a growing, engineering-driven organization, the power of product management could easily become an unstoppable force. Cindy's reports, including brand management, played a secondary role. We added the clear-coat finish on a precision automobile — our efforts invisible save for a glossy shine highlighting the beauty of the machine that lay beneath. My role still had value, because I worked on the language that went into the product itself. But thinking about how users perceived the product, and the company as a whole, was a low priority. The product would speak for itself, so what mattered most was the technology and the cool things that could be done with it.

The building's population density increased, even after we pushed finance and the ads team into an adjacent office, quickly dubbed the "MoneyPlex." Stacy in HR sent out multiple memos about office hygiene and our duty to respect the micro-kitchens, load our dirty dishes, put away the milk, throw out half-eaten bananas, recycle whenever possible, leave conference rooms clean, wash hockey gear, and keep animals out of the café, the kitchens, and the bathrooms. There were policies regulating dogs left alone, animal hair, and barking, barfing, and biting.

Charlie warned Larry, Sergey, and long-suffering facilities manager George Salah that he would expire without more space. A compromise was reached. A semitractor showed up one morning belching diesel and dragging a monstrous white trailer custom outfitted with ovens, dishwashers, pothooks, and prep counters. The leviathan was unhitched and beached in the parking lot adjacent to the café to bake in the sun like the victim of a drive-by harpooning.

The trailer contained a fully equipped mobile kitchen designed for use at large outdoor events. All it required was hookups to electricity and water. Those we had, though we lacked the permits that would have allowed us to use them legally. But what's a piece of paper compared with the happiness of hundreds of Google employees? Facilities plugged the trailer in and fired it up. With its painted sheet metal glinting in the harsh summer light and smoke pouring out of its vents, the "auxiliary kitchen" immediately lowered property values throughout the manicured office park in which Google was situated. All that was missing was a rusty Ford pickup on concrete blocks and an ugly mutt chained to a lawn chair. Charlie promptly had his crew run up the Jolly Roger on a pole jutting from the trailer's roof, proclaiming the auxiliary kitchen an interference-free zone. Charlie's outlaw kitchen crew operated unperturbed except for a lone fire truck that rolled up to investigate the smoke perfuming Mountain View with the aroma of a rib joint. Its crew left without citing us. Firemen. They do love barbeque.

CHAPTER 20

Where We Stand

U SERS WERE COMPLAINING again. We heard a rising chorus of annoyance with pop-up ads appearing when people did
Google searches. The ads opened new windows, cluttered users'
desktops, and irritated the hell out of them. Either we stopped running
pop-up ads, our users demanded, or they were prepared to stop using
Google.

Google never did run pop-up ads. Others just made it look as if we
did. A number of companies distributed free software for file sharing,
media playing, and the adding of smiley faces to email. When users
downloaded those programs, they unwittingly loaded their machines
with code that launched pop-up ads or even collected credit card numbers and other personal information.

Some software surreptitiously took ownership of computers and
made them "slavebots" that could be harnessed as part of a gigantic network to launch denial-of-service attacks or send spam. Techies called
these parasitic programs "malware," "adware," or "spyware." We lumped
them all together and called them "scumware."

Matt Cutts hated scumware. Intensely, personally hated it. His job
focused on blocking people who tried to trick or "spam" Google into
listing their sites higher in our results. He fought "black hats" every day,
and scumware distributors were the worst of the worst. It sickened him
that users thought we were the ones degrading their Google experience.

In late 2001, he began monitoring the rise of scumware and pleading with any Googler who would listen to do something about it.

I was with Matt. I loathed seeing notes from users threatening to quit Google because of something over which we had no control. I worked with him to draft a lengthy email response, in which we explained what was happening and how to fix it. People replied with apologies and thanked us for alerting them to problems they hadn't been aware they had. Matt wanted to do more. He proposed that the Google toolbar include software that killed pop-ups and that we forward complaints we received to the FTC. He also suggested we post a note on our homepage explaining that Google was not at fault.

Wayne Rosing supported the idea of a "full-scale crusade-jihad" against those responsible, but others worried about the danger of declaring war. We suspected there were hundreds of scumware creators, and we knew they could be . . . scummy. And spiteful. They didn't like to be thwarted, and they had no scruples about attacking those who tried to stop them. If we aggressively pursued them, they would target our site to make an example of us, causing even worse problems for users. Marissa suggested a compromise. If we could detect that a computer had been infected with specific scumware applications, we could show a message telling the user what to do about it. With that approach, we wouldn't confuse people who weren't experiencing problems and we wouldn't make ourselves too broad a target.

That solution turned out to be infeasible, so we fell back to posting a note linked from the homepage. We would tell users their pop-up ads weren't coming from us and casually mention that we did have our own, very discreet, very targeted, keyword-advertising program. Two marketing objectives satisfied simultaneously.

Larry didn't like the second part. Most of the people seeing our homepage would never advertise with us and might not even know we ran ads. Why disillusion them if they had no need to know? Larry never wanted to give people more information than he thought it was useful for them to have. I deleted references to AdWords.

In January 2002, we added a line to the homepage: "Google does not display pop-up advertising. Here's why." It was linked to a page that began, "Google does not allow pop-up ads of any kind on our site. We find them annoying." The response was immediate and positive, and I found it intoxicating. Google was becoming my own personal publishing platform. Mentalplex, the 9/11 news page, "Ten Things We've Found to Be True," and now "No Pop-Ups." The hits kept coming. We had built a global bully pulpit and my voice rolled forth from it. My thoughts, my ideas, my imprecations would be seen by more people than read the *New York Times* or watched a network newscast. I was the man behind the curtain giving voice to the all-knowing Oz. I tried to keep my ego in check.

The day after AdWords Select launched, the Associated Press ran a story about the service that said in part, "Online search engine maker Google Inc. is introducing a program that allows Web sites to be displayed more prominently if sponsors pay more money — an advertising-driven system derided by critics as an invitation to deceptive business practices." The article portrayed us as no better than Overture. It was flat-out wrong, yet major news outlets around the country ran it verbatim. The word "bastards" got a real workout in the Googleplex that day.

We had so carefully distinguished ourselves from the evil diminishers of search integrity, and all for naught. Cindy jumped on the AP to issue a correction, and they did, but she also reconsidered her original decision not to issue a press release about AdWords Select. She maintained a reporter-centric PR strategy of close communication with key journalists rather than "press-releasing" every burp, hiccup, and sneeze happening at the company. The strategy worked fantastically well most of the time, but when a reporter got a big story wrong, there was no official Google version to contradict it. Cindy and PR manager David Krane filed copy at two a.m. with the PR Newswire, saying, "Google's unbiased search results continue to be produced through a fully automated process and are unaffected by payment."

The AP story had been a fluke, an anomaly in a pattern of favorable press, but Cindy knew things would change. No one stayed beloved forever. Two days later she began formulating a "credibility campaign" to emphasize that not all search companies were created equal. We would use our own site to present our unfiltered messages in coordination with op-ed pieces in newspapers and executive speeches to select audiences.

"I want to kill the perception that we're selling our search results ASAP," she told us. "Our brand has been injured and we need to fix it. We're Google! Let's be outrageous and daring and have some fun with this."

Feelings ran deep on the subject of paid placement. When the topic of Google's refusal to sell placement came up on the geek bulletin board Slashdot, the first posted response was "I swear I want to make love to this company."

A self-identified Overture employee didn't share those warm and fuzzy feelings. "As for the claim by Google that they are pure," he asked plaintively, "why are they getting into the ad search business?" His implication seemed to be that the whole business was tainted. I didn't think so. You could present useful ads, but you needed to make it clear they were ads. It wasn't hard if you were willing to give up the revenue derived from deceiving users.

Larry and Sergey took the long view. Overture and the portals were training users not to click on links, because when they did, they felt cheated. It was our goal to make ads so useful that people would actually go out of their way to click them, even knowing that they were ads and not search results. To our founders, not being evil equaled sound business strategy.

My first contribution to Cindy's credibility campaign explained that principle. "Why we sell advertising, not search results," I wrote on our homepage in March 2002. The link led to a page that began, "In a world where everything seems to be for sale, why can't advertisers buy better position in our search results? The answer is simple. We believe you should be able to trust what you find using Google."

It didn't generate as much interest as our "No Pop-Ups" message, but our sales team loved it. It gave their clients a rationale for our refusal to offer pay-for-placement and detailed why that made us more ethical and more effective as an advertising medium. Our business-development team, though, had qualms about the closing: "Other online services don't believe the distinction between results and advertising is all that important. We thought you might like to know that we do." What about our partners like Yahoo? Would they view this as a swipe at them? After all, they ran Overture's ads above our search results.

It didn't help that with our Yahoo contract up for renewal, Inktomi suddenly got aggressive in attempting to win back the business, asserting that users introduced to Google on Yahoo's site would just search directly with Google in the future. Why would Yahoo let Google siphon off their audience? Inktomi even drove a mobile billboard around Yahoo's campus with the message "Do you, uh, Google? Google is stealing your users. A friendly reminder from Inktomi." We debated surreptitiously pasting the words "bringing you customers" over the phrase "stealing your users," but we decided not to legitimize our rival's feeble ploy.

Omid was not amused. He knew the perception was spreading that Google was not a friend of portal sites, especially since we were now openly seeking partners not just for search results but also for ad distribution. Sergey turned to marketing for data proving the perception false. We couldn't find any, though I spent months looking.

Our Earthlink win had cracked the icy stasis locking the search players in place. Suddenly conventional certainty was set adrift. Google had entered a new industry and won an account from a firmly ensconced leader. We had flawlessly implemented a substantial and complex advance in our back-end systems and transitioned from one economic model to another. Those accomplishments could easily have absorbed the full focus of a competent tech company for years. It was becoming clear that Google was more than just a competent tech company.

At the tail end of 2001, I had convened a group at Cindy's request to begin thinking about Google's evolving position in the marketplace. Since then, Susan, Sheryl Sandberg, Cindy, and a couple of other marketeers had gathered every few weeks to try and pin down Google's protean essence. We called our initiative "Baby Beagle," in homage to Darwin. Our corporate identity had morphed with our entry into ads syndication — but into what? We didn't want to be pegged as a portal, but we had outgrown the notion of being only a search engine.

Our group couldn't reach consensus. It was like the old story of sightless men describing an elephant by touching its leg, its trunk, its back. I needed to talk to someone who saw the whole picture. I needed to talk to Larry. The hour I spent with him and Sergey probing their vision for Google gave me my best look at their motivations and aspirations for the company. Cindy was the only other person in the room. It wasn't a press interview. They had no reason to shade their views or filter their thoughts. They expressed what they truly and deeply believed.

We spent the first fifteen minutes talking about what Google was not and what we would never do. Larry wanted Google to be "a force for good," which meant we would never conduct marketing stunts like sweepstakes, coupons, and contests, which only worked because people were stupid. Preying on people's stupidity, Larry declared, was evil.

We wouldn't mislead people like our partner Yahoo, which at the time was experimenting with a pay-for-inclusion program that sold placement in their results. Google wouldn't treat employees badly or sell products that worked poorly. We wouldn't waste people's time — a point Larry emphasized again and again.

We need to do good, he said. We need to do things that matter on a large scale. Things that are highly leveraged. When I asked for examples, he mentioned micro-credits in Bangladesh and the Rocky Mountain Institute and talked about changing business systems to make them environmentally friendly while saving money. He also talked about distributed computing, drug discovery, and making the Internet faster. And that wasn't all.

We should be known for making stuff that people can use, he said, not just for providing information. Information is too restrictive. In fact, we shouldn't be defined by a category, but by the fact that our products work — the way you know an Apple product will look nice and a Sony product will work better but cost more. We're a technology company. A Google product will work better.

We don't make promises and then break them.

If we did have a category, it would be personal information — handling information that is important to you. The places you've seen. Communications. We'll add personalization features to make Google more useful. People need to trust us with their personal information, because we have a huge amount of data now and will have much more soon.

Here his eyes took on a faraway look and his words came faster. Sensors are really cheap and getting cheaper. Storage is cheap. Cameras are cheap. People will generate enormous amounts of data.

Everything you've ever heard or seen or experienced will become searchable. Your whole life will be searchable.

Our conversation ended on that note. Not once did the subject of making money come up. Not once did he talk about advertising revenue or syndication or beating Overture or CPC or our new Search Appliance.

I was probably a naive middle-aged dreamer, because looking back at it now, I see there was nothing truly extraordinary about what Larry described. But when I walked out of his office I believed that for the first time in my life I had been in the presence of a true visionary. It wasn't just the specifics of what he saw, but the passion and conviction he conveyed that made you believe Larry would actually achieve what he described. And that when that day came, he would already be thinking another fifty years ahead. My respect for our two capricious, obstinate, provocative, and occasionally juvenile founders increased tenfold that day.

There were other glimpses of Larry's thinking. He and Eric shared a list of possible strategies that included Google as the publisher of all content, where users would pay us and we would reimburse the creators of everything from books to movies to music. Google as a provider of market research and business intelligence based on what we knew about the world. Google as an infrastructure platform and communications provider tying email and web data together. Google as the leader in machine intelligence backed by all the world's data and massive computing power that learned as it went along.

He had no small plans.

Eric, on the other hand, was the voice of corporate pragmatism. These grand schemes would have to be paid for somehow. "Any chart that goes up and to the right is good," he assured us. And, "I like to watch cash in the bank." I got the impression he shared my concern for all the things that could go wrong.

One fear I knew Eric had was of clowns. Specifically, the bozos who showed up at a company when it reached a certain size and bloated it with bureaucracy and bogged it down in mediocrity. Google's hiring guidelines explicitly stated we should only add people smarter than we were.

That's why we started running a line on the homepage that said, "You're brilliant. We're hiring." The engineers loved it.

I hated it. To me it reeked of arrogance and went counter to our "say little, do lots" brand strategy. I had opposed it when we ran it previously, but Marissa insisted the data showed it garnered more résumés than any of our other job-related lines. I got nowhere pointing out that a minuscule percentage of the people reading it on the homepage would be qualified to work at Google. Larry and Urs were willing to waste a few hundred million impressions to reach the dozen or so people they might consider hiring.

The page at the other end of the link had been written entirely by Jeff Dean. The word "exceptional" appeared three times in the first paragraph, and "problems" showed up four times in the next two sentences. I offered to smooth out the rough edges and nearly gave Wayne Rosing a heart attack.

"*No!*" he exclaimed. "Leave it alone! Please!" It was a page written for geeks, and if Jeff, our own über-geek, liked it, marketing's touch would only taint it. Cindy encouraged me not to let engineering roll over our department, so I sat down with Jeff and went through the copy line by line, making helpful suggestions. As I made the edits, Jeff said he liked most of them — then, as soon as I left, he undid them all. He knew what appealed to him and saw exactly how it would appeal to others like him.

It would be easy to assume from this anecdote that Jeff thought he was brilliant and was arrogant about it. That wasn't the case at all. In fact, Paul Bucheit told me, Jeff kept everyone humble. "You can't get up and be an asshole about being smart," Paul explained, "because Jeff's smarter than you and he's not an asshole." I think Jeff just looked at brilliance as a quantifiable asset. Since brilliance was a parameter for our search, it was best to specify that in a forthright manner.

I knew it would be pointless to keep fighting, and the page went up as written. I was learning to pick my battles.

The Copyright Crusade

One battle picked us. The Church of Scientology filed a complaint under the Digital Millennium Copyright Act (DMCA) demanding we remove links to Operation Clambake (www.xenu.net) from our search results. Operation Clambake, based in Norway, sought to expose what it claimed to be unethical practices within the church. The DMCA was a federal law requiring companies to remove content that an owner asserted was protected. In this case, that content included some of the church's internal documents and photographs on the Xenu website. We had no doubt the church would sue Google if we did not comply with the letter of the law and remove the references to xenu.net from our search results for the term "Scientology."

Ironically, while we were intent on keeping Google's internal processes private, many on our staff supported the first amendment rights of church dissenters to expose Scientology's secrets. I heard grumbling in support of those threatening to boycott Google for kowtowing to "an oppressive and censorious organization." The law was the law, however, and the DMCA was the status quo. But at Google the status quo was nothing more than an inconvenience to be improved upon as time allowed. Evidently, the time for fixing DMCA removal requests was now.

Matt Cutts led the charge. He proposed we put on our game face and drop pointed hints about how far we would go to defend our results, implying that we were committed to a more combative stance than we were actually prepared to adopt. He drafted a polite letter to his contact at the church (from whom we had received previous complaints) in which he laid out a number of paths Google might take, from publicizing that we had eliminated results at their request to letting the courts settle the issue.

Cindy was reluctant to stir the PR pot further. Larry and Sergey knew we couldn't bluff a group so famously litigious in protection of their copyrights. "Scientology will never back down," they advised Matt. "Focus on the per-search notification alerts. Figure out a way to let users know that some of our search results have been filtered."

Within a week, engineers Daniel Dulitz and Jen McGrath had come up with a solution. Any time a DMCA notice necessitated the removal of a search result, we explained that a result had been deleted and provided a link to a copy of the complaint on a website run by ChillingEffects.org. That way Google met its legal obligations while still letting users know what information had been removed.

Our user mail rapidly turned more positive. The *New York Times* ran an article about our innovative approach and noted that publicity about Scientology's complaint had pushed xenu.net to the second-highest spot in the search results for "Scientology" — just below the church's official site.

The xenu.net episode went a long way toward establishing our credibility with the hard-core, libertarian-leaning, free-speech army. I suspect some would have preferred Google go down in a blaze of glory, expending all our resources fighting the Scientologists in a Supreme Court smackdown, but they appeared somewhat appeased by Google's innovative way of "fighting without fighting." The outcome reinforced Larry and Sergey's optimism that there would always be a creative, technology-based solution when we got ourselves in a jam. We just had to be intelligent enough to see it, and if Google employees had anything, it was off-the-charts intelligence. Yeah, we could most definitely innovate our way out of anything.

That hubris would carry a price in years to come.

CHAPTER 21

Aloha AOL

I RAN INTO SOME Hawaiians," I informed our executive staff in March 2002. "They said Google had the best search technology in the market." Normally I wouldn't bother Larry and Sergey with compliments passed along at a marketing conference, but "Hawaii" was our code name for America OnLine (AOL).* We were scrambling to win their business from Overture, and the AOL vice-president I had spoken with gave every sign of being favorably disposed toward Google.

Overture was at the conference too. Their representative spent most of his time trying to convince our sales director, Tim Armstrong, to hire him. I took that as another good sign.

Our attack on Overture's business had been in the works for months, from the time Larry and Sergey had given the green light to AdWords Select. Launching an ad-syndication network was a major undertaking and new ground for Google. Omid realized it would take a unique combination of knowledge and skill to pull it off. Joan Braddi, the head of our sales team, could do it, but she was bogged down selling search services and managing the day-to-day sales effort. She would be part of the team, but she would need the help of a specialist. Omid knew exactly whom to call.

---

* AOL sounded like "Aloha," hence the nickname.

Alan Louie had worked with Joan and Omid at Netscape and now operated as an independent consultant. Lean, energetic, and given to wearing shades and safari hats, Alan had a degree in physics and had worked as an engineer at the Jet Propulsion Laboratory in Pasadena before moving into sales. He only took on unusual jobs and he only worked part-time. He didn't want direct reports. He didn't want to manage a team. He would handle the project, then leave when it was done. He started on contract at Google in October 2001. His assignment was to close the AOL deal, and he went about it with the dispassionate precision of an assassin stalking a high-profile target.

In addition to Alan and Joan, Omid pulled in Miriam Rivera, the second lawyer to join our legal group. John Barabino, who would head the syndication effort once the AOL deal was completed, became part of the team the day he was hired in February 2002.

Alan understood exactly what was at stake, and he knew the opposition. Overture had been born as GoTo in Pasadena, right down the street from the Jet Propulsion Laboratory. Even though they drew talent from Cal Tech and were plenty smart, they weren't Silicon Valley smart. They weren't really a tech company, and they didn't have the business intelligence Alan saw at Google. On the other hand, they had come up with the idea of marrying ads with search and implemented it before Google had.

When Omid called the AOL business-development unit run by David Colburn, AOL agreed to start talks with Google. Not because they intended to give us their business, but because they could use Google as a bludgeon to beat a better deal out of Overture when their contract came up for renewal.

Alan expected that. AOL was the giant of the Internet, with more traffic than any other site. They were doing deals every day and had enormous leverage. They had a reputation for being aggressive, foul-tempered, bloodthirsty, and brutal — and that was with their partners. Google was a pipsqueak trying to break up AOL's happy marriage to Overture with AdWords Select, an untested, unlaunched product with uncertain revenue potential. AOL was already making millions off Overture ads and had little incentive to put that guaranteed revenue at risk.

None of that fazed Alan or the Google team, who approached AOL as if we were already peers, not supplicants. "They wanted an emperor-to-toe-kisser kind of relationship," Alan recalls. "We came off as 'Okay, you can be emperor, but we'll be the pope.'" Part of the team's swagger came from their sense that AOL was heading up a blind alley toward a dead end. AOL was a walled garden offering screened, selected content to its subscribers. Google was coming from the Internet, an open system without limits. "We knew it was the overconfidence of youth, but it turned out to be correct," Alan told me. "It's just the confidence of knowing the industry and knowing what's going on."

Still, AOL was not going to come to Google to discuss the deal, so Google went to AOL. Their headquarters in Vienna, Virginia, was a sprawling complex not far from Dulles airport. It was hard enough on Omid's team that they were arriving at AOL's labyrinthine fortress armed only with an idea of what they wanted to sell, but all of them were also weakened by the five-hour flight and intense head colds. Their first stop was a pharmacy, where they loaded up on Cold-Eeze and Kleenex. Blowing their noses, they went to meet AOL's negotiating team.

AOL came on strong. The four staffers from Google, dressed in business-casual attire, were met by a dozen negotiators, product managers, and lawyers in expensive suits — a staffing ratio that AOL maintained throughout the negotiation. "They would always have this random cast of characters coming in and out," recalls Alan. "They'd have these people sitting in and we had no clear idea of what they were doing there."

Overwhelming presence was just one of many negotiating tactics. AOL also created artificial urgency, requiring the Google team to jet cross-country to address an issue that then dragged out over a week. The Googlers huddled in hotels, nursing their colds, while AOL's team went home to their families. If Google's negotiators were physically exhausted, they might cede key points, just to get some rest.

The tactic didn't work. "We've had enough," Alan finally announced to his AOL counterparts. "We're going back. We'll just do this over the phone."

"Great," they responded. "Go back home. You guys rest up over the weekend and just come back Monday."

Alan wasn't about to play that game. "Forget it," he said. "We're going home to rest up and we're inviting you guys out to California on Monday. You guys are much stronger and more able than we are, so you guys should come out to California. You guys are just supermen and we're not. I admit it. I'm a wimp."

AOL didn't fall for that. "Give it a rest," they told Alan. "We'll do it by conference call."

The deal would go nowhere, though, if we couldn't back up our claims about potential ad revenue with real data. While we had proven the value of our search technology with the Yahoo deal, Overture would make the most of our lack of a track record with syndicated ads, sowing FUD (fear, uncertainty, and doubt) about Google in the minds of AOL's execs. Overture was a known quantity and a reliable partner, and knew AOL would never agree to be our guinea pig. For a publicly traded company, the risk was way too high.

The only solution for Google was to sign a syndication partner ahead of AOL. Alan wanted someone who was already a good search partner and friendly toward us. Someone he could sign quickly. That was the real significance of the deal he negotiated with Earthlink in January 2002. Earthlink was our proving ground for AOL.

The Earthlink partnership was the ante that bought Google a seat at AOL's table. Now the real game began. There were no rules. David Colburn was an infamously intense negotiator sometimes called "the Butcher" for demanding — and getting — a pound of flesh from potential partners.[*] According to Alan, Colburn and the rest of AOL's team were the toughest negotiators he ran into during his time at Google. Their basic technique was to keep asking for more until the other team screamed uncle.

Colburn, Alan said, "would keep changing deal terms that had already been decided. We'd agree on certain things and then he'd just change them randomly — the prepay, the revenue split." These were key components of the deal, as was the amount Google guaranteed to deliver to AOL regardless of how the ads performed.

If we agreed to too large a guarantee, it could bankrupt us. The Google team knew the number would have to be big, because Overture was already providing AOL with a significant revenue stream. If Overture was delivering ten million dollars a year, AOL would build on that. They would argue they were growing at fifty percent a year, so the number Google needed to guarantee was actually fifteen million dollars. We would respond that there was a limit to how much Overture's flawed system could deliver, and that Google's method of ad ranking was so effective it would yield a much richer payoff. Ultimately, we would point out, Overture was training people to ignore ads altogether because their

___

system didn't automatically screen out irrelevant ads as AdWords Select did. "You think it's okay for your ads to get ignored?" Alan asked AOL. "No? So then you have to agree with our system."

No, AOL rejoined, Overture would clean up their system and make it more relevant. It wasn't in AOL's interest to admit that Google worked better, even after they came to believe it was true. "I think intellectually they agreed," Alan speculated, "but they wouldn't agree as part of the negotiation. They would always maintain that our system was worse. Their face to us was 'never give an inch.'"

Overture didn't sit idly by while we tried to steal their biggest customer. They struck back using one of the most powerful tools at their disposal: Google AdWords. Omid was in a meeting with the AOL team demonstrating our superior product when ads began showing up on searches saying "AOL sucks." The ads clearly hadn't been screened, so it was obvious to AOL that Google didn't have sufficient editorial controls in place. Omid excused himself and frantically called home to have the ads taken down.

AOL said, "This is a problem."

"It was a good move on Overture's part," admits Alan. "I would have done the same thing." The result was that the four members of Sheryl Sandberg's AdWords support team began hand-screening every single ad that was submitted. And AOL asked for a better understanding of Google's approval process.

"Here are Overture's policies," AOL said, dropping a phonebook-sized document on the table with a thud. "These are their editorial policies for what is allowed and what is not. Let's see yours."

"Fine. We'll show you ours," Alan replied. "Let's set up an appointment and do it right." We had no policy manual. But we would have one by the meeting the following Monday. Five minutes after that exchange, Omid was on the phone to Sheryl. "Overture has a binder," he told her. "*We* have to have a binder! We *have* to have a binder!"

Sheryl and AdWords staffer Emily White spent the weekend pulling one together. While they were at it, they pulled together an editorial team. AOL wanted to know how many people Google had dedicated to reviewing ads and approving them. By enlisting everyone in advertising operations who had ever looked at an ad, Sheryl stretched four to fifteen. "We didn't lie to them," she asserted, "but we included everyone we possibly could."

And Alan struck back by pointing out the weakness in Overture's system. He had the AOL negotiators search for "flight" to see the ads that came up. The top position wasn't occupied by American Airlines or Travelocity or Expedia. It was owned by a Midwest flight school for wannabe pilots that was willing to bid high for placement, knowing that thousands of people would see the ad but ignore it. These "squatters" paid only if someone clicked, so the exposure cost them nothing, but for Overture and AOL, it meant that the top position on a popular key-word generated almost no revenue. Google's more relevant ads would perform better.

Alan also showed AOL that we were willing to sweeten the pot at our own expense. Before Google entered the syndication market, Overture had owned a near monopoly. They set the terms for partners on rev-enue splits. For small partners the split might have been fifty-fifty, but for a large partner like AOL it would have been more generous. AOL might have been taking seventy percent of the revenue when some-one clicked an Overture-supplied ad on their site. Already, though, as George Mannes had postulated in his article, Overture's margins were slipping downhill. Our negotiating team gave them a helpful shove. We were willing to offer AOL eighty percent, a number we could afford because we kept all of the revenue for ads on Google.com.

AOL noted our strategic goals and our generous gesture and de-manded ninety-one percent. "We're going to make your network," AOL told Alan's team.

"No, you're not," Alan responded. Everybody knew he was bluffing. Larry and Sergey were desperate to kick-start our ad-syndication pro-gram, and a deal with AOL would leap across the Internet, creating a network effect that would bring in thousands of other sites. AOL had leverage and they used it to push harder and harder.

A key for Google was exclusivity for the placement of ads on AOL's pages. The more places to click on a page, the lower the odds a user would click on one of our syndicated ads. If Google was going to make the huge revenue guarantee AOL demanded, we would need every penny a page could generate. AOL kept offering "non-exclusive exclu-sivity." They drafted a ten-page section just on that topic, filled with loopholes and inconsistencies that would allow them to keep working with other partners. In the end, AOL kept the ability to run someone else's banner ads, and Google got exclusivity for text links in search re-sults.

Then Overture counterattacked. On April 4, they filed a lawsuit claiming that "bid-for-placement" belonged to them and that AdWords Select violated their intellectual property rights. They were taking us to court.

It's not ideal, when negotiating a contract, to have your rights to the technology you're selling be called into question. AOL immediately seized on our weakened position to push for even more concessions. Now they wanted access to the intellectual property behind our ad-serving system.

"Hey, they're suing you," AOL's team reasoned. "If you go down, we've got to go back to Overture hat in hand, so we want all of your intellectual property related to the ads system. Oh, and we want more money from you as well. Up front." It was the upfront payment that threatened Google's existence. If we miscalculated the revenue flow, we would be caught in a cash crunch that would kill the company.

Like bulldogs, the AOL team tightened their grip each time they sensed an opening, gradually moving closer to the jugular. As the far smaller partner, Google kept giving in.

Alan saw a need for a tactical shift. "I think we should say no and see what they do," he said to the rest of the team. "We can always go back and say yes." Step away from a deal and see what the other side does. If they were willing to walk away, we would run back, beg forgiveness, and throw an extra million dollars at them to show our sincere regret for offending them. It was that or keep acceding to every escalating demand.

For once, though, Larry and Sergey were unwilling to take the risk. "So we just kept agreeing until we screamed," recalls Alan. "Until they came back with something really egregious." AOL asked for *all* of Google's intellectual property—our code and secret search algorithms—if it ever looked as if we were headed for financial ruin. They had finally gone too far. Larry, Sergey, and Eric were furious at their demand for the very heart and soul of Google. No fucking way, they agreed. Their heels dangling over the cliff, they finally refused to take another step back. Alan recognized AOL's request for what it was: the closing gambit.

"That was the signal Colburn was waiting for," Alan told me. "Did he maximize his prize? Did he get everything he could get? As long as we were willing to give, we were the gift that kept on giving." It was a classic negotiation move. The only way to find the limit was to push past it. Once AOL knew they would get nothing more, the deal could be closed. Miriam was relieved. She had spent thirty consecutive days getting by on two to four hours of sleep each night, and her hair had become noticeably thinner. At one point David Drummond, our new VP of corporate development, had grabbed her wrist to keep her from throwing a pen at one of AOL's attorneys. Even by Google standards, the stress had been nontrivial.

We still needed a final number for the guarantee — the amount that we would pay AOL even if no one clicked a single ad. It was a deep pit into which Google would jump, with the faith that AdWords Select would pull us out before it collapsed. That faith relied entirely on revenue projections for the performance of AdWords on AOL. As CEO, Eric asked for three independent models, one from Susan, one from Salar, and one from Alan. They began pulling numbers from the limited data being delivered by Google.com and Earthlink. Neither, however, was AOL, so a lot of their assumptions primarily relied on SWAGs — scientific wild-ass guesses.

Alan was the sales guy. He was born optimistic. He looked at the numbers and saw a baseline. Google and Earthlink didn't have AOL's traffic or reach and their websites were not oriented toward consumer purchasing. People on AOL bought stuff. "I argued that as long as the advertisers were making money, they would create more ads," he told me.

As Susan and Salar saw it, that might be true theoretically, but in reality there were constraints that would prohibit meteoric growth. They plugged smaller numbers into their forecast assumptions. Salar was the most pessimistic; Susan was in the middle.

"I'm sure these are the three best models we could have," Eric said after they presented their scenarios. "And there's no way for me to know who's right. I'm not going to dig into the individual numbers, because I can't add any value there. So we're just going to take the middle one." It was a quick decision and strategically sound, but a gamble nonetheless.

AOL, meanwhile, nibbled around the edges, dragging out talks so that the cost of losing the deal would increase. "Oh, we just caught this and we need to change the language," Alan's counterpart would tell him, referring to wording that had been settled a dozen drafts earlier. Alan knew how to deal with middle managers trying to score points at the last minute to impress their bosses.

"Fine," he replied. "If you care that much about it, you call Dave Colburn tonight and have him call Eric Schmidt." Alan knew no one wanted to disturb Colburn for something insignificant and be lam-basted as an idiot. Suddenly the language was no longer an issue.

As negotiations dragged on, Overture continued to jab at Google. The patent lawsuit was followed by a deal with Hewlett-Packard that made Overture the default "search the Internet" link on new HP Pavil-ion computers. If HP thought Overture was good enough for Internet search, who needed Google? And Overture pushed Yahoo to renew their short-term advertising contract for a longer period. Omid had lost out to Overture with Yahoo once before. Now he burned to bring that business to Google. He would excuse himself from the negotiating table at AOL to entreat Yahoo on his cell phone to switch to Google's AdWords Select product. The Yahoo contract with Overture would ex-pire in June, so he knew time was short.

On April 24, 2002, Overture issued a press update on AOL. The ex-isting agreement, which had been set to expire, was being extended through May 1, 2002.

The next day, Overture announced they had renewed their deal with Yahoo. Two months early. The term was not the five months of the orig-inal agreement, but three years. It was a stunning surprise, and it rocked our world. Rumor had it that Overture had taken Yahoo's execs golfing and, over the course of eighteen holes, scored a major victory. Larry and Sergey had been blindsided by Yahoo again. They took it well, con-sidering. No one died that day.

Overture's Yahoo deal sent Wall Street's analysts into paroxysms of euphoria. Safa Rashtchy nailed the Google coffin shut. Investors had been waiting for the AOL deal and instead got the much more impor-tant Yahoo deal! Google clearly had no game. AOL was certain to sign with Overture now.

As May 1 approached, there was some nervous speculation about why AOL had not yet issued an announcement of a deal with Overture. "AOL must be raking Overture over the coals," read one online post.

On April 30, Omid's phone rang. It was Safa Rashtchy. Overture, he said, had announced they were not renewing their AOL contract. Did that mean Google had won it?

"Let me call you back," Omid replied. The deal still wasn't final.

Finally, Omid's fax started humming. Seventy pages chunked out, one text-heavy sheet after another. Miriam checked the document to make sure there had been no last-minute changes and then approved it. Joan signed it. It was done. But not over.

Overture's contract expired on Wednesday, May 1, 2002. AOL and Google were prepared to handle the transition throughout the day so that at midnight AdWords ads would begin filling the holes left by Overture's departure from AOL's pages.

But Overture threw one last wild punch. The contract would end on May 1, they agreed, but at exactly 12:01 a.m. Wednesday morning, not Wednesday night — twenty-three hours and fifty-nine minutes earlier than AOL had expected. "Overture were sore losers," Alan told me. "They said, 'No, no, no. Not at the end of Wednesday — at the beginning of Wednesday. We hate you guys. You're dead.'"

The Google team couldn't believe the depths of spiteful stupidity being displayed. Overture not only gave up a day's worth of revenue but pissed off AOL.

"You guys picked the right horse," Alan assured AOL. "We would never have done that to you." Overture's pettiness had AOL jumping through hoops to advance the schedule by a full day, just in the hope that Google would panic, drop the ball, and send AOL rushing back to their jilted partner. It didn't happen. Google's search results and syndicated ads launched at 12:01 a.m., May 1, 2002, and the world took note.

"The America Online pact now establishes Google as a major competitor in the paid-listings market, which Overture had dominated," wrote the *Wall Street Journal*. Overture's stock dropped thirty-six percent. Inktomi, whose search results Google had replaced as part of the same deal with AOL, dropped twenty-five percent.

"It represents an attempt to capitalize on Google's search brand," rationalized Overture CEO Ted Meisel. "Paid listings just came with the package." AOL switched because of the weakness of Inktomi's search results, according to Meisel's spin. Overture was just collateral damage.

Eric Schmidt's choice of Susan's mid-range revenue estimate proved unduly conservative. By the end of the contract's first year, we were far above the highest projections. Part of that success may have been attributable to a small shift made by an enterprising engineer. The day after the deal went live, John Bauer added code that boldfaced the keyword a user had searched for when it appeared in an ad, making it obvious that the ad was relevant. That single improvement increased clickthrough rates by four hundred percent. One engineer. One change. Four hundred percent.

I had plenty to do in the run-up to AOL's switch to Google. All of our advertiser communications had to be revamped; our new, more stringent editorial policies had to be communicated; and numerous slides showing the power of Google and AOL combined had to be prepared. It was clear that marketing had a role to play, and I plugged in to do my part as well as I could. It wasn't very exciting. Sheryl's support team was closer to the advertisers, and Jonathan's new product-management team did the deep thinking about integrating Google with AOL. I and my group were, as Jonathan described us to his team, "the ad agency" — a service bureau for implementing others' strategic visions. There was pressure, though. Everything had to be ready for the launch, which coincided with deadlines for the GSA team and Google answers, a service that used live researchers to answer complex questions for a fee.

I had no complaints, but after two and a half years, my job was taking the shape of a more traditional communications manager in a mid-sized firm. You wouldn't know it watching from the outside, but things were settling into a groove in my part of the Googleplex. Come in, work out, eat breakfast, answer email, put out fires, eat lunch, clean up messes, eat dinner, answer email, go home, write copy, answer email, go to bed.

Sheryl Sandberg, on the other hand, was sitting on a volcano. Her AdWords support team of four people could not possibly handle the incoming barrage of work AOL required. Google ads now had to meet AOL's editorial policies, and AOL was not as willing to embrace risk as Larry Page. They wanted every ad checked by hand before it ran. We had a hundred thousand ads in our system, and every day they didn't run, we lost money we needed to pay off our AOL guarantee.

Sheryl had been planning to double her department to eight full-time staffers. Now when she did the math, she realized she needed forty-seven people — immediately. She would need fifty more soon after that. The day the deal was announced, Sheryl put out a plea for staff volunteers to work on approving ads twenty hours per week for at least two weeks. The engineers offered some resistance.

"Doesn't everyone working here already have a job to do?" asked one, before pointing out that expanding the human component of the system was a flaw. Scaling by adding staff instead of algorithms and hardware would be a mistake. Salar came to Sheryl's defense and pointed out that there was a long list of tools that needed to be created, but not every task could be automated. Besides, Larry and Sergey had endorsed the idea of staff volunteers. Few were persuaded.

With almost no volunteers, Sheryl moved on to plan B. She called an agency and requested they send over fifty temps. Two days after the contract went into effect, dozens of temporary workers sat at desks in the open area we had used for TGIF meetings. Alana Karen from AdWords support stood at the front of the room and started walking them step by step through the process of approving an ad. Mass confusion ensued. The temps had no clue about online advertising, no familiarity with our approval process, and very little computer literacy. And the approval-tool software barely functioned. Sheryl watched with increasing frustration until she couldn't take it anymore. She marched upstairs to confront the half-dozen ads engineers.

"Come on," Sheryl said politely but firmly. "Come with me."

"Wait a minute," the group's manager protested. "You can't just take the entire engineering group with you somewhere."

"You come, too," Sheryl told him, using a tone she had developed as chief of staff to the U.S. secretary of the treasury. The engineers followed her downstairs and stood at the back of the training room as Alana tried to teach the temps to use the approval software they had written.

After a torturous hour, they stepped outside to talk to Sheryl. "The software doesn't work," they admitted. "We're going to rebuild it for you this weekend." Sheryl told the temps they would be paid for that morning and the next day, but not to come back until Monday.

On Monday all the temps came back, but they still weren't up to the task. Within two weeks, Sheryl had weeded out all but one of them.

On to plan C.

Sheryl cast her net at Stanford, which was stocked with recent graduates about to enter a dot-bombed local economy with few jobs. She promised them temporary positions that could convert to full-time if they worked hard and came up to speed quickly. The temp-to-hire program immediately took off, and dozens of history and sociology and philosophy majors unexpectedly had something to do the day after graduation. They would be AdWords reps.

Meanwhile, Eric Schmidt, the enormous AOL guarantee gnawing at his serenity like an ulcer, hovered about Sheryl's cube asking for updates. "So, how many advertisers do we have?" he'd ask. We needed to add tens of thousands to catch up to Overture.

"We're here," Sheryl would reply, pointing at a number on a spreadsheet.

"How many advertisers do we have now?" he'd ask a few hours later.

"Not many more than the last time you checked," Sheryl would say with the patience of a mom answering her child's query "Are we there yet?" We didn't pass Overture that first day, or even the first week, but it wasn't long before Google's ad network was as large as that of our biggest competitor.

More advertisers generated more ads, which required more AdWords reps to approve them. Sheryl's universe expanded from the AOL big bang until it filled half a building, and still it showed no signs of slowing. By October 2002, we had rented additional space in a facility as large as the one we already occupied. We officially called it the "Saladoplex" because it was on Salado Road, but everyone knew it as the "Honeyplex," because so many of the recent college grads Sheryl hired happened to be women. The outdoor patio lent itself to sunning on the warm California afternoons, and some AdWords staff members exhibited a predilection for clothing that facilitated tanning. Many a male engineer made the ten-minute walk from the Googleplex to enjoy lunch in the Saladoplex café.

Despite the sexist overtones, the Honeyplex name fit, as the building was a hive of nonstop revenue generation that paid for more machines, more engineers, and more AdWords reps to harvest the sweet bounty of our collective labors. The revenue engine driving Google's profits now hummed with a power equal to the search technology behind the growth of its user base.

Advertisers began finding us by word of mouth, so AdWords reps shifted from approving ads (a process that was increasingly automated) to persuading advertisers to spend more with us. Once they were in the system, Sheryl's organization — divided into tiers based on the budgets of the advertisers they served — assigned optimizers to improve performance. AdWords reps suggested more relevant keywords, set up multiple accounts for different product lines, and helped advertisers improve the sites linked to by their ads. Our AdWords reps didn't acquire customers, they just showed the ones we had how to make more money for themselves and for Google. By the time Sheryl left in 2008 (to become chief operating officer at Facebook), the AdWords group had grown from four people to four thousand, with most of the ad approvers stationed at offices in India and Dublin.

By winning AOL, Google had proved beyond a doubt the superiority of our ad-ranking technology and the value of maintaining a clear separation between ads and search results. So what happened next surprised everyone, including me.

We Walk the Line and Make a Misstep

"Is this new?" asked KeyMaster, a poster on the WebmasterWorld bulletin board. "Usually, ads are placed on the top of the search result page or boxed on the right side of the page. Now I see ads mixed in with the other search results."* KeyMaster was correct. For some users, on May 9, 2002, a Google search returned a paid listing embedded in our supposedly objective results. The paid listing was identified with the label "sponsored link," but it was the first time Google had displayed ads directly in line with regular results. It was essentially a form of paid placement, the exact practice Google had railed against so vehemently when it profited others.

By four a.m., a Google engineer using Matt Cutts' nom de plume, "GoogleGuy," had reassured the group: "This is a bug. Our new ad-distribution code had a flaw. It is mostly fixed already. It should be completely gone soon."

Not everyone was convinced. A poster named 4crests replied, "There is nothing like this anywhere else that it could have been confused with . . . was it a bug or a *test run*? Or is it something that is going to be served up to another search engine soon?"

Several other posters accepted the idea that Google was testing an interface for AOL and somehow it had slipped out onto Google itself. They weren't far off, but it wasn't AOL Google was conducting experiments for. It was Yahoo.

While our primary battle at AOL had been against Overture to provide advertising, we had also unseated Inktomi to provide AOL's actual search results. Inktomi wasn't ready to cede us the entire search market, however. Before taking AOL from them we had taken Yahoo, and they intended to win Yahoo back when their contract came up for renewal in June.

To Sergey's deepening frustration, I had been unsuccessful in finding third-party metrics to prove that adding Google search helped grow a partner's traffic. Without data to refute Inktomi's claim that we were

---

* http://www.webmasterworld.com/forum10003/3089.htm.

stealing Yahoo's users, we had to look for other ways to show our value. Perhaps we could provide unique new sources of revenue? Inktomi didn't offer ads.* Overture didn't offer objective search results. Google could deliver both in potentially lucrative ways. The Overture contract prohibited Yahoo from running Google's ads where Overture's ads appeared, but left an opening for our ads to appear as paid placements in the search results. Setting aside the irony, we planned to show Yahoo how that could work. We would test pay-for-placement AdWords on sites that used our "free-search" service.

We let free-search sites put a Google search box on their pages, but they couldn't run ads around the Google results. Only we could do that. We provided them with search service for free, and in exchange we kept the revenue generated by their users. Hardly controversial, but rolling out the new pay-for-placement test might be, so Larry and Sergey decided to show the ads to one percent of users for half an hour in the middle of the night — just long enough to gather some data on how much revenue they might generate.

We had made no commitment to actually implement such a system, and clearly there was no way in hell we'd ever actually do this on our own Google.com results pages. Marissa had a bad feeling, though, and expressed her concern that our test would be noticed and brought to the attention of the press. The only way that would be likely to happen was if the pay-for-placement ads ran on Google.com itself, which was not the plan. But things didn't go according to plan.

The paid-placement ads began showing up in Google's own search results. There was a bug in GWS, Google's web server, and it caused the ads to spread outside the limited test zone. Webmasters whose livelihoods increasingly depended on reading the entrails of Google's ranking system couldn't miss such a significant change. We stuck by our explanation that a bug had unintentionally caused the test of a partner interface to appear on our own results pages.

Engineer Howard Gobioff later let me know that there were other instances when engineering was instructed to code ads into search results. I never saw them because, according to Howard, "someone always cared enough to make noise." He laid the blame at the feet of new PMs and business-development folks who argued that what we did on part-

---

* Inktomi did have an extensive "paid inclusion" program that allowed websites to ensure they showed up in search results.

ner sites didn't matter and that, besides, the ads would still be marked as paid placements.

Howard said the engineers required to write the code buried some editorial commentary in its internal documentation. "This is evil but they made me do it," one engineer wrote. In Howard's opinion, the idea finally died because Sergey decided that it crossed into an ethically gray area and wouldn't play well in the press. We were willing to walk up to the edge of evil to get a closer look, but ultimately, Larry and Sergey were unwilling to cross certain lines. "Don't *be* evil" is not the same as "Don't consider, test, and evaluate evil."

Yippee! Yahoo!

On Friday, May 10, we celebrated the AOL deal with another company-wide luau catered by Charlie. Our executive team showed up in grass skirts. AOL sent over a giant blue lava lamp with their logo on it. Devin Ivester created a commemorative t-shirt with a traditional Hawaiian motif, but Larry made him change one element in the design: he insisted Devin remove the date. Larry didn't want anyone walking around wearing a reminder of when our AOL contract would be up for renewal.

Two months later, we took Ask Jeeves away from Overture. Overture CEO Ted Meisel remarked to the Associated Press, "We are still winning more deals than we are losing and I think we are winning all the right ones."* Now Overture had backhanded both AOL and Ask Jeeves. Not the way to make or keep friends.

Analyst Safa Rashtchy declared that the battle for audience share was over and that "Yahoo would probably accurately claim that they won, with something like 200 million worldwide users."† Yahoo must have felt far enough in the lead to keep working with us. In November 2002, they renewed their contract with Google. In fact, they expanded Google's presence, making us the primary source of their search results instead of delivering results from their own directory first. That came at a cost.

Miriam Rivera, the Google attorney who had worked herself to exhaustion on our AOL deal, also worked the Yahoo renewal. She remem-

---

* http://www.hollywoodreporter.com/hr/search/article_display.jsp?vnu_content_id=1548269.
† http://articles.latimes.com/2002/jul/21/business/fi-yahoo21.

bers Yahoo being wary of Google to the point of paranoia and hesitant to strengthen us as a competitor. As a result they put the screws in. Hard. "I would not have done the deal," she said, reiterating what she had told Larry, Sergey, and Eric at the contract-review meeting. "They wanted an open kimono from us, where we would alert them to all the technology we had in development. They wanted parity — everything we developed, they would get too." Miriam didn't think it wise to constrain ourselves that way. Besides, our billion-dollar deal with AOL made the tens of millions Yahoo offered seem insufficient compensation for all they sought in return.

In the end, Omid's friendship with Udi Manber at Yahoo and Larry and Sergey's desire to stay on Yahoo's good side won out. Keep your friends close, went the strategy, and keep your enemies closer. We accepted the offered terms. From that point on, we had to notify Yahoo before we launched any new feature. When Miriam went on vacation, she carried a copy of the contract with her and took calls day or night about product-disclosure issues. Given Google's aversion to process, it upset everyone that we now had to check with our competitor before moving ahead on new technology.

The relationship began on rocky terms — a marriage of convenience that bound the partners together so neither could run too far ahead of the other. It was a relationship between a fading name and a rising star and destined to fall apart. Just a month later, in December 2002, Yahoo bought our competitor Inktomi and began working to replace Google's search results once and for all.

CHAPTER 22

We Need Another Billion-Dollar Idea

THERE," CINDY SAID to Jonathan Rosenberg, pointing toward the parking lot. "That's my car." As she spoke, a stretch Hummer rounded the corner, impossibly long and large. It had once been white, but now it was coated with mud from hood to trunk. We had added that finishing touch at Cindy's request, and she was pleased with our efforts. It was a complete and utter mess. Jonathan looked stunned for a moment, then laughed and picked up a bucket and a sponge and began swiping at the mud-covered windows. That's when we unleashed the water balloons.

Jonathan Rosenberg came to Google to bring structure to product management. He arrived none too soon. By the spring of 2002, the PMs were driving me nuts. In one twenty-four-hour period, I found myself in the middle of disputes between PMs and engineering, PMs and advertising support, and PMs and other PMs. Communication among our swelling groups kept slipping into darkness and dragging marketing along with it.

Jonathan had the unenviable task of corralling not just the new hires but also big-name old-timers like Susan, Salar, and Marissa, all of whom now ostensibly reported to him. They didn't always act that way. It was a classic syndrome of a startup becoming a real company — old-timers refusing to acknowledge that there were new rules to play by. One of those rules for every engineering and product-management employee was filing snippets, the weekly reports of projects currently under way and the progress that had been made on them since the previous week. Snippets were compiled and distributed automatically, and the software that did this had been written to insert snide comments about those who failed to file.

Jonathan wanted his product-management group to improve its compliance, and being extremely competitive, he decided the best way to encourage his staff and bond them together as a team was to challenge Cindy and her corporate marketing group to a contest. The head of the group ending the quarter with the lower percentage of snippets filed would have to wash the other manager's car while the winning team assaulted the loser with water balloons. We became the first group in the company to attain a one hundred percent filing rate, an eventuality that Schwim, who had coded the system, had never anticipated.

When the day of reckoning arrived, we came prepared with Super Soakers, a blender churning out margaritas, and a boom box belting out carwash tunes. Jonathan was soon sopping wet and making little progress on the task at hand. He looked mortally betrayed when members of his own team joined in the assault against him. Cindy, sensing things were getting out of hand, stepped in and grabbed a sponge, putting an end to the deluge.

We had wanted to see Jonathan share our pain. Our lives had changed with his structured approach to product management. In July 2002, he reorganized his division and introduced the roles of APM (associate product manager) and PMM (product marketing manager) and promptly went on a hiring binge.* There were suddenly many more flavors of PMs, and they all needed more from me and my marketing colleagues. It was convenient to blame Jonathan for the hailstorm of their demands and for their apparent belief that we had no projects on our plates other than theirs.

It was all part of a shift that Eric Schmidt had outlined at our first mid-quarter ops review back in May, a meeting held at a restaurant adjacent to the municipal golf course just down the road. Lunch was lasagna. Forty of us — mid-level managers and execs — had gathered in a low-tech conference room that was sunny and hot. We kept the door open, despite the threat of ducks wandering in off the putting green and

---

*PMMs focused on marketing our revenue-generating products and working with sales on customer acquisition, market analysis, retention, and loyalty. APMs were usually recent grads in training to be PMs.

the irritating "beep—beep—beep" of golf carts backing up just out-side. Sergey sat at the front wearing a spandex biking shirt and shorts. Every few minutes he would launch a tiny remote-controlled flying sau-cer/hovercraft and send it careering around the room or try to make it hover over Larry's head. Susan coordinated the meeting, keeping time on presentations to ensure we stayed on schedule.* Eric kicked off the meeting by laying out the "Google Great Company Five," the areas we needed to get right in order to become a great company: global sales, strong brand and ethics, great financials, a good hiring process, and in-novation.

No major initiatives resulted directly from the get-together, but it marked, as Eric called it, "a phase change in our evolution." We were consciously leaving behind our startup days and becoming a big com-pany that made plans, communicated them to key managers, and then reviewed them on a scheduled basis. Eric established a mailing list called "VIPs" for directors and vice-presidents to keep us informed and to solicit input. And he offered a few directives of his own.

"Get a checkup," he instructed David Drummond. It had been a while since David had been to a doctor, and Eric wanted to be sure everyone was in good health for the challenges ahead.

"Buy a house with broadband," he lectured Bart Woytowicz, who complained about his slow Internet access at home. "Every one of you needs DSL or cable access."

"Develop better metrics for everything—from hiring women engi-neers to advertiser conversion rates," he reminded all of us. "And look for things we can patent."

I came away from the ops review determined to button down our marketing efforts and make them more systematic. My focus would be on supporting our revenue initiatives. And growing our international presence. And distilling our brand message. I had already put a fair amount of work into all three, but had really nailed the last one. The day before the offsite, I had sent our executives a list of five thematic messages for all Google communications—a distillation of a discus-sion I had been leading in our Baby Beagle group over the previous six months. We had started off looking for an alternative to "portal" to

---

* All important Google meetings after this one included a digital countdown clock that showed speakers how much time remained before they had to end their presentations.

describe our business and ended up looking more deeply into our core identity as an institution.

"Google drives better decisions," I wrote. "Google technology makes things more accurate, while making them easier to use. Google is ubiquitous. Google creates information marketplaces. Google is a clear channel for information." I offered brief explanations and showed how each point related to core elements for our business, from our mission statement to our privacy policy. I suggested we brand our approach to problem solving as "GoogleLogic," a blanket identifier incorporating all of Google's unique attributes — a one-word answer to any question about how or why we did what we did. Our new secret sauce, if you will.

I believed I had identified the deep benefit of our brand for users (enabling better decisions) and developed an identity in GoogleLogic broad enough to encompass everything from our technology to our hiring process. It moved us well beyond PageRank, the name for Larry's original ranking algorithm. PageRank only applied to Google's search engine, and even there it had been largely supplanted over time. GoogleLogic positioned us on a much bigger playing field of products and services. And it had that nice echo of the *g* and the *l,* almost as if "Google" and "logic" were mirrored halves of the same entity.

Jonathan and Cindy and Susan sent positive feedback, but I heard nothing from Larry or Sergey. I pinged them a couple of days later. Still no response. When, after another two months, I finally pushed Sergey for a thumbs-up or thumbs-down, I did it as an "assumptive sale": I assumed it was okay to publish our five thematic messages company-wide unless anyone had objections.

"I have an objection," came Sergey's long-awaited reply. "I think they need more thought." That was it. I'd been down this path before. I trapped him in his office and demanded more specific direction.

"Doug," he said, "I think you're slipping back into your old big-company ways. I don't know where this came from, but I don't see any point to it. Why do we need this kind of thing?"

Uh. Buduh. Duh. He apparently had no recollection of the six months of updates our Baby Beagle group had been sending him.

"I will not smite Sergey," I counseled myself. "I will not smite Sergey." I walked him through the process and the applications for a unified messaging strategy with press and our users. I explained the benefits of having a positioning platform that we could build brand extensions on.

He shrugged. He didn't see it, but if it was that important to me, fine. I could post it on the marketing page on MOMA. I was glad to have such an enthusiastic endorsement from the man who, just a week before, had been named "Marketer of the Year" by *Marketing Computers* magazine.

And, of course, Sergey turned out to have a point. I had convinced myself that our engineers would love the concept of GoogleLogic. They didn't. It wasn't impressive enough. They suggested "GoogleMagic!" Now that, they said, had some punch to it.

Other than my colleagues in PR, no one at Google was thinking much about our messaging strategy. Not yet. It wasn't all that important to people focused on building products, even when George Reyes joined us as chief financial officer in September 2002 — crossing another big item off our pre-IPO checklist. Presumably, if we ever went public, we'd need some coherent story to tell Wall Street, but no one seemed terribly concerned about that now.

I put it aside and dove into working with sales on winning more advertisers and helping our PMs prepare the products they were pushing through the pipeline. Tim Armstrong and his salespeople always seemed grateful for any effort we made on their behalf. Jonathan's group just got hungrier for more. We had a continual tug of war over who would do what and what was reasonable to expect, and Jonathan got tired of it. So when I copied him on a note confirming who would write a customer newsletter, his short fuse burned down to powder and he blew up.

"I don't want to get in an email debate over who owns what," he stormed to the group. "I can't get into monthly debates over ownership." There had been no debate in this case, just a reiteration of responsibilities. Unbeknownst to Jonathan, there was a performance issue with a member of marketing that needed to be documented in writing. My note had been intended in part to do that. Given Jonathan's VP role and his growing reputation as a forceful personality, it would have been easy to bow my head abjectly and apologize for the perceived error of my ways. I may have mentioned that I come from a stiff-necked people.

"Whoa," I responded, then let Jonathan know he had misinterpreted the intent of the email and that he was the only one sensing a conflict. I offered to take it offline with him if he thought clarifying responsibilities delayed execution rather than accelerating it. He backed down and came as close to an apology as he could without actually saying he was sorry. He privately explained his frustration about having a new team that had yet to mesh and seemed to be taking longer than necessary to get things done.

After that incident, we reached an understanding. Jonathan could be loud, insistent, and overbearing at times with his own staff, who seemed wary of his mercurial mood shifts. With me, though, he adopted a paternal air (despite my being three years older) and offered some level of respect — perhaps because I had not hesitated to return his fire.

So when Jonathan established a "chain gang" comprising new members of his team, he offered to have them work on low-level tasks in my department, such as checking that our partners were using our logo properly on their sites. Likewise, I offered his PMs my first-born son, Adam. At age fourteen, he needed something to get him out of the house over summer break. Jonathan threw some assignments Adam's way and, though he was too young to be paid, gifted him with a new iPod when the work was done.

I appreciated Jonathan's generosity and took his eccentricities in stride. "Look, I'm on a scooter!" he once shouted as he rode past Sergey and a reporter interviewing him. Later he told me he wanted the reporter to write about the wacky ways of Googlers — not one of the key messages in Cindy's PR plan.

"Look! I'm a human pop-up ad!" he exclaimed on another occasion, walking in front of me as I presented to a group of Wharton MBA candidates.

"Ladies and gentlemen, our VP of product management," I murmured as he strode on down the hall followed by their incredulous stares.

And I definitely picked up on tension between Cindy and Jonathan over his ambition to do greater things at Google. The first logical way to expand his empire would be to annex Cindy's small corporate marketing group. She made it clear that issues in his own backyard needed addressing before he made any moves toward her domain. "I was hoping *you* would tell *us* the next step," she pointedly responded when he offered to help resolve an issue about pricing for the Google Search Appliance (GSA). "Maybe a conversation with your PM? Or some decisive action?" At other times her tone was even terser, as when she insisted that she needed to interview any candidate for a job with "marketing" in the title. The tension ebbed and flowed with shifts in the overall barometric pressure within the Plex. One day Cindy and Jonathan were rivals, the next, the closest of colleagues.

My own issues with Jonathan's group settled into a low simmer and I hoped to keep them there. I admonished my group not to wallow in an us-versus-them mentality regarding the PM group. I admitted my own sins in demonizing Jonathan's team and suggested we focus on getting things done, not on the obstacles that might stand in our way. I said that if my direct reports came to me with a complaint about a colleague's demands or behavior, I would first ask if they had addressed the issue with the person involved and what thoughts they had about solutions.

Those rules didn't apply in product management, however. When Marissa felt too much marketing attention was being paid to the GSA at the expense of her Google.com initiatives, she came straight to Cindy. In particular, she felt we weren't sufficiently supportive of Krishna Bharat's soon-to-be-launched Google news service, a product in which she had developed a special interest. At the same time, the GSA team hammered us daily for more ways to generate sales leads, despite the relatively small revenue the Search Appliance represented. In trying to balance the needs of two different product groups, I was pleasing neither. I informed Cindy that going forward I would focus more effort on consumer marketing for Google.com, and I began thinking about ways to do that without spending any money on advertising.

I could not deny, though, that Jonathan was putting in place a strong and disciplined structure for product management. He understood the data-driven decision-making mindset of our corporate leaders and gave us sound guidance on how to move projects past them. "Board members don't want lists of possible ideas," he pointed out as we prepared a presentation about getting more users to download the Google toolbar. "They just want to know exactly what we're going to do and when we're going to do it." Time and again he sent slides back for more data, until they were dense with numbers and graphs and pointed to inescapable conclusions.

I learned things by listening to him. But that didn't stop me from bringing my bazooka-sized water gun from home and unloading on him as he washed Cindy's car.

The influx of PMs, APMs, and PMMs filling out Jonathan's org chart reinforced Google's meritocratic culture. Most were young. All had impressive credentials. Jonathan made sure everyone knew how high he had set the bar by distributing the résumés of those who had *not* made the cut. He wanted his staff to feel elite and Eric to rest assured there would be no bozo invasion on his watch. All these brilliant tyros caught on campuses and released in our cube farm impressed and unsettled me. Jonathan was right, I concluded. The quality of employees, at least on paper, was improving. I knew my questionable GPA and lonely BA would not make the cut if I had to meet Google's revised hiring standards.

I remember attending a product-review meeting in Larry and Sergey's office with Nikhil Bhatla, an APM so fresh out of Stanford that the ink on his sheepskin was still wet. When the meeting broke up, I stayed to harass Sergey about a marketing question he had been avoiding. Time like this was precious, because it was the only way to force decisions on issues not key to keeping the site up and running.

As the group filed out, I started making my case to Sergey, expecting to have five minutes mano-a-mano in which to persuade him. I was surprised when he looked over my shoulder at Nikhil, whose curiosity had caused him to linger. "What do you think of this idea?" Sergey asked him, then listened carefully as Nikhil laid out a cogent, well-argued response that poked enough holes in my idea to fill the Albert Hall.

I confess, I wasn't happy that this . . . this whippersnapper with no experience at Google was sitting in judgment of my proposal. Didn't he realize he was a junior staff member and shouldn't be within earshot to begin with? This would never have happened at the good ol' *Merc*, where proprieties of rank were carefully observed and it would have been unseemly, impolitic, and career-threatening to blatantly refute a manager in front of the company's top executive.

After walking briskly around the Plex a few times to cool off, I came to realize that Nikhil had made valid points. I also realized that I shouldn't have been surprised. It didn't matter that he'd only been on the job a short while. He was a smart guy. He didn't require immersion in Google's milieu to construct a logical argument when asked to do so.

That I took this lesson to heart can be seen in my own response, a year later, to an executive from another large technology firm with whom I was negotiating. I wanted his company's software for creating web pages to include an easy way to incorporate a Google search box. I had brought Priti Chinai, a recent hire from our business-development team, into the discussion. The outside exec let me know privately that, no offense, but Priti was too junior for him to waste time with. He only dealt with decision-making VPs.

"No offense taken, I said, "but you need to understand how Google works. We don't have senior VPs. We have Larry and Sergey and everybody else. The VPs we do have are involved in functional roles, like driving engineering projects. I understand your wanting to cut through bureaucratic layers, but if Priti recommends we do the deal, it will end up in front of Eric, Larry, and Sergey for sign-off. If she recommends against it, it won't go very far. If she needs more input, she knows all the people to ask." I found myself annoyed that he had the audacity to assume any Googler on our team couldn't have put the deal together after fifteen minutes of preparation.

Our work lives were too full of threats and opportunities to waste resources on bureaucratic redundancy. During the dog days of summer in 2002, we were juggling a dozen chain saws.

The Chinese government unexpectedly blocked our search results, as they had done once before in the spring of 2001. We didn't know why, exactly, but suddenly we had thousands of emails in Mandarin asking about other ways to access Google. Then the block was dropped. No reason was given. Eric had discussed getting Al Gore to mediate with the Chinese, but I don't think that actually happened. At least I didn't hear him talking about it outside my office door.

We set up a program called Google Grants to provide free AdWords ads to nonprofits. I had proposed a simple public service advertising (PSA) program months before and worked on the user interface, but Sheryl Sandberg was the one who crystallized the idea and brought it to life.

We fought a trademark lawsuit over a company using our name for its online store. I was deposed. I had never given a deposition before and had to be coached on how to approach it. I spent days learning not to answer any question I wasn't asked and to ask for the definition of any term that was ambiguous. I perversely enjoyed my four hours of sweating in front of a video camera sparring with the opposing attorney.

"Did you communicate this verbally?" he asked.

Pause. Think. "Can you define what you mean by 'verbally,' please?"

"Verbally! You know! Did you talk to him?" The attorney's frustration was audible.

"Well." Pause. "My understanding of 'verbally' is that it means 'expressed in words.'" Pause. "That can mean in writing. Or it can mean by speaking." Pause. "Did you mean 'orally'?"

We won that case. Our attorney Kulpreet was so happy with my Forrest Gump impression that he recommended me for a peer bonus — a thousand-dollar award any employee could receive for helping another department in its hour of need.

As our network of ad-syndication sites grew from Earthlink and AOL to include Ask Jeeves and the *New York Times* website, we needed branding guidelines to tell each new partner how to display our search results and our ads and where to put our logo. Creating them turned out to be complicated and time consuming, especially after we won the ad contract for InfoSpace from Overture. InfoSpace ran a number of metasearch sites, which included Google search results alongside those of other search engines. The deal was a big bite out of Overture's revenue, but we didn't want our brand to become just another generic ingredient in a salmagundi of results. I wouldn't allow InfoSpace to put our logo in their ads with all the other search engines, even after they had paid stiff penalties to Overture to break the exclusivity clause in their advertising contract with them.[*] The sales team backed me up but made me go to dinner with "the client" so InfoSpace could tell me how wrong I was. I didn't eat much, and swallowed less.

But the main thing Sergey was focused on that summer was finding a billion dollars. CPC AdWords was an unqualified success. It gave every indication it would pump dollars into our bank account for many years to come. That worried Sergey. Someone, somewhere, was undoubtedly watching that cash flow and working to come up with a new development that would make our search ads obsolete. If that happened, Google would end up a bit player in the Internet economy. We needed, Sergey believed, to uncover another billion-dollar business idea and launch it quickly. Larry agreed wholeheartedly, his paranoia every bit as deep as his co-founder's.

It was Paul Bucheit who showed them where to look.

Just for the Hack of It

Paul liked to hack things together. In his free time, he was constructing an email system he called "Caribou" — named for a poorly managed

---

[*] Overture subsequently sued InfoSpace, a move that sent other potential Overture partners a rather negative message.

project assigned to the comic strip character Dilbert. We would later call it "Gmail." He had been working on Caribou for a couple of years. Though dozens of Googlers, including Larry and Sergey, were using it, almost everyone he talked to at Google hated the idea of becoming a provider of email to the public. Some opposed it from a technical standpoint, some from a business point of view. But they all agreed on one thing. An email system should never display advertising based on the content of the email messages it sent or received. It was both technically infeasible and unacceptable from a product perspective.

"Before I was even working on Caribou," Paul told me, "Udi Manber[*] came in for a talk and I remember asking him, 'Do you think you could ever do content-targeted ads on email?' And he said, 'Oh no, we would never do that. That's a gross violation of whatever.' It was like, you should be fired for even asking that question."

Paul knew his mail system would never launch if it couldn't eventually pay for itself. He considered building in premium services or offering six-month free trials, but knew those models would inhibit widespread adoption. And Sanjeev Singh, a colleague helping out with the coding, kept bringing up content-targeted ads.

Paul liked to hack things together.

One night, he and Sanjeev went through his inbox one email at a time and tried to manually match each message to an ad already in the system. It wasn't that hard. Paul decided to put together a simple prototype that would do the matching automatically. He rummaged around his code files and came up with a classifier tool: software that could identify things that were related and group them. He had written it as part of Matt Cutts's porn filter project. Perfect for what he had in mind now. He reconfigured the porn classifier to match ads to the content of emails, flipped it on for all the users of Caribou at three a.m., and went home.

The next day, all the engineers using Caribou saw ads targeted to the content of the messages in their inboxes. They were not pleased. Paul recalls that Marissa, with whom he shared an office, was furious.

"We agreed not to do this," she insisted. "And then you went off and did it anyway."

"I don't remember ever agreeing to that," Paul replied. "Maybe you

---

[*] Director of search technology at Yahoo.

said not to, but I never agreed to anything. I'm not really that agreeable a person that I would ever agree not to do something."

Larry and Sergey weren't furious. They were impressed. The idea of content targeting had been around for a long time, but only as a theoretical concept. It was even on the engineering project list, but assigned a priority of one — the lowest — on a scale of one to five. Everyone assumed it would be hard to build and not terribly accurate. Yet Paul had built a working prototype in a couple of hours, basing it on a self-described "stupid hack" he had written for another project.

The founders, according to Paul, "were more open-minded about it than most of the rest of the company." They immediately saw the potential for targeting ads, not just to email, but to the content of *any* web page that contained text. They pulled together a team in September 2002 to start working on a more robust content-targeting system under the code name "Conehead." A month later, Google content-targeted ads started showing up around the posts in the old Deja News Usenet pages that had been incorporated into Google groups. A month after that we paid for low-cost remnant ad space — impressions that had not been sold and would have displayed house ads or PSAs — on small test sites like the ever-agreeable Wunderground.com to see if we could earn more from the ads than it cost us to pay for the media. In March 2003, Google's content-targeted ads publicly launched, expanding the places our ads could potentially appear to include almost every web page on the Internet. Google shared revenue with sites (which we called "publishers") that ran our ads, so small businesses, blogs, and even larger content producers struggling to sell their own ads could now turn on the cash spigot by adding a few lines of Google's code. In June 2003, we even made the sign-up process for publishers self-service (like AdWords for advertisers), calling the new service "AdSense."*

AdSense gave Google an incentive to help grow the amount of content online. The more content on the Internet, the more potential revenue for us. Larry's idea of digitizing all printed pages suddenly became a much higher priority. We launched Project Ocean in late 2002 to begin moving the "ocean" of offline content online. That initially meant sending Googler Cari Spivak to a giant used-book sale in Phoenix, where she bought twelve thousand volumes, loaded them in a

---

*There were still tweaks to be made. When the *New York Post* ran a story about a murder victim whose dismembered body was found in a suitcase, AdSense displayed an ad for a luggage store next to it.

WHERE WE STAND

rented truck, and shipped them back to Mountain View to be scanned. Soon Google would be signing agreements with university libraries to scan all their printed materials and battling publishers and authors in court over copyrights. And Google bought Pyra Labs, a small company offering tools for anyone who wanted to create and host a blog at its site Blogger.com.*

Google's second billion-dollar idea had been much easier to implement than the first.

For Paul, the experience confirmed the power of prototyping to give definitive answers far more quickly than theoretical discussions. "Experiencing something is much more powerful than just talking about it," he reflected. "I didn't think content-targeted ads would work, really, but I thought it would be fun. I spent a few hours working on it. It wasn't that I believed in it that strongly, it's just that it was really easy." Once people saw the prototype in action they realized, whether they liked Paul's implementation or not, that content targeting could be done.

Google learned a lesson, too. Paul had put together a prototype not specifically called for by his project, just because he found it interesting. He admitted to being easily distracted and had gone off on tangents before, but usually his manager reeled him in. When he added a primitive spell checker to the product search he was building, Urs admonished him for having too many side projects and asked him to stay focused. That attitude changed after he developed the content-targeting prototype. Not just for Paul, but for the company.

"I feel like the concept of twenty-percent time came out of that," Paul told me. "I don't think it was ever specifically stated, but it was more officially endorsed after that." "Twenty-percent time" was a mandate that all those in engineering spend one day a week thinking about something other than their assigned projects. Ad targeting in email had not been assigned to anyone, and most who heard about it vehemently opposed it. Paul built it anyway, and the company's thinking shifted overnight. Other engineers had also done side projects that looked promising, like Krishna's Google news service. Larry and Sergey wanted to encourage that kind of behavior.

At first, Paul observed, APMs ambitiously tried to organize the

---

* The founder of Pyra was Evan Williams, who left Google to found another startup that eventually evolved into the social-networking company Twitter.

twenty-percent time so it wouldn't be a wasted resource. "That was completely the wrong mindset," he said later. "'Oh, these engineers are working on random things. We need to coordinate them and manage it.' The real value is that people will do things that everyone thinks are a waste of time. That's where the big opportunities are. It's an opportunity because other people don't see it." Google itself was a canonical example. No other companies had thought search was important. If they had, Microsoft or Yahoo would have invested more heavily in technology and Google would never have gained such a big head start.

Overture observed our trials with content targeting. They didn't want us to have the "first mover" advantage in a new market, so in February 2003 they acted as if they had beaten us to the punch again — as they had with search-related advertising — by claiming that they would soon launch a "contextual advertising" service. A week later, our service was open and ready for business. As an astute poster on WebmasterWorld noted, "Overture announces first. Google launches first." Underpromise and overdeliver. I was gratified to see that people actually noticed. Google was again in front of the competition, and Larry and Sergey intended to stay there.

Overture's Content Match service didn't go live until the end of June. One reason for the lag may have been that Overture had planned to base their technology on content-targeting software from Applied Semantics, a company in Santa Monica. In April, Google bought Applied Semantics, bolstering our own capabilities while cutting the legs from under our competitor, which now had to look elsewhere for the technology or develop it themselves as we had done.

The firm was our largest acquisition to date, and we welcomed our Southern California colleagues at TGIF with beer and sushi served from atop a custom surfboard painted with a logo saying, "Google Santa Monica." The board was an apt metaphor. Content-targeted ads were the next big wave in online revenue, and we intended to ride it all the way to the beach.

CHAPTER 23

Froogle and Friction

MY THIRD YEAR at Google was rushing to a close. Everything shifted as the company transformed itself from startup to global powerhouse. New patterns and rituals slid into place, locked down, and began to feel permanent.

In October 2002, our department took up residence in the Saladoplex building with the AdWords team, my seventh (or eighth?) move since joining the company. I now had a closet office of my own with a wall-sized whiteboard and a window overlooking the patio. There was a micro-kitchen twenty feet away, and the gym — a converted computer mainframe room with an elevated floor and sub-zero air conditioning — was just around the corner. I felt completely embedded in my cozy corner of the organization and amazed at how many Googlers swarmed around me. (Ants, too. They found a hole in my window's insulation and a path into my Google gumball dispenser.) There were so many Googlers that the company stopped giving out stock options to new hires. Or, rather, deferred them. The government said that if we had five hundred shareholders we would have to make our financial records available, as if we were a public company. Instead, we kept hiring, but held back stock grants. The SEC would have some questions about that when we filed for our IPO.

I worked with the PMs on budgets for their 2003 initiatives, a task I could no longer complete satisfactorily with wild-assed guesses and a couple of bullet points. We had a CFO who paid microscopic attention to detail, and even Eric was heard to mutter, "Shit, we'd better take this seriously. We're going to be a billion-dollar company." He joked that we'd better not screw up things like audit trails that might send him to jail, an increasingly common destination for CEOs in the wake of the Enron meltdown. He said it so often, I came to realize he wasn't joking.

My world had grown large enough to split apart through mitotic division. Customer service was absorbed by Sheryl Sandberg's world o' AdWords, and marketing communications took up residence in Jonathan Rosenberg's product-management realm under the stewardship of Christopher Escher. Escher's groups would be devoted to supporting our revenue initiatives, which thankfully freed me from grinding out sales collateral and presentations. My new role revolved entirely around the products and services touched directly by users, so Cindy changed my title to director of consumer marketing and brand management.

My circle on Google's Venn diagram of responsibilities now overlapped Marissa Mayer's almost completely. She shepherded new services to market. I branded them. But branding originated with the products and the text included in them. So who made the final decision on what that text should say? The product manager or the brand manager? Ah, there's the rub.

Marissa let me know that she viewed me as the product marketing manager (PMM) for Google.com. I was comforted by the notion that I had a structural role defined within the new world order but unnerved by the realization that, according to her logic, I should be part of product management under Jonathan, not working in Cindy's corporate marketing group. I had nothing against Jonathan, but working for Cindy was like attending a small, high-caliber liberal arts college. Working for Jonathan would be like enrolling at MIT.

I didn't want to go to MIT.

My squabbles with Marissa over user-interface issues had ebbed and flowed, with the launch of Google news in September 2002 bringing both high points and lows. Marissa took particular pride in Google news, which automatically scanned thousands of news sources and extracted the ones that seemed most important. Krishna Bharat had started it as a side project, and after 9/11 had worked on it in earnest. Marissa made sure that Google news, like a favored child, moved to the front of the line for whatever goodies the company doled out. One of those was positioning as a tab right above the search box on the Google.com homepage. When the UI team questioned why we hadn't met to discuss such a major change, Marissa asserted it had always been planned that way.

It was hard to miss the shift in decision-making authority away from the UI team, where all members ostensibly had equal votes, to the product team, over which Marissa now held sway.

I saw it firsthand in working with Marissa on the language our site would use to describe Google news. As was often the case, the wording was still being finalized the night before the product launch. Marissa wanted to emphasize the automated nature of Google news by saying, "No humans were harmed or even used in the creation of this page." To me it sounded awkward and, worse, like a slap in the face to the journalists and editors whose stories we would be aggregating. I heard its tone as implying, "Look! We've built a machine that does your job better than you! You're not needed anymore, so why don't you take your Pulitzers and Polks and put yourselves out to pasture?"

Marissa didn't hear it that way. She found the reference to animal testing irresistibly humorous, though I pointed out to her that no humans were harmed in the creation of a printed newspaper either. "It's amusing," I conceded, though I didn't really believe it, "but it's going to wear thin very quickly. A lot of folks won't get it at all."

It all balanced out, though. Marissa was equally unhappy with the language I had written into the FAQ explaining Google news: "Google news is highly unusual in that it offers a news service compiled solely by computer algorithms without human intervention. Google employs no editors, managing editors, executive editors, or other ink-stained wretches."

She grimaced at "ink-stained wretches," a phrase I knew, from my seven years working at a newspaper, was a term of endearment among journalists. "It's a badge of honor," I assured her, "a tip of the hat to them to show we're on their side."

She polled the engineering team working on news, and they all hated it. Schwim, the ops guy, chimed in that he found it insulting. When the first iteration of Google news rolled out the next morning, "ink-stained wretches" was out and "no humans harmed" was in.

The "no humans harmed" line got noticed by the press. Some of the attention was positive, some not. Almost all the news reports I saw categorized the statement as boastful. Some also referred to the suffering of "ink-stained editors" who now would find their jobs threatened. I didn't point out that our critics had applied the "ink-stained" appellation to themselves without our prompting. Even years later, the line, which only stayed up a couple of weeks, is well remembered by journalists. When Google news began experimenting with adding human editors in June 2010, Phil Bronstein of the *San Francisco Chronicle* noted that our "no humans harmed" wording had "never made those of us who are, for the most part, human editors feel all that great."[*]

I can't honestly claim that my version would have been perceived any differently. It could very well have been much worse. The notion of automated news selection put journalists of all stripes on edge, and would have done so even if we hadn't placed any text explaining it on the site. What struck me, though, was my inability to persuade Marissa to see my point of view. And whenever that happened, Marissa's perspective prevailed.

By Any Other Name

Google news wasn't the only new product in the hopper. We had a product-search service scheduled to launch before the end of 2002 as well. The product team had assigned it the code name "Froogle."

"I was hoping you could help us out with a tagline for Froogle for the launch," Pearl Renaker, the PM for the new product, said to me in late August 2002.

"I'd love to," I told her, but thought to myself, "Uh-oh." It occurred to me that I had not been in any discussions about the "real" name that would replace "Froogle" when it went live. I suddenly got the feeling that the code name was no longer just a code name. Pearl confirmed it.

"We'd like to brand it as Froogle, but position it as a brand extension of Google." It was still a couple of months until launch. I had time to explain all the reasons that was a really bad idea.

My objections to naming our new feature "Froogle" were grounded in the brand architecture I had worked out with Salar, but more important, in Google's tradition of "underpromise and overdeliver." Salar and I had agreed when we launched the Google directory in 2000 that new products would all be under the Google name and just have descriptive

---

[*] http://articles.sfgate.com/2010-06-21/opinion/21919208_1_google-algorithms-human-editors.

titles: Google directory, Google image search, Google news. Froogle would be the first product to break that mold and set up an independent brand. Essentially, it would be saying that Google was no longer the one place to go for all searches. Users would have to choose one brand or the other. And it would set a dangerous precedent for future brand proliferation. Would we now create a name for every new service we developed?

I did see advantages to establishing an independent brand as a platform for commerce-related services. If Froogle was being positioned as a competitor to Amazon, with shopping carts and buyer reviews and one-click technology, it might make sense to give it its own Google-derived identity. But Froogle wasn't up to that challenge.

The Froogle prototype I had been trying out found products for sale on the web and ranked them according to "relevance," which didn't mean much when you had thirty identical waffle irons all offered at the same price. We did have "objectivity." Our partner Yahoo charged most merchants to be included in their product search, and Yahoo's search results sent users to Yahoo stores instead of directly to the merchants' sites. Yahoo had an editorial team making decisions, while we used a completely automated, and thus "purer," system, unaffected by paid relationships with merchants.

That was pretty much it.

There was no way to buy anything on Froogle without leaving the site. There were no product reviews. There were no merchant ratings. You couldn't sort by store, by brand, or by price. There was no way to do anything other than click on a link and go somewhere else. It was a search for finding products — a product search. That, I thought, is what we should call it: "Google product search." Calling it "Froogle" gave the impression that it was a comprehensive, full-fledged service, not a feature. People would bring to their first experience with Froogle all the expectations we had trained them to have for new Google services. They would expect "the Google of commerce." Instead, they would get — product search.

I went to Salar and the UI team to be sure they were aligned with my thinking. They were. Salar didn't like the name because the "frugal/Froogle" pun wouldn't translate internationally. Some English speakers might not get it either. Now I had to convince the people who could stop the runaway train before it got to the end of the line. I would argue my case at the Froogle GPS.

Each major product now had a forum dedicated to it. These get-togethers were dubbed "Google Product Strategy" (GPS) meetings and were attended by executives who could alter the launch timing, correct off-target plans, or completely change the features and purpose of the product in mid-development. Larry, Sergey, and Eric were there, along with Jonathan, Salar, Susan, and Marissa.

When my turn to speak came, I made my case to what I perceived as a hostile jury. I acknowledged the advantages of a memorable name for a product that was fully baked, but pointed out that our product search had barely gone into the oven. I laid out, logically and concisely, all the issues that made "Froogle" a poor choice, and I closed by suggesting that we should hold the name in reserve to apply when "Google product search" truly deserved its own brand. Better to underpromise now, I suggested, and overdeliver. I stopped talking and sat back, confident that Clarence Darrow could not have delivered a more cogent brief.

Sergey looked around the table. "I like 'Froogle,'" he said. "It's kind of funky and different. I think it's cute."

That wasn't the end of it. Eric charged Salar, Susan, and me with presenting an alternative to "Froogle" at the next GPS. We agreed on "Google product search," presented it, defended it, and were overruled.

That was the end of it. Of that part at least. But then the question of the tagline arose.

None of our other Google services had a tagline — a marketing slogan intended to get people to use a product. All our services had straightforward descriptive text on their homepages, explaining what they actually did. Text like "The most comprehensive image search on the web," or "Search and browse 4,000 continuously updated news sources." Perhaps because Froogle was a product dealing with commerce, there was suddenly a yen for a real marketing tagline.

The board of directors had saved the marketing department the trouble of developing one. "The board really likes 'All the world's products in one place,'" Eric announced at the November Froogle GPS. They wanted us to plaster it everywhere on the site. A great tagline, but obviously and provably false. I set about changing everyone's minds.

Fortunately, Marissa and I were in agreement that the board's wording promised too much. Unfortunately, we disagreed on whether the replacement should emphasize relevance (Marissa) or objectivity (me). We batted emails back and forth like Pong professionals, each making the case for our own word. That debate dragged on for weeks, until

Larry said "objectivity" was out. I think it may have cut too close to the bone for Yahoo, which was still a major partner.

I countered with the line "Find products for sale from across the web." It was a purely descriptive phrase devoid of any marketing spin, and it avoided insulting our partners. Five days before the scheduled launch, no one had objected to it. Pearl informed me my line would be the one on the site because it was the least controversial. I had lost the "Froogle" war but won the tagline battle. Small consolation, but I savored it.

The next day, the executive staff changed the Froogle homepage line back to "All the world's products in one place." The word came down that Larry and our board member John Doerr both liked the wording. No — they loved it. My teaspoonful of victory now tasted overwhelmingly of ashes.

On December 11, 2002, Froogle launched with little fanfare. We pushed it out the door quietly so as not to overly alarm Yahoo or AOL about our entry into an area they might view as competitive. But a new product from Google could no longer slip into the mainstream without making a splash. Froogle quickly became the center of a global media storm. Google was challenging the major players in e-commerce with a new shopping site. We were compared to Yahoo, to AOL, to Amazon, though clearly we offered few of the features of a full commerce site. Traffic to Froogle peaked high, then tapered off, and then, after the Christmas shopping season, plummeted sixty-five percent.

Also plummeting was enthusiasm for our tagline. Cindy heard feedback from her contacts in the press that our braggadocio was an unwelcome departure from our usual understated approach. "I don't like the tagline," one reporter told her. "I think Google as a search service never made any grand or best-in-the-world-type claims. The effect of this extreme form of 'underpromise, overdeliver' philosophy has been to make me feel certain that Google is supremely well conceived and fully worthy of every bit of trust that users place in it." Our new tagline violated that principle, and did so for a product that "was not equally well conceived nor equally worthy of users' trust."

Ouch. When you start getting marketing advice from journalists, something is seriously out of whack. Cindy agreed and even admitted regret for not having supported my recommendation more forcefully. The executive staff conceded that "All the world's products" might have overreached. Pearl asked me to prepare another slide explaining why it was a bad tagline. To all the reasons I had listed previously, I added, "It's blatantly and provably untrue." At the January 2003 GPS meeting, the executive staff agreed to switch to the line I had recommended. Eric even raised the possibility of killing the Froogle name and integrating the service directly into Google.com results.[*]

These developments left me with an unaccustomed feeling. I had been right in an argument with Larry and Sergey and Eric. Sometimes you just get lucky. It did embolden me, though. My instincts for our brand had been correct. Perhaps this would open a door and give marketing more credibility and access to the product-development process earlier in the pipeline. That way we could avoid last-minute scrambles and apply the same intelligence to branding as we did to the product's features. Perhaps the tension between product management and my consumer-marketing group would diminish.

I looked forward to exploring areas of interdepartmental cooperation in 2003, but I wouldn't get the chance for a while. Cindy had asked me to go to Tokyo. We had won Yahoo Japan's search business in November, and we needed to understand more about promoting our product in that market. I'd be operating out of our new office in the Shibuya neighborhood and would interview some job candidates, consult with ad agency Dentsu, and meet with a marketing group that had done some work for us. All very straightforward.

I let Cindy know I could probably squeeze the trip in, though it would be a hardship for Kristen, home with our three kids before the holidays. Japan was familiar turf for me: I'd been a Rotary scholar in Nagoya for a year after college. But the idea of taking my first international business trip secretly thrilled me. At forty-four, I was experiencing the same excitement I had felt the first day of high school. I had graduated to a new status because my company valued me enough to send me five thousand miles away.

Imagine, then, my elation when a couple weeks after my return from Japan, Cindy asked me to leave again. This time it was to help Sergey and our international PR team open a new office in Milan. We hosted a press conference and party at a trendy nightclub. I ate a dozen different cheeses at a single meal and discovered that wearing a nice suit from Macy's put me three fashion steps behind the barista serving me cap-

[*] Google changed the name from Froogle to "Google product search" in April 2007; http://news.cnet.com/2100-1038_3-6177393.html.

puccino. And cappuccino didn't look at all like what I got at Starbucks, but tasted like foamy caffeinated ambrosia. I cut the epaulets off my London Fog overcoat with a razor because no one in Italy wore epaulets, and I cursed my slick-soled loafers because they gave me no purchase on the rain-soaked marble streets. I carried deflated exercise balls around half the city looking for a place with an air pump to fill them for our coming-out party. It was all fantastic. By the time I got home I had convinced myself I should focus all my attention on building our international brand and keep a packed suitcase under my desk for quick getaways.

"Maybe you could take me next time," Kristen suggested, ironing my shirts as I regaled her with tales of couture and cannoli.

"Oh," I said unthinkingly as she maneuvered the heavy hot iron around a collar, "I was in meetings all day. What would you do on your own in Milan? You'd just be bored."

It's a testament to my wife's generous character that I'm still alive to tell that tale.

I would go to Japan again for Google, and to China, but there was too much going on in Mountain View to make constant globe-hopping feasible. I had branding guidelines to work out for new partners and language to draft for new products and site tours and newsletters. And I wanted to spend the credibility capital I had earned from Froogle. I decided to invest some of it to promote my ideas about the consumer brand we were building and how it should evolve.

CHAPTER 24

Don't Let Marketing Drive

N o, dad," i told my father as I watched pop-up ads spread across his screen, obscuring Google's homepage. "Google's not doing that. You've downloaded something you shouldn't have." I spent the next two hours of my vacation cleaning parasite programs off his computer.

Scumware was back. The malicious software that launched a thousand pop-up ads had never really gone away, but as 2003 began Googlers became increasingly alarmed by the proliferation of new mutant forms across the Internet. Matt Cutts, who dealt with the dark arts of the web every day in his battles against porn and spam, had reached a boiling point. On a visit to Omaha, Matt had spent an entire day cleaning scumware off his mother-in-law's PC. When he got back, his own computer had been infected. Worst of all, the company distributing the scumware afflicting him turned out to be a partner in Google's new syndicated-ads network. We were sending them ads to show on their website and then paying them every time someone clicked on one. We were bankrolling their scummy behavior. Matt and I were not the only ones enraged.

"I'd love to file a lawsuit and have a head on a pike," Matt recalls Larry saying about scumware creators and distributors. Matt's proposed solution was to post a screed on Google.com like the one we had launched previously about pop-up ads, but with a specific focus on identifying and removing scumware programs. I was a hundred percent for it, but this time, others had concerns. First, it would be hard to be righteous when we were doing business with a scumware site. We'd have to terminate that relationship before going any further. Second, several engineers were reluctant to launch an arms race against an invisible enemy while we were a sitting target.

Marissa proposed a compromise. We would be launching a pop-up blocker for the Google toolbar in a month or two. It would stop pop-ups from appearing, but not remove the programs that launched them. Could we fold Matt's language about scumware into the page talking about that new feature? She argued that simply taking a stand against scumware without context might seem self-serving, that people would think we just didn't want to lose revenue from users the programs hijacked to other sites.

I didn't want to compromise. Scumware was not a revenue issue, it was a privacy issue. I had personally experienced the invasive nature of a parasite program, and seen my dad's frustration as it crippled his computer. That infuriated me and perhaps clouded my judgment. I assured Matt I was prepared to wield a flaming sword and pursue those responsible to the ends of the earth. Or at the least, to make a positive assertion that Google was not behind the nasty behavior that irritated affected users. Google was righteous. "Google," I wanted the world to know, "would never screw its users."

Matt said he liked the idea of Google as a consumer advocate, fighting on behalf of users even on issues not directly affecting us. That encouraged me. The more I thought about it, the more I convinced myself that "consumer advocate" should be the next phase of Google's brand evolution. We would leave the sea of search and step onto the dry land of a new, more wondrous world in which we would become not just the source of information but the ally and protector of users who were searching for answers. In addition to being "fast, accurate, and easy to use," we would be a trusted friend.

So when a parallel discussion started in January 2003 about Google's own privacy policy and what we revealed to users about the data we collected from their searches, something clicked in my head. "We need to cross the streams," I thought. It was all related. Scumware. Privacy. The Google toolbar. "Yada," I realized in a moment of transcendental clarity, "yada."

Our "Not the usual yada yada" message had forestalled an uproar over our toolbar tracking users as they moved across the web. Now we could shelter ourselves from a PR cataclysm over privacy and fight scumware at the same time by employing a similar tactic. I knew a firestorm was coming. We were not immune to criticism about our privacy policy — from mild concerns to wild conspiracy theories. We had people's most intimate thoughts in our log files and, soon enough, people would realize it. We didn't know who searched for what, but, as I had seen after 9/11, there were ways to extract that information if someone was motivated to do so.

Chances are you've Googled yourself. Almost all of us have searched for our own names. When you do that, Google sees your IP address, the number corresponding to your computer's connection point on the Internet. If you connect to the Internet via a large commercial Internet service provider (ISP), a new IP address is theoretically assigned each time you log on* and then reissued to others when you turn off your computer. In practice, however, your IP address may not change for days or even months.

If you've used Google before, most likely you also have a Google cookie on your computer — a unique string of digits Google placed there so it can remember your preferences each time you come back (preferences like "apply SafeSearch filtering" or "show results in Chinese"). Google doesn't know your name or your real-world location, though your IP address may reveal your city if your ISP assigns blocks of numbers to specific geographic regions.

Looking at all the searches conducted from one IP address by a computer with a cookie assigned to it over a period of time could give a search engine data about individual user behavior. That information would be invaluable in improving both the relevance of search results and the targeting of advertising.

Why is the information helpful? Say that for a single twenty-four-hour period you threw all the search terms entered by one cookie/IP address combo into a bucket and analyzed them to establish correlations. Then say you compared those correlations with those found in other buckets: other searches conducted by other cookied computers. Patterns would emerge. So if you found that a search for "best sushi in Mountain View" was often followed by a search for "Sushi Tomi restaurant," you might associate Sushi Tomi with the best sushi in Mountain

---

* This is known as dynamic IP addressing.

View. A large search engine could compare tens of millions of buckets to determine how terms were related to one another. With that much data, you could derive some fairly definitive answers.

Using searchers' data, though, creates a fundamental dilemma. How do you protect user privacy while retaining the maximum value of the data for improving the search engine that collected it? Part of Google's answer was to anoint Nikhil Bhatla our "privacy czar." One of the first questions Nikhil raised was about identifying a user strictly from the stream of queries tied to one cookie over time. He shared an anecdote about engineer Jeff Dean, who had been working in the logs system where user search data was recorded. Jeff noticed that one cookie had been conducting a very interesting series of queries on technical topics, using highly sophisticated search techniques. He was impressed by the searcher's acumen. Only after studying the data further did he realize that the query stream he was looking at came from his own computer.

Nikhil's question kicked off a privacy debate among Googlers that dragged on for weeks. No one wanted to identify users or misuse the information we collected. But we also knew we weren't the only ones who might see the data in our logs. It was 2003. The Patriot Act had been the law of the land for a little more than a year, loosening restrictions on the government's ability to access email and other electronic communication records. The Justice Department could request data from Google, and we would be legally bound not to tell users that their information had been passed to law enforcement officials. Attorney General John Ashcroft might soon be knocking on our door.

The arguments raised were so complex and technical that it would be impossible to detail them all here.* The main issues, though, had to do with controlling access to logs data by Google staff, the length of time Google retained user data files, notifying users that we were storing their search information, and giving users the option to delete data we had collected. The tradeoff with each of these would be a reduction in Google's ability to mine logs data to make better products for all its users.

I trusted that my colleagues would make intelligent, ethical decisions on data access and retention. The point I cared most about was notification. I drafted a proposal outlining all the things we could do, *should*

---

*One example: If a user wanted to remove all her data from Google's logs, how would she prove it was hers? Her IP address was probably not unique, and family members might have shared her computer, meaning their search data would be tied to the same cookie.

do to lead the discussion on privacy and to set an industry standard. Instead of avoiding the issues raised by the collection of user data, I advocated we embrace them. We had nothing to hide. We could establish an advisory committee of outside privacy advocates, set up a public forum in Google groups, post tutorials about data gathering on our site, and give instructions on how to delete cookies to avoid being tracked.

Matt Cutts and Wayne Rosing, our VP of engineering, loudly and publicly supported the plan. I started thinking about ways we could build an area on our site for consumer advocacy. Then Cindy let me know privately that one Googler was not pleased with my proposal. Marissa, Cindy said, claimed that the idea of an advisory panel was hers and that I had neglected to give her credit. I rolled my eyes. I had suggested an advisory panel because we had had one at the *Merc*. I had not been in any meeting at which Marissa brought up the topic and so had no idea that she had suggested something similar.

I was tempted to fire off a note to that effect, but at my performance review a couple of weeks earlier Cindy had instructed me to stop waging email wars that went on forever. So instead of refuting Marissa over the ether, I set up a face-to-face meeting. It took me a week to get on her calendar, and even then her only available time was after dinner. As dusk fell, we went for a walk around the vacant lot next door to try and clear the air.

Marissa assured me that I was not the only one misappropriating her ideas. I was just the most recent. And, she wanted to know, why didn't she get credit for her work on the homepage promotion lines, which after all, should really be her responsibility, not marketing's?

I wasn't sure what credit there was to give for a single line of text on the Google.com homepage, or who else in the company might care, but I offered to publicly acknowledge her contributions whenever she made them. I wasn't willing to cede control over them, though. The marketing text on the homepage was the most valuable promotional medium we employed. It reached millions of people, and since promotion was a marketing responsibility, not a product-management one, I insisted that marketing should control the space.

As we headed back into the building, I assured Marissa, with complete sincerity, that I respected her intelligence and opinions and the enormous contribution she made to Google. I viewed her as my most important colleague in terms of the work that lay ahead. We had been working together to improve Google for more than three years, I reminded her. Despite our differing points of view in the past — and probably going forward as well — it was essential we maintain a direct channel of communication. I encouraged her to bring future issues to me and assured her I would do the same.

I told Cindy later that our chat had poured oil on some troubled waters. But, I added, I didn't expect it to be the last conversation of its kind.

Meanwhile, the privacy discussion had grown a thousand heads and was consuming vast quantities of time and mental effort among the engineers and the product team. Was our goal to make Google the most trusted organization on the planet? Or the best search engine in the world? Both goals put user interests first, but they might be mutually exclusive.

Matt Cutts characterized the two main camps in what he termed "the Battle Royal" as hawks and doves, where hawks wanted to keep as much user information as we could gather and doves wanted to delete search data as quickly as we got it. Larry and Sergey were hawks. Matt considered himself one as well.

"We never know how we might use this data," Matt explained. "It's a reflection of what the world is thinking, so how can that not be useful?" As someone who worked on improving the quality of Google's search results, Matt saw limitless possibilities. For example, "You can learn spelling correction even in languages that you don't understand. You can look at the actions of users refining their queries and say, if you see someone type in x, it should be spell-corrected to y."

Well, some engineers asked, why don't we just tell people how we use cookie data to improve our products? We could give Matt's example about the spell checker, which also relied on user data to work its magic with names like the often misspelled "Britney Spears."

We don't tell them, Larry explained, because we don't want our competitors to know how our spell checker works. Larry opposed any path that would reveal our technological secrets or stir the privacy pot and endanger our ability to gather data. People didn't know how much data we collected, but we were not doing anything evil with it, so why begin a conversation that would just confuse and concern everyone? Users would oversimplify the issue with baseless fears and then refuse to let us collect their data. That would be a disaster for Google, because we would suddenly have less insight into what worked and what didn't. It would be better to do the right thing and not talk about it.

Matt understood Larry's position. He also sympathized with Googlers who wanted to compromise by anonymizing the data or encrypting the logs and then throwing away the keys every month. That would keep some data accessible, but the unique identifiers would disappear.

Not that Matt thought it would do any good in stemming public concerns. "Part of the problem," he told me, "was explaining that in real-world terms. As soon as you start talking about symmetric encryption and keys that rotate out, people's eyes turn to glass." The issue was too complicated to offer an easy solution. Even if we agreed to delete data, we couldn't be sure we erased all of it, because of automatic backups stored in numerous places for billing advertisers or maintaining an audit trail. I began to understand the hesitation to even engage in the discussion with users.

What if we let users opt out of accepting our cookies altogether? I liked that idea, but Marissa raised an interesting point. We would clearly want to set the default as "accept Google's cookies." If we fully explained what that meant to most users, however, they would probably prefer *not* to accept our cookie. So our default setting would go against users' wishes. Some people might call that evil, and evil made Marissa uncomfortable. She was disturbed that our current cookie-setting practices made the argument a reasonable one. She agreed that at the very least we should have a page telling users how they could delete their cookies, whether set by Google or by some other website.

Describing how to delete cookies fit neatly with a state-of-the-brand analysis I had been working on. In it, I laid out my thoughts about redirecting our identity from "search and only search" to a leadership role on issues affecting users online. I forecast that user privacy, our near monopoly in search, and censorship demands by foreign governments would be the three trials to bedevil us in the coming year. We needed to prepare — to get out in front and lead the parade rather than be trampled by it. Marissa complimented my analysis but had reservations about my recommendations. Just as I had thought "Don't be evil" over-promised, she feared taking public stands about our ethical positions would result in overly heightened expectations and negative reactions if we failed to live up to them. I understood that perspective (and shared it) but believed we didn't need to *claim* to be ethically superior. We just needed our actions to demonstrate that we were. Users could draw their own conclusions.

Sergey's feedback was less encouraging. "I find documents like this frightening," he stated. "It's vague and open-ended, which makes specific feedback impossible." Lest I take his lack of comments for assent, he asked me to detail the next steps I intended to take. I had already done that, but evidently he hadn't read past the first page. I wondered if my communication with Sergey would improve if I took him for a walking chat, as I had with Marissa — perhaps along a high cliff overlooking the ocean.

Meanwhile, the privacy discussion bubbled and boiled until at last a meeting could be arranged to hash out once and for all policies on employee access to user data, data retention, and user education about privacy issues.

The meeting raised many other questions, and answered none of them. Eric Schmidt half-jokingly suggested that our privacy policy should start off with the full text of the Patriot Act. Larry argued we should keep all our data until — well, until the time we should get rid of it. If we thought the government was overreaching, we could just encrypt everything and make it unreadable. Besides, Ashcroft would most likely go after the ISPs first, since they had much better data than we did about what users did online.* The meeting ended, but the debate continued for months.

My idea for blazing a path on educating users about privacy never gained the endorsement of Larry and Sergey, and so did not come to fruition. Perhaps they were right that it would have opened a Pandora's box. The issue of privacy would never go away, and trying to explain our rationale might only make things more confusing. Why not let the issue come to us instead of rushing out to meet it? We weren't willing to talk about the wonderful benefits of users sharing their data with us, because we weren't willing to share any information about how we used that data. If we couldn't say something nice, why say anything at all?

That didn't stop me from assuming the most aggressive possible stance when it came to communicating with users about privacy each time a new product launched. I repeated the Yada Yada story to every Googler who would listen, though I found few converts to my vision of users making fully informed decisions about the data they shared with us. Most engineers felt the tradeoff was too high. If users came to Google looking for information about online privacy, they figured, we

---

* ISPs know every site you visit, including Google, though they probably don't retain the sort of historical data that Google has collected.

would help them the way we always did — by sending them somewhere else for answers.

Let the Good Times Scroll

Larry refused to talk directly to users about cookies and log files, and he tried to keep the public from getting curious by minimizing their exposure to the data we collected. He wasn't always successful.

For example, a display of "real time" Google search queries crawled across a video monitor suspended over the receptionist's desk in our lobby. I sometimes sat on the red couch and watched to find out what the world was looking for. The terms scrolled by silently in a steady stream:

 new employment in Montana
 scheduled zip backup
 greeting cards free
 nervous system
 lynyrd skynyrd tabliature Tuesday
 datura metal
 tamron lense 500mm
 mode chip for playstation
 the bone collector
 singles chat

Journalists who came to Google stood in the lobby mesmerized by this peek into the global gestalt and later waxed poetical about the international impact of Google and the deepening role search plays in all our lives. Visitors were so entranced that they stared up at the display as they signed in for their temporary badges, not bothering to read the restrictive non-disclosure agreements they were agreeing to.

The query scroll was carefully filtered for offensive terms that might clash with our wholesome image.* Offensive terms written in English,

---

* Early on, Larry asked Jim Reese to remove the filter. Jim objected, but Larry insisted. The two dozen people working for Google at the time watched the raw query stream in shock. A large percentage of the terms were pornographic. "Ohmigod," one staffer remarked. "That's what people are using Google for?" After fifteen minutes, Larry asked to have the filter restored. It stayed in place after that.

anyway. I recall a group of Japanese visitors pointing and smirking at some of the katakana characters floating across the page. The inability to identify foreign-language porn is just one of the reasons we never used the query scroll widely for marketing purposes, despite its ability to instantly turn esoteric technology into voyeuristic entertainment.

Larry never cared for the scrolling queries screen. He constantly monitored the currents of public paranoia around information seepage, and the scrolling queries set off his alarm. He felt the display could inadvertently reveal personal data, because queries could contain names or information that users would prefer to remain private (for example, "John Smith DUI arrest in Springfield" or "Mary Jones amateur porn movie"). Moreover, it might cause people to think more about their own queries and stir what he deemed to be ungrounded fears over what information was conveyed with each search.

Larry tried to kill the Google Zeitgeist, too. Zeitgeist was a year-end feature that the PR team put together recapping the trends in search terms over the previous twelve months. The press loved Zeitgeist because it gave them another way to wrap up the year, but to Larry it raised too many questions about how much Google knew about users' searches and how long we kept their data. Cindy asked me to come up with a list of reasons to continue the tradition, and my rationale evidently convinced Larry the risk was acceptable, because the year-end Zeitgeist is still published on Google.com.

All the while we wrestled with the issues of what to tell users, our ability to mine their data became better and better. Amit Patel, as his first big project at Google, had built a rudimentary system to make sense of the logs that recorded user interactions with our site. Ironically, the same engineer who did the most to seed the notion of "Don't be evil" in the company's consciousness also laid the cornerstone of a system that would bring into question the purity of Google's intentions.

Amit's system was a stopgap measure. It took three years and an enormous effort from a team of Googlers led by legendary coder Rob Pike to perfect the technology that, since it processed logs, came to be designated "Sawmill." The power of Sawmill when it was activated in 2003 gave Google a clear understanding of user behavior, which in turn enabled our engineers to serve ads more effectively than Yahoo did, to identify and block some types of robotic software submitting search terms, to report revenue accurately enough to meet audit requirements, and to determine which UI features improved the site and which confused users. If engineers were reluctant to delete logs data before Sawmill, they were adamant about retaining it afterward.

Larry's refusal to engage the privacy discussion with the public always frustrated me. I remained convinced we could start with basic information and build an information center that would be clear and forthright about the tradeoffs users made when they entered their queries on Google or any other search engine. I didn't really believe many people would read all the pages, or particularly care what they said. In fact, I somewhat cynically counted on that. The mere fact that we had the explanation available would allay many of their concerns. Those who truly cared would see we were being transparent. Even if they didn't like our policies on data collection or retention, they would know what they were. If they went elsewhere to search, they would be taking a chance that our competitors' practices were far worse than ours.

To Larry the risks were just too high. Once we squeezed the toothpaste out of the tube, we would not be able to put it back. And he would never do anything that might cost us complete access to what Wayne Rosing called our "beautiful, irreplaceable data."

Can't We All Just Get Along?

Ka-chunk. Ka-chunk. Over the rest of 2003, the product-development group under Jonathan worked with engineering to stamp out a series of features, services, and infrastructure updates.

Ka-chunk. Ka-chunk. The business-development group punched out partnership deals for toolbar distribution and advertising syndication.

I too ratcheted up my productivity. Writing copy for products and promotions was my primary activity, but there were other items on a list that perpetually expanded.

- Set branding guidelines for partners who kept trying to use our logo in unapproved ways.
- Arrange product placements. For example, I used Google to track down an email address for *Sex and the City*'s props guy on a German website and the brother of a *West Wing* producer in Los Angeles. Google appeared in both shows at no cost to us.
- Negotiate co-branding deals. Among other partnerships, I

worked with DK books in England to release a set of Google-branded reference works for kids, with *Time* magazine to do an Internet search guide for use in classrooms, and with the World Puzzle Federation to sponsor their international championship.
- Develop product identities. To brand our AdSense ads, I proposed "Ads by GOOOOOOOGLE," an idea that was rejected at first but implemented the following year.

No matter how efficient and productive I was, however, I felt hampered by the one thing that seemed to be moving backward. While I was communicating well with others in product management, my relationship with Marissa became more strained with each new project we worked on together. And we worked on an increasing number of projects together.

We disagreed about how to promote the Webby award won by Google news, which I thought was nice but no more exceptional than the four other Webbys Google had won and never acknowledged. Marissa wanted — and got — a special logo, a dedicated thank-you page, and a team picture on the site. Cindy stopped her from including the Webby in our online FAQ as well.

We had different views on Project Miles, a frequent-searcher program Marissa developed with no marketing input because, she claimed, Larry didn't want to use any resources to make it happen. In a test, the program put counters under the Google search box for some users. The number the counter displayed increased each time the users searched with Google. When Project Miles launched, someone from EPIC, a privacy rights organization, asked a *New York Times* reporter, "Do users know that Google is spying on them?"* Given Larry's hatred for frequent-flyer programs and his fears about raising privacy concerns, the test program was quickly canceled.

I argued against her idea to have staffers give away five thousand Google pens on the streets of Tokyo, which was opposed by our Japanese office and members of her own team. The promotion moved ahead anyway. Most of the Japanese pedestrians refused to acknowledge the Googlers, other than a handful of women who seemed quite comfortable accepting gifts from strangers.

All these instances of ignored or overridden input were eroding my

---

* http://www.nytimes.com/2003/10/06/technology/06goog.html.

authority to make decisions about our marketing. Worse, I had become a Cassandra — I could see bad things on the road ahead but couldn't stop us from recklessly rolling over them. Instead of having more credibility after the Froogle fiasco, I seemed to have less. I finally went to Larry to ask how we in brand management could align our efforts more closely with the company's goals. Work more closely with product management, he advised me. I assured him I would redouble my efforts to do so.

Two weeks later, Marissa closed the best window I had into Larry and Sergey's thinking about our brand strategy and the products in the development pipeline. She announced that Larry's weekly product-review meeting henceforth would be limited to Larry and members of the product-development team.

Product review was the meeting at which I learned about major initiatives while they were still the equivalent of a tropical depression forming somewhere in the Atlantic. At that stage, redirecting branding efforts might have some effect. Under the new system, I would not have input into products until they were full-fledged hurricanes five miles off the coast. I'd be able to do little other than board up the windows, huddle for cover, and pray for the best.

I thanked Marissa for trying to save me from an unnecessary meeting, but assured her I preferred to know what was happening with product development. Cindy reminded Marissa that since our product was our marketing platform, marketing needed to be part of the discussion that happened in the product-review meetings. The debate went on for a month, but the die was cast, and marketing was cast out.

Marissa told me that it was actually Larry and Jonathan who had suggested constraining the meeting to those in the product group. That may have been true, but since the word always came through Marissa, it was hard to know if something was lost in translation. I knew Larry hated large crowds, and now that the product group worked with engineering, perhaps he felt brand management's presence was redundant. Whoever instigated the change, it made my job harder. And it did not improve my working relationship with Marissa, who was promoted to director of consumer web products in mid-July 2003. I congratulated her and asked to set up a regular touch-base meeting so we could coordinate our efforts. It never happened.

Instead, our communication channel kept degrading. One day I heard from someone in product management that Sergey was furious at marketing. He believed we were holding up the launch of a new Google toolbar until it included a way for users to clear their search history. One of the most common questions we received from users was about removing previous search queries from Microsoft's Internet Explorer browser. The question came up because when people started to type in a Google search, their previous search terms would appear below it on the screen. Users didn't want that information displayed. Even though Microsoft was responsible for storing that data, our toolbar engineers thought they could fix it so the previous searches didn't appear.

I thought that would be great, but neither I nor anyone else in corporate marketing ever *asked* for it to be included. The toolbar engineers liked the idea enough to work over the weekend coding it anyway. Someone informed Sergey that our group was not only holding up the launch for the history-clearing add-on but insisting that the new feature delete Google's cookie as well.

"Why the hell are you letting marketing drive your product development?" Sergey demanded of the associate product manager, who spent a half hour well after midnight trying to calm him down and explain what was actually going on.

"There were only three people at Google at that hour," the APM vented, "Larry and Sergey and you-know-who. She found out about it and then all hell broke loose."

The UI team also struggled to retain access to the product-development process but we found ourselves marginalized, especially on design issues around Google news, which had become an entity unto itself under Marissa's stewardship. One of Marissa's APMs sent out a drastically different design for news search results and requested UI feedback forty-eight hours before the "code freeze," after which programmers would implement the design. Such major changes would normally be reviewed and tested for weeks, but Marissa informed us that Larry felt the project was behind schedule and so had asked her to form a task force to move it ahead.

The last straw for me was not about a major change, but about how a minor change was handled. Google's fifth anniversary as a company occurred in September 2003. Marissa reworked the wording of the alt-text of our Google birthday logo, the phrase that appeared when you rolled your mouse over the artwork Dennis had created for the homepage. I had written "Celebrating Google's 5th birthday" as the explanation for the cake and party hat decorating the logo. Marissa wanted "Happy 5th birthday, Google!" It seemed weird to me to congratulate ourselves on our own birthday, so I instructed Dennis not to change it. In the middle of the night, Marissa overruled me, claiming her wording was what we had always used. It wasn't. Mine was.

The next morning I drafted a note demanding that Larry weigh in once and for all about who controlled the copy on Google.com. He had already assured me privately that wording was my responsibility, but now I wanted it in writing and on the record. Cindy advised me not to send the note. I let her cooler head prevail. I don't know if Cindy said something to Larry, but after that things settled down.

Marissa and I still disagreed over wording on occasion, but, at least in the short term, we found ways to work out differences amicably. Maybe Marissa realized she had finally overstepped her bounds. Maybe I was adjusting to Google's new world order in which product management had a legitimate say in the brand messaging. Or more likely, keeping up with the overflowing load of projects kept us both too busy to waste energy debating passive vs. active voice and verb-subject agreement. By late 2003 I was getting more done, faster and more efficiently, than I had in any other job I'd ever held.

In Redmond, the Beast Awakes

One of my new responsibilities was running our weekly TGIF meetings. We had passed a thousand employees in April 2003 and our Friday get-togethers were now enormous gatherings held in a large open space on the first floor of the building next to the Saladoplex. Each Friday, a contractor named Michael "MLo" Lopez* helped me build an Apple Keynote presentation introducing just-hired Nooglers, highlighting department success stories, and providing insight into our financial health.

Larry and Sergey would barely glance at the script I gave them, then ad lib a comically surreal amble through the events of the previous week. "I can't really read this," Sergey might say, squinting at the revenue number on one of Omid's spreadsheet slides. "But you can tell it's big because it has a lot of pixels." I got my jollies by including horrible puns, juvenile animations, and absurd images in the slides projected behind them, which caused groans and laughs while they spoke.

---

* MLo now heads up the team of Google Doodle artists.

Because information tended to trickle in throughout the afternoon from around the company, preparation took an entire day — my twenty-percent time. I did my best to keep the TGIFs entertaining, playing world music as people assembled to munch on snacks provided by Chef Charlie and giving Nooglers propeller beanie caps so they stood out in the post-presentation mingling. Some weeks we had skits, such as the interpretive dance, caped superhero, and flaming laptop that intro-duced changes to our Help Desk organization.

Fewer and fewer old-timers showed up. The engineers already knew what they needed to know and found TGIF a waste of time. The ratio of news to fluff was not sufficiently high to draw them in, which alarmed Larry and Sergey. TGIF was intended to bind the company together. Instead, the culture was separating like the layers in one of Charlie's parfaits.

The founders weren't above bribing senior engineers to attend. Each December, Larry and Sergey "surprised" the staff by handing out a year-end thousand-dollar cash bonus at TGIF. Three days before the 2003 distribution was to take place, they asked me for ideas about how to do the presentation. I suggested a casting tape for a (fictional) Superbowl TV spot. Given how often we derided the profligacy of dot-com com-panies and their mass-market advertising, few staffers would fall for it, but it would give us a framework.

I drafted a script and gave it to Delicia Heywood, a marketing staffer, to shoot and produce. She came back forty-eight hours later with the tape we would use the following day. After a brief intro of scrolling text, we cut to a director's slate. Then Al Gore, giving an intense look of concern, asked with the emotional spark of soggy cardboard, "Are you searching for answers? Google.com can help you find them." A pause, and then Gore asked, "Was that too over the top?" Other Googlers appeared, including Chef Charlie and our sultry receptionist Megan, who leaned forward to whisper, "Looking for something? Need a good search?" as well as a guest appearance by the Pets.com sock puppet. When the video aired, the audience of Googlers went nuts. After it ended, Sergey announced that we had decided not to spend the money airing a spot after all, and instead would split the cash among the Google staff. That went over very well.

By the end of the next year, the amount of cash needed for the bo-nuses became unwieldy. Armored cars and shotgun-toting guards were needed to transport and watch over the funds until they could be distributed.

There was more good financial news in 2003. The slides at TGIF showing our corporate financial health kept pointing up and to the right. The board split our stock when it hit ten dollars a share in June.

Of course, we still faced competition, but we had momentum. Overture had bought the search engine company FAST in February to compete with us, but they were clearly too late to catch up on that front. We were not happy, but also not surprised, when Yahoo bought Overture in July for $1.3 billion. Now Yahoo owned the patents Overture had accused Google of infringing, which meant we would soon be in court with one of our biggest customers. The handwriting had been on the wall. Google had grown too big and threatening to be Yahoo's supplier. They would have to compete with us, and to do that they needed their own search-advertising technology.

More disconcerting was Microsoft's awakening to the power of search. "Google's a very nice system," Windows group VP Jim Allchin told the *Seattle Times* in February 2003, "but compared to my vision, it's pathetic."*

The threat to Google was real. If Allchin's vision included integrating search into the new version of Windows Microsoft was soon to release, it could eliminate the need to launch a browser and go to Google to search. Given the number of Windows users worldwide, our traffic could drop in a hurry. Without traffic, we would show fewer ads and make less money. Way less money.

"We will buy you," was Microsoft's ploy when it came to startups that threatened them, "or we will bury you." Google was not for sale. Nor would Google be foolish enough to partner with Microsoft, exposing our technology to them in ways that would let them "harvest" it and use it against us.† One business-development person warned me that Microsoft's MO as a company was to get close to startups, suck them dry, and then throw them away. Microsoft was methodical about it, giving generous terms to keep the startups alive, but essentially turning them into captive research-and-development centers. Microsoft would

---

* http://community.seattletimes.nwsource.com/archive/?date=20030226&slug=microsoft26.

† Larry told me once to change an underwriting tag on public radio so it didn't say Google was "a technology company." He didn't want to tip off Microsoft that we had bigger plans than just search.

become the startups' biggest customer and thereby drive the direction of their development, perhaps offering to provide informal technical help, which necessitated a look at the startups' proprietary code.

When Microsoft turned its gaze to us, Larry and Sergey huddled with our board of directors and determined to stay the course. There was fear, but no panic. To survive — as companies like Intuit, AOL, and Oracle had in direct competition with the Redmond giant — we needed to focus on our core strengths: search quality, a comprehensive ad network, and content targeting. And the key tactic for implementing that strategy was one we had been employing from the very beginning: hire brilliant engineers to do brilliant things.

First we needed to prevent Microsoft from luring away any of the talent we had already found. That might be difficult as stock options vested for the earliest engineers and Google grew larger and more bureaucratic. On the plus side, most engineers would not view a move to Microsoft as an improvement in management streamlining. It was Cindy who raised the question to me of how we might help engineering find more talent, perhaps in a way that would bolster our image with users as well. Ads aimed at engineers, but seen by consumers — consumers who would feel they were eavesdropping on a conversation intended for someone else. If users took joy from discovering Google on their own, such an indirect campaign would have an even deeper brand impact than one aimed directly at them. It was an inspired strategy, and I knew just the people to make it work for us.

A Brand-New Idea for Recruiting Engineers

Late in 2002, I received a poster in the mail. It was a montage of ads and PR stunts that had been put together to introduce the BMW Mini Cooper to the US market. Some of them made me laugh out loud. I dropped a note to the ad agency that had sent it, telling them we weren't in the market, but if they were ever in the Bay Area, I'd like to talk to them. Almost two years later, I convinced Larry and Sergey to put the agency, Crispin Porter + Bogusky, to work for us on my secret plan to do a consumer branding campaign in the guise of an effort to recruit engineers. I didn't tell Larry and Sergey the secret part. I just said we would hire an agency to help us find more technical talent, as they were desperate to do.

Advertising to engineers would be tricky. They don't like to be marketed to. I instructed the Crispin people not to tell anyone outside Google they were working on our behalf, and not to mention branding to anyone at Google. But I let them know I wanted a campaign to reinforce the positioning of Google as the world's best search engine because we had the best technology, created by the sharpest minds in the industry.

Crispin sent a team to spend a day interviewing senior engineers on our campus. A few weeks later, they came back with a presentation full of cutting edges and radiant brilliance.

They had realistic Google ID badges with pictures of real Google engineers on the front and coding challenges on the back to be solved and sent with résumés to our HR department. They planned to drop them in classrooms at top engineering schools.

They had a plan to get Google mentioned on *The Simpsons.*[*]

They had a billboard that was simply a mathematical equation followed by ".com." No logo or identification. Those who solved the equation and entered the solution as a web address would get another puzzle and ultimately a Google recruiting page.

They had a series of print ads with photos purporting to be from Google's office, where parking a car, sending a fax, or getting snacks from a vending machine required solving complex puzzles. Readers were invited to send in their solutions along with their job applications.

They had a plan to rebrand our recruiting effort as "Google labs," to emphasize we were working on much more than search, which many in our target audience considered to be an already-solved problem. To make that evident, they incorporated a handwritten "Labs" as an exponent above and to the right of our Google logo.

They proposed a "Google Labs Aptitude Test" (GLAT) to be inserted in school newspapers and magazines like *Science* and the *MIT Technology Review.*

Larry and Sergey didn't hate it. In fact, they were amused. One of the few elements they nixed was a video campaign called "Watch Your Ass," which showed gritty handheld-camera footage of Google recruiters hunting down engineering talent with dart guns and nets at their workplaces. It was too dark.

"Be careful not to upset those we don't end up hiring," was the gist of the founders' feedback. "Don't insult them if they can't solve the puzzles." For the rest, they gave the okay to go ahead. I quietly rejoiced. I had sold a branding campaign from the nation's hottest ad agency to two guys who hated anything to do with marketing. It had taken four years, but I had figured out a way to work the system.

The implementation of the campaign was almost flawless. Since challenging engineers fell outside Crispin's area of expertise, two Googlers, Curtis Chen and Wei-Hwa Huang (a four-time winner of the World Puzzle Championship), came up with most of the puzzles we used. I helped a bit.

"Write a haiku describing possible methods for predicting search traffic seasonality," I suggested for one.

"This space left intentionally blank. Please fill it with something that improves on emptiness," I offered for another.

For Wei-Hwa's question about the number of different ways to color an icosahedron with one of three colors on each face, I added, "What colors would you choose?" There were also nods to Chef Charlie, "Don't be evil," and an old computer game involving twisty, turny passages that I had played as a kid.

As we rolled out new elements in the campaign over 2004, the press ate it up. NPR, ABC, CNN, the *Wall Street Journal, Sixty Minutes,* and the Associated Press gave us widespread positive coverage and extended the reach of our effort substantially. Our own engineers praised the effort as fun and Googley. We received more than four thousand job applications at the specific email address we had set up. Everything worked exactly as I had hoped except for one small glitch.

We only hired one engineer because of the ads.

We had problems tracking applicants who sent in GLAT forms on paper and no way of knowing how many people the ads inspired to apply through our normal jobs@google channel. The ultimate number of hires may have been substantially greater, but I didn't have data to prove it. The branding effort worked. The recruiting component didn't.

Alan Eustace, the engineering director overseeing recruitment, didn't care. He wanted to run a modified campaign the following year. Urs liked the idea as well. The new head of business operations, however, didn't see it that way. The budget had come out of her department, and she had nothing concrete to show for it. I understood why she concluded it was a "complete waste of money," but I saw it differently.

For the rest of the year I tried to find a way to put Crispin back to work on promoting our brand, but the Google world had changed again. Now HR had recruiting specialists and Jonathan's product-marketing managers owned promotion of individual products. I could advise on branding, but they were responsible for the bottom-line performance. The PMMs were shopping for ad agencies, primarily to help with international promotion, which was a weak point for Crispin. And managers in Jonathan's domain — thinking outside the box — proposed we trade user data in aggregate for agency services. The agency would get inside information on the booming search-advertising market and we would get cheap ads. Win-win.

I disliked the idea. Giving out user data to cut costs seemed like a bad trade to me. But the loudest voice against it came from Marissa. For once we were standing on the same side of the fence. We had bickered in the past over issues of style, but we had never disagreed that our relationship with users was sacrosanct. Nothing should jeopardize their trust in us. Google's growth had brought in a new wave of managers, who were not "the bozos" Eric Schmidt had feared, but neither were they grounded in our core values. The PMs were impressed by the big international agencies that came wearing suits and bearing lofty titles. I wasn't. Crispin did some test campaigns for us, but their lack of global capabilities kept them out of the running. They moved on.* So did I.

---

* CP+B won Microsoft's $300 million account in 2008 and created the "I'm a PC" campaign.

CHAPTER 25

Mistakes Were Made

W E FIND OURSELVES today at the forefront of tremendous opportunity and worldwide attention," Sergey announced in October 2003. "This is, of course, an enviable position, yet it comes with substantial costs and risks."

Sergey wanted us to know that he understood how overwhelmed we might be feeling by the demands and issues coming at us from all angles. He didn't want us to become reactive and lose our ability to maintain the edge that had brought us so far. Prioritize, he instructed us. Don't let projects linger. Say no clearly when the answer is no. Don't create needless work for others or send emails that aren't worth reading. And he urged us to take care of our health and our families. Google, he assured us, wanted us to be productive *and* happy.

I was pretty happy at the end of November when my newly split shares fully vested. They were mine, though I couldn't do anything but admire their number in our online accounting system. Oh man. How incredibly liberating. I had no intention of leaving Google, but knowing that if I did leave I'd still fully benefit from an IPO eased some of the pressure I had been feeling. It put a spring in my step as I took my daily walk around the park.

"If the stock goes to thirty dollars," I mused, "I'll be worth X. If it goes to fifty, I'll be worth Y. Could it really go to fifty? What's Yahoo at? Ohmigod. What if it went to a hundred dollars a share? Nah. That could never happen." It was a fun game to play. I tried to wipe the goofy smile off my face by the time I got back to the office, but sometimes it would reappear of its own accord.

The office changed, too. We had completed our purchase of SGI's corporate headquarters in July 2003. In January 2004, it was corporate marketing's turn to follow engineering to our new home. I packed up my boxes on Friday and on Monday went to work in building 41. Not 42, which was where engineering lived, but next door and accessible by a series of elevated bridges and walkways that would have made a giant hamster feel right at home.

There weren't many corporate marketing folks left to move. Jonathan's product-management division had absorbed our internationalization group and our market researcher. I still managed Allegra, who was now our special events coordinator, and Dylan Casey, a marketing coordinator whose previous job had been cycling with Lance Armstrong on the US Postal Service racing team.

David Krane's PR group had grown considerably, with representatives in Google offices around the world, and Karen White, the webmaster, now had a much larger staff as well. I didn't mind that the branding group had not kept pace. Managing people always felt harder to me than doing the work myself. I liked sitting in my darkened office with headphones on, thinking about our brand and how to make it shine. I also knew that at the rate the product-management team was adding PMMs — marketing managers who worked with the product team much as I had — my fate would be either induction into the collective or elimination as a redundancy. Organizations grow. They change. I didn't worry too much about it. I loved my job, but I had stock options and they were fully vested.

We had come a long way from our cramped quarters in the original Googleplex, with its cereal bins relabeled to read "Larry-O's," "Raisin Brin," and "Porn Flakes," its intimate café with an unused cash register, and its walk-in-closet gym.

Our new facility had everything. There was a "Welcome home" pillow on my chair when I came in. We had a sand volleyball court, a bocce ball area, clean locker rooms, and an enormous café that doubled as our TGIF meeting space and included an upstairs balcony and an outdoor barbeque patio. There were a garden plot and an adjacent grassy field for Frisbee or soccer. There was even a mystery floor with a canted roof and oddly shaped windows creating a visual effect that nauseated the legal department staffers housed there. They quickly set up a portable bar and scheduled regular cocktail hours to ameliorate the effects.

There were snack rooms on every floor, foosball, Ping-Pong, and video games. Googlers brought in caged birds, threw camouflage netting over their cubes, and installed a traditional red British telephone booth purchased on eBay. We had massage chairs, massage rooms, and Japanese toilets featuring heated seats, "front cleansing," and built-in dryers. We had a stable housing a fleet of Segways and a video display Amit Patel created to show a spinning Earth with sample queries floating up from it in real time — each color-coded by language. And we had an enormous whiteboard on which any passing Googler could update "Google's secret plan" for taking over the world. It was filled with rumors, fake products, cartoons, and puns. Reporters sometimes asked if it was for real.

I always laughed. If it had been real, we would never have let them see it. Especially as, by the beginning of 2004, we were on the road to becoming a public company. Our obsession with secrecy had always been a shared cultural value. We didn't talk to anyone but other Googlers about what we did behind closed doors. Eventually we didn't even talk to them. When special key cards were suddenly required to access one engineering floor, the employees who worked there joked that they were working in the nude. By 2004, access to all information for all Googlers was no longer the norm.

Even MOMA, our free-for-all company intranet, began to show signs of becoming buttoned down. Our engineers had always obsessively collected every scrap of intelligence they could about what was happening within our servers. They analyzed it, kneaded it, and baked it into tasty little tidbits set out on MOMA where any Googler could consume them. The data was anonymized — you couldn't see individual queries or IP addresses, for example — but the number of searches, countries from which they originated, most popular search terms, and other key stats could all be viewed.

MOMA's homepage was originally dense and messy and full of numbers. At the center sat a large graph with colored lines labeled with the names of Muppet characters. The graph represented results quality across different search engines, and the top line, labeled "the Great Gonzo," belonged to Google. When another line veered close to ours, clarion calls could be heard above the gnashing of teeth, ordering that all energies be focused on improving the relevance of our results.

Larry and Sergey never forgot that the quality of our search drove our success and never took for granted that our lead was insurmountable. Ironically, the lack of a good way to search MOMA made it hard to use at first, though Google finally hooked up one of its own search appliances to fix that problem.

The most useful aspect of MOMA for me was the phone list, which contained the title, email address, and photo of everyone on the payroll. My picture was there. Sort of. My original photo captured more reflected flash than facial features, so I swapped it out for a press photo of Deputy Director Skinner from *The X-Files*. The resemblance was eerie, and his picture conveyed the gravitas and focus my own photo lacked. Other MOMA photos showed samurai warriors and masked figures with titles like "Shadow Ops" and "Black Ops." Yoshka, Urs's Leonberger, was listed as "Google's top dog." New Googlers looking me up for the first time would inevitably email me, asking about my uncanny resemblance to Mulder's boss. I'd assure them that the truth was out there.

In fact, the truth was on MOMA. I came to assume that any information I needed about Google could be found on the intranet, from the status of products in development to the number of employees at any point in the company's history. It was a shared wellspring of data that all Googlers could tap to test hypotheses, build prototypes, and win arguments.

In mid-2003, Susan put some product plans and strategic documents on MOMA that required a password to access. She was concerned that the sales team might accidentally spill too much to clients. As head of product management, Jonathan told her to make the documents accessible because Google so strongly valued the free flow of information among staff members. Only performance appraisals and compensation were off limits. "This is extremely unusual for a company to do," Eric Schmidt often reminded us at our weekly TGIF meetings, "but we will continue trusting everyone with sensitive information unless it becomes a problem."

In September 2003, it became a problem. Information about our revenue numbers and Larry and Sergey's stock holdings started showing up in news reports. Eric immediately clamped down, telling Omid and me to stop including revenue numbers in TGIF presentations. Passwords on MOMA were no longer forbidden. It was a shame, Eric observed, that reality had finally come to Google.

The source for the stories turned out to be a low-level administrator feeding information to an outsider. She was asked to leave. In January 2004, though, long after that first small leak had been plugged, a much bigger crack appeared in our wall of secrecy. The same month we hired our first corporate security manager, John Markoff from the *New York Times* wrote a series of articles in which he reported details of products in development and the results of an internal audit conducted in preparation for a possible IPO. The information had been extremely confidential and closely held. The leak was ultimately traced to a senior manager who had known Markoff for years. He left the company as well, though the true reason for his departure was not made public, leading to much speculation.

From that point on, I had to ask for access to the project information I needed to do my job. It felt odd, as if with each ironclad, password-protected gateway the company installed, it locked out a little more of its original corporate culture.

Shortly before going public, Google clamped down completely. According to SEC rules, every employee who had access to intimate knowledge about the state of the business would be restricted from freely buying and selling the company's stock. I, and most others, gladly traded ignorance about our bottom line for the bliss of being able to cash out whenever we were ready to do so. The days of innocence in the garden of data had officially come to an end.

The Antisocial Network

In February 2004, Yahoo dropped Google and began using their own Inktomi-based search results instead. We barely noticed. We stretched in the skin of our new headquarters and settled in to a new level of hyper-productivity. Everything needed to be done *right now* and everything was *very important*. New people were climbing onboard every week and taking control of projects in motion.

Cindy kept an eye out for any signs the news cycle was turning against us. She urged us not to let cracks appear in the shiny gold sphere of Google's public image, and every few months she sent reminders to all Googlers that when the press came calling, the calls should be forwarded to PR. "There is no such thing as 'off the record,'" she cautioned us, because "reporters are fiercely competitive and will tell you whatever you want to hear just to get the story." The last thing she needed was a very public slip on something as important as a new product launch. But sometimes things go wrong.

Engineer Orkut Buyukkokten came to Google in the summer of 2002 from Stanford, where he had become intrigued by the idea of social networks — a way to connect with friends and acquaintances online. As a student, Orkut had written a networking program for his classmates called "Club Nexus," and once he settled in at Google, he requested to spend his twenty-percent time coming up with an improved version. It was December 2003 before his project, code-named "Eden" and later renamed "orkut,"* was ready to be tested with a broader audience than just Googlers. That's when the fun began.

Orkut built his eponymous service entirely on his own. It was a prototype to gather data, to try things out, to experiment. He wrote the code, designed the user interface, set up the databases. He didn't intend for it to be a full-fledged Google product, so to accelerate the development, he used tools that were commonly available outside Google. They came from Microsoft. The server running orkut wasn't even located in a Google data center, but at the home of the weather site Wunderground .com. Orkut knew his system would never support Google-sized audiences, but it should safely scale to handle two or three hundred thousand users. Membership in orkut would be by invitation only, so he would be able to throttle growth by controlling the number of invitations the system distributed.

Marissa was the consumer product manager. She saw orkut as a small startup within Google, operating autonomously to prove that a single engineer with a new idea could build and test a product without enduring the delays of Google's increasingly bureaucratic development process. Larry and Sergey encouraged her to manage orkut as if it were an independent operation.

Other prototype projects by individual engineers were available in an area of our website called Google labs, but Marissa didn't believe orkut belonged there. It would be an exception — a standalone product, without Google branding, launched with lightning speed. If there were problems, few people would notice and there would be time to fix them. If anyone asked whether orkut was a Google initiative, we would an-

---

*The name was changed to "orkut" because the Eden.com domain was not for sale. It was intentionally not capitalized to distinguish orkut the service from Orkut the engineer.

swer that we could "neither confirm nor deny" a relationship between orkut and Google.

That did not sit well with Cindy, who had no desire to play coy with the press contacts she had so carefully cultivated over the years. "Reporters are not stupid," she warned the executive staff, "and we'll look silly saying this." All it took was one online search to find Orkut's connection to Google, and once the press had that, orkut would be branded a Google product whether we denied it or not. I worked on messaging to make it clear that orkut was developed by a Google engineer but was not an official Google project. Marissa rejected any such compromise. She was adamant that no explicit Google connection be revealed on the orkut site itself.

Sergey stepped in to resolve our standoff shortly before he, Larry, and Eric headed off to the World Economic Forum in Davos, Switzerland. "Let's make it an experiment," he said. "We'll launch without Google affiliation and neither confirm nor deny a relationship. If it gets out of control, then contact me in Davos and we'll come up with a new plan. Any problems with that approach?"

Oh yeah. Cindy had a big problem with that approach, and she let Sergey know it. This experiment, she pointed out, could destroy our brand reputation as well as her professional credibility. Sergey retreated to a fallback position. He endorsed launching orkut without any Google branding, but he conceded that if asked, we could admit orkut had been developed at Google.

On January 21, 2004, the day before the scheduled launch, Jonathan voiced reservations. He advised Eric Schmidt that we should wait to launch orkut until after our global sales conference and the company ski trip, a two-week delay. Cindy told Jonathan his effort was appreciated, but it was too little, too late. We had wasted weeks trying to live with the conditions Marissa had set while repeatedly advising that it was wrong to lie to the press. Product management of orkut had been bungled from day one.

Urs, our Google Fellow, raised his own questions about the timing. He had been hearing all day from engineers about unresolved issues: that orkut was running on a single machine with no easy way to scale, that there had been no proper load testing, no security review, and no agreement on the privacy policy. Clearly orkut would not be able to handle the influx of traffic once word got out to the geek news site Slashdot,* which would take about fifteen minutes. It would be smarter, he said, to clean things up for a few days, wait for the execs to return from Switzerland, and avoid a huge mistake.

We all breathed a sigh of relief when Jonathan confirmed that he had spoken with most of the executive team and they had agreed with Urs it was better to delay the launch. It was a commendable idea to accelerate the launch process, but just too risky given all the red flags that had been raised. We would begin moving orkut off its Microsoft.NET server to the standard Google technology platform so it could scale more easily and then, most likely, launch it officially on Google labs. I had proposed exactly that strategy and believed it would set user expectations appropriately — everything on labs was by definition an experiment, subject to drastic changes or sudden shutdowns. Marissa thought a launch on labs would irritate users, because they would be able to see orkut, but not to try it unless they were invited by someone who was already a member. That didn't worry me as much as users thinking, as with Froogle, that a half-baked orkut was Google's flagship product in an entirely new online sector.

I kept working on language for orkut's interface pages, user notifications, and community descriptions, so I was ready when, a day after Jonathan's reassuring news, Sergey sent word from Davos that we would, in fact, launch orkut that afternoon. Sergey had made a commitment to support a rapid implementation and he was standing by it. We would compromise by putting on orkut.com a small tag saying, "In affiliation with Google."

An hour before launch I sent Orkut text for his homepage: "orkut is an online community that connects people through a network of trusted friends. Join orkut to expand the circumference of your social circle." I included a disclaimer: "Great relationships begin with honesty, so we'd like to let you know up front that orkut is still a beta service. That means that it may appear a bit flaky at first. It may even require quiet time alone to work out some issues. We hope you'll bear with orkut as it strives to better itself. After all, that's what good friends do." At one in the afternoon, the first twelve thousand invitations to join orkut started going out via email.

---

* "Slashdotting" was a well-known online phenomenon: a site was mentioned on slashdot.com and all the users congregating there immediately went to check it out, causing the site's servers to crash under the sudden load.

In the social networks Orkut had built at Stanford, the users had been polite, respectful, and courteous. The users of orkut.com, however, were not. They immediately began looking for ways to break the system and to fill it with porn and spam. They found them. It was possible to search for every user in the system and then send them all email with hundred-megabyte attachments or write a script to add everyone as a friend. Orkut the project's creator had never seen problems like those before. He had to take the site offline almost immediately to fix them. I wrote an error message saying we were making improvements. It was to be expected given that orkut was just an experiment.

Google engineers didn't accept that excuse. They peeled back the skin of orkut's architecture and picked every bone they could find. Why hadn't orkut received a full security review? What was driving the rush to push it out the door? Wasn't it evil to place our need to launch before the security of our users? Why had we even tried to conceal Google's involvement? The questioners piled on. Marissa gamely defended the decision to move ahead by describing a startup-within-a-startup mindset that meant taking risks and patching things up as you went along. If decisions had been made differently, she indicated, and the Google name not attached to orkut at the last minute, everything would have been fine.

Engineer Howard Gobioff disagreed. "Don't be evil," he said, was a core value, which meant we needed to protect user privacy with any service we launched, whether it bore our name or not. It would have been no better if orkut users hadn't known Google was behind the service that was exposing their personal information.

Some defended the decision to prototype and launch quickly — to experiment and keep innovating. But their voices were drowned out by the angry mob clamoring for an explanation of why orkut had been allowed to go out with underweight technology, draped only in a thin association with Google that hid none of its problems. The criticism was not directed at Orkut himself or his admirable desire to try something new. The anger coalesced around the launch process. A number of engineers told me they had agreed with my original proposal to launch orkut on Google labs. I was glad to hear it, but their affirmation left a bittersweet taste.

When I first arrived at Google, I felt strongly about things and was often wrong. Fortunately, Larry and Sergey ignored my ideas. I had learned from that experience. Now I felt strongly about things and was often right. Unfortunately, my ideas were still being ignored. I wasn't sure which slight was more painful, but I suspected it was the latter.

Despite its rough start, orkut became a smash success — in Estonia, India, and Brazil.* Especially Brazil, where, Orkut informed me, a third of all the country's Internet traffic is still on the site that bears his name. When he visited Rio de Janeiro, he was recognized instantly and mobbed like a rock star. Brazilians bought computers for no reason other than to use the service he had built.

In the United States, however, orkut lagged. Two weeks after its launch, a student at Harvard introduced a social network for his classmates. He called it "The Facebook." Within six years that service would have half a billion users. Orkut continued to struggle to secure a toehold. The issue, according to most engineers I spoke with, was orkut's inability to scale to handle the influx of traffic from an audience the size of Google's, a task it had never been designed to do.

Paul Bucheit, the creator of Gmail, disagreed. The real reason was "Google's tech snobbery getting in the way of its success." Paul said orkut "was taking off. Lots of people signed up. And then it got really slow." But that was a problem other social networks had experienced as well — MySpace and even Facebook ran into capacity issues almost from the beginning. The difference, according to Paul, was that those services jumped in and did whatever it took to make things work. Facebook was just a bunch of college kids. It had no brilliant coders like Jeff Dean or Sanjay Ghemawat. And the final configuration of MySpace, which had hundreds of millions of users, wasn't much more sophisticated than what orkut had at its start.

"But at Google," according to Paul, "that wasn't how you did things." Because orkut had been written using Microsoft tools, Google's engineers deemed it "not scalable." "They turned their noses up at it and they didn't make the thing work. They just let it die. And by the time they managed to rewrite it in a way that was acceptable to the engineers at Google, it was already dead everywhere except for Brazil. Who knows? If they had actually done what was necessary to make it go, it could have been successful."

To launch a radically new product from an established company, Paul asserted, you needed someone who not only believed in it but also

---

* And in Finland for a brief time, because "orkut" in Finnish means "multiple sexual climaxes." Once people realized the site was not for romantic hookups, traffic quickly fell off.

was able to make the organization "do the right stuff." Two months after orkut's launch, he would personally put that philosophy to the acid test.

Bad News Arrives by Mail

I've never had much luck with email. For example, I had no idea that Microsoft Outlook had a two-gigabyte limit on how many messages I could save. I certainly didn't know that exceeding that amount would cause my inbox to explode and two years' worth of work to simply disappear. I found out, though, in 2002.

So I was receptive when Paul let me know he was working on an alternative to Outlook — a web-based email system he called Caribou — and asked if I'd like to try it out. I tried it, and it was pretty terrible. It didn't display well on my laptop, I couldn't sort messages from oldest to newest, and there was no way to select all the messages at once. Incredibly, there weren't even any folders for sorting mail by category. After a couple of weeks I told Paul, "Thanks, but no thanks," and went back to Microsoft Outlook.

A year later, I started hearing that Caribou had improved. Other Googlers were using it and not hating it, so I gave it another try. It still felt weak compared to Outlook, but it had some advantages. I could search through all my email quickly when I needed to find something, and it tied all my related messages together into an easily read thread. This time I stuck with it as Paul and a small team of engineers began prepping Caribou for launch as a Google product.

At the beginning of 2004, Yahoo, AOL, and Microsoft were the biggest players in online communication. They had created a balanced ecosystem of low expectations and commoditized email. Everyone knew web email came standard with a couple of megabytes of storage, inboxes littered with banner ads, and no easy way to find any message you had sent or received more than ten minutes earlier. Email addresses were disposable, and so many names had been claimed that almost everyone had to include a string of meaningless numbers in their user ID to open a new account. The major providers liked it that way and didn't want anyone rocking the boat. At one point during our negotiations to win the AOL contract, AOL had put terms into the deal specifying that Google could not do email. Before Google had to admit that might be a problem, AOL's own lawyers informed their negotiating team the language would violate anti-trust policies, so they pulled the wording.

According to Paul, fear of a radically new email system wasn't restricted to those outside the Googleplex. Some Googlers were so worried about how Microsoft might respond to Caribou, they proposed incorporating Microsoft's Passport identity-authentication system into our program. "Other engineers had so many complaints about Caribou that we had a meeting so they could list them all," Paul told me. "People were upset that we were using JavaScript. JavaScript was a huge mistake and we'd never get it to work. Just doing email was bad because we'd have to deal with spam, and all this data, and personal info, and security — anything you could imagine. Everything about Caribou was bad — that it even existed. Even right up to the launch, people were arguing we should just scrap the whole thing."

One positive asset Caribou did have was Georges Harik. Georges, as Paul describes him, was "an idea person," with a PhD in computer science, a background in machine learning, and relentless energy, which made him restless. And he had earned respect within engineering, especially from Larry, which made him priceless. "Ultimately," Paul said, "that's a really big advantage or liability for a project. What Larry thinks of the people involved."

Georges decided he would like to try product management for a while and became the product manager for Caribou. While he and Paul didn't always see eye-to-eye, Paul believed he was actually interested in shipping a product, not "playing power games." That kept the focus on the technology and steered the team away from damaging political conflicts that could delay the launch.

What I cared about was the name of the new service, the way we described it, and the date on which it launched. The choice of a name was complicated by our desire to have it tie to the Google brand but be faster to type than "Yahoo." The leading contender was "Gmail." The domain gmail.com was taken, though, and we were having a hard time connecting with the owners. Two weeks before the scheduled launch date, Rose Hagan, a Google attorney, tracked them down and offered them sixty-five thousand dollars. It was on the low end of what we were willing to pay, but more than they expected. Gmail.com was ours.

I was no longer the only one working on the text that would appear when the new product launched, though I insisted on reviewing every word to ensure we maintained Google's voice. Jonathan's product-management department had spawned a new position entitled APMM — associate product marketing manager — and the APMM assigned to Gmail was a hyperkinetic, hyper-focused Harvard grad named Ana Yang. Ana wrote copy, but she also thought strategically about the product's positioning, the reaction of users, and the perceptions of the press and our partners. She set up meetings, coordinated assignments, and worked closely with Georges to resolve issues. I could barely keep up with her. She sent out updates at two a.m., three a.m., and four a.m. in a single night. At one point I had to tell her that as important as Gmail was, I couldn't attend seven meetings about it in one week and still get my work done on the other projects I was juggling.

I looked at Ana and glimpsed my own mortality.

Product management was inexorably taking over the role of brand stewardship. The mass of Jonathan's world had grown so large, so quickly, that whole galaxies now tilted into its gravitational field. Things might have been different at a company like Procter and Gamble, which viewed its business from the outside looking in, searching the market for gaps between consumer desires and the products addressing them. Google looked at the world from the inside out. Engineers made products to their own specifications, not those of the consumers who would use them. If our technology found acceptance in the marketplace, great. If not, the technology was not inherently less worthy of being built. In a company where the products were the brand, brand management would become product marketing. I knew that was the natural order of things.

I still had a role, though, and I did my best to fill it. I positioned Gmail not as a better competitor to Yahoo mail, but as an entirely new way of thinking about communication. It wasn't just that we gave users a hundred times the storage capacity (one gigabyte) for free, but that we added a search capability that eliminated the need to manually file every email in a folder so it could be found again. It wasn't a home run compared with other email systems. It was an entirely new ball game.

The only remaining piece to be resolved was the launch date. In February 2004, Sergey suggested that we launch Gmail on April Fools' Day. It would be amusing to watch the press grapple with whether we meant it for real or as a joke. I didn't see the humor in playing our biggest new product launch for laughs. I told Sergey so and repeated my concerns at a launch review meeting in March attended by the Gmail team and the executive staff. Eric shared my concerns, and as CEO, he made a top-down decision. Given all the effort that had gone into creating Gmail and its potential to open up important new markets for Google, we would not make a joke out of the launch. Larry and Sergey argued that the joke was a Googley thing to do, but Eric was insistent. We could launch on April 1, but we would make it clear that Gmail was for real.

I hung around the meeting as it broke up and followed Eric out to the stairwell. "Thanks for that," I said to him as he climbed up toward his office. "You made the right decision. It has to be frustrating arguing with Larry and Sergey about such obvious things."

Eric stopped and looked at me. "I'm well compensated," he said with a smile. "Now please excuse me while I walk around the building a few times."

Thinking back to the weeks before Gmail launched, I'm amazed at how much we got done. I don't mean overcoming the technical challenges, which were mind-boggling, or resolving legal questions, which were Byzantine, or addressing partner-management issues, which were delicate — I mean just handling the elements lobbed into marketing's corner of the court.

Those elements would have kept us busy if we had been a startup focused only on the launch of one product, but the reality was that Google's product-release process had become a rolling-thunder operation of sustained, high-impact launches. Behind Gmail taxied personalized search, web alerts, local search, and "Total Recall," our code name for software that searched a user's PC files. Those products also required preparation that couldn't wait until Gmail was out the door.

I had my own projects, as well, including a nationwide engineer-recruitment campaign, a college promotion in Japan, an online tour of new Google features, and a response to users about JewWatch, an anti-Semitic hate site that we were showing as the top search result for the word "Jew." I felt my life shift into "bullet time," the effect from the *Matrix* movies, where everything slows to a crawl while the protagonist's perception of time expands, enabling him to see projectiles speeding toward him. I was operating at peak capacity. Every keystroke, every utterance, every thought moved me closer to my goal. I lost track of how much espresso I drank, but I remember being thankful that we had more than one machine, and that each one could make two cups at a time.

So the last thing I wanted to hear, five days before the launch of Gmail, was that we were going to make it a joke after all. It wouldn't be *the* April Fools' joke — we would go with my idea about a Google lunar office for that — but the executive staff had decreed we would do a hybrid announcement of sorts.

There would be a press release that was factual, but with enough humorous elements to leave people wondering if Gmail was for real. We would brief a few journalists in advance, but only on condition that they agreed to write funny stories about the launch. And we would incorporate the slogan Larry had come up with: "Gmail. It feels good."

Cindy was in Germany and largely offline, leaving PR Director David Krane to roll with the punches. "I knew we were going to be playing with people and challenging relationships if we shipped a communications vehicle written in such a way," he recalls. "Sergey insisted on it. I felt like we should hedge a little bit and deploy a few proven strategies in case things went haywire because our humor was misunderstood."

David recommended letting a few trusted journalists and analysts in on the joke, so the day of the announcement we could refer people to them with questions about Gmail's potential impact on the industry. "No way!" he remembers Sergey telling him. "It's a joke. We want to *surprise* everybody. No way. Absolutely no way. Categorically, *no*."

Meanwhile, Dennis Hwang spent the day before the launch coming up with ideas for a logo and trying to make it work in conjunction with the clown-colored Google brand. I suggested he make Google gray and let the Gmail logo carry the corporate colors. Even after four years at Google, I found it astounding that one twenty-something guy was sitting alone at his desk, sipping tea and developing the main branding element for a product to be used by millions of people — the night before it was scheduled to launch.

That's when Sergey stopped by to ask if we were making a mistake launching Gmail as a joke. I had assured him many times before that it was, but now, after running so hard to make it happen, I began to have doubts. "No," I said. "It's not a mistake. It's funny, but I think it's a missed opportunity. If people think it's a joke, they might not take it seriously when we tell them it's real." That didn't persuade him, as I knew it wouldn't. We chatted a few minutes more, then he wandered off.

Other cracks appeared as the pressure built in the final hours. There were miscommunications and dropped balls. Issues with version control on documents. Frantic revisions. Some bad assumptions. I apologized to our growing team of writers for being cranky and assured them they were doing great work. More worrisome, several engineers argued that the service itself wasn't ready. Paul pleaded for more servers to add capacity.

"We launched it with a couple hundred machines," he told me later. "We launched it with almost no hardware. We were able to support Googlers and a handful of other people. That thing we launched just barely existed."

At four p.m. on March 31, the press release went out. The Rubicon had been crossed.

The phones in the PR department started ringing almost instantly. Once reporters got beyond annoyance at the ambiguity of our announcement, they were impressed. Their stories the next day were positive. We had dodged a bullet. Cindy was thrilled with the new breezy tone and style of our press communications, though she thought it unfortunate that we had rolled it out on April Fools'.

On the first day, a quarter of a million users put their names on the waiting list for Gmail accounts.

Then things started to go sideways.

Reporters complained to Cindy that we had mishandled the announcement. A journalist friend of hers had assured people it was a joke and been embarrassed to be proven wrong. Even more than most people, reporters don't like to be proven wrong. Cindy was taking considerable flak, but that was hardly the worst of it.

The ads in Gmail, targeted to the content of messages in the inbox, freaked people out. They didn't like it that Gmail was going to read their mail to serve them targeted ads. They called it "creepy" and an invasion of their privacy. Stories started showing up on TV and the Internet about Google's scary new email system. Conan O'Brien joked about it in his monologue. Why was Google even getting into email in the first place? Google was a search engine. Those who had urged the government to punish the advertising company DoubleClick for tracking users' online behavior put Gmail in the same camp.[*] Only worse. We were reading people's email.

On April 12, California State Senator Liz Figueroa announced she would introduce legislation outlawing Gmail. She did not have a Gmail account. She had never seen a Gmail account. Almost no one had. In a

---

[*] Google bought DoubleClick in 2007 for $3.1 billion.

press release, she quoted from a letter she had sent to Google: "I cannot urge you strongly enough to abandon this misbegotten idea. I believe you are embarking on a disaster of enormous proportions."

When Sergey called the senator to explain that Gmail ads were placed automatically by computers, the same way emails were scanned for viruses, she didn't want to hear the details. She did not, in fact, like email, she informed him, and she certainly didn't want hers scanned by Google.

I had never heard of Liz Figueroa, but I looked her up online and saw that she soon would be forced out of office by term limits. I wondered if she hoped attaching her name to a "pro-consumer" issue would help her win her next election.*

A law against Gmail would certainly be a problem, but it wouldn't matter if we continued to be hammered by privacy groups and the press. No one would sign up for the service anyway.

The day after Figueroa's announcement, I headed to Washington, DC. The trip had nothing to do with Gmail. My mother's sister had passed away and I was going to her funeral. It was an emotional experience for me during an already stressful time. As I stood graveside, all the pressure that had been building within me found an acceptable release. I found myself crying uncontrollably when I dropped a handful of dirt onto my aunt's coffin as it was lowered into the ground. I hugged my mother and sister for what seemed like a very long time. With all that had been happening, I had not had a chance to breathe, let alone process the events bombarding me. I knew the avalanche of new problems back home was accelerating in my absence.

When I returned to the office, the atmosphere had changed. I sensed gloom and recrimination and frustration about the negative response to ads in Gmail. Sergey paced the office like a tiger in a tiny cage, commanding us to set up a war room to deal with the problem, demanding we put up more information on the site, and insisting that we tell everyone, "There is *no privacy issue*."

It was a perspective shared by Paul and other engineers as well. Computers did the scanning, and computers were good at keeping secrets. It was a closed system. If there was no loss of privacy, there was no privacy issue. Why couldn't people understand that?

---

* Figueroa ran for lieutenant governor in 2006 and came in third among three candidates in the Democratic primary.

"Just tell them spam filters and virus detectors have done this for years," Sergey instructed David Krane, who told me the founders dismissed critics as misinformed and intimated that they should "trust us, we have no record of doing anything bad." Sergey in particular seemed to take the criticism personally, and his frustration deepened with each passing day as Georges and Ana worked on a statement defending Gmail to post on the site. They had begun work on it while I was in DC, and when I rewrote it to make it more user-friendly, Sergey insisted we change it back. Though the writing was an improvement, he said, our users were not the target. He wanted a direct response to the points raised by privacy advocates, and he didn't care if users read it or not. In this time of crisis, Google would once again be a platform for expressing his personal perspective.

Cindy's mood also darkened by the hour. She was stung by the criticism from her professional colleagues and unhappy with the response of our group to the conflagration we had ignited. Googlers from other departments were asking why we were not responding to all the misinformation circulating. What was our PR strategy?

David and his group pushed Gmail accounts into the hands of journalists and analysts so they could see the service for themselves. Once they tried it, most backed off their alarmist tone about privacy, but that took time, and we were now on the wrong side of public opinion. Cindy demanded to know how soon we could launch a corporate blog to respond more quickly to controversy — a project I had been working on for weeks.*

Cindy seemed on edge, though not more so than anyone else, and not just with me. Sergey got singed when he repeated a rumor suggesting that PR had missed an opportunity to defend Gmail.

I began dreading Cindy's late-night emails asking for updates on all the projects she thought I should be leading more forcefully. I had set up my inbox to color her messages bright red so I'd be sure not to miss them in the sea of spam. Now I switched the color to a subdued maroon and began taking deep breaths before opening each note. Still, I was unprepared for the missive she fired at me at three in the morning one Saturday, telling me a full plate was no excuse for letting the product-

---

* There were technical issues integrating software from Pyra Labs, the blogging company Google had bought, and there were legal questions about whether launching a new communications vehicle so close to the time we were planning to file for our IPO would violate an SEC-mandated "quiet period."

management team assume ownership of the Gmail privacy issue. User communication was my job, and once we lost control of it we would never get it back. There was more, and none of it was pleasant to read. I felt as if I had moved back to square one — with a difference.

One of the tasks keeping me too busy to lead every charge was rewriting the language of our S-1 filing document. Google was finally ready to go public, and I knew that would change everything.

PART IV

CAN THIS REALLY
BE THE END?

As Google blossoms,
We grow together, then part.
I'm feeling lucky.

CHAPTER 26

S-1 for the Money

WHY 'TECHNOLOGY' AND not 'technologies'?" asked the lawyer sitting ten bankers down from me.

"We always refer to technology in the singular," I replied leaning forward so I could see him. "As a collective noun." I had no idea if that made any sense. I prayed there weren't any other English majors among the thirty attorneys, bankers, and venture capitalists in the room, all of whom were looking down at their own copies of our S-1 filing statement and following word by word with mechanical pencils and highlighters. If there were, they didn't speak up. We moved on to the next line of the text.

The printing firm RR Donnelley had been putting ink on paper for almost as long as the *Mercury News*. Their facility in Palo Alto, however, bore little resemblance to my former place of employment. The conference room we met in was packed with the latest communication electronics and decorated in muted contemporary tones. A fully stocked kitchen was just down the hall, as were an entertainment lounge, a pool table, a gym, showers, and rollaway beds. A massage therapist was on duty in case the stress of editing became overwhelming. Located directly behind Silicon Valley's premier law firm, RR Donnelley was the place companies went when they were ready to go public.

I had arrived late on Tuesday afternoon, April 27, and parked down the street from the Mission-style building as instructed. The license

plate frame on my Taurus sported Google's logo and the words "I'm
Feeling Lucky." If seen near Donnelley's, that could be enough to give
away the secret we wanted to keep; that Project Denny's — our public
filing — was under way.[*]

I had not expected to be involved, but late the night before, Cindy
had emailed me a draft of a letter Larry had written to Google's future stockholders. In it, he laid out the principles by which he, Sergey,
and Eric intended to run Google after it went public. The sentiments
were true, but the sentences stacked together like computer commands.
Cindy asked if I wanted to take a pass at putting it in "Google voice." I
made some quick edits and sent it back to see if I was on the right track.
At eleven-thirty p.m., Larry sent me an instant message asking me to
keep going. He was in his office with Salar, Susan, and Marissa hashing
out the text. I kept going. At around one-thirty a.m., I sent my finished
draft and went to bed.

Larry's revised draft was waiting for me the next morning. Not much
had changed. The style was still all Larry's. Cindy let me know that, at
the board's urging, he had also asked Kara Swisher, the lead reporter
covering Internet companies for the *Wall Street Journal,* to take a stab
at improving it. Larry regarded Kara as family because she was married
to Megan Smith, a Google manager, but Cindy upbraided him for con-
tacting a journalist without her knowledge — especially one who wrote
frequently about Google for the national media. Kara found Larry's request endearingly naive, but declined because of ethical considerations.
Undeterred, Larry turned to James Fallows of the *Atlantic.* Larry always
believed in hiring the best talent, and while Fallows did not accept payment, he offered a few editorial suggestions to make the language flow
as if it had been written by a native speaker of English.

Meanwhile, I had moved on to the business section of the document,
a sixteen-page description of every product Google offered, our partners, our technology, and our corporate culture. I had a lot of changes
there as well. Larry seemed more willing to incorporate input on that
aspect of the filing, and I was invited to join the group finalizing the
document at the printer's.

When I arrived, I sat quietly. The room was intimidating and filled
with suits worn by men of importance. Jonathan Rosenberg was in the

---

[*] Larry and Sergey have always had a thing for cheap restaurants. They celebrated the initial funding of Google at a Burger King and negotiated the $1.65 billion purchase of YouTube at a Denny's.

chair to my left. He greeted me warmly and introduced me as "the voice of Google." "If Doug says it's not Googley, we need to change it," he informed the group.

Everyone opened their books to the business section and someone began to read aloud. "'Google is a global leader in web search,'" he intoned, "'a web advertising innovator, a top Internet destination, and one of the most recognized brands in the world.'"

"I rewrote that," I said, clearing my throat. "It should say, 'Google is a global technology leader focused on improving the ways people connect with information.'"

"Why?" piped up a guy in an ironed polo shirt. "What's wrong with what we have?"

"Google's mission is not limited to search," I told him. "Just last week we launched an email service. We're more than a search engine."

And so it went for hours. At one point I tried calculating how much it would cost to hire everyone in the room for just one minute, assuming five hundred dollars an hour was probably the least any of those around the table charged for their time. By that estimate, my talk was not cheap, but Jonathan prodded me to speak up each time he sensed I was being reticent. When I got home at two a.m., I sent him a private thank-you note for his encouragement before collapsing into bed. He answered at seven the next morning, and it was unclear if he had slept in the interim.

"You did a great job," he wrote. Your changes were all well written, thoughtful, and you defended them based on your understanding of Google, the founders, and the history of how we've handled prose for the last five years. There is no one in the company who could have been more effective. You came through in a big way last night for the cause." He copied the message to the entire executive team.

Suddenly I felt bad about the whole carwash thing.

I'd like You to Be the First to Know

"Please come to a company meeting today at 11:30 in the TGIF area," said the email that went out to all Googlers on Thursday, April 29, at eleven a.m. "Full-time employees only, please. Be prepared to show your ID badges."

The TGIF area was Charlie's Café. By the time I arrived at eleven-fifteen, the building was packed. Every Googler I'd ever seen, and many I'd never met, either sat in the rows of folding chairs or leaned over the balcony railing.

At the front of the room, four microphone stands stood on the low stage, waiting, each mic covered with a windscreen in one of the Google logo colors. The mics were not the wireless ones Larry preferred, because our security manager worried that someone outside the building could pick up the signal from a wireless mic. The wall at the back was made of three-foot-wide perforated metal panels that curved in a semicircle and stretched to the ceiling. A row of potted plants marked the front of the stage, and two banners printed with enlarged Google doodle logos hung at the back. On one banner, Albert Einstein peered out of an *o*. On the other, two aliens sat on the letter *g* and looked down from the moon on a rising earth.

Craig Silverstein, Google's first employee, sat on the floor facing the stage, and an interpreter for the deaf faced the other way, signing for one of our hearing-impaired engineers.

Larry and Sergey walked in with Eric and Omid. Larry leaned against the railing as Sergey walked onstage. Sergey grinned and stepped up to the microphone with the bright green cover. He wore a black long-sleeved t-shirt and gray jeans.

"Thank you for coming," he said to the hushed assemblage. Pause. "I just wanted you to be the first to know . . ." Nervous giggles from the crowd. Pause. "that I just saved a fortune on my auto insurance."* The laughter shook the walls. We all knew why we were there. In the half hour after the note went out announcing the meeting, our press release had crossed the wire. Google was going public.

News vans were parked in a row down the street outside, microwave antennas extended, satellite dishes up, and light-diffusing scrims positioned for on-camera interviews. A helicopter buzzed overhead as security guards stood watch from the parking lot entrances.

Omid gave an encore performance of his greatest TGIF hits, with slides showing what we hadn't been allowed to see in months. Our revenue was so far up and to the right that the purple bars were pushing off the top of the screen.

Eric spoke and reminded us not to be distracted by all that was about

---

* The line was from a GEICO insurance commercial popular at the time. A week after Google went public, GEICO sued Google for allowing their competitors to place ads on search results for their name.

to happen. Not to let the company's culture change, not to get caught up in the hype.

When the floor was opened for questions, Keith Kleiner, an early employee from operations, walked to the mic. "I just want to say," he began, looking at Larry and Sergey, "thank you. You guys have done an incredible job building this company." The applause burst like a thunderclap from the seats, the aisles, the balcony. Within seconds, every employee was standing and cheering. Larry put his arm around Sergey's shoulder and beamed at the crowd. Sergey reciprocated. For two minutes, waves of unadulterated appreciation rolled over the founders as Eric stood to the side and pointed like a conductor at two virtuoso violinists.

After the meeting we went back to our desks and back to work. I stayed there until after six, before packing up my laptop and heading to the Sports Page bar and grill around the corner. Affectionately known among Googlers as "The Shit Hole," it was a funky wood-and-plaster hut with a large back patio perfect for informal celebrations. Lori Park, one of the first engineers hired, had arranged to rent it out for a get-together of old-time Googlers. Salar was there, and Susan brought her kids. Bart from advertising operations and the biz dev guys who had come over from Netscape. Orkut, Ben Smith, and Ben Gomes showed up. Radhika, Ed Karrels, and Wayne. The Blogger guys. Craig and Georges. And Babette, who now supervised an army of Google massage therapists. I flashed back four years to Google in early 2000 and felt as close to my colleagues as I ever had. We had made this climb together, and for just a brief moment, we could pause and reflect on the journey that had brought us here.

I had printed out a copy of the S-1 (as had most of the company — the printers hadn't stopped all day), and I walked around with a red Sharpie, collecting signatures on it from Larry and Sergey, Craig, and our chief legal officer, David Drummond. I wanted something tangible to prove I had been there, to freeze the moment when my Silicon Valley fantasy solidified into reality.

I finished my beer and headed home.

Money from Nothing

The months that followed were not much different from the ones that had come before. The Gmail privacy issue finally settled down. Liz

Figueroa abandoned her legislation. Cindy and I talked out the issues she had raised in her late-night flame mail. The tension eased, but the pressure didn't. I continued to put in long hours working on principles regarding scumware, and I fought for a Users' Bill of Rights that didn't make it past the executive committee.

We launched a corporate blog, though it was risky given that we had entered a government-mandated "quiet period" as soon as we filed our S-1 statement. We couldn't post anything that might be perceived as promoting sales of our stock in the IPO. My first post was about recruiting for our European office. My second post was an apology for editing the first post after it had already gone up. I was still learning new things, like blogger etiquette.

I kept knocking my head against the wall between corporate marketing and product management and got little more than a migraine for my efforts. I went to Marissa's weekly launch meetings but had only occasional glimpses into products that were early in development. One of those was desktop search, which now was called "Fluffy Bunnies," because its original name, "Total Recall," had been deemed too scary from a privacy standpoint. Fluffy Bunnies would index the hard drive on a personal computer and make it searchable. I argued vehemently that we needed to give users a warning up front — "This product is not like others you may have used. Please read the privacy policy carefully" — but my tone was considered too alarmist. I did convince the team to use the descriptive line "Search your own computer," though Marissa found it colloquial, redundant, and "lame, lame, lame."

The CIA bought one of our Google Search Appliances for their intranet and asked if they could customize our logo by replacing an O with their seal. I told our sales rep to give them the okay if they promised not to tell anyone. I didn't want it spooking privacy advocates. "Do you think they can keep a secret?" I asked her.

I hired a writer to take on some of the load — Michael Krantz, a funny, gifted journalist who had covered Silicon Valley for *Time* magazine and understood technology. He got the job because he put together a prospective April Fools' joke that made me laugh.

Having writing help freed up some of my time, giving me the opportunity to attend the series of finance fairs Jonathan had arranged for the company, with representatives from firms like Morgan Stanley, Salomon Smith Barney, and UBS explaining how to invest prudently and avoid excessive taxes. Many of these advisors had been randomly dialing every phone extension at Google for months, trying to line up clients before the IPO. I had ignored the calls, but now I was curious about what the professionals had to say. The IPO was coming in August and I needed to think about what it might mean for me.

The road to the IPO was rocky. Larry and Sergey wanted to sell stock directly to the public through a Dutch auction, in which the stock price would be gradually lowered until all shares were sold. They thought that would be democratic and allow broad participation. They saw the traditional way of going public as a broken system. Wall Street investment banks insisted on pricing shares artificially low so that they popped up on the first day of trading and the banks made a killing on the shares they owned. To Larry and Sergey, it was deceptive and inefficient and only the banks benefited. They spurned the bankers and told them Google would do it differently. The bankers fought back, constantly bad-mouthing Google's stock, its management, and its idiosyncratic IPO process.* Estimates for the opening price of Google shares sank below the high end of one hundred twenty-five dollars because there was less demand than anticipated amid all the disparaging chatter and a sagging stock market.

Admittedly, Larry and Sergey didn't help much. The report from their road show, in which they traveled to various cities flogging our offering to institutional investors, was that they weren't taking the presentation any more seriously than they took our weekly TGIF meetings. In other words, Sergey didn't look at the slides before speaking about them, and commented that the information they contained was wrong, or not very good, or of dubious origins. The energy levels were low, the handoffs sloppy, and the attitude so laid-back as to be disrespectful.

People noticed. *BusinessWeek* reported that when Sergey was "asked about Google's strategy for growth," he said, "'If I tell you, you'll just ask again.'" The article also quoted "a different money manager with a billion-dollar Internet fund" as saying, "'They seem to think you should feel privileged [to buy Google stock]. That's the attitude — and it's a bizarre one.'"† The writer questioned whether Sergey had the maturity or the humility to run a major technology company and whether our

---

* For example, the founders' insistence on valuing the company at $2,718,281,828, which is the product of the mathematical term *e* times $1 billion.

† Timothy J. Mullaney, "My Google Grubstake," *BusinessWeek*, August 16, 2004; www.business-week.com/technology/content/aug2004/tc20040816_6051.htm.

founders would "be blinded by the sort of success that would go to any-one's head."

"How can I win, Doug?" Cindy, who was on tour with them, asked me.

"It's like living in a Greek tragedy," I told her. "These guys define hubris. I'm afraid it will be our downfall."

The lack of deference seen as an asset in Silicon Valley didn't play well among the status-conscious players of the Wall Street establishment.

Nor did the twenty-three million shares of stock we had neglected to register with the SEC before giving them to employees. Or the interview Larry and Sergey had done with *Playboy* the week before filing the S-1. We didn't think it would come out until after the IPO date, but on August 12, there it was on the PR department's fax machine, with a cover sheet from *Playboy*'s editors saying, "Enjoy and Congrats!" We didn't enjoy, because the SEC made us include the full text of the article in our filing statement and pushed back our IPO a week.

I took advantage of the unexpected break to arrange a quickie vacation to San Diego with Kristen and our kids, who barely recognized me anymore. A day before our planned departure, though, my wife's grandmother passed away. Kristen flew to Seattle for the funeral, and I stayed home with the children, doing loads of laundry, shopping for groceries, and playing board games while running to my laptop every few minutes to respond to emails about budgeting, trademarks, and trade show giveaways.

It was an odd interregnum. My life had been moving so quickly, I hadn't taken a break in what seemed like years. Now I was overcome by lethargy, perhaps induced by exhaustion or by the knowledge that I had become part of something larger and that, consequentially, my individual contribution had become less essential. In my early days at Google, if I didn't do the marketing tasks, they didn't get done. Now Google overflowed with PMs, APMs, PMMs, and APMMs eager to showcase their abilities.

The Saturday before our scheduled offering, Jonathan put out the word that he had hired a director of product marketing. The era of corporate marketing had truly ended and the era of product marketing had formally begun.

I cut my vacation short and returned to work early on Thursday, August 19 — IPO day — to watch the circus. I drove by the TV trucks and into the parking lot. The auction for Google shares had ended, the initial price was set at eighty-five dollars, and when the markets opened, the world would tell us what it thought of the business we had built.

There was no company meeting scheduled. Sergey was with us in Mountain View to set the proper tone: it was a Thursday like any other, and we needed to stay focused on the work ahead of us. The rest of the executives were at the NASDAQ, preparing to start the day's trading. Larry called Sergey, according to David Krane, and gave him a rundown. Not on the valuation he expected, but on the technology being used by the traders. "Here's what I'm looking at," Krane heard Larry tell Sergey. "Here's what the systems look like, and here's how much data is passing through. This is how fast it's updating. This is the resolution of the displays. This is how big the displays are, how many they have . . ."

I joined a half dozen employees gathered around a TV mounted on the wall above the PR cubicles. On the screen, a bunch of people in suits stood before a large electronic display. I didn't recognize Larry at first, wearing a gray jacket, a white shirt, and a red tie. Was this the guy I had seen sweating on a locker room bench as he struggled out of his hockey pads? Eric stood to Larry's left and Omid looked over his shoulder, as Larry picked up a marker and signed his name on a glass screen, and by so doing, made them all billionaires. Someone standing behind me opened a single bottle of cheap champagne, poured it into paper cups, and passed it around. Then we went back to our desks.

"The thing I remember about the IPO," Paul Bucheit told me recently, "is how much of a non-event it was. I was at Microsoft the day Windows 95 went gold,* and that was a huge party. I got in a little late, and the place was just destroyed. The carpet was torn up because someone brought a motorcycle inside. Tables were smashed and they had gone through some enormous amount of alcohol. It was a big deal. The IPO was not that big a deal. Everyone was just working. Kind of remarkable."

Larry and Sergey did all they could to keep the company culture as it had been. Wayne Rosing told the engineers that he would personally greet anyone who showed up the next day driving a Ferrari, and that he would gladly redecorate the new car with his baseball bat. That didn't

---

* "Going gold" meant the code had been finalized and was loaded on a master disk, ready to ship to the manufacturer for production.

worry engineers Ed Karrels and Chad Lester. They hadn't bought sports cars; they had purchased airplanes.

"It's not a Ferrari," Chad told Ed. "It's not a Lamborghini. Let's bring our planes in and land them on the road outside Google."

They didn't. And anyone else who had splurged on a new toy left it at home. But things did change.

Bart, the advertising operations guy who had so eagerly anticipated the IPO, took to practicing his putting on the lawn outside the front door at every opportunity. People tucked stock tickers discretely into corners of their laptop screens, though Larry and Sergey threatened to fine anyone they caught doing it. It became harder to hold meetings because the conference rooms were occupied by Googlers huddled with people wearing polished shoes and toting expensive leather briefcases.

I was back at work and busy, but not as crazily busy as before. I had seniority plus a large group of product managers eager to pick up any slack. Cindy agreed to send me to China to learn the market and find a new Chinese name to replace our current brand there. While Yahoo's name translated as "elegant tiger," ours was rendered with characters that meant "old dog."*

In October, Cindy asked me to run the logistics for our first earnings call, in which we would reveal our quarterly results and take questions from brokers and analysts. It would be our first time talking directly to investors, and the desire for perfection was amped even higher than usual. Larry, Sergey, Eric, and George, our CFO, sat in a conference room with an armed guard outside. I was next door, looking through the window with Cindy, Jonathan, and our operations and legal teams. There was a last-minute breakdown in communication with the outside investor-relations firm, but we established an instant messenger link and no one was the wiser. To the rest of the world the event came off flawlessly, keeping the focus on the reported numbers, which stunned the market. Google's stock shot up to almost two hundred dollars over the following week.

Also stunned were my colleagues, when, at a party at Zibbibos after the earnings call, Cindy announced she was leaving Google. I had seen it coming. In fact, I had entertained thoughts along the same line. It seemed as if we had come to the end of a long story, and I wasn't sure

---

* I liked "Gu-Gu," a nonsense sound reminiscent of a bird's song or a baby's cry. Our Chinese staffers felt it was too informal. In 2006, Google chose Gu-Ge, or "harvest song."

I wanted to begin a new one. Cindy said she would stay another two months and leave in January. I decided to wait at least that long to see what the future held.

Cindy had been my last and strongest ally in defending the role of branding that went beyond research, analytics, testing, and iteration — and now she was heading out the door. After her departure, I would report to the director of product marketing. He seemed very well-qualified for the job. He had earned degrees in electrical engineering and computer science from MIT, had worked as a business strategist for a consulting firm, and had been a VP of global product marketing for a major networking company. He was exactly what Google was looking for, and that meant I no longer was.

Three weeks after Cindy left, the director of product marketing called me into his office. I knew he wanted to talk about slotting, the process established in product management to determine where on the org chart an individual best fit.

"Doug," he said, "I'm having a hard time slotting you. I don't really see where you fit. There doesn't seem to be a place for 'brand management' in the organization as a functional role."

I could have made the case that I deserved one of the predefined jobs in product marketing and negotiated for the most senior position available. I had no desire to do that. I could have protested, tried to explain the value of my work, and insisted a slot be created for my function. I knew I would never be able to provide sufficient data to back that up. Instead, I agreed with him. There was no longer a role at Google for what I did. I would wind things down as Cindy had, and leave in two months.

I picked March 4, 2005, as my last day: "Three. Four. Five." I liked the architectural purity of it.

When the day arrived, I said my farewells. There were many people at my sendoff I hadn't seen in a long while. Larry shook my hand and wished me well. Charlie baked me a cake. Marissa surprised me by giving me a hug and saying she had always respected my judgment, though she hadn't always agreed with it. I surprised myself by admitting I felt the same about her.

I went back to my office to finish some edits on Sergey's letter for the annual report, emailed it to him, then shut down my computer and turned it in to the help desk. I cut up my corporate credit card and left it on my manager's chair.

My exit interview was brief and with an HR staffer I had never met before.

It was late when I went out to the parking lot and climbed into the Taurus. I put the key in the ignition and turned it. I sat for a moment, breathing. In my mirror loomed a large array of buildings occupied by a powerful global enterprise. Its logo stared at me from across a grassy embankment, a motley assortment of brightly colored letters on a white signboard.

I had started at a small startup as a big-company guy. Now I was leaving a big company as a small-startup guy.

I put the car in reverse, backed out of the slot, and drove home.

You Must Remember This

A cold fog wafted out of the open freezer in front of me. It was a week after my last day at Google, and Kristen had sent me on a night run to Safeway to pick up some milk for the next day's breakfast. As always, I was going off-list; picking up a few items with more sugar and fat than nutrition. I squinted at the tags on the shelf below the different brands of ice cream. What I really wanted was Starbucks Java Chip, but I only bought that when it was on sale. I reached for the Safeway store brand.

My hand froze, but not from the cold. "I want Java Chip," a voice said inside my head.

"It's not on sale," another voice answered automatically, in a monotone.

"It's. Not. On. Sale," the first voice replied with mimicking sarcasm. "So . . . ," it went on, spacing the words for emphasis, "*what?*" I picked up a carton of Java Chip and put it in my cart.

For the very first time, I was doing something differently because of Google's success.

Hitting the startup jackpot was like leaving Flatland, the world hypothesized in a geometry-based novel I had read as a kid.[*] In Flatland, the characters moved along a single, two-dimensional plane and only perceived objects as points or lines. That had been my life, and I had never realized it. Go to work, make money, come home, sleep. Repeat. Now, though, I had the ability to move in all dimensions. The tethering

---

[*] *Flatland: A Romance of Many Dimensions,* by Edwin Abbott (1884).

constraints of grocery bills and mortgage payments had been severed and I was floating free.

Some Googlers used their new freedom to change their lifestyles, their cars, their homes, their careers, their spouses. For me, all that open sky was disconcerting. I clung to the familiar to anchor myself. It was surprisingly hard to do that without a job.

I had practiced the marketing arts in one form or another for twenty-five years, and I didn't want to do it anymore. The position I left at Google had been the pinnacle — the best job I could imagine for someone in my field. I had watched over a brand that exploded from obscurity to dictionary definition in five short years. My colleagues were some of the most brilliant people on earth. I traveled the globe and made my fortune. I learned things about my limits and my capabilities. And I like to think that, in some small way, I helped advance the human condition. Or at least that I did more good than harm.

I've heard the speculation about Google since I left. That it's a monopoly. That it's tracking users. That it's in cahoots with the government. That it spies on people. That it's evil. Well, maybe it is all that. I haven't worked there in more than five years. Things change. But from what I know about my coworkers in the Plex — many of whom are still there, putting in long hours perfecting a product used by millions every day — I'd say that's highly unlikely.

Is Google secretive? No question. Arrogant? Maybe. Tone-deaf to the concerns of the very users it claims to serve? Occasionally. But evil? I don't think so.

I started my career working at ad agencies. It was fun, challenging, and potentially well paying. I quit because I didn't like the idea I might have to sell something I didn't believe in. I worked in public broadcasting and then newspapers, where I found coworkers who sacrificed material rewards to be part of something connected to the common good. I got that same sense at Google, but with greater intensity and urgency. And stock options. This was no institution continuing a long tradition of public service. This was a headlong rush to reshape the world in a generation. And therein lies the company's biggest flaw, in my estimation: impatience with those not quick enough to grasp the obvious truth of Google's vision.

"When were we ever wrong?" Larry asked me.

Not often. But "not often" is not never. If Google's leaders accepted that reality, they might understand why some people are unwilling to suspend skepticism and surrender to Google's assurances the company can be trusted.

After Google, I find myself impatient with the way the world works. Why is it so hard to schedule a recording on my DVR? Why aren't all the signal lights synched to keep traffic flowing at optimum speed? Why, if I punch in my account number when I call customer service, do I have to give it to them again when I get a live person? These are all solvable problems. Smart people, motivated to make things better, can do almost anything.

I feel lucky to have seen firsthand just how true that is.

Timeline of Google Events

11/29/99	My first day at Google
12/4/99	CableFest '99
12/13/99	Inktomi partners with MSN
1/27/00	Premium Ads (original) launches
1/30/00	First OKRs set
3/14/00	Google directory launches
3/22/00	Larry becomes chief of products; birth of product review
3/27/00	Affiliate program launches
4/1/00	MentalPlex April Fools' joke
6/26/00	Yahoo replaces Inktomi with Google
9/27/00	AdWords launches (do-it-yourself CPM ads)
12/10/00	Google toolbar launches with "Not the usual yada yada" warning
1/17/01	Wayne Rosing starts full-time as VP of engineering
2/10/01	Acquisition of Deja News
3/20/01	Eric Schmidt named Chairman of the Board
3/29/01	China blocks access to Google
7/5/01	Engineering reorganization
8/1/01	Chad bikes America
9/11/01	Response to September 11 attacks
10/8/01	GoTo renamed Overture
10/24/01	Trakken CRM system installed
11/13/01	Yahoo-Overture deal announced
11/20/01	"10 Things We've Found to Be True"

11/28/01   Launch calendar instituted
12/13/01   Google catalogs launches

1/24/02   "No pop-ups" linked from Google's homepage
2/4/02   Earthlink switches from Overture to Google for ads
2/19/02   AdWords Select launches (auction-based CPC pricing)
3/5/02   "Why we sell ads, not placement" on homepage
4/4/02   Overture files patent lawsuit against Google
4/25/02   Yahoo renews with Overture for three years
5/1/02   AOL drops Overture and Inktomi for Google
5/2/02   Sheryl Sandberg begins building AdWords team
7/23/02   Yahoo renews contract with Google for search results
8/31/02   China blocks access to Google results again
9/11/02   Content-targeting project starts
9/22/02   Google news launches
10/1/02   Expansion to Saladoplex
11/20/02   Project Ocean launches (digitizing offline content)
12/12/02   Froogle launches
12/13/02   Yahoo buys Inktomi

1/6/03   Milan office opens
2/14/03   Google acquires Blogger.com
2/25/03   Overture buys FAST
3/12/03   Microsoft calls Google "pathetic"
4/11/03   1,000 Googlers
4/24/03   Google acquires Applied Semantics (content-targeting firm)
6/6/03   Yahoo to spend $10 million on branding campaign
6/17/03   Google stock splits
6/18/03   AdSense launches (self-service content-targeted ads)
9/25/03   Leak of financial data
12/3/03   All logs data available in Sawmill system

1/16/04   Yahoo drops Google
1/22/04   orkut launches
1/28/04   Leaks to the *New York Times*
4/1/04   Gmail launches

4/29/04   S-1 filed, "quiet period" begins

7/8/04   Financial planning fairs for Googlers

8/9/04   Yahoo/Overture settles patent lawsuit with Google

8/10/04   *Playboy* interview with founders published; one-week IPO delay

8/19/04   IPO

10/21/04   Earnings call

2/1/05   Earnings call

2/3/05   Microsoft announces $200 million ad campaign for search

3/4/05   My last day at Google

Glossary

This book is written in English but contains some phrases in Geekspeak. Here's what they mean.

AdSense: Google **CPC** ads that appeared on other websites next to content other than search results and were **content targeted.**

AdWords: The second Google advertising program, after **Google Original Ads.** AdWords gave advertisers the ability to create and manage their own **CPM** ad campaigns using an online tool and a credit card. The ads contained only text, no images, and would automatically appear next to Google.com search results when a user searched for the keyword(s) targeted by the advertiser.

AdWords Select: The successor to **AdWords.** The system that introduced auction-based **CPC** pricing for Google ads.

Affiliate program: A program by which one website pays other websites to send it traffic. The sites sending the traffic are called "affiliates." For example, Amazon pays a commission to affiliates that promote specific books it offers for sale. The affiliate gets paid only if one of its users clicks on a specially encoded link pointing to Amazon, and then actually purchases the book there. Google's program paid affiliates if their users conducted searches using special Google search boxes that could be added to almost any website.

Algorithm: A set of instructions (such as a computer program) for solving a specific problem, like finding a particular bit of information in a database. Also, a stiff, rocking motion modeled by a former vice-president.

Canonical: When engineers don't want to say "the preferred" or "the usual" way of doing something, they talk about the canonical example, which is pretty much the same thing but conveys a more exalted sense of correctness to the practice in question. The canonical way to avoid spending an hour in traffic is to go to work at noon.

Clickthrough rate (CTR): The percentage of people seeing an ad who actually click on it. A high CTR means an ad is effective at driving traffic to the advertiser's website. Anything better than 1 or 2 percent is considered high for most types of ads, but CTRs improve the more targeted an ad is to the interests of the person viewing it.

Content targeting: The placement of ads relevant to the text of the page on which they appear. This requires analyzing the page's content and then matching ads from a database that are likely to appeal to someone reading that content. For example, a news story about vacationing in Florida might include ads about theme parks there, airlines, and hotels.

CPC: "Cost per click" — a method of paying for online advertising in which the advertiser pays only when a user actually clicks on the ad and is transferred to the advertiser's website. This is a form of "pay-for-performance" advertising.

CPM: "Cost per thousand impressions" — a method of paying for online advertising in which advertisers pay a set rate to have their ads displayed a thousand times, regardless of whether anyone actually clicks on them. The *M* in CPM comes from the Latin word "mille," which means one thousand.

CPU: Central processing unit — the part of a computer that does the actual "thinking" or processing of code to execute instructions.

Crawler: An automated computer program that follows links from website to website, collecting information about the pages it finds and the **URLs** at which they live. See **Spider.**

Cruft: Cruft is bad. Like the stuff that grows under ungroomed toenails. Like barnacles on a speedboat. It usually refers to old code or dead links on a web page, but it can be applied to any unwanted material that accumulates anywhere. The men's locker room in the Googleplex was filled with cruft, much of it unwashed and hockey-related.

Database: Information collected and stored in a computer in a structured way, so that it can be easily accessed and searched. Like a dictionary that contains words in alphabetical order.

Google Original Ads: The first ad system developed and deployed by Google, it offered **CPM** ads that were sold by sales representatives. These ads, which appeared above the search results, became known as "Premium Ads" when **AdWords** ads were introduced.

Googler: A Google employee who is neither still a **Noogler** nor yet a **Xoogler.**

GoTo (later renamed **Overture**): An advertising network founded in Pasadena, California, that pioneered the idea of a **pay-for-placement** search engine, in which companies bid for the most prominent position in search results for specific terms. GoTo was Google's key competitor in supplying ads to major Internet sites like AOL, Yahoo, and MSN.

GWS: Google Web Server (pronounced: "gwiss"). The software that interacts with users when they enter searches and when Google sends results back to them. It doesn't determine the results, it just delivers them. It also controls the look of the pages on Google's website, so when those pages need to change, a new GWS needs to be pushed out (sent) to the servers.

Hardware: Any part of a computer you can touch with your hands. Anything with wires, disk drives, cables, or a power cord coming out of it.

Incremental index: An **index** that is continually refreshed with new data and is integrated with another index that changes less frequently. For example, an incremental index might include daily-updated pages from news websites to be mixed in with infrequently changing pages that form a much larger index.

Index: An organized list of web pages that can be searched much more quickly than the original pages listed within it. There are many ways to organize an index, and the more efficient the technique used, the faster an **algorithm** can find and retrieve a specific piece of information.

Inktomi: A search-technology company from Berkeley, California, that supplied search results to the majority of web portals, such as Yahoo, AOL, and MSN, before Google entered the market.

Intellectual property (IP): The output of a creative effort that can be legally protected. It often refers to patented technology, such as search **algorithms,** but can also refer to music, movies, artwork, and so on.

Internet Service Provider (ISP): A company that provides a connection to the Internet, whether by phone line, cable modem, or wireless network.

Keyword (also query or search term): The word or words that users type into a search box — that is, the thing they are trying to find. Advertisers specify (target) keywords when they purchase ads. When a user searches for one of the targeted keywords, the results page may display the targeted ad.

Machine: A generic term for a computer or a web server. Also a box, a PC, a **server.**

Nontrivial: A euphemism for "impossible." Since engineers are not going to admit anything is impossible, they use this word instead. When an engineer says something is "nontrivial," it's the equivalent of an airline pilot calmly saying you may encounter "just a bit of turbulence" as he flies you into a Category 5 hurricane. See also **Trivial.**

Noogler: A new Googler. The tag usually sticks until another Noogler is hired into the same group.

Orthogonal: Engineers often talk about things being orthogonal to each other. The first time I heard the term, I thought it meant something like "eleven-sided." It doesn't. It's some kind of technical way to say "unrelated." I still don't really get it. But that didn't stop me from casually dropping it into conversations with engineers: "Oh, yeah, that press release is totally orthogonal to the ads we're running on Yahoo."

Overture: The name assumed by the advertising network **GoTo** in October 2001.

PageRank: An **algorithm** used for analyzing the relative importance of pages on the web. Written by, and named for, Google's co-founder Larry Page. PageRank's breakthrough approach was to look at the sites linking to a particular page to determine how many other websites deemed that page authoritative or important.

Pay for inclusion: Some search engines accept payment from website owners to guarantee that their sites will be included in search results. These search engines don't necessarily guarantee the site prominent *placement.* Web-crawling software can take weeks or months to find new sites; pay for inclusion gives those sites a way to accelerate the process.

Pay for performance (PFP): A method of paying for online advertising in which the advertiser pays only when users actually perform an agreed-upon action, such as clicking on the ad or registering for an account on the advertiser's website.

Pay for placement: The practice of some search engines to accept payment from website owners to give their sites more prominence within search results, as opposed to in a separate, clearly marked advertising area.

Query: The words a user types into a search box, or a single search. See **Keyword.**

Server: A computer that has been configured to hold large amounts of information and provide it to other computers quickly across a network.

So . . . : This all-purpose word is not a word at all. It's the sound of an engineer clearing his or her throat before beginning to speak. The first week I worked at Google, it seemed as if some linguistic virus had infected all the technical staff. Every sentence in every conversation began this way. So . . . , eventually, I got used to it.

Software: The part of a computer you can't touch: the programming and applications that instruct it what to do. All the bits and bytes that are stored in a computer's memory.

Spam: As a noun, "spam" is any unrequested and unwanted electronic material sent by one person to another, whether it's junk email sent to thousands of people simultaneously or a chain letter sent by your very close friend who swears something bad will happen if you don't forward it to ten others. As a verb, "to spam" means to send spam and can also mean to try to obtain an advantage, such as a higher ranking in search results, through deceptive practices, including hidden text on pages or unnecessary repetition of certain words.

Spider: Web-crawling software that gathers data from websites that are the basis for an **index.** See **Crawler.**

Targeting: Matching an ad to a trigger that causes it to be displayed. The trigger may be a **keyword** a user enters for a search, or the content of a web page determined to be relevant to the subject of the ad. The better the targeting, the more relevant the ad is to the keyword or content that triggers it, and the more likely the user is to click on it.

TGIF: Short for "Thank God it's Friday," and the name of a weekly meeting where Googlers are updated on the week's events, usually while munching on chicken wings and drinking beer.

Trivial: As defined by Google engineer Georges Harik: "I say that a task is 'trivial' if I think it is possible. It's 'easy' if I can't see a way to do it but I'm certain it can be done. It's 'hard' if several people have declared it impossible but I disagree with them. It's 'impossible' if I am too tired to do it."

URL: Short for "uniform resource locator." A URL is the address of a particular page on the web. Many URLs begin with "http://www." and end with ".com" (for example, http://www.google.com).

User interface (UI): The look and feel of the part of a website visible to visitors. The UI

is the website's face and includes the graphics, the text, the forms, and any other elements with which a user can interact.

Web server: A computer that delivers content, such as a web page, when requested to
do so by another computer on a network. Or the software that runs on the computer
that delivers the content. See **Server.**

Xoogler (pronounced "zoogler"): A former Googler. I coined this term as the name for
a blog I maintain at Xooglers.blogspot.com, a gathering place for former Googlers to
reminisce about the company's early days.

Acknowledgments

I was lucky long before I'd ever heard of Google.

My parents Marvin and Helene Edwards raised all their children with love and fairness, and instilled in us a desire to be upright and do good in the world. Not once have they wavered in their commitment to our happiness or hesitated to sacrifice to bring it about. When they could ill afford it, they helped fund my dreams and then gave me the confidence to pursue them. I can never repay the debt I owe them for their guidance, their patience, and their understanding.

My wife Kristen experienced all the pressures and insanity of a Silicon Valley startup without the compensating perks that I enjoyed. She didn't divorce me. For more than twenty-five years she has encouraged me, supported me, engaged me, and endured me. She is a ruthless editor and a stickler for facts. She has, on occasion, been the only reason I've remained sane. She is my best friend. "Gratitude" is an inadequate word for all I feel for her, but the end pages of a book about search technology hardly seem the place to delve deeper.

My children, Adam, Nathaniel, and Avalon, not only survived my frequent absences but became intelligent and accomplished beings despite my inattention. For that I thank them, as my guilt at being a negligent father is somewhat offset by their achievements. I hope that my becoming a more constant presence in their lives doesn't destroy the strong foundations upon which they have built such admirable success.

Many people deserve to be in this book but aren't. Some people are, but in a way that trivializes their contributions to Google's meteoric growth. I apologize to all who were truncated by the constraints of page limits or foreshortened because this tale is told from one marketer's perspective. You have earned recognition, and I hope this effort inspires others to publicly sing your praises.

To those Googlers and Xooglers who generously shared their time and their stories with me, I offer my deepest gratitude. Because of you, I understand more about Google now than I did when I was working in the Plex. I offer a special note of thanks to those who explained not once, not twice, but many, many times the complicated systems I still may have managed to mangle in these pages. Any such errors are clearly of my own making and not the fault of those who attempted to impart technological insights to a nontechnical mind.

Among that number are Gerald Aigner, Anurag Archarya, Mieke Bloomfield, Paul Bucheit, Orkut Buyukkotten, Bay Wei Chang, Matt Cutts, Jeff Dean, Ron Dolin, Sanjay Ghemawat, Ben Gomes, Urs Hölzle, Zain Kahn, Salar Kamangar, Ed Karrels, Deb Kelly, Keith Kleiner, Ross Konigstein, Chad Lester, Jane Manning, Amit Patel, Jim Reese, Larry Schwimmer, Ray Sidney, Craig Silverstein, Shawn Simpson, Ben Smith, Eric Veach, and Will Whitted.

Howard Gobioff would be on that list, had he not passed away in 2008. Howard was bright, funny, and full of opinions he happily shared. I respected his acumen and his principles and was saddened by the loss of his talent and his humor.

Those who provided much appreciated perspective on our business-side systems and our corporate culture include Charlie Ayers, Heather Cairns, Devin Ivester, Katina Johnson, Jim Kolotouros, David Krane, Alan Louie, Miriam Rivera, George Salah, Sheryl Sandberg, Stacy Sullivan, and Susan Wojcicki.

Sincere thanks also to Cindy McCaffrey for sticking her neck out to hire me, when clearly my academic credentials were marginal at best, and then for helping me survive in the maelstrom of daily life at Google for more than five years. It was a joy standing with her to keep the marketing fires burning while the wolves howled just outside the light. She inspired and supported me and always lived up to her promise: "My door is always open. Except when it's closed."

Larry Page and Sergey Brin must also be acknowledged here for handing me a ticket to the most amazing ride I will probably ever experience. Had they changed the way I thought about work, expanded my assessment of my own capabilities, or altered my view of global communication, it would have been enough for me. But they did all that while creating a new technology that reshaped the way everyone thinks about everything. To quote Larry, "Kewl."

To my friends Andy and Lita Unruh, Jan Kerans, and Al and Joanne Riske for enduring the teeth gnashing and mood swings while I struggled to churn out more pages, to my in-laws Maggi and Merritt for tiptoeing around the house so as not to disturb the creative process, to my siblings Jeff and Carolyn for their restraint in not asking me constantly about my progress, to Emily Wood of Google PR for scheduling interviews and shepherding me to them and Karen Wickre for her thoughtful comments and gentle encouragement to stake out my own narrative, to my agent Amy Rennert and my editors George Hodgman, Tom Bouman, and Camille Smith — to all who have helped me get this story out of my head and into print — I extend my true and heartfelt appreciation.

And to those who have read this book and are left with questions about how to get a job at Google, how to improve a site's ranking in Google results, or how to share a great idea for a new Google service, I invite you check out the same helpful resource I would use now that I've been away from the company for half a decade. You can find it at www .Google.com.

Index

Doerr, John, 52, 54, 117, 332
Dolin, Ron, 9n, 130–31, 225
"Don't be evil." *See* corporate culture
Doodles (Google Doodles), 122–23, 122n, 349n
dot-com bubble, 107, 112, 115, 129
DoubleClick, 6, 60–61, 371, 371n
doug@google email address, 17–18
Drummond, David, 302, 314
Dublin, Ireland, data centers, 110–11
Dulitz, Daniel, 294
Dutch auction, 383
dynamic IP addressing, 337n

earnings call, first, 386
Earthlink deals, 279, 298
easy, defined, 397
eBay, 155–56, 269
e-commerce, 332
editorial controls and policies, 259, 299, 305, 330
Edwards, Adam, 317
Edwards, Kristen
    on marketing projects, 118
    on stock option purchase, 115–16
    visits to Google, 47, 214–15
    and work/family life balance, 84, 127, 188, 333–34
efficiency/functionality, focus on, 12, 23, 26n, 48, 68–69, 110–11, 201–2
eGain, 207
eGroups, 34n, 179
"email-a-friend" program, 76–77
emails, customer
    automated response text, 198
    and Deja News purchase, 211
    flame circles, 72
    responding to, 204–9
email systems, 322, 366. *See also* Gmail
end user licensing agreement (EULA), 195
engineering group, 35–36, 38, 80–83, 223–25
engineers. *See also* product development; recruitment/hiring
    advertising to, 352–53
    arguments, questioning attitude, 66, 134, 143–45, 262–63, 316
    code reviews, 81–82, 188–89
    decision making by, 29, 101, 248
    Google Two development, 168–69
    independence, 147, 225–26, 227

language used by, 396–97
lines of authority, 283
old-timers, at TGIF meetings, 350
and pay-for-placement code, 309–10
phase-shifted work schedules, 12
pressures on, 169, 198, 206
roles/responsibilities, 39, 197, 328
stereotypical view of, 143
twenty-percent time, 324–25
EPIC (privacy rights organization), 346
Epstein, Scott, 8, 42, 117
equity share, 43n
Erdstein, Max, 204–5, 205
error messages, humor in, 191
Escher, Christopher, 327
eStaff, 205
Eustace, Alan, 354–55
evil, avoiding. *See* corporate culture
Excite@Home, 53, 138, 283
exclusivity, 300, 321
exit interview, 388
Exodus data center, 20–23, 22n, 111–12, 155–59, 176

Facebook, 307, 365
FAQs, 191, 328
FAST Search and Transfer (search engine), 28–29, 161–62, 161n, 351
Federal Trade Commission (FTC), 264
fifth anniversary logo, 348–49
Figueroa, Liz, 371–72
Filo, David, 175
foreign-languages, addressing, 343–44
Fredricksen, Eric, 193–97
free meal plan, 90–91, 90n
Froogle, 329–32, 333n
Fujii, Shari
    departure, 152
    hiring of, 13
    marketing contributions, 40, 48, 71, 73, 117
    role and responsibilities, 24, 51–52, 56, 136–37

gap analysis, 53
Gates, Bill, 194, 353n
Gatt, Erann, 266n
geek chic, 248
GEICO, 380n
gender equality, 222
generalists, hiring, 129–30

Schwimmer, Larry (*cont.*)
  and response to email inquiries, 198
  snippet software, 313
  on traffic increases, 201
  and user interface, 59
scumware, 148, 286, 286–87, 335–36
search bots, 148
search engines, search industry
  competition/changes within, 18–19,
    46–47, 137–38, 161–62
  costs, 201–2
  directories *vs.*, 68–69
  how they work, 31–32
  optimizers, 150, 340
  and paid search, 60, 149, 271
  as passé, 6
  speed *vs.* scale, 33, 46
  technology and, 27, 34, 139
  traffic, 157–58, 166, 200–201
search results. *See also* pay for placement
  and ad quality, 267–68, 270
  content-targeted ads test, 323
  delivery speed, 26–27, 33, 45, 69–70,
    93, 164
  DMCA-mandated removals, 294
  duplicates in, 134
  ethical considerations, 66
  following 9/11 attacks, 230
  integrating ads with, 309
  organic, 65, 65n
  pop-up ads accompanying, 286
  quality of, as driving force/source of
    pride, 32–33, 161, 201–3, 202n, 252,
    352, 359
  real time query scroll, 343
  relevance of, improving, 32, 54–56
  retaining history of, 348
  targeted, 61, 61n, 323, 337–38
  unbiased, affirmation of, 288
search scientists, 129, 129n
second-price auction approach, 269
secret sauce, Google's, 32, 149, 315
Securities and Exchange Commission
  (SEC), 373, 373n, 382, 384
security concerns, 359–60
Senkut, Aydin, 13, 51–52
Sequoia Capital, 7, 45, 52, 141, 161
servers. *See also* data centers
  capacity issues, 155–57, 162–63, 201
  corkboard design, 19n
  crashes and repairs, 19–20, 87

design, 19–20, 22, 111
  failures of, impact on search results,
    164–65, 165n
  functions, 395, 397
  power needs, 22
  server farms, 20–22
SGI (Silicon Graphics), 62, 110, 163n, 357–58
Shazeer, Noam, 82, 82n
"show matches," 95–96
Shriram, Ram, 52n
Sidney, Ray, 78–79, 87, 97, 150–52
Silicon Valley, 5–6, 43n, 140, 178–79, 186
Siliconvalley.com, 4, 66
Silverstein, Craig
  background and skills, 31–34
  code reviews, 81–82
  crawler/index development, 166–67
  on engineer attitudes, 143
  Google Two development, 168–69
  index patching efforts, 166
  at IPO announcement, 380
  MOMA, 55
  on Netscape partnership, 158
  on project review team, 94
  on start-up companies, 42
  Verdana font decision, 28
simplicity, as value, 27n, 58, 139, 240
The Simpsons, 353, 353n
Singh, Sanjeev, 322
Singhal, Amit, 129n, 149, 202–3, 202n
Skeet, Annie, 11, 140
ski trips, annual, 213–14, 217
Slashdot, "slashdotting," 288–89, 363, 363n
slavebots, 286
slotting, 387
"Smart Ad Selection System," 266n
Smith, Ben
  game playing skills, 87, 87n
  incremental indexing, 172–73, 173n
  on Larry, 173
  on overcrowding, 108–9
  on role of project managers, 224
  on Urs Hölzle, 35, 130–31
  and Yahoo launch, 168–69
snippets, 312
"So . . . ," defined, 397
social networking (orkut project), 179, 361,
  363–64
software, defined, 397
S-1 filing document, 374, 377–78, 382
space tethers, 105, 105n